W9-BRK-162

Books by Tom Shachtman

DECADE OF SHOCKS
THE DAY AMERICA CRASHED
EDITH AND WOODROW
THE PHONY WAR, 1939–1940

for children

GROWING UP MASAI
THE BIRDMAN OF ST. PETERSBURG

Tom Shachtman

DECADE

Dallas to

OF SHOCKS

Watergate, 1963–1974

 POSEIDON PRESS • NEW YORK

A Poseidon Press Book
Published by Pocket Books,
A Division of Simon & Schuster, Inc.
Simon & Schuster Building
Rockefeller Center
1230 Avenue of the Americas
New York, New York 10020
POSEIDON PRESS is a trademark of Simon & Schuster, Inc.
Designed by Eve Kirch
Manufactured in the United States of America

10   9   8   7   6   5   4   3   2   1

Library of Congress Cataloging in Publication Data

Shachtman, Tom.
  Decade of Shocks.
  Bibliography: p.
  Includes index.
  1. United States—History—1961-1969.
  2. United States—History—1969-   . I. Title.
E839.S23 1983   973.923   83-13891

ISBN 0-671-44252-x

for Noah

Contents

Photo section follows page 96.

If I were standing at the beginning of time, with the possibility of a general and panoramic view of the whole human history up to now, and the Almighty said to me, "Martin Luther King, which age would you like to live in?"...I would turn to the Almighty, and say, "If you allow me to live just a few years in the second half of the Twentieth Century, I will be happy." Now that's a strange statement to make, because the world is all messed up. But I know, somehow, that only when it is dark enough, can you see the stars.

—Martin Luther King, Jr.
Speech in Memphis,
April 3, 1968

Foreword

THE "SIXTIES" WHICH PEOPLE REMEMBER did not begin in 1960 or in 1961 with John Kennedy's inauguration; nor did they end when Johnson yielded to Nixon or in 1970. They began with the assassination of Jack Kennedy and ended with Nixon's resignation at the end of the Watergate scandal. The Johnson-Nixon years were of a piece, suffused with shocks to the body politic and to our societal assumptions which were massive and very nearly continuous. We had political assassinations, urban riots, an undeclared war, runaway inflation, technological breakthroughs and breakdowns, energy price rises, the near impeachment of a president. "In the sixties—it can almost be dated from the assassination of President Kennedy," wrote historian Henry Steele Commager,

> Americans awoke with a sense of shock and incredulity to the discovery that the American dream was largely an illusion. Twenty million Negroes were second-class citizens—or worse. Thirty million poor made a mockery of the proud claim of an affluent society. For two hundred years Americans had laid waste the exceeding bounty of nature . . . and now at last an outraged nature was revolting. Cities were everywhere rotting away; crime flourished not only on the streets but in high places; the supposed demands of security had qualified the institutions of democracy and of constitutionalism, and permanently shifted the balance in the relationship of the military to the civilian power.

After Gerald Ford's assumption of the presidency in August of 1974, *Atlantic Monthly* columnist L. E. Sissman wrote,

For the first time in eleven years, I am not ashamed of my citizenship. From the day of John Kennedy's assassination in 1963, through the slow, painful escalation of the Vietnam War and the grudging, snail-like revelations of Watergate, hardly a week has passed that I haven't felt slightly sick over the course—and the presumed destination—of our country.... I've braced myself almost daily before settling down with the morning paper.... Now it is suddenly different. In the silence of a late-summer Saturday after the change in Presidents, I feel myself suffused with a new, unfamiliar circulation of hope. And pride, after all these barren years, pride in a country I'd given up for lost.

This is a book about the ways we perceived the events of 1963–1974 at the time, and the ways we were changed by those events and by the trends those events dramatized. This book aims to be neither historical chronology nor exhaustive survey; rather, it is an attempt to make sense out of the flash points and transformations of a difficult period.

As such, it is a book of personal observations. I am emboldened to make them for I belong to that extensive generation whose lives for some time now have been irreversibly shaped by the events of the Decade of Shocks. Part of the reason that we are a generation, and not simply a birth cohort, is that we have been commonly touched by the events of this era. We have been shaped by the Decade of Shocks just as surely and as deeply as those before us were shaped by the twenties, the Depression, World War II, and by what I. F. Stone has termed the Haunted Fifties. The events of this decade affected our generation more deeply than others, because we were of the most susceptible age. Sociologist T. Allen Lambert contends that:

> There is a most probable or best time during which events are most "impactful" in the development of consciousness. And because the period is of limited duration, after which consciousness is relatively set and the person turns his attention to other concerns, the stratification of experience in consciousness makes some experiences more important than others.

Lambert puts at eighteen to twenty-six the age when "politico-cultural consciousness" normally develops, "because the requisite levels of intellectual and moral development and resolution of emotional concerns have only then been stabilized."

I would widen Lambert's eight-year span a bit when referring to my generation, to include those who were, at the time of John Kennedy's assassination, in the years from adolescence to late twenties. I was twenty-one when Kennedy died, and people my age were deeply affected; research shows also that teenagers ranked among the groups most highly disturbed by that event—thus, the rationale for my extension of the "susceptible" group. In 1983 this group, who range in age from the late twenties to the middle forties, represent about a quarter of the population. For we who came of age or who lived through a substantial portion of the Decade of Shocks when we were in a formative "politico-cultural consciousness" stage, the time remains a touchstone, a benchmark to which we compare all our later experiences and sensations. We shall probably do so for the rest of our lives.

In the pages that follow, I shall argue that during the decade certain assumptions about the nature, structure and purpose of American society and of individuals within that society were controverted. Those assumptions were the unwritten but powerful working rules that informed the lives of adult Americans. Adults for the most part accepted them as "givens." It was these assumptions that were the subject of great questioning by youth. At the time, the term "identity crisis" was used to label and often to disparage the "phase" youth was going through. However, as Richard Sennett points out, the identity crisis

> is not simply a crisis of "what my personality is like"; it is rather the conscious attempt of the growing human being, for the first time, to formulate rules or patterns of the relations between a self-image and an image of the world outside the self.

During the era, as we tried to elucidate working rules for ourselves, we recapitulated (and contributed to) the whole society's reworking of the rules. Thus for us the events and struggles of the era were doubly meaningful.

Many of us experienced the events directly, but most of us learned about them through television, and this book speaks about the events as television transmitted them to us. It was through the living room pipeline that we experienced them together.

Stephen R. Graubard has recently suggested that what television brought us during this time was a faulty view of history:

War, riot, assassination, civil disorder, public protest—the eye of the camera recorded it all, for two-minute presentations interrupted only by the more insistent demands of the advertiser. Whatever pleasure or pain such fleeting images inflicted on their mass audiences, they communicated a public distress and anger that could not be ignored.... How is one to interpret the events of these long, difficult, and agitated years? Why, in the end, do they matter? What, in fact, is their residue?... May the greatest change not be in the collective memory of the American people?... Have we been so preoccupied with watching a drama (indeed, more recently, a cheap melodrama) that some significant events, occurring offstage (off camera), have largely escaped us?

Under Graubard's editorship, the journal *Daedalus* devoted a book-length issue to exploring those offstage phenomena—but the writers of the chapters of that issue had constant reference to the onstage events, for the years make no sense without reference to them.

I contend that the greatest change has been in the collective mind of the American people, because these events have had a tremendous impact on the assumptions which underlie our lives. Today, in casual conversations, we say "before King died," or "during the peace movement," or "after JFK," or "before the blackout," or "before inflation." Those conversations tend to be about how our lives have changed, how we perceive people and events differently now than we did before the Decade of Shocks. It is to understand the changes that I have undertaken this inquiry.

TOM SHACHTMAN
New York City, 1983

1 American Colossus

AMERICA IN THE POSTWAR ERA was a homogeneous country, its social constructs well understood and accepted by the majority of its citizens, who perceived the United States as the foremost power in the world. Dormant within our society lay a conflict in values of potentially great proportions. Some perceptive observers tried to pinpoint it. In the 1960 edition of the influential textbook *American Society: A Sociological Interpretation*, Robin M. Williams, Jr., stated that we were holding to our traditional ideals of "freedom," "democracy," and "equality," but that first among the actual values of the day was

> a central stress upon personal achievement, especially secular occupational achievement. The "success story" and the respect accorded to the self-made man are distinctly American if anything is.

The values of the businessman "dominate and permeate national life," and our society was highly competitive, Williams said. In fact,

> Economic success has been so heavily stressed . . . as to impose a widespread and persistent strain upon institutional regulation of means used to attain this goal. . . . There is growing evidence that performance in consumption is partly replacing performance in work: how one spends his income, rather than what he did to earn it, appears increasingly to be a mark of "achievement."

The commerce so characteristic of our culture was action-oriented, full of hustle and bustle. An aggressive people, we were used to dominating, to being first among many. This characteristic described us as a nation and as individuals. Williams noted a distinction between Americans and other peoples:

> In this culture the individual tends to "face outward"—to be interested in making things happen in the external world. In ideal type, he seeks to dominate the world of nature, to subdue and exploit the physical world around him.

An observer could tell much about our values, Williams wrote, from our

> high sensitivity to such epithets as "backward," "inefficient," "useless"...One of the blackest public curse-words we have is "impractical"—in the culture at large, the practical man is the good man, an embodiment of a major value.... "Practical" (pragmatic) orientation is basically short-range adjustment to immediate situations.

We believed wholeheartedly in the "cult of progress," with its relentless optimism and faith that the future would be much better than the past. Such a belief was almost a religion with Americans, Williams noted.

We saw ourselves as ruggedly individualistic, but actually we were subject to a good deal of "external conformity," and defined tolerance of nonconformity "largely in terms of sanctioning technological and economic innovation," not originality of thought. We canonized Henry Ford, not Eugene Debs. Perhaps this was to be expected in a society in which upward social mobility was highly prized and regularly achieved. We were rapidly becoming "an engineering civilization" (shades of Herbert Hoover!) interested in "order, control, and calculability."

Moreover, Americans were increasingly viewing the world in moralistic terms. We had, Williams noted, a proclivity for dividing the paths before us into Right or Wrong, Good or Bad, Ethical or Unethical; this was clearly "an element of moral overstrain" which might well engender "hypocrisy, ritualism, and vacillating or compensating behavior." It had already done so in the McCarthy era. Williams wrote that the reflexive moral stance we so often took on problems got us into trouble, for it was exacerbating a split between our humanitarian concerns and our conception of rugged individualism. Increasingly we were caught in a bind: we espoused a value, yet acted in a way that belied our espousal. We said and believed that all men were created equal, yet we had a segregated society.

The dichotomies in our value system also troubled Francis L. K. Hsu, in his 1961 study "American Core Values and National Character." With breathtaking scope, Hsu reviewed fifty years of value studies in the United States. Many observers had noted that we seemed to hold simultaneously in our minds such things as autonomy and obedience to authority; individuality and conformity; freedom and totalitarian tendencies; a belief in egalitarianism together with stubborn class, race, and ethnic superiority tenets. Observers had tried in many ways to gloss over these apparent contradictions. Hsu did not. He said we must accept that we held the contradictory values simultaneously. Hsu traced our ambivalent attitude to a single "core" value upon which all Americans agreed: self-reliance. We all wanted to be self-reliant, dependent upon no one. We all feared dependence. No wonder, Hsu wrote, that we suffered from insecurity, for "the very foundation of the human way of life is a man's dependence upon his fellow man, without which we shall have no law, no custom, no art, no science, and not even language." Hsu mourned our inability to see that we were all interdependent, that under our democratic, free-market system "success, superiority, and triumph on the part of some must of necessity be based on the failure, inferiority, and defeat" of others, and therefore "the best of America is directly linked with her worst, like Siamese twins. The way out of the worst is not to deny it but to recognize it for what it is."

In an early television series called "The Search for America," broadcast on public stations in 1959 and later made into books, one contributor was theologian Reinhold Niebuhr, who tried to delve a bit further into the contradictions in our value system:

At the time when man's dreams of bringing history under control is troubled by a nuclear nightmare . . . the American mind is still influenced by the optimistic illusions of a bygone era. The dream of progress still envelops us. Generations of Americans have grown to maturity believing that the present is the culmination of the past and the stepping-stone to a brighter future.

This, Niebuhr said, was an illusion which sprang from American history, where the frontier connoted freedom and where our idealism was furnished by a recent break with tyranny. Without doubt America had a mission in the world, but

> What is likely to keep us from doing as well as we otherwise might with our historical opportunity is our conviction of our own wisdom and virtue. So convinced are we of the purity of our motives that we find it difficult to believe that anyone should dislike us. Criticism of our actions is attributed to malice, or to envy of our material prosperity, which prosperity (overlooking differences in natural and historical situation) we brashly offer as proof of our superior ideology.

This image of superiority and innocence of wrongdoing had left us "ill-prepared for the moral ambiguities that our rise to power has forced upon us." It also left us, Niebuhr thought, ill-prepared to deal with the coming complexities of the world. Niebuhr saw our weaknesses as several-fold. First,

> in our continuing pride: moral pride which inclines us to dismiss the criticisms that are raised against us, and pride of power which glories in the accumulation of physical and economic might. A too-confident sense of justice always produces injustice. And pride in power intensifies the temptation to use it without considering the views and interests of others.

Second,

> we have yet to perceive as a people that, in fulfilling responsibility, the choice is seldom clearly defined between good and evil. Power often confronts a nation with the necessity of sacrificing a high value for the sake of a higher one—a truth we are reluctant to credit because it means that guilt cannot be avoided.

Third,

> we have not learned that power does not increase a people's freedom to do as it pleases. The power that has extended our influence over many peoples has inevitably bound us into the vast web of their conflicting wills and aspirations. We cannot have our way, not even when we are acting "for the good of mankind."

* * *

Niebuhr concluded that the central problem was that we had no cognizance of our limitations, and such a realization would be essential for dealing responsibly with the challenges of the future.

Niebuhr, Hsu, and Williams were depicting the dichotomy between the ideal and the real, or, more precisely, the gap between our true values and our operating assumptions. In the 1830s de Tocqueville had pinpointed a gap between word and deed in American life. He saw it as the inevitable result of the tension between our legacy from the French Enlightenment (human beings were perfectible; an egalitarian democracy could endure in which the state existed to serve the common well-being) and that bequeathed us by the English mercantilist policy of *laissez-faire* (the social order and the state existed to meet the needs of "economic man," or the chief businessmen of the society).

To phrase it another way, we can say the problem was caused by misapprehensions of the concepts of "freedom" and "equality." We had once known precisely what freedom meant—freedom from the tyranny of King George III. But since the Revolutionary era the definition had changed. No longer in thrall to tyranny, we construed freedom in other ways. We thought of freedom primarily in the terms Roosevelt and Churchill had used in the wartime Atlantic Charter, and which translated into our enjoyment of "rights" which the Russians did *not* have—free speech, free assembly, and especially free enterprise. Over the course of United States history, we had come increasingly to define freedom as residing in the economic sphere—freedom meant being loosed from trade restraints, or from shackles on individual license. As the English mercantilist would define it, freedom meant *laissez-faire*.

We had also once known what equality meant—equality of condition. In this, too, our definition had changed. Opposite us we saw a Soviet system in which equality of condition was imposed on everyone. We did not think it should be imposed, and so we rather thought of equality as equality of opportunity—which might be translated to mean that everyone had an equal shot at becoming rich (or becoming president). This was a serious redefinition of the prime value we had taken from the French Enlightenment.

These redefinitions encompassed certain contradictions between the guarantees embodied in the Declaration of Independence, the Constitution, and the Bill of Rights, and the current moral assumptions. We gave much honor to the guarantees, but we lived by our assumptions.

All peoples have a set of beliefs about how the real world operates, and these assumptions differ from their ideals. At certain times, the split between ideals and assumptions seems particularly acute. The postwar era was such a time, for during it there crystallized a set of assumptions that were widely held, honed to a fine point, and were most important to those who held them.

It was just these assumptions which the decade of shocks challenged, and so we must outline these assumptions here in some detail. They were:

1. We believed firmly in the safety, sanctity, and legitimacy of our leaders. Having survived war and depression, our society was stable. We believed our leaders would not be physically harmed, because if we did not like them we could replace them by our votes. Bullets took away leaders only in banana republics. Our leaders' motives were beyond question, their goals understood. Since the war our presidents had been exemplary men. Kennedy, the war hero, had faced the enemy in Cuba. Eisenhower, the commanding general, had been the benevolent grandfather. Truman, low-born, had grown in office. All had proved themselves to us under fire, and of them all it could be fairly said that during their terms they represented and held the confidence of the majority. They were authentic and legitimate.

There had been smooth transitions between administrations, smooth enough to give reason for confidence in our government. Though there were jolts, in postwar American history there were no major discontinuities. It had been inevitable that Russia would get the bomb. Sputnik, the Russian satellite which in 1957 beat the U.S. space program into orbit, was a jolt, but almost an expected one. Little Rock, where Negro schoolchildren were escorted into a previously segregated school, was a triumph of gradualism, not a true shock. The continuity of the times, their understandable nature, their measured pace had given us a baseline conviction that the character of change itself was gradual and predictable. The train to the future was on the track, and few believed it would encounter any major derailments or serious detours.

2. The belief in the gradual nature of change informed our conceit that the various minorities in our society would stay in their "place." As with the rest of the citizens, minorities would continue to accept their lot—even if their lot was second-class citizenship. By 1963 there was plenty of agitation for change in civil rights, but only for public civil rights such as desegregated waiting rooms. Any brilliance or accomplishment on the part of a member of any nonwhite race in America was treated as a unique and nonrepeatable instance, an anomaly. We believed that as a group,

blacks were inferior to whites and were unable to radically alter that fact.

Most leaders of minority groups, and certainly those few people in government who were responsive to minority demands, spoke of the changes to come in terms of integration and gradualism. The courts would rule, and concessions would be wrested from the overt and covert segregationists through the pressure of the legal system backed by the sanctions of the federal government, both prodded by nonviolent marchers and sit-ins. There was a slight belief that registration of black voters would change the political balance of the South—but that it would not change suddenly. Those, like Malcolm X or the Ku Klux Klan, who advocated separation rather than integration of the races were considered irresponsible or fanatic.

The interlocking web dedicated to gradualism was itself predicated on a belief that the structure of our society was fixed and not fundamentally in flux.

3. Cardinal to the notion of the immutability of society was a belief in the basic health and superiority of the American economy. The 1940s and 1950s saw rapid and sustained economic development and, as measured by the GNP and other indicators, the early 1960s showed an ample supply of goods, the absence of uncontrolled market downswings, and a manageable unemployment problem. Americans had an almost unlimited sense of prosperity; those young enough to have been born after the Crash and the Depression knew nothing but prosperity. The dollar was a symbol of economic might worldwide and the most widely used unit of international monetary understanding. We owned and housed much of the world's gold. Though war had destroyed the economies of Japan, Germany, and Western Europe, we had rebuilt those countries and made them strong; however, we had also trained them in the buying of American goods. Our allies were not viewed as serious competitors. The balance of payments was still in our favor.

As individuals, we could agree that the American economy was good to us. We saw little to stop us from doing better each succeeding year. Inflation, a small cloud in the U.S. during and immediately following the war, now troubled only badly managed countries. Though in the early 1960s wages had not kept pace with profits, jobholders nevertheless felt secure in their positions and expected in their paychecks ever-larger slices of the American pie. Automation had not proved to be the bugaboo once imagined; it was actually helping some workers cut excess manual labor from their tasks.

Because our economy was sound, because our jobs were secure, Americans did not shrink from undertaking large future obligations—mortgages, car payments, tuition loans—in order to possess ever-greater concentrations of material goods and services. It was our constant belief that tomorrow would be better than today; even those scarred by the Depression no longer predicated all their pocketbook decisions on fear of what the future could bring. The American economy was as sound and as triumphant as the dollar.

4. Economic strength was one leg of the American colossus; the other was military strength. We believed we were militarily superior to the rest of the world. Our might bordered on the invincible. After forcing victory in World War II we had turned Japan and Germany into admiring allies; we dominated NATO, SEATO, and other alliances. In Korea we "won" while using only a fraction of our resources. We had never lost a war. The confrontation over the missiles in Cuba showed that we would not lose even that kind of showdown. Our power was supreme not only in nuclear armament, but also in conventional arms, bombers, submarines, carriers, even in the equipment, training, and fighting spirit of the individual GI. Our CIA, with an annual budget which exceeded that of the State Department, functioned as an adjunct to military pressure, and had engineered coups in Iran, Vietnam, and in several Latin American countries. If we didn't know all that our spy boys were up to, we usually approved it in retrospect and thanked God they had done it. Our foreign aid was 60 percent military; we had many "client states."

The basis of our foreign policy and our military outlook was anticommunism. In order to fulfill our mission of defending the free world against Communist encroachment, our might must continue at a high level; we were, in fact, prepared to fight simultaneously both a major and a minor war. Only the Soviets had enough power to give us pause, and they lagged behind us. Though we were winning the bilateral struggle of giants, we would remain eternally vigilant.

5. Only we and the Soviets really counted. We acted as if the small and emerging nations had no possibility of affecting the strategic balance. Their fate was to be vassals or prizes to be won. China was seen as wholly under the thumb of Moscow; the emerging African countries were economic and ideological battlegrounds for the superpowers; Latin American dictatorships were accepted as bulwarks against communism. Vietnam was an exact replica of Korea, divided into two halves—the North, Soviet-controlled; the South, a right-wing anti-Communist dictatorship.

In the Kennedy years this simplistic world-view had begun to change—

the president spoke of the necessity of recognizing the needs of the 70 percent of the world's people who lived in the "have-not" nations—but the American people, speaking through a recalcitrant Congress, did not do much to support or recognize a multipolar world. We considered the lands of the Southern Hemisphere to be tropical, backward countries to whom we need pay no attention because they had no militarily or economically effective weapons with which to oppose our will. It was axiomatic that the poor, the colored, the helpless, the technologically weak could never alter the prevailing balance of power.

6. We believed that our environment and natural resources were virtually limitless. Our military, economic, and other perceived superiorities required that there be no limits to the satisfaction of our demands. In regard to natural resources, only pessimists saw problems that were beyond our capacity to solve. While cities were crowded, there were millions of countryside acres that could be used for expansion, and with new agricultural technologies we were actually using fewer acres to feed more people. Birth control methods and the "Green Revolution" would offset the geometrical advance of births over deaths and would finally give the lie to Malthus.

Plentiful and cheap energy was available to run Western civilization's machinery. Gas and oil were abundant, and by the year 2000 atomic power would provide between a third and a half of our electricity, thus enabling us to conserve our fossil fuels. The oil which flowed from the Middle East wells backed up our own abundant supply. There were also adequate and reasonably priced supplies of uranium, copper, tin, molybdenum, and other mineral resources in the world; it did not give us pause that most of these deposits lay underneath the "emerging" nations. They would be able to sell the resources only to developed countries, who were the only ones who could utilize and pay for them, and so the cost of resources could be controlled.

Pollution was unsightly, but only a minor price to pay for our advanced standard of living. Soot in the air connoted a factory going at full blast while employing people and paying them well. The diluting capacities of the air and the water would take care of our excess; there was no need to heed doomsayers who contended that we were permanently fouling our nest. Garbage was not wholly unlovable; we liked to produce it, and in fact believed that its production was inevitable. The successful conspicuous consumer necessarily made a mountain of castoffs. Advertising, which made us buy packaging (and thereby contributed to the accumulation of garbage), was the grease that oiled the wheels of our economic machinery.

7. We believed that somehow American ingenuity, technological virtuosity, and money would solve all our problems. We were a nation of mechanics and tinkerers; we could "fix" anything. In the future we would fix the problem of pollution just as we would fix the problem of reducing the size of bulky communications equipment. Modern medicine was already eradicating smallpox and malaria; agriculture was undergoing an American-sponsored "Green Revolution," and our eggheads and technicians were already discussing the best way of landing a man on the moon. Soon technology would free the average American from the drudgery of work, and we could lie back and watch our Dick Tracy two-way television wristwatches.

At the far end of the belief that we could fix anything was the notion that nuclear missiles, those ultimate weapons of death, might by their technological preponderance obviate future wars.

Our experience since World War II validated the idea that "progress" was "our most important product." Progress was on view in our greatly expanded creature comforts, in television (which was changing the way we looked at the world), in the computer (which was changing the ways we worked). Instant Polaroid pictures replaced the old film and cameras, inoculations replaced childhood diseases, jets replaced propeller planes— and so on, and on and on. The cornucopia was incredibly varied; technology could work miracles.

Increasingly we sought the solutions to our problems in technology. Ingenuity and innovation in material goods we pursued for their own sake, to further the perpetual alteration of styles, the dance of planned obsolescence that had become the mainstay of the consumer goods sector of the economy. Products labeled "new" or "improved" or containing some important (and obscure) chemical formula or additive were those we bought most eagerly in the marketplace.

We had a fear of standing still. As Americans, our heritage was to conquer frontiers, our myth, to constantly pierce through obstacles to reach a newer and larger destiny. Not to be in motion—in forward motion— was to be in the process of dying. We said of a jobholder whose income did not increase yearly, that he was not doing well. We said of a company that did not annually boost its gross sales, that it was stagnating; if publicly held, that company's stock would plummet. Growth was all, and we defined growth as progress toward greater size. Grandness had become the sole measurement of greatness. As a country we were large and good, and we measured the potency of our corporations and of our people by the same standards.

All Americans lived along a single scale of valuation. We knew that scale; it was the ladder of upward mobility, it was the never-ending stair of consumption. We knew exactly how much those above us were earning because it was reflected in the things they were able to own. Here was a six-room family, there a family with a boat; when we became rich we would buy a Cadillac. But the scale was more than a continuum of consumption; it was a codified belief system in which the goals of the nation became those of the corporation, and those of the nation and corporation became those of the private individual. The only way to go was up, up along the ladder of money and power.

On that ladder, youth was expected first to take its place on a lower rung, and to creep upward in the manner prescribed by the system. One showed aggressiveness and sought achievement, one went along with the company, and one got there—"there" being success. Parents and educators communicated to the young that in the United States one person could achieve as much as the next—but that in order to go far, one had to climb a recognized ladder to success.

Here was the ultimate consequence of the belief that the structure of American society would not fundamentally alter: Youth was told to keep in line. It was a time of world stability and of reasonably dynamic growth, a time when the shape of the future seemed known. It seemed logical that if its shape were known, one could systematically prepare for that future. Thus the forces of conformity and of the wish for material rewards both pointed youth (and their education) in a single direction. Margaret Mead wrote in 1961 that these pressures conspired to work on people's lives, to lead them to

> learn how to present a career line which shows even and continuous conformity to existing educational and social standards. . . . High school and college have become progressively vocationalized, and statistics on successes and failures in national contests for scholarships and for admissions to especially desirable institutions have increased the widespread sense that to succeed today it is necessary to conform and to compete in terms of national norms.

The consequences of such behavior, Mead suggested, were

> a marked shift throughout this (younger) generation from the pursuit of longtime goals...to the "more, more, more now" philosophy.... Immediate sex gratification as represented by early marriage, early attainment of full adult status including parenthood, and the possession of the material attributes of economic independence, such as house and car, TV, a full and complete way of life on the installment plan rather than saved for....

Young people were labeled trainees, both as jobholders and as assimilators of their parents' culture. The early internalization of societal mores and patterns of consumption—the pursuit of stability, the purchase of material goods—underlined youth's junior status, and showed how firmly the steps of youth were fixed on the one correct ladder to success. You did not flail about helplessly in life, not knowing what to do; you took a pre-med course and went steady.

Despite all this certainty, there remained for the generation approaching adulthood in the early 1960s a serious problem, one pinpointed in an article by Liston Pope, dean of the Yale Divinity School. Pope said contemporary adults were presenting to youth

> a hazy picture as to the very ideas on which they will base their lives. Belief in the essential goodness of man is tempered by a recognition that man is a selfish creature capable of almost anything. Belief in social progress is still widespread in America, but we doubt that we are making any net gains except possibly in the field of mechanical gadgets. We continue to teach that hard work is a great virtue, but the work week grows ever shorter. We praise virtues of frugality, temperance, and modesty, but we live as the most spendthrift and boastful nation in the world.... In our personal lives as well as in public matters... we give confused answers to life's challenges and opportunities, and our young people sense the confusion.

It was the old, perhaps unbridgeable gap between the ideal and the real, coming into ever-sharper focus.

9. If youth's place was relatively fixed, so was the relationship of the nuclear family to society. The nuclear family consisted of a man and woman, married for the first and only time to each other, living together with their natural children. Each member of the family assumed "traditional" roles, such as husband/breadwinner, housewife, student, infant.

Single-parent families, families with stepchildren, single-person households, and other permutations of households were considered socially inferior and statistically insignificant alterations of the basic familial setup. The nuclear family was the model for society.

The man provided; the woman directed the family's consumption and raised the children. He operated daily out in the "real world"; she did not. Her influence was supreme in the "ideal world" of continual hope. Though she brought in no money, the woman was the center of the nuclear family. In the 1950s and early 1960s the women workers of the war years fled to the suburbs. The younger women married earlier and had children earlier (and more of them). Social scientists saw these trends as affirmation of women's traditional roles. Women might well be entering the work force in record numbers, but they were dropping out of that force permanently once they began to bear children. Women were considered inferior to men in terms of brawn, practicality, aggressiveness, and worldliness. The chief task of a female child was to find and hold a husband.

Traditionalism also informed our sexual mores, whice were intertwined with the sanctity and continuity of the nuclear family. The technological innovation of the birth control pill had just begun to free intercourse from the consequence of unwanted pregnancy, but the ramifications of such freedom were not yet apparent. Pre- and extra-marital sex were still outside the bounds of morality and law. Sexual promiscuity, experimentation, homosexuality, and explicit verbal or pictorial representations of sex were considered pornographic, outlawed by statute and custom. All were understood to be affronts to that central social and personal relationship of husband and wife which was also the heart of the nuclear family.

10. Just as we took the nuclear family to be the reflection of American social order, and the best possible relationship that could obtain for man, woman, and child—we regarded our society as being the best possible realization of our potential, the model for the rest of the world and for the future. We believed that, as a nation, as individuals, we were constantly striving toward more democracy, peace, personal freedom, stability, justice, and happiness. We knew what we were doing. We could only hope that the rest of the world would follow our leadership. If our aspirations at times stretched beyond our grasp—what was a heaven for? We were the future.

Polls showed that President John F. Kennedy and his young wife and family were the most admired people in America. In John Kennedy we had a rich man's son who had gone beyond the mere consumption of riches in order to seek public service. In his last press conference Kennedy said that the exercise of power "along lines of excellence" was its own reward, and a working definition of happiness. Similar sentiments had come in their own time from Eisenhower, Truman, and Roosevelt, and fitted with what often came out of the mouths of revered artists and high executives of business and industry. All these people appeared satisfied with their rewards, their nuclear families, their environment, their employment, their safety and sanctity, their future, and their own personal place in the world. America worked, and was in the process of perfecting itself.

We have come full circle. The set of assumptions about America's place in the world and about the individual's place in American society was a fixed and closed set, one which seemed to many to be invincible and unalterable. They reflected our recent history.

At the end of World War II, at the inception of the modern era, the United States bestrode the world like an omnipotent colossus, our technology, reach, and moral fervor exemplified by our recently demonstrated capacity to destroy at will a portion of that world.

During that war it had been fashionable to hate the Nazis and to proclaim the moral leadership of the United States. As we conquered the Nazis and repaired Europe and Japan with our benevolence, the Soviet Union moved into Eastern Europe. In the Cold War our fervor translated into a hatred of everything Communist, and into a continued exaltation of the American way of life.

In 1948, Representative Richard M. Nixon of California began to pursue suspected American Communist and State Department official Alger Hiss. In 1949 the Soviets exploded their atomic bomb, and when in 1950 Soviet "puppets" from North Korea invaded the Korean peninsula to the south, the Cold War seemed as dangerous to us as the previous global conflict. In 1950, Senator Joseph McCarthy of Wisconsin sought to uncover evidence of Communist influence throughout all of American life—in the government, in the universities, in private business. The ethic of Cold War was driven into the minds of millions, until it became a personal as well as an international matter. The Cold War was the U.S. against the U.S.S.R., Americans against un-Americans, light against darkness.

This was not new in American history. A period of witch-hunts had followed many of our major wars. After the Revolutionary War there were reprisals against former Tories. After World War I, Attorney General A. Mitchell Palmer used wartime sedition acts as the basis for a "Red Scare" which besmirched the reputations of many good people and succeeded only in deporting a number of harmless ones. In these instances, as in the time immediately after World War II, the sequel to wartime hatred was peacetime terror.

McCarthy played on the idea that evil was not within us but could be located outside, over there. In the 1950s the evil could be pinpointed overseas in Communist encroachment, and at home in the person of the secret Communist. Senator McCarthy said the atheistic, Machiavellian U.S.S.R. had the power to "dupe" us, and suggested that those who would not admit the extent of the Communist menace at home were either blind to it or unknowingly in its service. To be a dupe was almost as bad as being a fellow traveler, a card-carrier, bomb-thrower, home-wrecker, or an enslaver of lost souls.

The effect of anti-communism in this era cannot be overstated. The prevailing ethic, it insisted not only that citizens be profoundly and actively anti-Communist, but also that all must agree with the majority on everything or be labeled as dupes. Thus a Negro bootblack in the Pentagon, who had given money to help the Scottsboro boys, was questioned seventy times by the FBI; thus men called before congressional subcommittees were repeatedly asked what newspapers they read or whether or not they happened to own a phonograph album by singer Paul Robeson. The number of "political firings" at colleges and universities will never accurately be known. There were similar dismissals in private industry, based on hearsay or on whether a man was a friend or relative of a suspected Communist. Anti-communism stifled dissent. Millions conformed internally without ever having been asked to sign a loyalty oath, for they feared coming to the attention of any who might accuse them of the slightest deviation from the majoritarian line.

The spirit of conformity dovetailed with Americans' attempts to obtain for themselves the materialistic version of the good life which had been denied during the Depression and the war. The marketplace was flooded with consumer durable goods, new foods and luxuries. Now people had the money to buy, and after sacrifices for the war effort they felt entitled to relax and to enjoy life. The good life was the carrot leading to adherence to the majority viewpoint. The stick was the threat of being hounded for holding views which differed from those of the majority—those people championed, whether they liked it or not, by Joe McCarthy.

Most vulnerable to such pressures were the new parents of the war and the postwar period. Since the baby boom of the postwar era was the greatest in history, those parents constituted a great body of people. And the new parents were the Americans who could least afford to compromise their jobs, their mortgaged homes, their children's future. Having had enough of apocalyptic struggle, they sought mostly to enjoy their time of peace, to make their homes pleasant for themselves and for their children. Encouraged to pursue refrigerators and larger cars, they were discouraged from nurturing any doubts as to the quality, goals, or methods of American life.

Eisenhower, the victorious general elevated to the presidency in the manner of George Washington (and with nearly as much popular support), seemed to aspire to be the grandfather of his country. He projected an image of benevolent remove. His cabinet officers had grown up in the 1920s, when Calvin Coolidge had said that the business of America was business—and the 1950s shared the same atmosphere of *laissez-faire* in the business world.

For most, it was a good time. Union members climbed into the middle class and became less concerned than they had been in former years about broad-scale social change. In the blossoming suburbs women forgot about Rosie the Riveter and looked to "I Love Lucy" as a model for behavior. Two-thirds of the nation's children lived in two-resident-parent households where the mother held no job outside the home. The unemployment rate for Negro teenagers was still below the overall unemployment figure. Black leaders were derided for saying that for them the American dream was not coming true fast enough. The will of the majority in racial equality, reflected accurately by the Eisenhower team, was that change ought to be gradual.

National defense was still the clarion call and rationale for actions ranging from the production of weapons to the overproduction of highways. In 1957, when Sputnik ascended into the heavens and there was a consequent increase in science and mathematics training, the reason given for the increase was to ensure the United States a good supply of technicians for the country's future military needs. The same reason was given to revive our lagging space program and to convince ourselves that we must have rocket thrusters capable of carrying a satellite into orbit and back to earth again.

In the 1950s, William H. Whyte, Jr., looked at American society and found it peopled by achievement-oriented, conformist organization men. David Reisman's more scientific appraisal concluded that American men were no longer "inner-directed" as their fathers had been; rather they were motivated by the mores, rewards, and punishments transmitted to them from those higher up in status in society. Recruitment officers and sociologists found college students to be a "silent generation." Gone were the high jinks of the 1920s, the intellectual ferment of the 1930s, the intensity and valor of the 1940s. Business recruiters were astounded to find that students asked questions not about the possibilities in the jobs being offered but about pension plans and womb-to-tomb coverage. To excel was not as important as to obtain security.

Conformity, security, anti-communism and a firm orientation toward business characterized both candidates for the presidency in 1960. Viewed today, the most remarkable aspect of the campaign was the similarity of the notions of Democratic candidate Senator John F. Kennedy and Republican candidate Vice President Richard M. Nixon. In their "debates," they agreed on how to conduct foreign affairs, get rid of Communists within the country, balance the budget, maintain a steady rate of economic growth, and do something about mounting unemployment. "Senator Kennedy and I are not in disagreement as to the aims," Nixon said during the debates, and at times Kennedy expressed similar sentiments.

Social scientists found that many viewers of the "debates" could not distinguish between the candidates except by image. Democratic viewers were no more likely to recognize statements made by Kennedy than by Nixon, and the same held true for Republican viewers. By those who saw the "debates" on television, Kennedy was perceived to have won; Nixon was declared winner according to those who listened on radio.

By less than a majority of the votes cast, though with a plurality and a good margin in the electoral college, Kennedy was elected president on November 8, 1960. The result underscored the virtual unanimity of outlook in American leadership at the moment. After such a close election, the president had no clear mandate to make sweeping changes. The Democratic party had lost ground in both House and Senate; a coalition of southern Democrats and conservative Republicans still held most of the power in the legislative branch.

It is often stated that Kennedy's inauguration ushered in a new era which made a sharp break with the past. At the time, and to some people in retrospect, the rhetorical style, promises, and youth of the New Frontiersmen were fresh and appealing. The new president's utterances had a strong moral tone—"Ask not what your country can do for you; rather ask what you can do for your country." This combined with an affable and breezy personal style, and he became popular within a few months of taking office—polls in late 1961 showed few who remembered having voted against him. Kennedy held the first-ever regularly televised press conferences. He played touch football on the White House lawn. He founded the Peace Corps. All of this was new; what was old were his constant warnings to the Soviet Union to keep its distance.

Beyond a small circle of liberals such as John Kenneth Galbraith, Arthur Schlesinger, Jr., Walt Rostow, and the Bundy brothers, Kennedy's advisors were solid, middle-of-the-road men who might have come from the ranks of the Republicans. Dean Rusk, secretary of state, was a John Foster Dulles protégé. The president of Ford Motor Company, Robert S. McNamara— a Republican—became secretary of defense. Douglas Dillon, an undersecretary of state for Eisenhower, became secretary of the treasury.

Kennedy initiatives in Medicare, federal aid to education, urban affairs, tax reform, postal reform, and long-term foreign aid all went down to defeat or emasculation in the president's first brush with Congress. Kennedy blamed the recalcitrant legislators, but part of the problem was his own unwillingness to back up his initiatives with presidential arm-twisting. Kennedy's task force on schools recommended that he ask for $1.5 billion a year for education; he requested of Congress half that amount. The AFL–CIO suggested he build 400,000 new units of low-income housing; he asked for 100,000. In administration circles it was widely believed that Kennedy's 1960 phone call to Coretta King, while her husband was in jail, helped swing enough black votes to Kennedy to give him the election. Blacks had high hopes for Kennedy's involvement in their cause; however, in 1961 the White House issued a statement that the president "does not think it necessary at this time to enact civil-rights legislation."

At the end of the administration's first year in office the liberal Americans for Democratic Action (ADA) called Kennedy's record in the domestic arena one of "callous expediency" marked by "an astonishing indifference to real national needs." The victories had been modest—for example, a Kennedy-sponsored day-care bill for working mothers passed, but it provided only $5 million in facilities to care for 4 million children a year, equivalent to $1.25 in rent per child per year.

On reaching the Pentagon, McNamara had found no missile gap between the United States and Russia. During the campaign Kennedy had insisted there was such a gap. The president told the secretary to forget his new information. There was a 100 percent increase in the production of Minuteman missiles. Funding for the Polaris submarine program was increased by 50 percent. The number of nuclear bombers on standby alert was raised.

The most obvious and disastrous continuity between the Eisenhower and Kennedy administrations lay in their dealings with Cuba. In Ike's last year an invasion of Cuba was planned that would be executed by a United States–supplied force of Cuban emigrés. The Bay of Pigs operation was mounted in Kennedy's first months, and it was a disaster, ill conceived and ill executed. Shortly after the Bay of Pigs, Kennedy reiterated publicly that the U.S. had the right to overthrow a Communist regime that was 90 miles from American soil, a position entirely consistent with Cold War anti-Communist dogma.

Further foreign policy setbacks for Kennedy came from his unproductive Vienna summit meeting with Khrushchev, from the erection of the Berlin Wall, and from the Soviet resumption of atmospheric bomb testing. In reaction Kennedy tripled draft calls, told Americans to build fallout shelters, asked Congress for $207 million to build the shelters, and raised the national defense budget in order to mobilize 150,000 National Guardsmen and to send 40,000 troops to Europe.

As 1962 began there was a widening rift between the president's rhetoric and his actions. He embodied the promise of youth; his witticisms were already legend; his style had influenced fashions; his family were folk heroes—but he had achieved no significant victories other than his election, and his presidential prestige was at a low point.

In April of 1962, while the stock market was in a slump, Roger Blough of U.S. Steel met the president at the White House and simultaneously released a statement that his company was raising steel prices 6 percent. It was a blatant attempt to make it seem as if the administration backed the steel-price rise. Kennedy sprang into action. He put heavy pressure on smaller steel companies to resist the increases and began to switch government steel orders to companies that held the price line. U.S. Steel caved in, the price increase was rescinded, and Kennedy claimed victory. He seemed delighted that the business community now considered him an enemy, for that burnished his image with the working public.

It was Kennedy's image, not his substance, that attracted the country's young people and began to galvanize them. More of the Harvard class of 1962 wanted to go into the Peace Corps than sought jobs with the Fortune 500 companies. Idealism became something around which one might plan a life. There were increasingly more volunteers to ride buses South for sit-ins, even though the Kennedy administration had not yet openly supported the civil-rights movement. It was the president's idealism, Tom Hayden later reported, that inspired him in the spring of 1962 to write the Port Huron statement, the charter of SDS, Students for a Democratic Society:

> We are people of this generation, bred in at least modest comfort, housed in universities, looking uncomfortably to the world we inherit. . . . We regard men as infinitely precious and possessed of unfulfilled capacities for reason, freedom, and love. In affirming these principles we are aware of countering perhaps the dominant conceptions of man in the twentieth century: that he is a thing to be manipulated, and that he is inherently incapable of directing his own affairs. . . . Men have unrealized potential for self-cultivation, self-direction, self-understanding, and creativity. It is this potential that we regard as crucial and to which we appeal.

Hayden wondered about the probability of obtaining justice and equality and redistribution of income from a business-oriented civilization.

In general, President Kennedy's course of action was good for business and for the established priorities of the United States. While he was in office corporate profits went up 43 percent, a figure proportionately higher than the growth in the gross national product (GNP), and also higher than the increases in wages. Kennedy's tax reform proposals called for extremely generous depreciation allowances for business. Thirty percent of the savings realized by the proposed tax cut would go to that 2.2 percent of the population which earned over $20,000 a year; a family with a $200,000 income would save $32,000 in taxes, while a family with a $3,000 income would save $60.

In the summer of 1962 the president, *Time* and the Congress all became concerned with Castro's island. Congress authorized the use of American arms in Cuba, should that prove necessary; the midterm elections were approaching, and there was nothing like rattling sabers to jingle ballot boxes. In October, a month before the elections, spy flights revealed the presence of Russian missiles in Cuba, and presented Kennedy with an opportunity for confrontation which he could not refuse.

The Cuban missiles were few in number and of doubtful strategic value, for the American capacity to react to a Russian/Cuban first strike was so enormous that it was unlikely that Cuba or Russia would use the Cuban missiles in the near future, if ever. But Kennedy decided that United States prestige demanded that the missiles be removed.

Meeting in the White House, the Executive Committee of the National Security Council (NSC) urged a U.S. air attack on the missile sites, followed by an invasion which would topple Castro. Nearly alone among the Cold Warriors, Attorney General Robert Kennedy managed to convince his brother to downgrade this idea to a blockade by a fleet of 180 ships. Squadrons of nuclear bombers, 156 ICBMs and a quarter-million troops were held in readiness should the blockade fail. Negotiation was not seriously considered. Kennedy wanted victory, not a trade.

For several days in October, the planet teetered on the brink of Armageddon, until Khrushchev agreed to remove the missiles and to send in no more. We had stood eyeball-to-eyeball with the Russians, and they had blinked. However, as Khrushchev wrote to Kennedy in his long and emotional letter during the crisis, "only lunatics or suicides, who themselves want to perish and to destroy the whole world," would have triggered a thermonuclear war.

Soon after the Cuban missiles confrontation the Soviet Union began to manufacture missiles at a greatly accelerated rate; there had been a gap between the number of missiles the Russians had and the far greater arsenal of the United States. The jump in manufacturing missiles would enable the Soviet Union to make that gap disappear in the future. Thus Kennedy's actions in Cuba pushed the nuclear arms race to a higher level.

Although his actions did not result in a diminished Communist presence in the Western Hemisphere, Kennedy became a hero because of the Cuban standoff. A few days after the crisis the voters certified his popularity by returning a new Congress whose party makeup was virtually unchanged from that of 1960. In combination with other victories this gave Kennedy the mandate which previously had eluded him.

In Kennedy's third spring in office the administration began to move on a number of reforms. There was progress in civil rights, in reversing the escalation of the Cold War in Berlin and in Laos, in tax policy. The president's rhetoric continued to move the generation of apathetic youth; more and more became active and involved.

In June, Kennedy called for a nuclear test ban treaty with Russia, which was ratified with incredible speed in July of 1963. Although there had been an informal test-ban during the Eisenhower years, this new treaty was perceived as a great victory for peace.

Also in June, Kennedy called for civil-rights legislation and announced that even without the new legislation the administration would be pushing forward to defend black rights. Black students in sit-ins, Freedom Riders and voter registration campaigns had been bloodied in defense of these same rights which the administration was only now preparing to defend. Although Robert Kennedy's Justice Department had taken part in several highly publicized confrontations, the overall might of the federal government had so far not been used by the administration in support of civil rights. Over the summer the White House moved steadily to an advocacy position, but as the moment approached for the August March on Washington, the president was still opposed to the gathering. Behind the scenes Kennedy stalwarts labeled the march as embarrassing and warned that it might prove counterproductive by provoking a backlash that would halt the progress of civil-rights legislation through a balky Congress. Only at the last moment did the president change his mind and welcome the march to the nation's capital—and then only when its focus was changed to be a demonstration in support of his own legislation.

In his last months Kennedy was quite concerned with Vietnam. Southeast Asia was the one place in the world where the United States could openly and with firepower oppose communism. Berlin was in stalemate, and Cuba was too close, but Vietnam was an open and faraway war. Kennedy announced he would increase counterinsurgency forces 600 percent; such forces would provide the country with an alternative to nuclear bombs as a way to throw its weight around. The president personally supervised the selection of equipment for the Green Berets.

Up until mid-1963 it had been the American position that our military advisors in conjunction with native South Vietnamese forces could rid South Vietnam of communism. But during 1963 the fight seemed to grow larger and more desperate. Asked on television in September if he doubted the reasoning of the domino theory, Kennedy replied, "No, I believe it.... If South Vietnam went, it... would give the impression that the wave of the future in Southeast Asia was China and the Communists." By October, 16,732 Americans were in South Vietnam training the GVN army under combat conditions, flying combat support, surveillance and reconnaissance missions, and patrolling the waters off North and South Vietnamese territory. The Diem regime was corrupt and unable to govern without United States support; when a group of generals in Saigon asked for U.S. approval to make a coup, the Kennedy administration did not directly give support but did cut off economic aid to Saigon. This stopped all South Vietnamese military salaries and effectively showed the rank-and-file soldiers that in order to be paid they would have to agree to oust the Diem regime. On November first the generals set the plot in motion.

As it unfolded, Diem telephoned Ambassador Henry Cabot Lodge (who had run against Kennedy as Nixon's vice-presidential candidate) and asked the U.S. attitude toward the coup attempt. Disingenuously Lodge replied that he was not well enough informed about the situation and could say nothing. Not fooled, Diem tried to escape; within a day, both he and Nhu were dead. The generals took over. Washington was pleased. The new rulers pledged to root out communism and to prosecute the war with vigor—in return for even more U.S. aid and an increased American military presence.

Kennedy had backed the coup as a way to continue the fight against the Red Menace. It was an important step on the road to escalation in Vietnam, and one that was taken without too much soul-searching. It was simply one more step on a line that linked the present policies to the consensus foreign policy forged after the destruction of Pearl Harbor and repledged at the end of World War II.

As I. F. Stone would later put it, Kennedy was

> a conventional leader, not more than an enlightened conservative, cautious as an old man for all his youth, with a basic distrust of the people and an astringent view of the evangelical as a tool of leadership.

That evangelical talent had begun to move the country as Kennedy neared the end of his life, but during most of his thousand days there had been a surfeit of rhetoric and only a modest amount of forward movement in the society. Kennedy was a realist, but even more, he was a man who seemed to believe in making progress an inch at a time.

As he prepared to go to Dallas on a fence-mending political jaunt, Kennedy told aides that many of the administration's measures now before Congress, as well as some of his more visionary plans, might well have to wait for his second term before he could afford to push them. In that second term, he was looking forward to leaning more to the left. He expected that a big 1964 election victory would bring in a Congress weighted heavily in his favor. Then he would make his big moves.

At Amherst in October, Kennedy gave his last major speech, at a gathering held to honor poet Robert Frost. He first spoke in praise of art and dissent:

> The men who create power make an indispensable contribution to the nation's greatness, but the men who question power make a contribution

just as indispensable... for they determine whether we use power or power uses us.

And he offered his vision of the promised land, now in more specific terms than he had been willing or able to use three years earlier in the debates:

> I look forward to a great future for America, a future in which our country will match its military strength with our moral restraint, its wealth with our wisdom, its power with our purpose. I look forward to an America which will not be afraid of grace and beauty, which will protect the beauty of our natural environment... and... build handsome and balanced cities for our future. I look forward to an America which will reward achievement in the arts as we reward achievement in business or statecraft.... I look forward to an America which commands respect throughout the world not only for its strength, but for its civilization as well. And I look forward to a world which will be safe not only for democracy and diversity but also for personal distinction.

It was an exciting vision but one which Kennedy had not yet begun to translate into reality—nor even into legislation which might have been precursor to systemic change. At the time of his trip to Dallas, John Kennedy and his helpmeets were working within the set of assumptions that had existed, virtually without change, since the Second World War.

"Handsome and balanced cities" were not being sought with much more than words; the beauty of the natural environment was not being protected in any more efficacious way than it had been in Theodore Roosevelt's day; our military strength was not being especially tempered with moral restraint; and the achievement ethic was not yet supporting artistic or intellectual accomplishments to anywhere near the degree that it pushed monetary success.

In the years since 1945, in fact, the assumptions had hardened rather than softened. They had become transformed into what Lionel Rubinoff calls "causal myths,"

> covert value judgments which determine the limit of human responsibility.... There is nothing more dangerous to the health of a society than to be [overly] influenced by critically-accepted values.

Kennedy had inculcated the "critically-accepted" values of his time, and they had mitigated against his making much change in that society.

Yet change was in the air. There was a sense, expressed to a university audience by Columbia University provost David B. Truman, that the decade to come would be one in which the choices to be made would be critical.

> because so many of the particular decisions to be made are irreversible. They are irreversible not in the sense that once they are made there is literally no turning back from them, but rather in the sense that human and material resources once expended cannot be recaptured or readily replaced, and that the range of choice may be a good deal narrower tomorrow or the day after tomorrow than it is today. A generation ill-educated cannot be sent back to school; under-investment in basic research cannot be made up in a day; land relinquished to haphazard private exploitation instead of being kept for public uses cannot easily be re-captured. . . .

Truman was sure there would be crises in the years ahead. If in the heat of the crises, he argued, priorities could be formulated and coherent policies drafted—if the difficulties could be treated as challenges, as they had been in America during the Depression—then the crises might be productive. On the other hand, if naught would be thrown up but a succession of emergencies as chaotic and as unpredictable in their effect as typhoons, and if we reacted to them in the same helpless way people react to a tropical storm—then the crises might be unproductive, obstructions rather than challenges.

One thing, alone, was certain: youth would bear the brunt of the changes of the next decade. On that all the seers were agreed, especially those who gathered at the outset of the decade for a White House Conference on Youth. The baby boom of the postwar years had created a bulge in the population: the numbers of teenage and prepubescent youth were immense. Several conference members wondered about what would happen to them. For the youth of the coming decade, Margaret Mead wished a period of intensity. She suggested that although American civilization in the past quarter-century had provided for many of its children's material wants and needs, and even for their emotional needs, it had wiped out the traditional moratorium time when youth could find itself, free from all sorts of training and from the restraints of acquiring a mate and a vocation:

American Colossus   *41*

In those periods of history which we think of as golden ages, such a time of freedom from the immediate consequences of any act was permitted to a small number of youth. . . . There was . . . time to sleep, to grow, to experiment, to change, and to choose. In such periods the fiercest political idealism, the hardest religious choices, the acceptance of stringent artistic discipline belonged to youth.

Mead fervently hoped youth might find such a moratorium time, during which they might reach

the special degree of great questioning, high dedication, uncompromising search for something greater than mankind has yet attained, a willingness to search and wait and search again.

Echoing Mead, Dr. Charles Janeway of the Harvard Medical School suggested that *all* people need to be challenged, to lose themselves in struggles for something bigger than themselves in which they could believe deeply. These days, such a struggle would not be easy to come by, Janeway observed:

War, which provided such a challenge in times past, is unthinkable. Purely intellectual challenges, such as the pursuit of science, technology, or scholarship, will suffice for a few, creative activity in the arts will satisfy others . . . but . . . for the majority of our citizens a sense of purpose and satisfaction . . . is . . . harder to sustain when the economic and social systems provide for our material needs so lavishly.

It remained for Liston Pope, dean of the Yale Divinity School, to outline the ultimate battleground of the years ahead—the value system of the country:

Despite the necessity of facing the facts of the world in the 1960s, the problem of young people remains the same as for their elders, namely, that of finding ideals by which life's motion may be made meaningful and values by which intelligent and ethical decisions can be made. . . . The next ten years will be crucial ones for determination of man's aspirations and ethical standards.

Aspirations and ethical standards have always been at risk in times of change, especially for the young. But this is not a negative idea. When he was an old man, Oliver Wendell Holmes looked back, noted the terrors of the Civil War and of the struggle against slavery which had been the flash point of his own generation in its youth, and was grateful: "Through our good fortune in our youth our hearts were touched with fire. It was given to us to learn at the outset that life is a profound and passionate thing."

2 The President Has Been Shot

DURING THE LUNCH HOUR in Dallas on November 22, 1963, while he was riding through the downtown streets in an open limousine and smiling and waving to sidewalk crowds, President John F. Kennedy was assassinated.

Apart from the detonation of the atomic bomb at Hiroshima, the murder of President Kennedy was the single most shocking event of our time. Reverberations from the act are still being felt today. The assassination shattered the time of complacency that had existed in the United States since the close of World War II and ushered in an era of uncertainty and anguish.

Kennedy's position, age, and personality added to the shock of the assassination. Young, smiling, popular, the president embodied a great spirit, an eagerness for the use of power that was tempered by vision and purpose. Though many disagreed with his policies and methods, there were few who disparaged his engaging personality or who wished him bodily harm. There was every expectation that the remainder of his term would be filled with progressive ideas, and that he would win a second term in 1964.

The reaction of the country to Kennedy's death was nearly as instantaneous and as explosive as the rifle shots themselves. This was a moment of intense emotion, a public and private tragedy. A housewife in the Midwest summed up how many people felt when they heard the news:

Well, when I first heard, my husband ran back in and he said, "You know, Mary"—he was on his way back to work—he says, "You know, the president has been shot." I said, "Oh, turn the television on quick, quick." He turned the television on and...I felt terrible, just awful, so I said to myself, "Well, he'll be all right, he'll be all right, I know he'll be all right." And then a few minutes later here it came, he's dead. Well, then I just went all to pieces and said, "Well, he will not die in vain," and I cried.

Bad news traveled fast: according to a study made by the National Opinion Research Center, before the end of the afternoon 99.8 percent of the population knew that the president was dead. Half learned by word of mouth; then for verification most turned to the electronic media.

Americans shared a tremendous sense of loss. From the time of the assassination on Friday until mid-Monday when the slain president was laid to rest, the three television networks broadcast without commercial interruption every detail of the event and its aftermath. This was the greatest simultaneous event in the history of the world, and it bequeathed to us a series of indelible images. We watched television ten hours a day and saw: the assassination site from every angle; the unloading of the casket from *Air Force One* in the rain; Lyndon Johnson's agonized face and his plea for our help and God's; the murder of Lee Harvey Oswald by Jack Ruby; the stream of high-level mourners in the East Room of the White House; dignitaries and heads of state of ninety-two nations come to pay homage; the stoic honor guard; the funeral cortege with its riderless horse and reversed boots in the stirrups; little John-John's salute; Mrs. Kennedy's remarkable fortitude; the grave and the eternal flame in Arlington National Cemetery.

Sociologist Martha Wolfenstein studied natural disasters such as tornadoes, and compared them to the assassination of President Kennedy:

> The impact of the sudden violent death of a leader resembles other disasters that affect large numbers of people simultaneously. People react differently to such large-scale events than they do to more exclusively individual or family catastrophes. In a large-scale disaster the individual does not feel singled out by fate as he may when misfortune befalls him alone. He feels to some extent sustained by the realization that many others have been affected by the same event, that he is sharing a common experience.

Wolfenstein outlined the sequence of events that follows any enormous shock. The first stage is real shock, when people are disorganized, distressed, "dysphoric" (insulated against the full impact of the shock because they are stunned with disbelief). They feel that other disasters lie in wait—that another tornado will come, or, as Lyndon Johnson thought after Kennedy had been killed, that the assassinations were part of a larger plot and that people would come next to kill him. In the second stage the disastrous event is recapitulated repeatedly in an effort to assimilate and understand it, to master the distress it has caused. In the third stage the projection is toward the future: people are filled with fantasies about how the event could have been prevented and how similar events may be prevented in the future. This stage is characterized by a feeling of utopia—the disastrous event is felt to be the low point, so things will have to get better for they could not possibly get worse. In this phase larger questions spring to mind. If he wasn't a bad man, why did he die? Is there a God? Is the moral order benevolent? Such questions revolve around the difficulties of continuing to exist in a world in which evil thrives despite man's good intentions. There is a final stage of equilibrium, wherein the effects of the disaster are permanently incorporated into individual and societal consciousness.

Reactions to Franklin Roosevelt's death in 1945 had been extreme, but not so severe as to Kennedy's, for Roosevelt had been both old and sick. To cut down a young president by violent means was more of a shock. Then, too, through his continual television exposure, John Kennedy had been more intimately known to more people than had Roosevelt. Kennedy was as near and as familiar as our living rooms; we saw more of him than we saw of family members who lived away from the hearth.

Television, a critic noted at the time, was at the center of the shock. With its indelible images, information, immediacy, repetition, and close-ups, it served to define the tragedy for the public and added a new dimension to grief:

> The viewing ordeal was almost uncannily strange, a battle within one's self not to hear more and an uncontrollable hunger to obtain more information.

Television gave us a window through which to participate in the private grief of the Kennedys and of the official family. It also bore witness to our own grief, and helped us integrate the event into our lives.

Every great and unexpected crisis has the capacity to produce behavioral extremes—to send people into hysteria, or to numb them into apathy. As sociologists James Coleman and Sidney Hollander have suggested,

> There are events that cut through the apathy and chronic "know-nothingness" as if the public were hard of hearing and had suddenly turned on its collective hearing aid. The assassination of President Kennedy was such an event.

In extreme situations the wrong kind of information can precipitate violence, but the right kind can reduce anxiety. Sociological researchers found that the three days and nights of television coverage reduced Americans' fears of conspiracy, demonstrated to the public that the presidential succession was working smoothly, and facilitated discussion of feelings about the event and its aftermath.

The classic functions of media are the enforcement of societal norms, the conferral of status, and the narcotization of action. Television coverage of the assassination and its aftermath provided all three—with an emphasis on the third. An enormous energy charge had built up in the body politic, and somehow had to be dissipated. After Pearl Harbor, a similar charge had been transformed into hatred of the Japanese and channeled into the war effort. But the Kennedy assassination provided no easy targets for hate—Oswald was soon dead, and no conspiracy could be found or proved— and so the energies floated about and were not so quickly discharged. Television was a narcotic and a purgative; so were the grand displays of grief, the endless renaming of boulevards, high schools, and airports. But some of this energy remained, a free-floating emotional distress load that did not completely disappear.

That it took years to dissipate is testimony to the tremendous nature of the loss. Kennedy was taken from us both as man and as symbol. Chief Justice Earl Warren said President Kennedy was "chosen to embody the ideals of our people, the faith we have in our institutions, and our belief in the fatherhood of God and the brotherhood of man." These are mystical, even religious terms which may seem inappropriate to our large and complex democracy, but they accurately describe the nature of the loss. As Emile Durkheim had pointed out many years before, politico-economic units (governments) do not easily become the direct objects of emotional attachments, but a common symbol that stands for the government does attract emotion. In large societies even more than in smaller ones, Durkheim contended, the emotional connection between the symbol and the people was important, because the large society, "owing to its dimensions, the number of its parts, and the complexity of its arrangements, is difficult to hold in the mind." As the person through whom our complex government was encountered by the public—especially on television—the president was such a symbol.

Studies made after the assassination revealed that women were more affected by Kennedy's death than men, children more than adults, and blacks more than whites.

It was suggested that women were more affected than men because, in general, women had a more emotional response to life than men did. Kennedy had been handsome, young, and attentive to women, and there was every reason (researchers said) for women to have responded emotionally to his death. What was more surprising to researchers was the extent of men's responses. Many men wept openly and became depressed. Researchers said that men, in general poor mourners who were not supposed to cry, were enlarging the event of the president's death to encompass the many previous occasions when they had never been able to mourn properly.

Blacks were more affected than whites, it was suggested, because they had more reason to perceive Kennedy as hope. In his last months the president had become the symbol of a federal government committed to moving forward on civil rights, as no other had for a hundred years. Kennedy's sudden death instilled fear in black communities, a fear that was exacerbated by the fact that his successor, Johnson, was a southerner.

Historically, children have been the group that most readily identifies the president with the government. For children the president *is* the government. The president is near to God; he is the idealized father of the child's culture, the benign and omnipotent protector, the ultimate boss who tells everyone what to do. Children took Kennedy's death as a threat to their own security; they required reassurance that the government—and their world—would continue without serious consequences to themselves.

For months after the assassination many children drew dark pictures and suffered traumas. The incidence of mental distress among children was notably higher than it had been before the event. To help such children in distress, to assuage their fears of being submerged in a tide of anarchy, many psychologists and psychiatrists began to discuss with children the mechanism of the government. In the schools, educators began to spend more time on "civics" courses, giving the same reassurance to children who were not disturbed but who were nonetheless concerned about the assassination.

Similarly, many parents took the opportunity of Kennedy's death to discuss the democratic system with their children. Thus the assassination served as impetus to learn about and to question the political machinery of the country. How did we know the best man was now president? If there was another assassination, who would govern us? Many children began to think of the president as less powerful, since less omnipotent.

The group with the most profound reaction to the president's death were adolescents and college students, people born in the late 1940s and early 1950s. Martha Wolfenstein studied this group, and concluded:

> For adolescents (as opposed to adults) the feelings of loss tended to persist; they had difficulty working it through. The problem of giving up a loved and admired leader coincided with the basic unresolved task of their time in life, that of giving up their childhood attachment to their parents.

As a Princeton senior put it, "I guess this is part of growing up. This is the first time anything like this has hit our generation."

The first time, but not the last. In the ensuing decade, three other major assassinations and one assassination attempt took place; these left three men dead and the fourth severely crippled. The deaths of Malcolm X, Martin Luther King, Jr., and Senator Robert Kennedy and the wounding of Governor George Wallace made it plain to everyone that the assassination of President John Kennedy could not be dismissed as an isolated incident or as a complete anomaly in the life of the United States.

Though unique and quite dissimilar individuals, the five men were all charismatic; that is, they gave to ordinary people who acknowledged their leadership some sense of exaltation and surpassingness. Their intensity and visibility were high and their symbolic qualities were much in evidence, though each man was very much a realist.

As a country, as a people, we have spent an inordinate amount of time and energy analyzing the causes for each man's death, the possible assassins and the conjunctions between suspects. We have summoned up conspiracies too numerous to consider. Even where the "facts" of an assassination are well known, we have doubted them. The most important fact remains: in a ten-year period, four prominent men were assassinated and one was severely crippled.

Just after President Kennedy's death the black leader Malcolm X made a public comment that the assassination had been an instance of white people's "chickens coming home to roost." It was a reference to what Malcolm saw as America's violent way of treating people. For this remark, ostensibly, Malcolm was suspended from Elijah Muhammad's Nation of Islam. The comment was widely excoriated in the press—but similar comments voiced by other Americans drew no fire. Sentiments that the climate of violence and irrationality contributed to the president's death came from Chief Justice Earl Warren, from President Lyndon Johnson, from psychiatrist Dr. Karl Menninger, and from columnists for *The New York Times*. Malcolm's quip was anathema because it came from a man whom many viewed as an extremist, a man who had often seemed to advocate violence as a means to redress the grievances of the oppressed black minority of the country. In the years just prior to 1963, Malcolm X had transformed a small, local (Detroit) religious organization into a nationally based voice of the ghetto.

The rift between Malcolm and Elijah Muhammad had appeared even before Kennedy's death; it grew steadily wider thereafter, especially when Malcolm learned that Muhammad had transgressed his own codes and the generally held canons of sexual behavior. Suspended, Malcolm then broke with the Nation of Islam and formed a rival organization, the Muslim Mosque. As Malcolm's group prospered, Elijah Muhammad's group stagnated. There was bad blood between the two men, and Malcolm was viewed as a traitor to the cause. After a trip to Mecca, Malcolm converted to the orthodox Muslim faith and renounced the truncated and muddled version of it which Elijah Muhammad had taught. Malcolm became El-Hajj Malik El-Shabazz; his mosque became the Organization for Afro-American Unity. He suggested that his conversion taught him that blacks and whites could exist peacefully, side by side, though he continued to reject as unachievable an integrated society. Early in February of 1965 he flew to Selma, Alabama, where moderate leader Martin Luther King, Jr., was in jail as a result of leading a march for voting rights. Malcolm had often been contrasted to the "nonviolent" King. While in Selma, Malcolm spoke with King's aides and told Mrs. Coretta King at a banquet that he was "trying to help," and felt "it might be easier for whites to accept Martin's proposals" after hearing his own, more radical ideas. After returning to New York from Selma, he was awakened one night by firebombs exploding in his house. He helped his pregnant wife Betty and four small daughters escape to safety. After this there was little doubt in his mind that he was being pursued by Elijah Muhammad's men, and that they planned to kill him. On Sunday, February 21, 1965, just as he had begun to speak to an all-black meeting in Harlem's Audubon Ballroom, Malcolm X was assassinated by several black men wielding revolvers and shotguns. With eighteen slugs in his body, he died within minutes.

In the years between 1965 and 1968, over a dozen civil-rights figures and black leaders were killed, among them some Black Panthers and various workers in the South. With each passing year the times themselves seemed to become more violent, perhaps a reflection of the escalating war in Vietnam. Crime against persons leapt up in the annual FBI statistics. Crimes with guns, and especially homicides with guns, increased at a rate of 15–20 percent a year.

Some progress had been made in relieving the grinding poverty that was the lot of most blacks in America, but not much. In 1964, Martin Luther King, Jr., received the Nobel Prize for Peace. Despite his youth, he was the most visible and widely respected black leader in the United States. For more than a decade he had helped make the cause of the black voter a matter of national public concern. By 1968, however, people with more militant views had captured the imagination of the media, and the tactics which King had originated in the Montgomery bus boycott of 1955 no longer seemed workable nor the best answer to current crises. The emphasis swung to confrontation with the white hierarchy through whatever means possible. Appeals to morality were *passé*. Civil rights had become black liberation.

King decried the violent tactics which many blacks had embraced; he felt they would lead to further violence. To prove the violent tactics unnecessary, in April of 1968 he sought a new victory for nonviolence in a Memphis, Tennessee, garbage collectors' strike.

A march in support of the strike did not go well. It had been badly planned and inadequately controlled, and it got out of hand. Young blacks looted and randomly vandalized a neighborhood. This led to violent reprisals against the marchers in which one young black man was killed and sixty-two were injured.

King's worst fears were realized. Violence was not the answer, it was the problem. Frustrated and despondent, he talked of a Gandhian "fast until death" to force all blacks in the country to refuse to use violence in pursuit of their goals. As the prime mover of the coming Poor People's March on Washington designed to bring home to the politicians the inadequacy of current measures being taken to assist the poor, King obviously did not feel that the quest for equality was finished. He wished to reinstate the balance in the black movement between just goals and judicious means. On the evening of April 3, King spoke to a Memphis audience, and told them that all he had done had been God's will:

And He's allowed me to go up to the mountain. And I've looked over, and I've seen the promised land. I may not be there with you, but I want you to know that we as a people will get to the promised land.

The next evening King was relaxing in a motel room with his close associate Reverend Ralph Abernathy. He went out on the balcony to speak with Jesse Jackson and some others who were in the courtyard below. He asked a musician with Jackson to sing "Precious Lord, Take My Hand" at the coming rally. A rifle shot rang out, apparently fired from a nearby motel. The bullet severed King's spine and he died within hours. Like Malcolm X, he was thirty-nine years old.

When King was assassinated, Senator Robert F. Kennedy was in the midst of a campaign for the presidency. Kennedy and King had been in close touch for the past five years and more, working both sides of the street on matters affecting the poor and black in the United States. Though Kennedy had allowed the FBI to place a telephone tap and to tail King, he had done so (he now said) in order to prove to J. Edgar Hoover that King was *not* being influenced by foreign Communists. By 1968 the tapping was long in the past, and Kennedy and King had most recently been collaborating on ideas and planning for the Poor People's March.

It fell to Robert Kennedy to tell the people of the black ghetto of Indianapolis, Indiana, the news of King's death. After his brother John Kennedy's death in 1963, Robert had begun to read Edith Hamilton's *The Greek Way,* and from it had progressed to a study of the Greek dramatists and poets; he drew some solace in his own grief from the Greek conceptions of character, tragedy, and fate. In the ghetto of Indianapolis, Kennedy mounted a platform, cited the first evidence of King's death, and said that he, Kennedy, had also suffered the killing of a member of his family, a killing by a white man:

But we have to make an effort in the United States, we have to make an effort to understand, to go beyond these rather difficult times. My favorite poet was Aeschylus. He wrote: "In our sleep, pain which cannot forget falls drop by drop upon the heart until, in our own despair, against our will, wisdom comes through the awful grace of God."

What we need in the United States is not division; what we need in the United States is not hatred; what we need in the United States is not violence or lawlessness, but love and wisdom, and compassion toward one another, and a feeling of justice toward those who still suffer within our country, whether they be white or they be black. . . . Let us dedicate ourselves to what the Greeks wrote so many years ago: to tame the savageness of man and to make gentle the life of the world.

Later in the evening, Robert Kennedy remarked to friends, "You know that Harvey Lee Oswald, whatever his name is, set something loose in this country."

Following King's death there was proportionately less rioting in Indianapolis than there was elsewhere in the country. Kennedy won the Indiana primary, and looked strong in other spring primaries.

In the four and a half years since his brother's death, Robert Kennedy had steadily become more liberal. He was a Senate champion of the needs of the disadvantaged and a critic of the Vietnam War. Even though he emphasized these concerns, he had won in Indiana. Though many disparaged Kennedy as a political opportunist who entered the fray only after President Johnson had withdrawn and after Eugene McCarthy had shown there was political capital to be gained from the anti-war issue, Kennedy's positions on major social issues appealed to a substantial number of voters.

Victories in the next round of primaries would make RFK the prime challenger to Vice-President Hubert Humphrey's seemingly secure hold on the Democratic nomination. On June 4, Kennedy won the California primary and the South Dakota primary; in the latter, he outdrew Humphrey and McCarthy combined. In his victory speech early the next morning in the ballroom of the Los Angeles Ambassador Hotel, he stressed that he had won both in the most urban state and in the most rural state. As he left the ballroom through the kitchen to go to a press conference, Robert Kennedy was shot by Jordanian immigrant Sirhan Sirhan. He died the next day.

After Robert Kennedy's death many white voters who had supported him now told polltakers they would vote for Governor George C. Wallace of Alabama. In June of 1963, Wallace had stood in the doorway of the University of Alabama to block two black students' entrance to the school;

only under pressure from Robert Kennedy's Justice Department and from President Kennedy's action which federalized the Alabama National Guard had Wallace capitulated. That action, even though it ended in defeat, had made Wallace a national figure; during the next several years he became the foremost anti-integrationist in the country. By 1968 his anti-black stance had widened to include openly reactionary positions on many issues. As Robert Kennedy had in other ways, Wallace appealed to the dissatisfied. He stood against the federal government on most issues, for states' rights, and for a tough "law and order" program which was actually a cover for a racist design that would keep black and white societies separate and unequal. In a time of national difficulties and division (represented by the split over the Vietnam War), Wallace's simplistic answers to complex national traumas won him supporters among blue-collar workers, small businessmen, urban ethnics of recent European origin (particularly those who lived on the edge of black neighborhoods), and among those who worried about riots, permissiveness, student protesters, and losing the Vietnam War. Wallace loudly opposed gun control, long hair, "pointed heads" (intellectuals), the Supreme Court, school busing, liberals, poll-takers, and *The New York Times*. He said those who opposed him were anarchists and Communists, and he accused candidate Nixon of stealing his thunder by copying his positions on many issues and claiming them as Republican.

Wallace was a charismatic candidate and leader who focused people's negative energy, rather than marshaled positive, popular support for progress. In the 1968 election Wallace received 13½ percent of the popular vote and 46 electoral votes. This was the largest number of people ever to vote for a third-party candidate, and Wallace polled only slightly lower in percentage of total votes than had Theodore Roosevelt and the Bull Moose party in 1912. The Wallace votes came more from Nixon than from Humphrey. Nixon had been so concerned about the potential loss of the upper South to Wallace that he had made an alliance with arch-segregationist Strom Thurmond, and had put on his ticket Maryland's Governor Spiro T. Agnew, whose anti-black and rabid law-and-order pronouncements rivaled those of Wallace.

Even after having won the 1968 election Nixon feared a renewed Wallace candidacy, and in 1970, using leftover campaign funds, Nixon financed the campaign of Wallace's opponent for the Alabama governorship. Wallace won anyway, and used the governorship for a serious try at the presidency in 1972.

By the early spring of 1972 Governor Wallace was boldly stalking through both southern and northern states, seeking votes. In the Florida primary he beat the leading Democratic contender, Senator Edmund Muskie, and was making generally good showings in other primaries against a weak and divided field of Democrats. During a campaign stop in Laurel, Maryland, Wallace was shot and paralyzed by a young white man, Arthur Bremer. This ended Wallace's campaign for the presidency.

These five shootings were the decade's most obvious shocks. But what effects did they have? Murray Clark Havens, Carl Leiden, and Karl M. Schmitt, authors of *The Politics of Assassination*, suggest that the possible impact of an assassination can range over many areas: the system can radically alter, personnel and policies can change, institutional relationships can be modified. It is important to differentiate between the shock of the event and systemic change. Emotional displays such as public mourning, the renaming of streets, even the riots which followed Martin Luther King's death, were all responses to shock. They were not alterations of the system of government. In fact, because these events were so shocking, they may have allowed the system to absorb stress and to remain unchanged. In this sense, the authors conclude, "Shock is a ritualized substitute for change." In other words, the riots that took place after King's death—or the public mourning after John Kennedy's death—absorbed energies which might have gone into changing the system, and so the system survived.

However, even if the assassinations did not result in *coups d'état*, or in the substitution of another form of government for our participatory democracy, there were, indeed, changes produced by the assassinations. Alterations in personnel, policies, and institutional relationships were many, especially if we consider the multitude of entities outside the mammoth federal bureaucracy which governs us—institutions such as churches, ethnic groups, economic classes, as well as charismatic individuals who lead causes of the spirit. The Kennedys, Malcolm X, Martin Luther King, Jr., and even George Wallace led not only by virtue of their elected positions but also by the force of their personalities. Their removal forced some changes.

In *War and Peace* Tolstoy debates two theories of history. One says that history is made by exceptional men who achieve and wield power. The second suggests that tides of emotions (liberty, equality, fraternity) or of invention (the industrial revolution) are what make history, and that great men merely embody the direction of those movements. The question is as it was in Tolstoy's time.

However, in Max Weber's concepts of charisma and routine there are possible explanations of the changes that the assassinations wrought, changes that meld the theories of great men and great movements. Weber suggested that there is in all organizations (and societies) an opposition between charisma and routine. Charisma, the primary force, appears at the outset of a civilization. As organizations and societies age, charisma yields to routine, leadership to bureaucracy. When charisma suddenly disappears, as in an assassination, there is a dramatic shift toward routinization. Malcolm X's death deprived his nascent organization of its only acknowledged leader, and it very nearly dissolved. Also, since the actual influence of Malcolm extended far beyond the OAAU or the Nation of Islam, his death affected constituencies greater than those organizations. Many whites at the time were incredulous at the outpouring of affection and respect accorded Malcolm in death by even the least radical element of the black community. Had not the chickens come home to roost for Malcolm as he said they had for Jack Kennedy? Blacks understood, as whites did not, that Malcolm's rhetoric had been directed toward building, rather than destroying. Blacks understood that Malcolm had made himself over as a man, bootstrapped himself out of the gutter and the prison to become an exemplary moral figure whose genius was articulating the concerns which many held but few could voice. His rhetoric insisted that blacks recognize their state of oppression for what it was, and take steps to free themselves from that oppression. This was a positive, not a negative goal. Malcolm's death left blacks who agreed with his assessment of society without leadership.

The death of Martin Luther King, Jr., altered his own organization, the Southern Christian Leadership Conference (SCLC). When King was gone, it was neither as vibrant nor as effective. If Malcolm's death removed the apostle of anger, King's death removed the apostle of hope, and the conjunction of the two losses left the black community directionless. The riots which followed King's assassination showed this lack of direction, and were counterproductive. It took a major repressive action to stop the riots, and this helped to establish the climate of backlash. Richard Nixon rode that backlash; when elected, he used his mandate to change policies which affected the black and the poor, discontinuing or cutting back governmental programs benefiting these groups. In this way the deaths of the black leaders resulted in governmental policy changes. Without the voices of Malcolm and King, the black community had less charisma with which to resist the policy reversals of the Nixon years.

The Kennedys, King, Malcolm X, were all shamans, spiritual as well as political figures. Following them was more than a political act; it was an expression of inner conviction. Their emotional appeal was part of what made their deaths so shocking.

In the case of Robert Kennedy's death, a political cause foundered when he died: its name was postwar liberalism. The Democratic presidential nomination in 1968 went to a tired and lackluster Hubert Humphrey, whose earlier liberal positions had been eroded in the Johnson years, and whose compromise with power struck many as unseemly. After Nixon's election, liberal ideas fell steadily from favor. No obvious standard-bearers emerged to lead the cause of the left—the remaining Kennedy suffered a blow at Chappaquiddick, and other liberal senators and non-congressional leaders could not hold people's attention. McGovern's 1972 candidacy illustrated the lack of leadership: liberal ideas abounded in his campaign, but no charismatic appeal enlivened them.

The wounding of George Wallace proved it was not only liberalism that was under attack, but rather any kind of leadership coupled with celebrity. Anyone visible enough to attract attention could be the target of an assassin. Wallace's charisma was not so strong as that of the other men; his conservative appeal did not seem to belong to him alone—indeed, it had long been usurped by Nixon—and it outlived his candidacy. The wounding of Wallace showed that anyone could be hit; the bell could toll for any person at any time.

With each new assassination, stories surfaced about the earlier ones. In the public mind one murder ran into another; one reinforced the fears and added ramifications to the last. Taken together, as they had to be by the end of the decade, the assassinations seriously affected our perceptions of our leaders, and of our society.

First and foremost, the assassinations forced Americans to accept death as a threat to political life in the United States. From Jack Kennedy's death onward, on the national scene we lived with death constantly in the wings. Assassination was no longer only a happenstance in banana republics or in corrupt, old world societies. It happened here. It happened in front of us, on television. It happened repeatedly. We could no longer dismiss political murder as an aberration. Now it was endemic.

Foreign observers since de Tocqueville had unfailingly noted that Americans do not understand or even accept the possibility or inevitability of death. Death to us was a disquieting event, an interruption or discontinuity that introduced chaos rather than order. To a future-oriented, progress-besotted society, death was anathema. It meant that tomorrow might not be better than today. Under the shadow of death, a man, a policy, an institution, a deeply held belief could suddenly and unexpectedly come to an end. We seemed astonished to learn this truth.

The assassinations forced upon us an acceptance of death-in-life, and the impact ranged far beyond the understanding that death came to all individuals. Reinhold Niebuhr had seen a need for the United States to have an understanding of its limitations. The series of assassinations began to provide us with this sense of the finite. We slid from charisma toward the ultimate routinization. We found that our human resources were severely limited, because no Martin Luther King, Jrs. or Bob Kennedys sprang up to replace the originals. Our stock of men who could command allegiance beyond duty was declining. We could not rely on any one man; we had to rely on many. Thus the assassinations moved us from a world view that saw unity to one that encompassed multiplicity, from a simplistic sense of events and causes toward a more complex apprehension of the world.

These are large shifts, and none of them was completed by the assassinations alone. We will return to these themes throughout the rest of the book. But with the assassinations, the shifts began.

Concurrent with the assassinations was a narrowing of our field of information. Through television we were presented with less knowledge and perspective about seminal events just at those times when we might well have profited from a broader view. When the total focus of the media was on the events in Dallas or the mourning in Atlanta, we could do little but pay attention to that focus and ignore others.

It was during the assassination crises that we seemed to need television the most, to need the pictures and the intimacy that television brought; we needed television to verify that each new death was real and important. But even as television salved our needs for proximity and participation, it rubbed salt in our wounds. The close-up was not close enough, it had to be more clinical, more revealing; the detail had to be compared to others; the knowledge had to be in our eyes and ears and brains ever more quickly. Truth would slip from our grasp if we had to wait for the morning's newspaper or for next week's or next month's magazine analysis. To indemnify our loss we demanded payment in images. The suddenness with which change came reinforced our tendency to rely on television, which seemed most able to transmit that change as it was happening. We got hooked on the short-term. Our sense of the long-term atrophied.

In these years television presided over an ancient ritual, the death and rebirth of the king. Through television we participated as had celebrants of old—for the transference ritual is found in one form or another in nearly every culture throughout history. It has profound emotional components, among them the longing of the human spirit to overcome death and assert life's continuity. While grieving for the lost president, we celebrated the fact that a new man had assumed the office; the president was dead, the presidency lived on. Similarly, when Martin Luther King, Jr., was killed, the invariable comment that came from black leaders and news analysts was that the Poor People's March would go on, that civil rights would not die. When Robert Kennedy died, some took comfort from knowing there was yet another Kennedy brother available to assume the mantle of the family.

As with all essential rituals, the death and rebirth of the leader emphasizes the immortality of the system over the mortality of the individual. It is expression of the wish—and the need—to return to *status quo ante*. In having survived the assassinations the social and governmental systems appeared strong. In fact, it was in such times of crisis that the durability, continuity, and flexibility of our societal institutions became most apparent.

However, just as being overly calm in the presence of overwhelming danger is not necessarily an indication of mental health, so having rocklike faith in the immutability of our institutions in the face of shocking assassinations was not altogether salutary. Research on grief suggests that a mourner goes through several emotional stages, from acute grief through a less intense but longer period of recovery to a last phase of reintegration into the world. Too rapid a return to normal life after the death of a close friend or relative often results in psychic trauma. The healing process takes time—months, usually, and often years—until new life patterns are established, patterns which show some acceptance of the death that has occurred, and some alteration of old habits.

In late 1963 and early 1964, people marveled at how quickly national life returned to "normal" after the president's death. Similar observations dot the record subsequent to the other assassinations of the decade. In these rapid returns to *status quo ante,* in the celebrations of systemic stability which followed the assassinations, the mourning process was incomplete. Unnoticed at the time, some psychic damage remained in part of the body politic, covered up but still potent, a load of unfinished emotional business.

One can see some of this emotional overload in perusing the vast amount of materials about John Kennedy and his death, which reflected a fixation that bordered on idolatry. It was only after the fact that the Kennedy administration became a Camelot, that touch football was retroactively elevated to the status of court gavotte. It was only after John Kennedy was dead that he was pronounced to have been a martyr to a moral crusade— civil rights or international peace, depending on the mourner's need. Hagiographers compared him to Lincoln. Kennedy memorabilia became nearly as valuable as that of saints; his portrait kept watch over households. In retrospect the Kennedy years took on the air of being better than they actually were—youth remembered through the seamless gauze curtain of middle age.

Perhaps this retroactive transformation sprang from the yearning for rational explanation of an irrational event. Perhaps it came from the need for a hero. Whichever, the young and unfortunately victimized president was metamorphosed into a martyred philosopher-king. Similarly, after Martin Luther King, Jr.'s death he was lionized by whites as the moral arbiter of the nation—a notion closer to the truth than that embodied by Kennedy's transformation—while many in the majority conveniently forgot the years during which they had looked upon King as only an uppity black.

America had long been inordinately fond of such denials of historic fact which helped us maintain our self-image. We had pretended to be a peaceful society, had believed that all our wars had been fought for good causes, that the lawlessness and viciousness of the Old West was merely an unconnected series of frontier incidents, that the extermination of Native American tribes could be dismissed as an unfortunate sidebar to the fulfillment of manifest destiny. Public murder after public murder gave the lie to pretensions of the peaceable kingdom, and legitimatized violence. The assassinations began a period in which violence became an accepted part of the country's life. Sirhan Sirhan and Arthur Bremer were influenced by the instant fame acquired by Lee Harvey Oswald; James Earl Ray was swayed by the violent rhetoric and extralegal aggressions practiced by the Ku Klux Klan and other antiblack groups. The chickens had indeed come home to roost.

Through the decade the rate of murder among Americans increased to near-epidemic proportions, and the rate of all violent crimes doubled. According to the FBI, in the late 1970s a violent crime was committed in the United Sates once every twenty-four seconds, and one American was murdered (usually by a handgun) once every twenty-three minutes. It is not too farfetched to assign some fraction of this increase to the influence of the assassinations, which highlighted violent death and made it possible to incorporate the results of such death into our society.

The assassinations also raised doubts about the legitimacy of the successors of the murdered leaders. This was most serious in the case of Lyndon Johnson. Through his tenure Johnson had to work to make the public accept him as the true president, rather than as the accidental and temporary occupant of the Oval Office. Robert Kennedy, in the four and a half years between his brother's death and his own, was most often compared unfavorably to President Kennedy. A sympathetic reporter noted on the last campaign trail that at every whistle stop the ghost of John Kennedy dogged Robert's tracks.

Loss of authority continued throughout the decade. As vice-president under the "upstart" Johnson, and as the winner of the Democratic nomination only after Robert Kennedy had been removed from the field, Hubert Humphrey was viewed with a taint of illegitimacy on him; Richard Nixon was viewed as the ultimate political benefactor of the deaths of the two Kennedys and of Martin Luther King, Jr. After Watergate had begun to unravel, this loss of authority hampered Nixon even more, and it was bequeathed to his successor, Ford, a man who had not been elected either to the vice-presidency or to the presidency.

The loss of legitimacy at the highest level was reflected in a serious doubting of authority on all levels. We came to doubt the legitimacy and authority of the doctor pounding our chest, and of the cop pounding the beat. The rising crime rates fed on this doubting of authority; it became less immoral to do something illegal. The father figure no longer had unquestioned title to his position; he had proved to be less than omnipotent; his capacity to demand obedience, tribute, and even respect was undermined. The superego seemed to have gone into hiding: it was as true in the personal and familial spheres as it was in the arenas of national politics and international affairs.

The questioning of authority is an emotional response to the shock of the father's death. Two other, even more fundamental responses grew out of the assassination of the president, and it is these responses that crystallized into basic patterns which remained in place and would characterize the decade ever more strongly as the years went by.

When a gunshot is fired, in response we crouch, take a defensive and apprehensive stance. We fortify ourselves against further attacks; we take cover. Physiologically as well as psychologically, our actions are motivated by the desire to *preserve* and to defend what is left to us after the shock. We cherish what remains, for now that we have suffered a grievous loss what we still retain seems all the more precious to us.

A second response to the gunshot, often delayed a bit, is to scan the horizon and the near vicinity to discover why and whence the attack has come and how to prevent further attacks. Psychologically speaking, we *search* to find the causes of our misfortune, to understand what has happened to us.

These two courses of action—to be more precise, of reaction—normally coexist. Both characterize the responses of any individual to shock. In this era, both immediately characterized our national responses. Both are normal, healthy, and necessary responses.

After the president was assassinated the impulse to *preserve* translated into beefing up the Secret Service to insulate the former president's family, as well as the new president, from further shocks, After the Robert Kennedy assassination this protection was extended to presidential candidates and later to some other elected officials, as well as to ex-presidents and their families. Private organizations also took steps to provide similar protection for their own leaders. But while providing such protection, as a society we acknowledged that attack could come at any time and from any direction. If those who were carefully protected were vulnerable, then who was safe? No one, it seemed, could be completely insulated against attack; nevertheless, we began to develop a fortress mentality, protecting our persons, then our property, then whole communities, behind ever-higher and more isolating walls.

After the president was assassinated we also pursued a *search* for the truth of what had occurred, and explanations of why it had occurred. Many people excoriated the Warren Commission for never satisfactorily establishing the motivation of the most likely assassin, Oswald. And searching led into ever more murky waters, for as we looked into the existence of violence in our society, difficult questions were raised. Was violence societally condoned? Was violence due to inequities in our system, or to misperceptions of individuals? Why would men ever want to kill one another?

With each subsequent assassination and attempt, the questions became stronger and more insistent, and seemed to demand action on their logical sequel, the attempt to redress the fundamental imbalances which were uncovered through the questions. But such imbalances were so thoroughly entwined in the structure of our lives and in the institutions of our society that any attempt to redress them seemed as futile as securing for anyone of complete protection from a determined assassin.

3 The Fire This Time

ON JUNE 11, 1963, President John F. Kennedy introduced his civil-rights bill:

> The heart of the question is whether all Americans are to be afforded rights and equal opportunities, whether we are going to treat our fellow Americans as we want to be treated. If an American, because his skin is dark, cannot eat lunch in a restaurant open to the public, if he cannot send his children to the best public school available, if he cannot vote for the public officials who represent him, if, in short, he cannot enjoy the full and free life which all of us want, then who among us would be content to have the color of his skin changed and stand in his place?

In equating the "full and free life" with voting rights, desegregated restaurants, and a single school system, Kennedy barely grazed the surface of Negro Americans' second-class citizenship. At the time blacks lived mostly in segregated areas, in substandard housing, had few rights of any kind, held menial and low-status jobs, had inferior education, and were haunted by discrimination from cradle to grave. Kennedy made no mention of the economic disparities, nor of the social barriers to blacks' participation in mainstream American life, nor of the ineradicable scars of discrimination. If in 1963 civil rights was popular with the majority, that was because the administration's program for civil rights was limited to the public sphere, and because it did not go very deep and would not cost the white majority very much. Even so, the modest program endorsed by Kennedy was bottled up in Congress, with slim chance for passage.

In August of 1963 a quarter-million people, 80 percent of them black, 20 percent of them white, gathered at the foot of the Lincoln Memorial. It was one hundred years after Lincoln had signed the Emancipation Proclamation, and the rally was to spur the completion of the major unfinished business of emancipation, the integration of dark-skinned citizens into the mainstream of American life. The march was the culmination of three years' work. Under the hot sun the idealistic marchers waved placards, sang songs, pledged support to the government's program for civil rights, and listened to speeches. The most telling speech came from Dr. Martin Luther King, Jr., who proclaimed that he had a dream, a dream that his children would one day enjoy the advantages already extended by birthright to the children of the white majority.

On this same day black novelist James Baldwin wrote out another dream in a letter to his fourteen-year-old nephew:

> This innocent country set you down in a ghetto in which, in fact, it intended that you should perish.... You were born where you were born and faced the future that you faced because you were black and *for no other reason*.... You were born into a society which spelled out with brutal clarity, and in as many ways as possible that you were a worthless human being. You were not expected to aspire to excellence; you were expected to make peace with mediocrity.

Though the novelist was more bitter than the preacher, their dreams were two sides of the same coin. Which foretold the future? In retrospect it has become clear that the peaceful, biracial, legislation-focused March on Washington was not the harbinger of the crusade to come but the final celebration of a gentle era.

That era began with the Supreme Court decision in *Brown vs. the Board of Education* in 1954, and it was focused on the South. The Montgomery bus boycott of 1955–1956, which first brought Dr. King to prominence, was an instance of moral judgment being brought to bear on the unjust, archaic remnants of the Confederacy. Starting in 1960, sit-ins swept Negro campuses and nearby towns, and the imagery of the peaceful strike entered the nation's consciousness. Across the ocean, in Africa, new black nations were emerging; here, too, black men and women could stand up for respect and self-governance. The style of the nonviolent protests was as important as the targets: such decorous civil disobedience could be celebrated by the majority for being within God's law, if not within Alabama's. It was mostly Southerners who agreed with William Simmons, editor of "The Citizens' Council," who wrote that

> The Caucasian and the Negro have never been integrated in our land. Racial segregation is, and has been since the founding of this country, a pervading characteristic of American life.... It is a remarkable—and encouraging—fact of contemporary American life that... our population as a whole has remained almost totally impervious to [proposals for integration].... I have known professors who teach integration, preachers who preach integration, and politicians who would stand on their heads for the Negro vote, but I have yet to meet (or even hear of) a law enforcement officer or anyone else whose daily business brings him into intimate association with our most publicized minority who thinks integration is a good thing.

Simmons's apostrophe to the law enforcement officer was an apt image, for in the early 1960s it was southern law enforcement officers who were the leading edge of the segregationist ethic. "Bull" Connor of Birmingham sent fire hoses and police dogs to battle black (and some white) students trying to stage a sit-in to integrate lunch counters in his town; publicized, his tactics helped to widen the base for protest.

Blacks from the North, some from the South, a few white students, and some of the media came to the rural South in the first few summers of the 1960s and began to see at first hand the abysmal conditions in which blacks lived: housing without heat, water, or indoor toilets, jobs without security, conditions little better than serfdom. The volunteers (and their hosts) also experienced the hard work and exposure to continual hatred and beatings which had to be endured to advance the cause of black equality.

Those who went South in the days before it became fashionable to do so were in many ways the most dedicated young people of their time; their concerns went beyond themselves; they worked for the future, to add small, incremental pieces to an American dream of brotherhood. Sensing this, the majority gave them support. Even when CORE (the Congress of Racial Equality) and SNCC (the Student Nonviolent Coordinating Committee) began to cast out their white workers and to insist that blacks alone must win their rights, popular support did not appreciably narrow. So long as the goal continued to be integration, such groups were applauded. Civil rights was merely a way station and a means to achieving integration.

Civil rights was also about public rights and public places, *de jure* segregation. It is a commonplace that legislation is often passed to assure rights already won, not to win new rights. Such was the case with the 1964 civil-rights package which Congress passed at Lyndon Johnson's specific request as a "memorial" to John Kennedy: this legislation assured rights which were already the law of the land. But there was more to the black cause than civil rights, and even as Congress debated the 1964 civil-rights bills, Johnson initiated a new phase in the fight for equality: a war on poverty.

As it was so often in this era, the genesis of the War on Poverty was solid anti-communism, which translated into President Kennedy's request for a task force report on manpower conservation in the military. Its findings, as summarized by Johnson, were

> 1) that one-third of the nation's youth would, on examination, be found unqualified for military service; 2) that poverty was the principal reason these young men failed to meet those physical standards.

From this report sprang the Economic Opportunity Act of 1964, and from that, the War on Poverty and the Great Society. The goal of all the programs was to lift 35 million Americans out of poverty. Of the total, 78 percent were white, and 11 million were children. But while only 22 percent of the poor were nonwhite, nearly half of all the dark-skinned people in the country lived in poverty and another quarter lived one or two months' wages per year above the poverty line. Clearly, dark skin and poverty were intertwined in the United States; and so it came to be perceived that the War on Poverty had as a primary focus the aiding of minorities, in particular those who lived in inner-city ghettos.

The War on Poverty was hardly a giveaway. Funding for its first year was $750 million, or about $20 per poor person. The aggregate amount was what it took to sustain the still-small American commitment to Vietnam for one month. It was one-tenth of one percent of the gross national product, a figure so small that it made few demands on business or on taxpayers.

At its outset the War on Poverty enjoyed the same majority approbation and the same congressional enemies as had the fight for civil rights. After much fuss, the first batch of War on Poverty measures passed Congress in August of 1964, during what was known as "Freedom Summer." In Mississippi, that summer was marked by efforts to register voters, and the murder of three young men from the North who had come South to help with the task. Many black civil-rights workers had been harassed and murdered before, but two of these three were white, which gave these murders media attention not accorded the others.

In November of 1964, Johnson won a landslide at the polls. The victory seemed to ratify the nation's desire to help the poor and the black. At about the same time, Dr. Martin Luther King, Jr., won the Nobel Peace Prize: this was ratification of another sort.

In early 1965, Dr. King decided to put his powers to the test in a voter registration drive focused on Selma, Alabama. Selma was a tough place. Segregationists pointed to it with pride as one town that wouldn't give in. The black community of the nation looked at Selma as a test not only of themselves, but of the government's commitment to defend its citizens' rights. It was in Selma that Malcolm X came closer to the ideals of Dr. King, just weeks before Malcolm was murdered. During the Selma voting drive there were some murders of marchers and of sympathizers by state troopers and by the Ku Klux Klan. The government did send in some help. On March 15, after demonstrations of solidarity with the Selma marchers had been held in Detroit, Chicago, Los Angeles, and Washington, President Johnson spoke of Selma. The events there, he said, were

> part of a far larger movement which reaches into every section and state of America. It is the effort of American Negroes to secure for themselves the full blessings of American life. Their cause must be our cause, too. Because it is not just Negroes, but really it is all of us, who must overcome the crippling legacy of bigotry and injustice . . . and We Shall Overcome.

He asked Congress to pass the strongest voting-rights bill ever proposed. On June 4 the president echoed his themes in an important address at Howard University. He outlined the needs of poor black Americans:

> Negro poverty [is] . . . solely and simply the consequence of ancient brutality, past injustice and present prejudice. . . . The task is to give 20 million Negroes the same chance as every other American to learn and grow—to work and share in society. . . . To this end equal opportunity is essential, but not enough.

The Fire This Time 69

These were lines that could have been written by Baldwin. Johnson's address signaled a commitment to go beyond legal protection of publicly visible rights and into the provision of resources for blacks. Here was the interweaving of the strands of civil rights and the War on Poverty, two attempts to redress grievances of the minority. Years before, Eric Hoffer had shown how both were related to a man's sense of worth:

> Individual self-respect cannot thrive in an atmosphere charged with...discrimination. Both the oppressors and the oppressed are blemished. The oppressed are corroded by an inner agreement with the prevailing prejudice against them, while the oppressors are infected with the fear they induce in others. Finally, even in advanced and wholly egalitarian societies millions of people are robbed of their sense of worth by unemployment....

The interweaving of the two strands had begun to create a "revolution of rising expectations" among blacks. In history there had been many such revolutions. De Tocqueville characterized the French revolt of 1789 in such terms, but warned of the dark side of the ferment:

> A people which had supported the most crushing laws without complaint, and apparently as if they were unfelt, throws them off with violence as soon as the burden begins to be diminished....The evils which are endured with patience as long as they are inevitable, seem intolerable as soon as a hope can be entertained of escaping from them.

The problems of inequality in the North were more complex, more related to economics, and more private than the public segregation of the South. Yet the "revolution of rising expectations" now informed the belief that *de facto* segregation, with all its subtleties, was under attack and might soon yield. And then, five days after the Voting Rights Bill was signed, two months after the Howard University speech, and as the first antipoverty monies were flowing into the nation's ghettos, the city rated by the Urban League as first among 68 as to the quality of black life possible within its invisible walls—exploded.

The night of Wednesday, August 11, 1965, was sweltering and windless in Watts, the black section of Los Angeles. An old Buick weaved to the corner of 116th and Avalon, and a white California highway patrolman thought its driver must be drunk. By the time he finished administering a sobriety test to Marquette Frye, who was driving with his brother Ronald, a crowd had gathered. So had more patrol cars, and the Fryes's mother. Marquette resisted arrest, and when the police were rough with him, the other Fryes joined in. A woman bystander was thought by police to have spit at a cop; she ran into the crowd and the police lunged in after her with nightsticks flying. Heads were battered, and moments later patrol cars and the four suspects left the area in a hail of rocks, bottles, and epithets about police brutality.

The general allegation of brutality had broad substantiation in a history of shoddy police patrol work and blatant discrimination. Left to its own devices, the crowd began to exaggerate the Frye incident. It was said that the woman bystander had been pregnant and that the cops had beaten her. The crowd began to pull passing white motorists from cars and beat them; they threw more rocks and bottles; they started a few fires. When newspaper and television crews (along with police reinforcements) arrived, 1,500 people milled around and engaged in various angry activities. In the melee 19 cops and 16 blacks were injured, and 30 blacks joined the Fryes under arrest.

Had the incident ended there, it would have been minor, and considerably less fervent and bloody than the disturbances in the summer of 1964 in New York, Rochester, and a few other cities. But it didn't end. On August 12, while resentment smoldered, the streets were quiet during daylight hours. A "Human Relations Commission" meeting with the community turned into a shouting match, and no wounds were soothed. In the early evening the previous night's violence was on display on every channel in the television-conscious city. When darkness fell, despite the presence of more police, or perhaps because of them, people again took to the streets and looted and burned retail stores. In general their rage was directed against businesses owned by whites which had long exploited blacks through extra-high prices, shabby merchandise, and merciless credit terms. By morning 75 stores had been "torched" and 103rd Street was becoming Charcoal Alley.

On the morning of Friday, August 13, when crowds continued roaming the streets, LA Police Chief William H. Parker called in a thousand National Guardsmen. They did not arrive until after nightfall, and before they got there, looting and burning went on at will. Firemen were prevented from doing their job because of the risk of being hit by rocks or sniper fire. When 30,000 people controlled the streets, the community's normal life was totally disrupted. Media attention fanned the flames of disturbance.

When the troopers arrived, they were given pep talks such as this one by the commander of the 77th LAPD precinct:

> "I can't tell you to go out and kill," he said [Robert Conot reported]. "But when someone throws a rock, that's a felony. When they throw a Molotov cocktail, that's a felony. And don't you forget it!"

> A murmur went through the ranks. The officers knew well enough that anyone resisting or trying to escape from a felony arrest, could be shot.

In the fifteen hours following this speech eighteen men died; most ot them were "suspected looters."

With the advent of Saturday morning daylight, the troopers and guardsmen began actively to take back control of the streets. Curfews, roadblocks, checkpoints, and guardsmen riding with fire crews, as well as jeeps which carried machine guns, enforced virtual martial law. The tide of disorder was turned. Yet the agony went on, for there was little food left in the stores, and conditions were bad. As the riot waned on Sunday, Monday, and Tuesday, the forces of law loosened their trigger fingers; repeatedly they shot at suspected looters, too-inquisitive bystanders, people who did not immediately halt at checkpoints, a man who suddenly lit a cigarette in a darkened window. By the time the curfew was lifted on Tuesday evening thirty-four were dead. Not a single law officer had been killed by a sniper, though two had died at the hands of brother officers, and a fireman had gone down under a burning wall. Nearly 4,000 blacks had been arrested and commercial Watts lay in ashes, with property damage estimated between $35 and $200 million. It was the worst riot in the U.S. since 1943, and its violence, intensity, and duration shocked the nation.

Four days after the riot Martin Luther King, Jr., and Bayard Rustin—respectively the orator and chief organizer of the 1963 March on Washington—walked together through burned-out Watts. Some black kids recognized them, surrounded them, and shouted, "We won!"

"How can you say you won," King asked, "when 34 Negroes are dead, your community is destroyed, and whites are using the riot as an excuse for inaction?" "We won," the youngsters repeated, "because we made them pay attention to us."

The comment, and the riot itself, underlined the basic fact of the ghetto: it was populated by the powerless. They had the right to vote, but that was a weak and not-well-understood kind of power; what they lacked completely was the power to alter their circumstances. The only power they had was to destroy some property.

Watts was a turning point for blacks and for the white majority which had to react to them. Watts was black rage, and after black rage was established, civil rights lost steam. The 1965 crop of volunteers for the cause in the South were, Elizabeth Sutherland observed in *The Nation*, of "poorer quality than last year's; less inspired and more frustrated." Rustin knew the transition time had come:

> In the past you could both call attention to an evil and correct it with a handful of people who were prepared to go to jail. When you come to housing, to schools, to jobs, no demonstration can do more than call attention to an evil. It is a political problem requiring a political strategy, numbers, planning, reading, requiring knowing something about the nature of revolution.

The rage displayed in Watts at first seemed to give impetus to "political" solutions to the problems. As if in response to the Watts action, antipoverty programs were stepped up. Also, as if in response to the Watts riot—though actually prepared before the Howard speech—there came a semi-official "explanation" of black behavior in the form of a report by presidential counselor Daniel Patrick Moynihan of Harvard. He contended that the structure of black families was crumbling, and that unless the black family was shored up by new measures, none of the weapons of the War on Poverty would go very far in changing the lot of the poor.

Based on erroneous assumptions, the misreading of statistical trends, the Moynihan Report was inept at best. It overlooked the fact that all families were crumbling at the same rate, and the possibility that poverty, not blackness, might be the most significant factor affecting black families. It ignored the way in which the structure of welfare grants encouraged black fathers to leave home so their kids could eat. Surfacing in the wake of Watts, the Moynihan Report was an especial disaster. It gave whites a way off the hook; they could say black families were crumbling and ignore the extent to which white society had oppressed the black minority. The report had been designed to shore up the attack on poverty. Johnson's plan had been to triple the Great Society appropriations in the coming year. Because of Watts, and the escalating war in Vietnam—and at least in part because of Moynihan's wrongheaded observations—the new appropriations were doubled to $1.5 billion, rather than tripled. Now they were $40 per poor person per year.

In early 1966 the slogan "black power" emerged. It called up images of Watts burning, and although it was not meant that way, in the mind of the majority there was little separation between slogan and image. Actually, black power meant black access to power; it was interpreted, however, as embracing separatism. Black leaders echoed the sentiments of the newly martyred Malcolm X and called for blacks to unite spiritually with African black nationalist movements. As Thomas Wagstaff suggests,

> The strength shared by all American Black Nationalist movements has been their ability to engage the pride and imagination of the Black community, in ways that integrationist leaders cannot. For a Negro to seek integration into American society means to identify with the values of a society that has oppressed and degraded him, to repress his natural hostility against a people who have mistreated him and to seek their approval and acceptance by continually proving his worth.

Blacks sought acceptance of their worth as human beings without continually having to assert that worth.

Congress was unimpressed by this new idea—or perhaps Congress was negatively impressed. In early 1966 it began to reassert the prerogative of the legislative branch to control the country by controlling its purse strings. In 1964 and 1965 the Johnson steamroller had rammed through the Great Society programs. Now Congress was belatedly discovering that the "maximum feasible participation" of the poor which was mandated by the new laws could be political dynamite. Congressmen had not historically paid much attention to the poor; they owed more to City Hall, and to local political machines. The idea of decentralizing the bureaucracy didn't appeal to them, for it sapped patronage and meant that newly enfranchised local groups would be able to go around mayors and other officials to obtain funds directly from the federal government. Such an affront to the established edifice of power could not be sustained indefinitely. In 1966, Congress specifically tied much of the new spending to popular but systemically harmless programs such as Head Start and the Neighborhood Youth Corps. The first benefited pre-schoolers, the second gave temporary jobs to teenagers. "Maximum feasible participation"—the only potentally revolutionary aspect of the poverty programs—was damped down.

In the broadest of terms, Congress was giving expression to the majority's shifting view of the needs of blacks. Whereas before Watts the consensus held considerable sympathy for black aspirations, after the battle moved North and blacks began burning down property, that sympathy was replaced by fear. Blacks might still be downtrodden, but they might also be enemies in our midst.

In his definitive study of black violence in America in this era, James W. Button details two sets of explanations for Watts and subsequent riots. The liberal view held that "collective violence" was generally inevitable under certain historical conditions, and under the present conditions it was particularly understandable. In the riots, blacks were expressing justifiable rage at ghetto conditions. Their violence was a collective reflection of the group's anger. It was natural, not criminal, and the violence might well prove to be a spur to societal change. To prevent new outbreaks of violence, the underlying, deplorable conditions must be ameliorated. There must be a search to comprehend why the rioters had done their damage, and an effort to change the basic conditions of the ghetto.

The conservative explanation said such collective violence was "rare, needless, without purpose, and irrational," possibly instigated by outsiders and certainly committed by pathological and criminal elements rather than by the whole community. Since existing institutions (democracy, capitalism, free education, fair trials) were "adequate for advancing the interests of deprived minorities," the violence neither was necessary nor would it facilitate societal change. The correct response to the riots was not federal handouts but "repressive, control-oriented measures" such as improved riot-containment materials, techniques and police training, to protect the majority from such violence. The rioters themselves would be changed through the "moral restructuring of violent individuals through the basic institutions of the home, the church, the school."

Before Watts it was possible to be neutral or merely charitable about the needs and actions of blacks. After Watts it became increasingly necessary for the majority to choose one or the other of these two positions. As a society we chose both: we cautiously allotted more money for poverty programs, and provided more training and equipment for police and guard forces.

The 1966 riots began in March and continued through the summer. Chicago and Cleveland had bad riots, though not so bad as Watts. Television and other media, now alert to the dramatic possibilities of the riots, sent ever more reporters and cameramen to the scenes to transmit images of destruction and pillage. What did not often filter through to home viewers was much understanding of the rioters' grievances, since these grievances were harder to film or tape. It was difficult to see how poverty wasted a child's life, or to identify the discrimination behind the rejection of a particular job applicant. Fires in the streets were comprehensible—but not the metaphorical grease-stained rags or splintered wood which had given the fires their start. From behind police barricades cameras got, mostly, the police point of view, which shaped the public's image of what happened.

A backlash was felt in the 1966 midterm congressional elections. Many candidates claimed that the disorder of the riots had to be contained, and that antipoverty monies must not be given to "reward" cities which had riots. In the election forty-five congressional supporters of the War on Poverty lost their seats. After it, Congress scaled down and nearly disemboweled the Model Cities program, perhaps the most ambitious of all the Great Society measures. The continuing escalation of the war in Vietnam also slowed the momentum of the attack on poverty. So did the new and troubling inflation, which ate away public as well as private dollars.

Vietnam was becoming an issue. In a move which placed him at a distance from his old moderate constituents, but which aligned him with the more radical among the blacks, in 1966 Martin Luther King, Jr., spoke openly against the war. At this time most white people in the country still embraced the war and could not understand why blacks might be against it. White refusal to understand the new sore point hurt black causes. Among the majority, there was growing impatience with the black issues of poverty, racial discrimination, civil rights, which had been on the agenda too long. What a society would do when it was feeling flush and magnanimous (as in the early 1960s), that same society would not do when it felt tight—and threatened.

In the spring of 1967, disorders broke out at three southern black universities. In June there was a major riot in Tampa, followed by other large-scale outbreaks of violence in Cincinnati, Atlanta, Newark, in other cities in northern New Jersey, and, worst of all, by a catastrophe in Detroit.

In the dark of Sunday morning July 23, 1967, police entered the last of five Detroit "blind pigs" (after-hours clubs) which they raided that night. They expected to find a handful of blacks, but arrested 82 who were celebrating the return of two Vietnam vets. Had the gathering been held in a suburban country club rather than in a quasi-legal ghetto establishment, it might have been ignored. But the police were there, and they did their duty. It took an hour to ready transport for so many suspects. As the last cop car left, a bottle smashed its rear window. Within hours flames had ignited whole blocks. By the next night several were dead.

As in twenty-one of the twenty-two major disturbances in the previous three years, Detroit's troubles were triggered by inept police work. As in all the other riots, Detroit's involved more young people than old, more long-term than short-term residents, more unemployed than employed. The street crowds included a hard core of the chronically dissatisfied, which was augmented by substantial numbers of people from all sectors of the community. The rioters were no worse off economically, no more radical politically than most of Detroit's black citizens. Psychologist Ernest Harburg had found in an earlier study that the immediate community around 12th Street, the heaviest damage area of the riot, ranked high in stress and tensions; conditions were so bad that 93 percent of the residents interviewed wished they lived somewhere else.

Detroit's riot flames were whipped by summer winds. One arsonist set off a building, then watched as fire swept down the block of nine tenements until it engulfed his own, the ninth. For twenty-four hours the fire department was unable to enter the area, held back by thrown rocks and by suspected snipers. As in Watts, the community's rage was directed against businesses. This time, however, "soul brother" scribbled on a shop window did not protect a store. Also new in Detroit was the anger passing whites showed; several blacks were killed by civilians from nearby communities.

Local police were unable to control the streets. First the state troopers, then the National Guard, then Army paratroops were called in. The White House became directly involved in decisions on how to control the Detroit riot; questions were raised as to whether this was an "insurrection," or part of an organized plot to overthrow all authority in Detroit. The decision to send in the Army was made because of the "revolutionary" aspects of the riot. Detroit dominated the news for days with images of havoc.

Young and inexperienced National Guardsmen who had not learned the lessons of Watts fired their guns too often and hurt people. The Detroit police, more experienced, acted savagely. On Tuesday night, in response to a report of snipers, police, guardsmen, and state troopers entered an annex of the Algiers Motel, where they found ten black men with two white girls—and no guns. The police left an hour later without having made an arrest, but three of the black men lay dead and all the others had been severely beaten. At station houses men and women suspects were harassed to extract confessions. One woman was forced to strip while police took photos of her. There were 7,200 arrests, and there was some sniping from rooftops, but of the 27 people arrested for sniping, 24 cases were dismissed and the other three were never proven.

Police and the guardsmen killed most of the 43 victims of the riot. The Army killed only a few. In general the Army did a good job: mostly it picked up trash, helped residents clean the streets, and rendered assistance where it could. Such behavior calmed the streets, whether performed by the Army or by block associations.

While the embers of Detroit still smoldered, President Johnson used the language of the "search" modality to suggest what had to be done about the chaos:

> The only genuine, long-range solution for what has happened lies in an attack—mounted at every level—upon the conditions that breed despair and violence. All of us know what those conditions are: ignorance, discrimination, slums, poverty, disease, not enough jobs. We should attack these conditions—not because we are frightened by conflict, but because we are fired by conscience. We should attack them because there is simply no other way to achieve a decent and orderly society in America.

Johnson established a National Advisory Commission on Civil Disorders chaired by Illinois Governor Otto Kerner, and charged it to discover what had happened in the riots, and why, and to recommend how to prevent such riots in the future.

In as forthright language as any ever published, the Kerner Commission responded that the basic causes of the riot were, as Johnson had guessed, the conditions in the ghetto, and that the prime factor in these conditions was "white racism":

> What white Americans have never fully understood—but what the Negro can never forget—is that white society is deeply implicated in the ghetto. White institutions created it, white institutions maintain it, and white society condones it.

The commission outlined three choices facing America: 1) to continue the present push toward equality with the present proportion of resources devoted to the task; 2) to enrich the ghetto but to work for separation rather than integration; and 3) to make a "commitment to national action on an unprecedented scale" whereby large portions of the nation's resources would be put to the task of achieving a fair and just society. The commission rejected the first two choices and said that if the United States did not embrace the third choice, there would be chaos. They imagined a bleak 1985: swollen metropolitan areas which were black at the core and white at the fringes, with intensified problems of inadequate education, massive unemployment, welfare dependency, and roving bands of violent youths beyond hope of salvation. To make that picture reality, the Kerner Commission warned, all America had to do was fail to make the third choice.

The report was handed in on March 1, 1968, several months before it was expected, but the timing was bad. At the end of March, Lyndon Johnson refused to run for a second term, and a few days after that Martin Luther King, Jr., was assassinated—and there were more riots of the intensity of Detroit and Watts.

The news of King's death at the hands of a white man moved many black Americans to react in a paroxysm of rage and grief. In 150 cities looting and burning took place. The worst damage was in Washington, D.C. Dr. King's assassination certified in the minds of blacks that white America would never give its black minority anything of worth; Dr. King had been the most moderate of black leaders and the most honored by white society—and he had been cut down. In the riots which followed King's death, forty-six people died, all but five of them black. That was not new. But what was new—and important—was the amount of power marshaled by the state to put down the disturbances across the nation. To maintain order 34,000 National Guardsmen, 21,000 federal troops, and uncounted numbers of local police were brought out—the largest single deployment of military and paramilitary forces for a civilian purpose since the Civil War.

In the front row at the funeral of Martin Luther King, Jr., were all the major presidential candidates, including Richard Nixon. The former vice-president had recently pilloried the Kerner Commission for blaming

> everybody for the riots except the perpetrators of the riots. And, I think that deficiency has to be dealt with first. Until we have order we can have no progress.

The theme of Nixon's presidential campaign was "law and order," which most whites understood to stand for cracking down on crime believed to originate in minority-dominated ghettos. Polls showed that a substantial majority of "middle" Americans queried now believed blacks had already obtained too much from white society—too many programs to redress grievances, too many federal handouts, too much in the way of bending over backward to help blacks catch up with whites. Candidate Nixon said the answer to poverty was not federal handouts, or more federal jobs, or equality in housing programs, but "more imaginative" approaches, which he refused to define.

With Nixon taking a patently anti-black stance, and with the sympathetic Robert Kennedy dead, blacks did not come out strongly for a candidate in the 1968 election.

Nixon's electoral margin came largely from "middle Americans," from white southerners, from white ethnics in and around cities who perceived themselves as having gotten the short end of the stick while blacks received federal largesse.

A major difference between the Nixon and Johnson administrations was soon evident in Nixon's treatment of minority issues. Early in 1969 the new administration simply stopped federal enforcement of voter registration, and then stopped enforcement of antidiscrimination laws. Funding for the Office of Economic Opportunity (OEO) was continued at $1.5 billion (a figure cheapened by inflation), and more money was allotted for summer job programs which were seen as palliatives to buy summers without riots. Indeed, after the chaos of the latter Johnson years, 1969 and 1970 were described by the Lemberg Center for the Study of Violence as summers of only moderate civil disorders. The Nixon administration advocated pumping money into the new Law Enforcement Assistance Administration (LEAA), which gave police departments money to buy such things as tanks, armored cars, helicopters, riot-control equipment, walkie-talkies, and to take part in a national computerized identification system for criminals. LEAA got $63 million in 1969, $268 million in 1970, and $700 million in 1972. The administration also sponsored the Washington, D.C., Crime Bill, which would allow judges to jail suspects 60 days before trial (preventative detention) and gave police the right to break into a house without a search warrant (the "no-knock" provision). Congress, not wanting to be accused of being "soft" on crime, was coerced to pass the bill.

The Nixon administration also introduced the Family Assistance Plan. FAP was to replace the cumbersome bureaucracy of the War on Poverty with a streamlined direct handout procedure. There would be outright grants to needy families. That sounded good, but the details were bad. Under FAP, a family of four would receive a guaranteed income of $1,600 a year. The poverty line was then $4,000 a year, and forty-five of the states granted more to poor people than FAP would. George Wiley, head of the

National Welfare Rights Organization, dubbed FAP "guaranteed poverty." The plan also imposed work requirements, placed restrictions on recipients' ability to change residences, choose doctors or lawyers, and could penalize recipients up to half their grant should they refuse an offer of job training or referral to a psychological counseling service. Mothers of children in school could be forced to work at three-quarters of the minimum wage.

Congress defeated FAP soundly—but Nixon, by having presented a plan which ostensibly helped poor people, looked good for a time. The administration also put a public relations effort into "black capitalism," a program to encourage entrepreneurship in the ghetto. But without access to credit, without strong tax incentives, and without any commitment from white businesses to give up lucrative near-monopolies catering to ghetto inhabitants, "black capitalism" was a plan that could not succeed.

While these black-oriented programs won headlines, a campaign of repression against blacks occurred behind the scenes. The most active and successful repression was directed against the Black Panthers. The Panthers preached independence from the white man's way, wore guns, and had attractive Green Beret–type uniforms. The Panthers provided free breakfasts for black children and organized some educational projects, but their main accomplishment was to embody the idea of black personal power.

The arrogance of the Panthers outraged Johnson, who decided they were foreign-influenced and subversive and ordered the FBI to collect information on them. Under Nixon, the FBI surveillance escalated into infiltration of Panther ranks and outright repression. In a few years twenty-eight Panthers were killed, and many more were sent to jail, some on questionable charges. Several Panther leaders were executed in their Chicago beds by police working with the FBI. Others were killed in Oakland. Against this campaign of suppression there was no sustained white outcry. The campaign against the Panthers came to light at a time when the furor over social injustices had been superseded by anger over the war in Vietnam. The majority no longer had the time to be concerned with suppression of an arrogant, anti-white group, nor to be concerned with questions such as whether too many blacks were being sent to jail, or whether the welfare "budgets of despair" were being cut back beyond endurance, or whether more strict criteria were keeping minority families off the welfare rolls and without governmental help. By 1970 newly armored police forces around the country were asserting the majority's wish to "preserve" their society, and the will of those who could "search" out the causes of inequality and change them had grown faint.

More than the Panthers had been ruined: the whole leadership of the black movement had been decimated. Blacks believed that if a black man became important enough, white society would cut him down. Medgar Evers, Malcolm X, Martin Luther King, Jr., Adam Clayton Powell: all were dead. James Meredith was wounded. Stokeley Carmichael, H. Rap Brown, and Eldridge Cleaver were in exile or in jail. Men who would have moved into the leadership, such as Robert Moses, John Lewis, and Robert Williams, had been so beaten down that they had moved to other pastures. A strike in support of the Panthers in New Haven was overshadowed by Earth Day. The killings at Jackson State were overshadowed by those at Kent State.

In September of 1971 the bloodiest prison riot of the century took place at Attica, which was a concentrated ghetto. "We Are Men," said the prisoners. "What has happened here is but the sound and fury of those who are oppressed." The prisoners miscalculated: the sound and fury belonged to the state, which, at Governor Nelson Rockefeller's command, took the prison back in a heavy-handed show of force. The police assault killed many prisoners and guards, and it was made with new riot-control weapons and with techniques gleaned from the years of working to subdue urban violence.

After reelection in 1972, Nixon more actively worked to reverse the tide which had resulted in black gains. He cut back OEO and then dismantled it; HEW, HUD, and Model Cities withered. Community Action, Nixon stated, was "no longer...either necessary or desirable," and was abandoned.

For blacks, the Decade of Shocks was one of some gains and nearly as many losses. Most of the progress toward equality and a larger share of the national pie was made from 1964 to 1969. Thereafter the progress slowed, and in many areas it was erased. Between 1960 and 1970 the proportion of blacks aged 18 to 24 who enrolled in colleges rose from 10 percent to 18 percent, more than double the rate of white increase; from 1970 to 1974 there was virtually no further increase. During the 1960s blacks went from filling 3.5 percent of new jobs to 7 percent, or near their own national population percentage. From 1970 to 1974 the proportion of new jobs filled by blacks declined to 6 percent though blacks grew to 11 percent of the population. Blacks moved upward a bit from menial jobs, but by the end of the era blacks had not reached the occupational level whites had been at in 1940. A black was likely to hold a low-wage or service job, to be the last hired and the first fired. Blacks did not join whites in the upper levels of management, despite increases in black educational levels and "affirmative action." Even in government service, though blacks came to be a substantial fraction of the work force, they made large gains only in the postal service, and filled less than one percent of top-level government jobs. By the decade's end, blacks made up less than 4 percent of the work force at such important and powerful places as the Department of Justice.

The openhanded years of the Johnson administration were perceived as good for blacks, but in fact everyone benefited. More whites than blacks, for example, joined the welfare rolls in those years. "Poor people" declined from 17.3 percent of the population in 1965 to 12.1 percent in 1969—but the percentage went up again thereafter. Black unemployment dropped from double digits in 1964 to approximately 5 percent in 1969—but from then on until 1974 it resumed its steady climb and in 1974 was well over 10 percent. What was worse, as the years went on, black unemployment seemed far harder to reverse than white unemployment.

The ratio of median incomes between black and white families—a clear index of equivalency—underwent a dramatic shift. In 1963, black families earned 53 percent of what white families earned. In 1970 they earned 64 percent of what white families earned—but by 1974 blacks had dropped down to earning about 50 percent of what whites earned, less than they had before all the ferment began.

Nevertheless, during the decade fundamental changes were made in the relationship of blacks to the country.

Though black demands might be held down, they could never again be cavalierly ignored by the majority. Laws were on the books, guidelines had been established and court opinions written. These had to be obeyed. Moreover, blacks had a number of exemplary citizens among their community in whom many could take pride; also, they had forged a strong alliance with liberals that would not soon be broken. Most important, blacks had tasted upward mobility, and they were no longer invisible.

Blacks came out of the decade more united as a group than they had been in the past. The majority had always considered the black community as a unit, but as a group blacks had been less like-minded than whites. Grinding poverty had a lot to do with the fragmentation. At the bottom of the economic heap, sociologists have long observed, men are driven one from another by the fierce competition necessary just to survive; this works against a sense of community. But while taking pride and hope from the civil-rights years, and while tasting some of the fruits of the system, blacks began to close ranks. Many moderate blacks resented the heavyhanded brush which tarred them with the excesses of a few. After the riots, if a black man made it into the middle class, his consciousness of being a "soul brother" still remained in the forefront of his mind. He might live in suburbia, but he knew his roots and did not forsake them. In the fires, a community had been forged.

For a hundred years the goal of those who fought for black rights was integration. But no one was certain what integration would mean, should it ever come to pass. In the late 1960s and early 1970s, the black-white coalition which had carried on the fight for civil rights went into hibernation (according to whites) or died (according to blacks). One result of this parting of the ways was the death of the goal of integration. Curiously, as we approached it, the ideal seemed less applicable and unworkable.

It did not appear, after all, that enhancing equality of opportunity would automatically result in equality of condition. The passage of federal legislation and the loosening of purse strings had not made most whites accept blacks as next-door neighbors. Nor did these things make either race more accepting of interracial marriage. Nor did these things in any great degree alter our economic system so that the poor would be more able to become rich. There was some softening: individual whites who lived cheek-by-jowl with blacks became less racist and more tolerant in their outlook, and the same was true for whites who worked next to blacks. Studies showed that what people were afraid of was the anticipation of difficulties, and that actual mixing of the races in communities, schools, and work places proved rather harmless.

But if integration faded as a goal, nothing else sprang up to take its place. Separatism was not workable either. So the more things changed, the more they stayed the same.

In retrospect, nobody liked the War on Poverty. Liberals claimed it had been a failure because not enough resources had been devoted to it. Liberal experts said the redistribution of $15 billion a year would have pulled everyone who was below the poverty line over into solvency—and at its height OEO had only $1.5 billion a year, most of which went for salaries and office rent. Actually, the programs of the Great Society had never aimed directly at redistributing income, but merely at redressing some of the more obvious discrepancies in blacks' educational and job-training levels. Redistribution of income would have had to be accompanied by massive infusions of money into schools, medical care delivery systems, and the like to have made a War on Poverty really work. That was never in the cards.

Conservatives said the War on Poverty was a failure because in a capitalistic economy you could not legislate away the poor. There had to be some winners and some losers in the system, some who did well and some who did less well: that was the nature of our economy and the way the world worked. Conservatives and liberals said the constellation of social difficulties that beset blacks was intractable.

Had anything good come out of the violence and rioting? Ghetto uprisings had achieved some limited social change in that they got the majority to throw a bit of money toward the ghetto and to pay a bit of attention to it. In his study of black violence James Button asked the rhetorical question, "When does the squeaky wheel get the grease?" He found it did so under several distinct conditions. First, "when those in power have relatively plentiful public resources available to meet the basic demands of the partisans of violence," which happened prior to 1968. Second, when the episodes of violence are heavy enough to be noticed, but not so severe or so frequent as to scare the majority into repression. The episodes were noticed in 1965 and 1966, but by 1967 the frequency and intensity had begun to scare the majority. Third, when those in political power and a substantial portion of the public are in general sympathy toward the goals of the perpetrators of violence. When the rioting had become so massive as to engender a backlash, the sympathy dissolved, and with it went the will of the majority to redress black grievances. Fourth, when the demands of the violence purveyors are "relatively limited, specific, and clear to those in political power," and have not become vague, complex, or beyond the scope of ordinary changes. Civil rights were legislatable; antipoverty money could be found; but black power was an unacceptable demand. Fifth, when violence is used in conjunction with nonviolent strategies "as a means of asserting the demands of the politically powerless." The people of Watts felt at one with the people in Selma; later on, this sense of common purpose dissolved. When, by the end of the summer of 1967, riots had preempted civil-rights protests, the rioters' effectiveness in loosening the purse strings of the majority came to a halt, and the course of change soon went into reverse.

One of the unexpected side effects of the ghetto violence was to bring out into the open the police power of the state. For years the police had been the arresters of drunks, the chasers of petty criminals, the directors of traffic, the issuers of summonses. When the riots occurred, a new aspect of the police function in our society hove into view. The police became the purveyors of the organized, concentrated, officially sanctioned violence—an expression of the power that could put down riots, a power which by its very existence certified ghetto residents as powerless.

During the years of the black riots, crime in the country escalated in all categories. While this frightened the white communities, the crime wave had the most impact on the black communities. Poor blacks were the most likely victims of burglaries; they were raped more than twice as often as whites, and murdered six times more often. Police power to answer such crimes was overwhelmingly white, and the capability of police officers to distinguish "good" blacks from "perpetrators" was low and did not rise as crime statistics grew. Ghetto residents perceived that the police were in the ghetto not to stamp out crime but to maintain order.

For whites, order had been a condition passively accepted. However, in the riots, people watching television, or on the wrong end of a night stick, could see that order meant a definite diminution of personal freedom. Order was a construct that could be—and in the riots, was—forcibly impressed on sectors of the citizenry. At first the majority found the police power to be good and salutary. But as the years of riots went on, television viewers began to see the full price of police power, and wondered: if a cop clubbed a youth rumbling in the ghetto streets, or a protester with long hair, might he not eventually be provoked to club a middle-class middle-aged white? The riots made it clear that "law and order" and a free-but-restrained society existed at a price that could at times be quite high.

The major dividend of the era was the articulation of a black critique of American society, an adamantine mirror of great clarity. This critique said all Americans must realize that we lived in a racist society, egalitarian neither in fact nor in aspiration. As to this "fact," the everyday experience of blacks provided eloquent testimony. The woman whom John Langston Gwaltney called "Hannah Nelson," and who was a piano teacher in the black community and a domestic worker on the outside, told him that she was *drylongso*—ordinary—and summed up her attitude thusly:

> Every reasonable black person thinks that most white people do not mean him well. Every reasonable black person knows that many other black

people cannot afford to treat him fairly. . . . It is the greed and cruelty of white people which is at the root of all this business. . . . The existence of white people has meant for many of us that it is sometimes hard to tell whether life is more to be desired than death. . . . I am tired of standing in pointless lines and filling out the same papers for somebody to lose. I am tired of being governed by people who are not as considerate or as intelligent as I am. Most black people feel that way. Most black people are intelligent enough to know that the trouble we have in getting value for our money and recompense for our wrongs is not accidental.

In the black view racism, segregation, and discrimination suffused North as well as South, liberal as well as conservative. There was not much to choose from between the overt segregation of southern washrooms and the covert segregation of excluding blacks from high-level government positions. To blacks it was clear that whites defined themselves as an upper class and defined all nonwhites as a lower class. Such a subversion of the egalitarian ideal made a mockery of the notion of a classless society. Democracy was a facade; an autocracy held power and it catered to the rich, who were the white. "Capitalism" was a fancy word for naked exploitation. Blacks believed much of the country's wealth had been made by slave labor and now came from black labor kept cheap by racist suppression. The black critique recognized economic power as fundamental to any achievement of equality, and saw that equality would never be achieved so long as the economic deck was stacked against blacks.

Increasingly larger numbers of American blacks were residing in big-city ghettos. In the black view, these ghettos had been encouraged and nurtured by the white majority in the United States. If the nurturance had been mostly unconscious, that did not excuse it, because the ghettos served the same purpose for white Americans as the European ghettos had for the Nazis: to concentrate and contain a minority which the majority believed to be dangerous. When white society built walls of police protection around the ghettos and fenced off the suburban enclaves of the white and the rich, this was more evidence to label majority society as racist.

Translated into more philosophic terms, the black critique held that the majority told itself that it was good, and that the black minority was evil. In fact, blacks believed, such a division of the world was essential to whites in order that they might see themselves and their oppressive actions as correct, proper, and morally justified. Such a "naive dualism," as Jean-

Paul Sartre put it in an earlier context, such a simplistic division of the universe into good and evil, is

> reassuring to the anti-semite himself. If all he has to do is to remove evil, that means that the Good is already *given*. He has no need to seek it in anguish, to invent it, to scrutinize it patiently when he has found it, to prove it in action, to verify it by its consequences, or, finally, to shoulder the responsibilities of the moral choice he has made.

In other words, as an attitude and an operating assumption, racism was a way to justify maintaining the *status quo*—whether that be continued segregation in the South or inequality of opportunity in the North. Blacks believed that the majority would give up nothing, would make no essential change in society. The majority was a crowd. Sartre characterized the racist as the quintessential man of the crowd, part of the community of the mediocre. Lionel Rubinoff extends this concept in calling racism

> a passion which rationalizes aggression by concealing the aggressive impulse under the cover of a rational purpose. The behavior engaged in is not just immoral; it amounts virtually to a pornographic celebration in bestiality. . . . Racism is an apocalyptic phenomenon which proceeds from the exhausted imagination of a defeated culture, a culture which has lost faith in its basic values.

In the most benevolent interpretation of the racist society, some blacks believed that many whites who were overtly or covertly racist did or thought as they did because they themselves were hopelessly exploited by a system which operated for the benefit of the few and to the detriment of the majority, whether the members of that majority were white or black. Racism was a response to an oppressive system, a downward translation of the sense of being had.

The black critique saw even the most openly liberal of the help-the-blacks programs as subtly racist. It saw a terrifying sameness to the ideology that championed compensatory education for black children, the retraining of unemployed blacks, the restructuring of black families, and the razing of slum buildings.

That ideology William Ryan of Boston College characterized as "blaming the victim." He found it in the 1965 Moynihan Report, which said blacks came from broken homes, environments which the report associated with emotional maladjustment, poor school achievement, and criminal records. However, when the statistics which underlay these correlations were controlled for socioeconomic status rather than color, there were no more poor school-achievers from broken homes than there were from nonbroken homes. Poor whites proved to be as likely as poor blacks to come from broken homes, drop out of school, and go to prison. "Blaming the victim" also informed treating black children as ineducable because they came from the ghetto. In ghetto schools less was usually expected of black pupils, and they were subtly rewarded for poor performance; with each passing school year they performed progressively worse, until they opted out or were pushed out of the system. In a Harlem experiment where poor pupils were systematically encouraged, they became brighter and got better grades than expected. In the War on Poverty victim blamers such as teachers, social workers, and government bureaucrats designed and operated programs based on the notion that blacks and other poor people were "caught in the cycle of poverty" and must themselves be made to change so that they were more acceptable to white society.

When blacks appeared to resent the programs established for their benefit, they were considered ingrates. Although private doctors who saw patients on a one-to-one basis were the middle-class standard for medical care, poor blacks were sent to clinics and treated not as individuals but as members of a stigmatized group. Blacks resented rehabilitation programs in prison because they knew that no matter how rehabilitated they became, once outside again it would be nearly impossible for them to get a job. When the government razed neighborhoods of low-rise, individualized, spread-out slum housing to make way for new high-rises, there was normally a hiatus of years before the new buildings went up, and during it, the old residents would melt away and all sense of community would disappear. When the new project was erected, there would be application forms and regulations on the incomes and the habits of successful applicants. Thus, in the housing projects the poor were concentrated and ostracized, and when they did not "properly" take care of apartments which they were not encouraged to view as their own, they were castigated for having no sense of responsibility and no respect.

Victim blamers are not crude racists, Ryan contends, but people of good will who submit to the ideology because it gets them off the hook of having to alter a system which has benefited them, while giving them a chance to appear sympathetic to the system's victims. In this way the "humanitarian" can

> all at the same time, concentrate his charitable interest on the defects of the victim, condemn the vague social and environmental stresses that produced the defects (some time ago) and ignore the continuing effect of victimizing social forces (right now). It is a brilliant ideology for justifying a perverse form of social action designed to change, not society, as one might expect, but rather society's victim.

Thus the black critique could show that the Great Society programs had been conservative wolves in the clothing of sheep: they had deflected attention and energy from the task of changing the system to changing the individual to make him fit the system.

The black critique said that the campaign to lift up poor folks was indistinguishable from the campaign to control riots and crime-in-the-streets. When the Man felt flush, he opened his palm a bit; when the Man felt pinched and threatened, he showed you the back of his hand. In the 1970s when the budget for LEAA began to match that of OEO, blacks were not surprised.

The black critique was hard for whites to accept. A mild distillate of it, in the Kerner Report, was enough to get the report shelved and its recommendations ignored. The black critique went beyond black-white relations and cast into bold relief many of society's inconsistencies and philosophical hiding holes. It questioned the future of the cities, the nature of equality, the soundness and flexibility of the economy.

You could not be neutral to this great critique. It had to be accepted or rejected wholesale.

In the acceptance or rejection of this critique there lay deeper and further definition of the two channels of reaction which had first seriously begun to diverge at the time of President Kennedy's death. Acceptance of the tenets of the black critique meant that beyond the "search" for root causes of black Americans' poverty and inequality and the wish to ameliorate those conditions, was the need to go to the foundations of our society's structure and to lay them open to discussion—and alteration. This was an extension of the liberal viewpoint into more and more radical modes of inquiry.

If the black critique was rejected—and many people did reject it—then the implications for behavior were equally difficult. For beyond the "preserve" mode, with its wish to protect the integrity of the society we had, lay the need to maintain that society even if it condoned overt and covert segregation. Rejecting the black critique meant rejecting also any need for fundamental changes in the societal structure, and accepting as irrevocable the differences in quality and station between the life of the majority and the life of the minority.

4 The Silent Killer

IN 1963 THE DOLLAR was the supreme currency of the world. The United States had the world's highest standard of living and the world's strongest economy. Our products were technologically superior, our productivity was high, our balance of trade and our federal deficits seemed manageable. Our rate of inflation was 1.2 percent a year, so low as to be discounted by economists and by everyone else in the country.

John Kennedy's "new economics" proponents said the country was recovering slowly from a 1957–1958 recession and a 1960 dip and was performing below its capacity. They spied a gap between the current gross national product figure and the figure the GNP might reach if the economy were to operate at full steam. This gap they estimated at $35 billion a year. They also said that 5.5–6 percent unemployment was too high and should be brought down to 4 percent, which was considered an irreducible minimum. To close the GNP gap, to cut unemployment, and to stimulate the economy the advisors called for a $13 billion tax cut. Since consumers would have to pay less in taxes they would have more money to spend; this would create additional "demand" for goods and services. To fill the new orders expected from consumers, companies would have to increase production; that would mean the hiring of new workers. Output would soar and unemployment would drop. Although the plan anticipated that federal tax revenues would initially fall slightly, the economists believed that when the companies and their workers both became prosperous, the later tax revenues would jump and more than make up the initial loss.

The 1964 tax cut was enacted in the flood of legislation that passed as a testimony to the late president. It, too, was a legacy of Kennedy's martyrdom. President Johnson hailed the measure as "the single most important step we have taken to strengthen the economy since World War II."

It worked like a charm.

Soon after the tax cut went into effect, consumers started spending and corporations started hiring. Unemployment fell dramatically, down to 5.2 percent in 1964, 4.5 percent in 1965, and 3.8 percent in 1966, which was termed "full employment." True to predictions, federal tax revenues were sluggish in 1964–1965, but in fiscal 1966 they easily made up the lag. The GNP surged upward steadily and devoured whatever gap there had been between potential and actual. The GNP stood at $573 billion in 1963, at $612 billion in 1964, at $654 billion in 1965, and at a whopping $721 billion in 1966.

By mid-1965 the "demand" unleashed by the tax cut was making the economy hum at an unprecedented growth rate—but with increased purchasing power came a whiff of inflation.

The last time the United States had experienced worrisome inflation was at the end of World War I, and few people remembered that far back. In the years 1919 to 1921, inflation had been licked, at the cost of a small depression. There followed twenty-five years of price stability. Many people could recall that during the Depression of the 1930s prices had been stable—in some cases they had even dropped ("deflation"). Prices and wages were controlled during World War II; after the war both rose in quick spurts and there was a mild inflation. The same thing happened after the Korean War. By 1965 these inflationary bursts had long since subsided. Prices were stable. Inflation was a serious issue only with those European countries that had not fully recovered from the war, or with those badly run South American dictatorships. We thought that a country with an annual inflation rate of 5 to 6 percent was touched with primal economic sin. Double-digit inflation meant that a country was entering its death throes; the classic example was Germany in the 1920s, where people carried satchels full of banknotes to bakeries in order to buy a loaf of bread.

In the United States a dollar was an invincible and inviolable measure of worth. A lower-middle-class income for a family of four was $10,000 a year.

Then something happened. In mid-1965 here and there a supplier, certain his products would be bought by consumers whose new money was burning a hole in their pockets, hurried things up. He raised a price to make a quick profit while demand was high. Or he granted his workers an overgenerous wage settlement in order to keep his factories on their output schedules. In the summer of 1965, as Watts burned, the fire of inflation was being fueled by Americans buying out the stores. As they did so, they not only helped hike prices and wages, but they also created new markets for imported French wines, German automobiles, and Japanese electronics products.

Helping the buying along was a tremendous new influx of consumer credit cards. The first such cards had been issued to good customers of department stores and gasoline stations in 1914. Montgomery Ward soon found that the average charge customer bought two and a half to three times more than the average cash customer. In the early 1960s, oil companies found that the average credit card purchase at the pumps was about $5, while the average cash sale was less than $3. In 1965, bank credit card programs went national; BankAmericard and Master Charge began to flood the country with consumer cards, and people began to use them.

Credit cards raised prices in two ways. First, merchants who accepted credit cards paid between 2.5 percent and 7 percent to the card system—a charge which was usually passed along to the consumer in the form of a higher price. Second, people who used the cards often paid interest on the balance of their purchases, which was an indirect way of making an item cost more.

In 1965 there were 5 million bank credit cards in circulation; by 1970 there were 20 million, and by 1974 there were 50 million cards. Robert A. Hendrickson listed some of the consumer items that could be paid for by credit cards:

> tooth extractions, tombstones, taxi rides, driving lessons, diamonds, dog kennel fees, ambulance service, apartment rent, auto license fees, music lessons, movie admissions, rented cars, savings bonds, scuba diving instruction, church tithes, college tuition, garbage removal and psychiatric care.

In 1970, Hendrickson reports, there was $123.7 billion in consumer credit outstanding, including $99 billion of installment credit, and $23 billion of non-installment credit—of which credit card purchases made up a significant part:

The credit card revolution has extended the availability of unsecured credit to purchase volumes of consumer goods and luxuries far beyond the circle of the affluent members of society to the middle-income and low-income members of society who once had little or no access to credit of any kind.

In 1965 the American people also began to buy something else on credit—the escalation of the Vietnam War. That was when the war began to heat up. In the previous ten years, defense spending as a percentage of the GNP had actually decreased; in August of 1965 defense spending reversed directions and started upward. There was a virtual deluge of orders to defense contractors—only some of which were immediately paid for. There had been a budget surplus for the first half of 1965; by virtue of the added defense spending that became a budget deficit in the second half of 1965. Such a sudden surge in defense spending fueled inflation—as it had in each of the previous major conflicts of the United States.

Wars promote inflation in several ways. First, since the economy must produce guns, butter becomes scarce. In the U.S. this meant that money spent on war-related items was no longer available to be disbursed (for example) to riot-torn cities. Second, wars mean higher prices for defense-related goods: if the government wants rifles pronto, it will pay "unavoidable" cost overruns. Third, because wars are costly they create an incentive for a government to finance them by recourse to the printing press. During the Revolutionary War the Congress printed "Continentals" and used them to pay soldiers and to purchase supplies—until the Continentals became worthless. Fourth, wars add to the national debt, since many of the costs are not paid immediately and have to be borne by later generations. Annuities and indemnities related to the War of 1812 were being paid into the 1920s; those relating to the Civil War, into the 1950s. Budget deficits have to be serviced by borrowed money: in 1965 the largest fraction of the government's debt was from costs incurred in World War II, and the second largest fraction was from our action in Korea.

Toward the end of 1965, the Council of Economic Advisors issued its annual report, which said:

> The objective of promoting balance between overall demand and productive capacity pointed to tax cuts in recent years when demand was inadequate. The same criterion now calls for tax action to moderate the growth of private spending.

President John F. Kennedy waves to crowd, Dallas, November 22, 1963.

Malcolm X.

Senator Robert F. Kennedy.

Supporters of
Governor George Wallace.

Martin Luther King, Jr.,
among civil-rights leaders
in Montgomery, Alabama.

Robert F. Kennedy
assassinated.

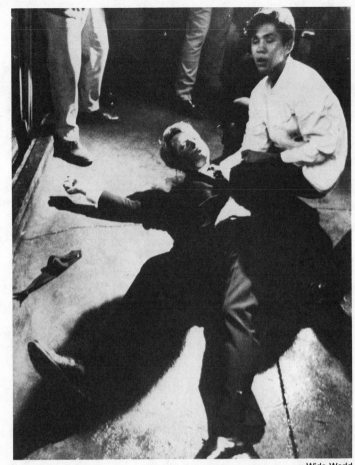

Cortege at the funeral of Martin Luther King, Jr.

The view from the Lincoln Memorial one hundred years after the Emancipation Proclamation.

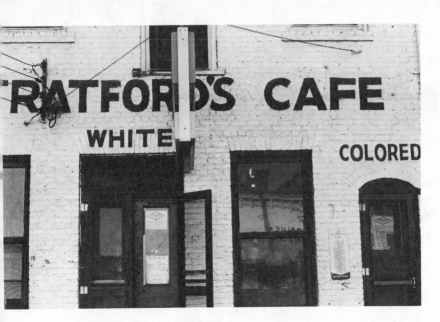

Segregation.

A ghetto riot—occupants' view.

The Fire This Time.

Inflation linked with the war.

"Levitating" the Pentagon.

Woodstock. *Don't Trust Anyone Over 30.*

President Lyndon Johnson decorates General
William Westmoreland for services in the war in
Vietnam.

Chicago business executives picket the White House to advocate
ending the war, June 1969.

South Vietnam, *The Scarlet Thread*.

Children of the war. Vietnam and Kent State.

On the moon, July 20, 1969.

Anti-pollution rally.

The wreck of the *Torrey Canyon*.

Women's Liberation.

President Richard M. Nixon leaving the White House grounds after resigning the presidency, August 9, 1974.

UPI

Shorn of expert language, it was a call to the president to raise taxes in order to curb spending before inflation got out of hand. Inflation was a silent killer, as dreaded in economic affairs as was high blood pressure in medicine—and as little understood by laymen. Or presidents.

Federal Reserve Board Chairman William McChesney Martin understood inflation, however, and in late 1965 pushed the Fed to raise its rediscount rate dramatically. The rediscount is the rate at which banks borrow from the central system; when it went up, so did the cost of borrowing money at local banks, in what became known as the 1966 "credit crunch." Money for mortgages and for business expansion dried up or was unduly expensive to borrow, and so individuals and businesses postponed or forgot their spending decisions. In a year, housing starts dropped 21.3 percent, corporation profits fell from 21.1 percent in 1965 to 9.7 percent in 1966. All this as the Fed cut the rate of growth in the money supply from 4.9 percent to 2.2 percent a year.

The rate of inflation slowed, but the number of complaints rose, and the latter reached the sensitive ears of Lyndon Johnson, who pressured Martin to ease the money supply. Martin refused. Johnson had ignored the CEA's call for a tax increase. At the end of 1965 and in 1966 he ignored it again but tried to creep up on the problem with a package of small taxes, pre-payment of some corporate and self-employment taxes, and a postponement in scheduled reductions of excise taxes on cars and telephones.

As this made only a small drop in the bucket, chairman of the CEA Gardner Ackley pressed Johnson for a 2–4 percent general tax increase. He told the president that the country could not sustain three things together without a tax rise: 1) the Vietnam War, 2) the War on Poverty, and 3) no inflation. Johnson was already committed to the first two, and so he said:

> I don't know much about economics, but I do know the Congress. And I can get the Great Society through right now—this is a golden time. We've got a good Congress and I'm the right president and I can do it. But if I talk about the cost of the war, the Great Society won't go through and the tax bill won't go through. Old Wilbur Mills [chairman of the House Ways and Means Committee] will sit down there and he'll thank me kindly and send me back my Great Society, and then he'll tell me that they'll be glad to spend whatever we need for the war.

Johnson held a series of meetings with congressional and business leaders in which he estimated the cost of the Vietnam adventure at $800 million a month. His figures were wrong, in part, because the Pentagon's accounting system deferred the cost of a tank until that tank was delivered— a cost which might not show up for a year but which was incurred right away. In part, his figures were overt lies. The annual cost of the war, which even Pentagon experts were then underestimating, was nearer to $2.5 billion a month. Thus the total underestimate for 1966 was $20 billion, and there were even more costs hidden away that would come due in future years. Having been given the figure of $800 million a month, most of the congressional and business leaders, including Wilbur Mills, advised the president that a tax increase would not be necessary to cover that amount and, therefore, he should not ask for one. At $800 million a month, all seemed to agree, the United States could have both guns and butter.

It was a disastrous nondecision. In its wake, inflation took off. In 1966 consumer prices rose 3.3 percent, nearly three times the previous yearly average rise. Prices floated up, and so did wages. In August of 1966, when airline machinists won a 4.9 percent wage increase, the old voluntary guideline of 3.2 percent hikes became meaningless.

Since the war in Vietnam showed no signs of abating, many businessmen decided that continued war would mean continued prosperity, and they expanded their businesses. In fact, the increased defense spending superheated the economy to the point where new jobs were created even for the chronically unemployed. The boom was out of control.

In September, in an attempt to slow the boom, the president suspended business investment tax credits. Businessmen howled that in conjunction with the "credit crunch" the suspension was damaging business futures. Johnson at last struck a deal with Federal Reserve Board Chairman Martin: in exchange for a Johnson request to Congress for a general tax increase, Martin would loosen the Fed's purse strings. Martin did his part: the money supply grew in 1967 at 6.5 percent, up from a restrictive 2.2 percent. Under this impetus, demand surged, and imports flooded into the country. But because there was no counterbalancing tax increase, inflation also surged.

In January of 1967, when Johnson asked for a 6 percent surcharge on income taxes, Wilbur Mills insisted that such a surcharge be accompanied by cuts in domestic spending—and Johnson backed off and would not even transmit the revenue bill to Congress for another six months. When he did send it, the surcharge was up to 10 percent. Mills bottled the tax bill in committee. Mistake followed mistake: government calculations of federal income that year included the surcharge, and without the expected surcharge dollars the federal deficit rose like a hot-air balloon. In 1965 the deficit had been $2 billion; in 1966 it was $4 billion; in 1967, it was nearly $9 billion; and in the first half of fiscal 1968 (when the surcharge had been expected but was not in place), it was already $11 billion.

In January of 1968, Johnson reintroduced the surcharge and began dickering with Mills, who wanted $6 billion cut from domestic programs in line with rising public dismay over "giveaways" to the poor. (The OEO budget was, for instance, $1.5 billion.) In February the Tet offensive shocked the United States and helped to tip the balance of public opinion against the war. In addition, many European countries, led by France, angry at the way the U.S. was handling the Vietnam War, started selling off their dollar holdings and buying gold. The previous November the pound had been devalued, and the dollar was the only remaining currency to which the 1945 Bretton Woods agreement could be pegged; that agreement had fixed within narrow limits the relative prices of European and U.S. currencies. Now, in order to keep the dollar up, the U.S. had to sell much of its own gold holdings. By March the administration was forced to announce that it would no longer openly sell gold to buy dollars. For a time this kept the dollar stable against the French franc, the German mark, and the Japanese yen, but at the cost of adding inflationary pressure on the dollar at home. The combination of military problems, pressure on the dollar, urban and campus unrest, and the inability to get the necessary tax surcharge all besieged Johnson. His popularity sank to an all-time low. On March 31, he announced that he would not run for another term.

In June, Wilbur Mills got his $6 billion cut and Congress passed the Revenue Expenditure and Control Act. As soon as the surcharge took effect, it balanced the federal budget for fiscal 1969—but the 1968 deficit had reached $25 billion, and because the tax increase had been delayed, it came too late to curb much of the inflation, and too late to help Lyndon Johnson remain in the presidency.

Richard Nixon became president in January of 1969. Shortly thereafter, he casually remarked that businessmen should not overly restrain themselves on prices because "they have to be guided by the interests of the organizations that they represent." A financial journalist translated Nixon's statement: "the president just said you could raise prices."

The new Republican administration had a plan for halting inflation. The federal budget would be cut gradually and the money supply restricted gradually, and then inflation would drop. The key to "gradualism"—as explained by Geoffrey Maynard and W. van Ryckeghen—was "monetary policy," that is, the regulation of the money supply:

> If money supply is kept constant, inflation comes up against a monetary barrier (where no money is available for further expansion), so that although prices may continue to rise for some time, output and employment will be falling simultaneously. After a time, the rise in unemployment may check wage demands and the rate of inflation will diminish. The crucial question which then faces the government is whether to allow the money stock to rise to prevent or limit unemployment, or to keep firm control on it in the interest of bringing inflation to an end.

In other words, Nixon planned to slow the boom in order to slow inflation. Some unemployment would result, but before there were too many jobless, the government would again ease the money supply. The final result would be a sound economy with modest unemployment and no inflation.

Slowing the behemoth proved easy. The Fed immediately cut off the money spigot: from an 11 percent aggregate growth in the money supply over the past two years, money supply went to *zero* growth. Defense spending was cut a bit. Soldiers were brought home from Vietnam. Domestic programs were curbed. The income-tax surcharge was extended an additional six months, though at only 5 percent. As predicted by Nixon economists, in the autumn of 1969, after 105 months of boom, the U.S. went into recession and stayed there. Unemployment rose at first slightly, and then, in 1970, it rose sharply. That much was expected.

But the unexpected also happened: inflation did not abate; it got worse.

Economists were astounded. The "Phillips Curve," which demonstrated that when unemployment went up, inflation must come down—simply wasn't working this time.

As economists got around to sorting out the figures, they discovered that inflation seemed to have entered a new phase. It was no longer a straightforward response to "demand." Everything contributed to inflation: demand, war costs, attacks on the dollar, and especially people's expectations. Believing the prices of raw materials and labor would be higher tomorrow than they were today, businessmen raised their own prices. Labor followed suit. When unemployment rose, labor was supposed to be weaker at the bargaining table; all the extra idle hands were supposed to mean that management could buy labor more cheaply, and blue-collar workers were supposed to be willing to take less in their paychecks so that others could be employed alongside them. But the theory no longer worked. The same blue-collar resentment which helped to elect Nixon now was reflected in the fear which workers brought to the bargaining tables—fear of being replaced, fear of not earning enough of the cheapened dollars to get by.

The anger of the working man turned increasingly against the poor, the black, the women, the young, the part-timers who made up a substantial fraction of the new workers and of the unemployed. In the working man's view, such people were cutting into his ability to put bread on the table, and they were getting handouts and other assistance from the federal government. But it was the nature of work that was really changing. We weren't "producing" any more in the old sense of turning out cars; more and more people were employed in service industries—social work, fast food, government—where output was hard to measure and reward. Once U.S. workers had led the world in output per man-hour. By 1970 the U.S. had the lowest productivity rate of all the industrialized nations. Less output for more pay also was inflationary.

Inflation also was helped along by the propensity of the young to obtain jobs outside the usual economy. If someone worked underground and paid no taxes, that was inflationary. If someone did not work at all (in the productivity sense) but continued to take advantage of government services (food stamps, student loans, highway maintenance) while paying less than equivalent amounts in taxes, this lowered government revenue, raised government deficits, and was inflationary. Youth opposition to the work ethic also exacerbated a growing reluctance among all workers to put in the same time and effort for what were now cheapened dollars. Adding to the inflationary burden was the new "ecological consciousness": pollution controls were popular in 1970, but few understood that they reduced the efficiency of machinery and added cost to products—costs passed along to consumers.

Inflation grew. People thought they saw it in the inferior quality of goods, in the more perfunctory nature of services, in the flood of imports that replaced domestic goods in the marketplace, in the pervasive cynicism and "I've-got-mine-the-hell-with-yours" attitude that poisoned daily interchanges. People thought it was inflation that forced them to stay at home and watch television rather than to go out to the movies, and to wear clothes for an extra year rather than to buy new ones. Fewer men's suits were sold in 1969 than in any other year since the Depression.

Part of this cheapening was an illusion, for the real incomes of Americans were still rising. Higher prices create some winners and some losers. In ordinary times winning and losing are taken as part of the game of economic life. But in inflationary times, as Robert Heilbroner and Lester Thurow suggest,

> The losers in the economic game are those whose incomes rise less rapidly than the rate of inflation.... In a world without inflation, losers blame their lower incomes on bad luck or bad judgment or other things. During inflation, when they are pinched *despite higher incomes,* they lay the blame on the system.... College professors blame inflation for their sagging real incomes, when the real trouble is the oversupply of Ph.D's. Factory workers blame inflation when the culprit is the rise in female and part-time employment that has cut into the work week, lowering weekly wages even though hour rates go up. Thus inflation has the effect of distorting our ability to measure our own well-being accurately.

Television fed this distortion with its simplistic reporting about inflation: it often tried to pinpoint the "cause" of inflation as if it were a medical virus. But by 1970 the causes were so numerous and intertwined that it was impossible (and not particularly helpful) to label any single cause as the villain. John Maynard Keynes had once said of inflation:

> There is no subtler, no surer means of overturning the existing basis of society than to debauch the currency. The process engages all the hidden forces of economic law on the side of destruction, and does it in a manner which not one man in a million is able to diagnose.

Unable to diagnose, we looked for scapegoats, and found them in the young who were degrading the work ethic, the blacks who were getting handouts, the unions who were gorging themselves, the businessmen who were reaping windfall profits. All these resentments were exacerbated by inflation, and by reportage which depicted these charges as confrontations. There was a modicum of truth in all the allegations, but the larger truth was more complicated.

The GNP dropped in 1970 for the first time since 1938.

In this land of growth, not to be continually enlarging meant that you were dying. Worried about the economy's health, President Nixon remonstrated with his old friend and advisor Arthur Burns (now head of the Federal Reserve), and Burns opened the money spigot a bit. He did so warily, pointing out to Nixon that inflation was slowing and if the administration would just hold a steady course inflation would soon be licked.

That proved to be impossible. Conditions on the stock market were reminiscent of 1929. The Dow-Jones average was down nearly 200 points from its recent 1968 high. Conglomerates, computer leasers, and other new glamour stocks (which were *not* in the Dow-Jones averages) were down as much as 75 percent. Nearly a hundred brokerage firms were on the edge of bankruptcy, and a portfolio that contained one share of every stock listed on the Big Board of the NYSE was worth half of what it had been at the time Nixon took office.

Echoing Herbert Hoover's statement just before the 1929 crash, on April 28, 1970, Nixon said that if he had the spare cash now, he'd buy stocks. But confidence in government pronouncements was low. With one hand the government was selling bonds, while with the other it was buying back $3.5 billion in old Treasury bills. Abroad there was new selling against the dollar. And as American forces went into Cambodia despite a previous indication that the war was winding down, there was violent domestic reaction. In the week after Kent State, stocks dropped fifty points. Bernard J. "Bunny" Lasker, chairman of the NYSE and another old friend of the president's, convinced Nixon that he had to shore up confidence in the market or there would be a disaster. At a White House dinner for business community leaders, Nixon told his guests that the Cambodian invasion was the greatest military coup since MacArthur landed at Inchon and wondered why people were so upset about it. In turn the guests told Nixon that a stock market recovery depended on his removing troops from Cambodia on the schedule he had announced, and on an immediate loosening of the money supply. On the strength of the dinner, the Dow-Jones went up thirty-two points.

Then another crisis peaked. Over the past several years tightened credit had forced corporations to borrow from one another as well as from banks. Newly amalgamated Penn Central railroad was one of the biggest borrowers, and in June of 1970 Penn Central was on the brink of becoming the largest business failure in world history. Should it collapse, the numerous corporations which had lent it money might also fold, and then the Stock Exchange might be in trouble; should the Exchange get into trouble, there might be runs on the banks for cash, which could lead to a national money panic and chaos. With such a possibility looming near, the Federal Reserve leapt into action. It opened wide its rediscount windows, which enabled commercial banks and their corporate customers to borrow money, so that when the Penn Central declared bankruptcy, that didn't bring down the Stock Exchange.

Though the Penn Central's crash did not bring down the system, when the Fed turned on the hose to put out the potential liquidity fire, the "monetary barrier" to inflation drowned.

As the market started to creep up again, people assessed what had been lost: some $300 billion by 30 million investors, or $10,000 per investor. By late 1970 this translated into recession. The federal government was forced to bail out not only Penn Central but the failing Lockheed Corporation. To save some of the country's largest brokerage houses there were several shotgun marriages. Thirty-five metropolitan areas had substantial unemployment; one was Seattle, where defense and space industry cuts contributed to an unemployment rate over 12 percent. With a population of half a million, Seattle had 200,000 people receiving or applying for food stamps. The country as a whole had lost two million space- and defense-related jobs in two years.

Unemployed this time were many of the "baby boom" generation born after World War II. There were more of them than there were jobs. Nearly 40 percent of the unemployed were in the 16–24 age bracket, while workers over 40 made up only 6 percent of the unemployed. White employment kept pace by age, black employment did not: black teenage population grew at 4.5 percent a year, but jobs for black teenagers grew at only 2.2 percent a year. The employment gap widened between blacks and whites.

Democrats said that the state of the economy was such that we required wage and price controls and attached authorization for such controls to a defense bill. Nixon signed it, but avowed:

> I will not take this nation down the road of wage and price controls, however politically expedient they may seem.... Wage and price controls only postpone a day of reckoning, and in so doing they rob every American of an important part of his freedom.

The midterm election result disappointed Republicans. In January of 1971, after a year in which unemployment rose and the GNP dropped, the president announced, "I am now a Keynesian in economics." Keynes had advocated that governments spend their way out of the Great Depression even if they had no cash on hand. The application of Keynes which Nixon sought to realize was that once explicated clearly by Franklin Roosevelt's amanuensis Harry Hopkins: "Tax and tax, spend and spend, elect and elect." For conservatives such a deficit-spending policy was anathema. Nevertheless, Nixon embraced it, but to cover all bases he said confusingly that he was proceeding on the assumption that the budget would be balanced if there were full unemployment. He explained his tortured logic as follows: since unemployment was high and rising there was, regrettably, a deficit, but "by operating as if we were at full employment we will help bring about that full employment." That was sand in the eyes. Real were new programs that would spend money on non-Vietnam-related defense, and on such politically helpful causes as Medicare and a "war" on cancer. The deficit for fiscal 1971 had been about $2 billion. Nixon's fiscal 1972 budget multiplied the deficit more than ten times—to $23 billion.

By stimulating the economy the new budget made many people happy. But in spending considerably more than the government had, Nixon adopted a discredited Johnson policy of pursuing proximate goals while letting the future go hang. The new budget encouraged inflation.

In January of 1971 inflation control was dealt another severe blow by the Federal Reserve Board. Chairman Burns decided to increase the money supply at the phenomenal rate of 11 percent a year. This would expand the economy but would also virtually guarantee continued inflation. By the spring the value of the 1965 dollar had shrunk a third and was worth about 67 cents. The inflation rate was 4.4 percent for the first half of 1971, but during that first half wholesale prices climbed at an annual rate of more than 8 percent. Prices of everyday necessities were up sharply: carrots, 40 percent in a year; fish, 14 percent; postage, 25 percent. Wages for selected industries were also up: in 1971, steelworkers obtained a 30 percent increase package spread over three years, and railroad workers got a 46 percent increase spread over 42 months.

Abroad, the dollar was in worse straits. Because the Bretton Woods agreement bound international exchange rates within narrow limits, no matter how strong the German mark or Japanese yen became, they were officially worth only a fixed amount of now-cheapened dollars. For years Japan and Germany had been forced to buy dollars and keep their price high so that their own currencies would remain stable; by the spring of 1971 neither country could afford to do so any longer. Their economies were suffering, and even U.S. pressure could not continue to force them to defend the dollar. In May of 1971, after long internal agonizing, the German government revalued the mark upward. It was like putting a finger in the dike to stop a flood: the action worked only for a short time, and then the dam burst. The flood was an outflow of U.S. dollars into German marks, Japanese yen, and other currencies and commodities which seemed more valuable than our own. In the first half of 1971 our balance of payments was down $12 billion, the largest deficit in years. All our selling of gold to keep the price of the dollar artificially high came back to haunt us, for our gold reserves were down to $11 billion. Now there was sustained selling against the dollar all over the world, and we didn't have gold to buy dollars. When private individuals sold dollars to buy German marks or (illegal) gold, we called it speculation; when the government of France did the same thing, we called it repositioning. Both actions were disastrous for the dollar.

For years the Europeans, led by the French, had claimed that the arrangement which kept the price of the dollar artificially high had allowed the U.S. to export inflationary pressures. When our imports exceeded our exports we forced European countries to accumulate overvalued dollars. As our inflation rate got worse, it doubled Europe's problem of accepting our dollars. During one week in August of 1971, France sold off $150 million in dollars. Neither Japan nor Germany could buy all that France wished to dump. Speculators also were selling dollars, and were buying German marks, which were consequently revalued up again. The sellers were betting that the dollar would soon have to be devalued, and were getting rid of the dollars now while they were still worth something. This wave of selling reached crisis proportions in August and finally forced the United States government to act.

On August 15, 1971, President Nixon announced a "New Economic Program." He proposed 1) a 90-day freeze on wages, prices, and rents; 2) tax cuts, mostly for business; 3) government spending cuts of $417 million from temporary deferral of revenue-sharing and of welfare-reform programs then before Congress, and from a six-month deferral of a federal pay hike; 4) a 10 percent surcharge on all dutiable imports; and 5) a complete embargo on government sales of gold to foreign banks at $35 an ounce, which would put the world on a "dollar standard." In his speech the president linked these various items:

> We must protect the dollar from the attacks of international money spec-
> ulators. . . . Whether this nation stays number one in the world's economy
> or resigns itself to second, third, or fourth place, whether we as a people
> have faith in ourselves or lose that faith . . . all that depends on you, on
> your competitive spirit, your sense of personal identity, your pride in
> your country, and in yourself.

Nixon's proposals were a bit of political sleight-of-hand that would have far-reaching ramifications. In the New Economic Program (a name which unwittingly aped Lenin's title for the redevelopment of Russia), everything was not as it seemed.

In the international arena the NEP killed the Bretton Woods agreement, which had been effectively dead since 1968; the closing of the gold window was not new, it simply acknowledged what was already the fact, that the U.S. was not selling gold. The NEP threatened a new round of tariff reprisals against the United States—in Japan the NEP was referred to as Nixon *shokku,* for the impact the program would have on Japan's many exports to the United States. In response the yen was revalued upward. The only positive international message of the NEP was to signal the coming devaluation of the dollar.

The heart of Nixon's program was the domestic and price controls. Just weeks prior to the announcement, CEA Chairman Paul McCracken had told Congress that controls were a liberal panacea that wouldn't work. They "would be a serious threat to individual freedom," he said, for "wages and prices would be in upward motion from the first day" because millions of workers were covered by contracts which had built-in escalators. Moreover, pressure to raise prices would be deferred only temporarily until controls came off. McCracken concluded that a freeze and controls would be highly inflationary on both supply and demand, since such controls would be undoubtedly accompanied by "liberal" pump-priming tax cuts. What McCracken had disavowed, Nixon then championed—and, in a cruel irony, put McCracken in charge of the controls.

In the latter months of 1971 inflation did slow. This was as much due to the taking-hold of prior tight-money policies as it was to patriotic appeals to business and labor to hold down prices and wages. For 90 days, anything could be deferred. The Nixon tax cuts passed Congress, but the budget cuts did not; they were illusory in any event, since they were to come from programs that would have gone into effect only sometime in the future.

George Meany of the AFL–CIO grumbled that controls held down wages, while neither corporate profits nor dividends were controlled. Democrats complained that Nixon had stolen their thunder. Economists and historians pointed out that similar controls had failed in Holland in 1965, that France's controls had not survived 1968, and that Canada's 1970 experience with controls had been equally fruitless.

The reason and the timing of the controls was political. Nixon had long believed that he had lost the 1960 election because the country had been in a period of stagnation following the 1957–1958 recession, and because he had been hurt by the Federal Reserve's 1960 action to constrict the money supply in the election year. So, some fifteen months prior to the 1972 election, Nixon took measures both to halt inflation and to selectively stimulate the economy; these actions would get the country out of economic stagnation just in time for voters to feel a bit prosperous as they went to the polls. Such schemes were not new. In a study of election-year economic conditions, political scientist Edward Tufte found that since the war years presidents had often stimulated the economy in time for the elections, but had let the economy cool in years when the presidency and congressional posts were not at stake. In four out of the last eight presidential election years, presidents had managed to reduce both unemployment and inflation simultaneously, but they had managed the same trick only two out of 24 years when there was no president being elected.

Phase One was like a new honeymoon for the Nixon administration. The public cooperated. Of 120,000 prices spot-checked, more than 80 percent were unchanged through the period, and of the remainder, half went up and half went down. On November 13, 1971, Phase One ended and the hard part began. The president decreed that a Cost of Living Council (COLC) rather than the Pay Board or the Price Commission would be the final arbiter of settlements. This was a first blow to labor cooperation. Both labor and management agreed to a 5.5 percent guideline for future wage packages and left a bit of slippage for fringe benefits. But this guideline was broken almost immediately by a COLC decision to grant soft-coal miners a 16 percent hike—and it was nearly invalidated altogether when the Price Commission refused to allow the coal companies to pass on all this increase to consumers. That was a blow to businessmen, for it warned them to hold their price increases until Phase Two was done.

In December 1971 the major world trading nations met in Washington at the Smithsonian to set new currency parities. This was when the yen was revalued upward, and when the mark went up yet another time. Until the last minute Treasury Secretary John Connally denied vehemently that the U.S. would devalue the dollar; then he lost a battle to Arthur Burns and Henry Kissinger and was forced to announce that the price of gold would go up slightly, which meant a dollar devaluation of about 8 percent. However, since the U.S. still adamantly refused to sell gold to anyone, one result of this maneuver was to up the paper value of the 300 million ounces of gold which the U.S. still held in reserve. Now our gold was worth about $10 billion.

As the 1972 election year began, Nixon announced that inflation was pretty much under control. That was not so. It was a smoldering ember: it had been damped, but the fire coals would burst into flame anytime the restraints were taken off. No one seemed able to understand the decisions of the COLC, Pay Board, or Price Commission; from week to week they seemed to differ so widely that no pattern could be discerned. Most people just held on, and waited for controls to come off.

Meanwhile, Arthur Burns and the Federal Reserve continued to expand the money supply at a rate of more than 7 percent a year, which economic historian Allan S. Blinder characterized as "exuberant monetary growth . . . excessive, even reckless." In addition to stimulating the economy through easing the money supply, during 1972 the administration made many federal handouts. The most obvious, though deserved, was a 20 percent increase in Social Security benefits just prior to election time. (Johnson had done a similar thing in 1964.) An overall deficit-spending policy continued, lauded by liberals as well as conservatives, who each had favorite packages that needed funds. Discernible now was the widening gap between what people paid in taxes and what they were obtaining in the form of direct transfer payments such as grants-in-aid, Social Security, and veterans' benefits—yet those programs continued to mushroom in size. The federal budget became an ever-larger fraction of the GNP. All this transformed 1972, in Blinder's words, "from a year of healthy growth into an unsustainable and inflationary boom."

Johnson had fueled inflation because he had not wanted to lose his social programs; Nixon fueled inflation because he did not want to lose the election. After the election, the president vetoed a number of measures passed by Congress, calling them inflationary. In January 1973 he declared, "The surest way to avoid inflation or higher taxes or both is for Congress to join me in a concerted effort to control Federal spending," which he described as the cause of inflation. In this spirit he vetoed spending bills, impounded funds for legislated programs, and cut benefits in others. Also to cool inflation, Nixon once again influenced Burns to contract the money supply. The contraction occurred so suddenly, and without the usual time lag, that economic activity began to plummet in 1973 and stayed down thereafter for quite some time.

Even as Nixon tried to tighten the federal budget, the budget totals were rising. As a result of inflation, however, receipts also were up. When people's dollar incomes rose, they became victims of "bracket creep," and paid higher taxes even though their real incomes were falling. Another blow to wage-earners' pocketbooks came from a quantum jump in Social Security paycheck deductions.

Phase Two of the wage and price controls ended, and Phase Three began. Rife with internal dissension, the Pay Board and Price Commission were abolished, their functions absorbed by the COLC. In Phase Three, rigid adherence to guidelines was relaxed, and prices and wages both rose. Before anyone could get upset over 6 or 8 percent wage hikes, though, there was a spectacular 22 percent rise in food prices. All over the world the 1972 harvests had been bad, and the price rise was the inevitable result. Rising food prices pushed inflation to over 9 percent a year. In a June 1973 action that observers said might have been taken to shift focus away from the imminent Ervin Committee hearings on Watergate, the Nixon administration announced "Freeze II." Its most obvious goal was to hold food prices in check. By August, Freeze II had given way to Phase Four, a less-strict period of controls on prices and wages. During this phase there was gradual decontrol: one week an industry would be under supervision, but the following week it would be off the controlled list and able to set whatever prices it wished.

As Phase Four went on, nothing seemed to lower the inflation rate— not the constriction of the money supply, not the sale of grain to Russia (which was supposed to ease our balance-of-trade deficit), not the cutting of the budget deficit by impounding funds and lowering benefits.

One reason none of these actions helped was that by 1973 the entire world was in the throes of an inflationary boom: in every country around the globe where a semblance of free market conditions existed, prices were rising. In 1973 there was another forced devaluation of the dollar, which meant that since 1971 it had lost nearly 20 percent against the mark and yen. The price of gold shot upward sharply, which meant that the dollar was worth even less.

The penultimate blow to stability came in October of 1973, a result of the Yom Kippur War. Because the West was supporting Israel, the Organization of Petroleum Exporting Countries (OPEC) cut off oil to America and to Europe. Between late 1973 and early 1974 OPEC quadrupled the price of oil; at the U.S. pumps, prices went up 40 percent.

This last shock sent inflation into double digits. Then, on April 30, 1974—at the worst possible moment—Phase Four ended, and all price and wage controls were lifted. In a different political climate the Nixon administration might have attempted to maintain the controls, but in the spring of 1974 the president was not expending his little remaining political clout on inflation. The controls had been, in Blinder's phrase, "a remark-able act of national self-flagellation." Now that the nation was released from the controls, prices and wages shot upward instantly.

By August of 1974, when Nixon was forced to resign, inflation was more than 12 percent a year—fueled by the remnants of excess demand, by war costs, by rising federal expenditures and deficits, by the worldwide boom, by the bad harvests of 1972, by inflated commodity prices led by OPEC oil, and by the sudden burst in domestic wages and product prices which followed the demise of Phase Four, as well as by our now nearly permanent expectations of rising prices.

Though economically we were still the strongest nation in the world, at the end of the Johnson-Nixon era we had many afflictions. Inflation seemed the worst, but there were others. Unemployment was higher and more persistent than it had been when the era began. The money supply had been subjected to so many abrupt reversals that it had nearly lost its power of gentle restraint and encouragement of the economy. Federal budgets and federal deficits were sky-high. The 1974 GNP was heading toward another net loss, a loss which would wipe out several previous years of gains. The sum of all our troubles was the state of "stagflation": a stagnating economy coupled with inflation. Stagflation was the economic legacy of the era, the characteristic of what later became known as the Great Recession of the middle and late 1970s.

In his speech of August 15, 1971, President Nixon had identified areas at risk because of inflation. As was often the case with Nixon, he accurately pinpointed some of our cherished assumptions, even though he conjured them up only to legitimatize actions which were of immediate political use to him. He said the dollar was in danger of being held hostage to foreign interests; he said the central question was whether we would remain number one among the world's economies; he told us our competitive spirit was in jeopardy and equated that spirit with pride in our country and in our sense of personal worth. Nixon was entirely correct: all these elements, all these assumptions, were compromised by inflation.

Persistent inflation meant that the dollar was continually hostage to currency speculators, gold bugs, Swiss gnomes—and to OPEC oil, Eu-rodollars and petrodollars, and even to countries that held resources in the ground and wouldn't sell them to us. The world was littered with excess dollars, the detritus of our trade deficit, which in foreign hands helped to devalue those we still retained.

While at the end of the decade it was clear that we were still the world's largest economy, we were no longer alone at the summit of power. Rather, we were the largest among a number of strong economies, many of which were considerably strengthened in relation to ours. We were no longer able to dictate how world trade would be run. OPEC held the oil card, Russia had low-priced technology and was willing to sell it, the ten European Common Market countries were trading among themselves at such a rate that the U.S. was forced to curtail exports to the European continent, and Japan (the most changed and most advanced country) was taking business away from us everywhere in the world.

We had replaced the Japanese and German factories after World War II, but we had not replaced our own. With modern plants, our former enemies took greater and quicker advantage of technological breakthroughs. By the mid-1960s the U.S. edge of technological superiority had been blunted: our cars lasted a full year of use less than they had formerly, our steel was not cast continuously, our television sets did not have the sophisticated wizardry of foreign models.

We spent an enormous dollar amount for research and development, but most of it went for military hardware; Japan and Germany spent proportionately less on defense and more on consumer R&D than we did. And, as Jordan D. Lewis commented, the proportion of U.S. industrial R&D always varies inversely with inflation:

> At low inflation rates, technical advance contributes to productivity growth, which in turn reduces the growth rate of prices paid for goods and thus dampens the rate of inflation. But at sufficiently high rates, inflation inhibits the predictability of future business conditions, frustrating the selection of long-term R&D goals. . . . Higher inflation rates also inhibit capital investment, an important vehicle for the introduction of new technology.

Inflation forced U.S. companies to look for short-term gains rather than long-term improvements. This pressure was so intense that it helped delay decisions to replace outmoded plant or to start up new generations of equipment. Thus the designs for cars which could get higher gas mileage stayed on the shelf—and while we were not in production our former markets were saturated by competitors who were already manufacturing such designs. Inflation reduced both our willingness and our ability to invest.

Even with inflation, the American economy was still the world's most stable, but as with a man who becomes a hypochondriac after listening to his heart beat, we were continually aware of our shortcomings and were always on the outlook for symptoms of ill health. Over the course of the decade we lost confidence in the government's ability to control inflation— the tools no longer seemed to work, or they seemed so arbitrarily applied as to render them ineffective. The economic superiority of the United States could no longer be taken for granted.

It often seemed as if the government itself were responsible for inflation, so much did the government tinker with the economy by use of its various agencies. H. L. Nieburg observed that "creeping inflation" had become a way of life,

> softened and maintained by periodic injections of public funds through tax reductions, welfare programs, subsidies to education, and the maintenance of employment and income levels through non-growth government expenditures for R&D, space, defense, and intellectual make-work projects. This dynamic distorts the public R&D investment—however justified in terms of valid government missions—into a species of pump-priming and gold-plating. This dynamic also endows the centers of concentrated economic power with a vested interest in government spending, including welfare programs that do not threaten the status quo. Thus the most powerful elements of American business have converted to Keynesianism—but this new Keynesianism produces growth only as a by-product of other processes which enhance the distortions of power and income, and postpone but intensify underlying problems, forcing the government to maintain an ever larger subsidy system to prevent recurrent crises.

By using such measures, the government intensified the public's perception that whatever Washington was doing to the economy, it was doing because the system was neither as healthy nor as legitimate as it had been in the past. A dollar no longer bought what it once had, and an honest day's work did not seem to generate an equivalent amount of pay. Thus the economy became tinged with that same lack of legitimacy and authority which also colored the presidency, the government as a whole, the corporations, the war, and every other institution of the country.

Economic historian Robert L. Heilbroner wondered if the malaise which had attacked our economic health lay deep within our society, in

> the industrial foundation upon which our society is based. Economic growth and technological achievement, the greatest triumphs of our epoch

of history, have shown themselves to be inadequate sources for collective contentment and hope. Material advances, the most profoundly distinguishing attribute of industrial capitalism and socialism alike, [have] proved unable to satisfy the human spirit.

President Nixon had said that we should fear for our competitive spirit, for pride in our country and in ourselves: it was on these deep-rooted beliefs that inflation and materialism took their greatest toll.

Inflation helped make a mockery of the old Protestant work ethic. Workers felt powerless; it seemed next to impossible to get ahead, because more dollars did not mean more rewards. The ordinary person hoped to get an edge on life by working hard, saving money, sacrificing for the kids' education, and building a nest egg for retirement. Inflation hurt those strategies, and therefore hurt the assumptions about American society on which they were based. "Own your own home." "A penny saved is a penny earned." "Neither a borrower nor a lender be." "All things come to those who wait." These old adages no longer applied.

A man's home was no longer his castle. On the average, it had shrunk in space 20 percent during the decade. It might have gone up in value during the decade, from, say, $50,000 to $75,000, but if you sold it, you didn't actually realize a profit, for you simply ended up buying another house for the same or more money and making a larger mortgage payment. Value was relative, not absolute. Pennies saved might become pennies lost, and if a dollar kept in a bank became worth progressively less the longer it stayed in the bank, people saw little reason to save at all. Rather, they were encouraged to spend dollars when they had them, a process which was itself inflationary as well as profoundly materialistic. You might not have a savings account, but you had a new living room.

Those who bought the furniture outright seemed foolish, for if you took delivery for the furniture now but paid for it next month and next year in cheapened dollars, it seemed as if you were a winner. Most people paid for their purchases by credit. For a time, when inflation outran the charge rates on the credit cards, it seemed to make sense to go into debt. In 1970 the 20 million active bank credit card users owed an average of $150 each on their cards, or $3 billion. The Charge Account Bankers Association prescribed this formula for a rosy future to its members:

> To generate the major sources of income, card-holders must use their cards more and more often, from more and more merchants, for more

and more purposes, and for larger and larger amounts, and on more and more extended terms.

For the public, this was a prescription for disaster. During the decade personal bankruptcies doubled from 125,000 a year to 250,000 a year. Larger and larger fractions of a wage earner's income went to paying off his debts; and as charge card rates finally crept up to meet (and then to surpass) the rate of inflation, it became more and more difficult to get out of debt.

Something else happened when the price of credit soared: the entrepreneurial spirit was sapped. The American enterprise system had been built on individual initiative, on the idea that if a man made a better mousetrap, the world would beat a path to his door. But during inflationary times it was the already-established firm—with a good credit rating, with dollars enough for advertising—and not the better mousetrap which brought in the business. Here was another piece of mounting evidence as to the infinitesimal nature of the individual in a world of big government, multinational corporations, and immutable economic forces. Inflation took responsibility from a man: if a large and unknowable economic force was beating him back, it was not his responsibility to counter it, but the government's. As a consequence of inflation, individuals felt not only smaller but less powerful and less responsible for their actions.

During the decade, government grew at an alarming rate, a rate which both fueled inflation and exceeded inflation's growth rate. In ten years the federal budget more than tripled. By 1974 there were 81,299 governmental entities in the country, many of them employing thousands of people. Our one-to-six ratio of civil servants to private-sector workers was the highest in the world. Great Britain, often thought of as a country filled entirely with government bureaucrats, had a ratio of one to eighteen. Rising governmental spending meant a continual escalation of the share of the GNP funneled through official hands. There seemed no way to reverse this trend. Caspar Weinberger, at the time head of the Office of Management and Budget, observed that "a pilot program turns into an essential program in three years....The distance from an urgent priority to a sacred cow is usually no more than five fiscal years."

Nowhere was this more evident than in the military. When the end of American troop involvement in Vietnam was envisioned, there was supposed to be a "peace dividend" of $20 billion a year which could be made available for social programs. It never materialized. The money was eaten up in defense budget increments. Cutting back on defense spending was also virtually impossible because such spending was so great a share of the GNP that if it were cut the country's economy would suffer. Similarly, to cut back on the "transfer payments" from Social Security, Medicare, food stamps, veterans' benefits, and the like would leave many Americans without dollars to spend on consumer goods—and also would adversely affect the economy. So very little in the federal budget was ever cut back. And as the budget rose, so did its deficits, even though taxes were taking a larger fraction of each American's income than ever before.

Not only were individuals paying more taxes, but the taxes on individuals made up a greater fraction of the government's income. Once business had paid a substantial share of the tab: in 1964, corporations paid $23 billion, but by 1974 they paid only $30 billion, an amount which, when adjusted for inflation, translated to proportionately less than what they had paid at the outset of the era. In contrast, individuals paid $48 billion in 1964, and more than $90 billion in 1974. In 1974, direct levies took 25 percent more from a paycheck than they had in 1964. Federal taxes were up more than 80 percent, state taxes up more than 100 percent, local taxes up more than 150 percent. In addition, a taxpayers' foundation reported there were more than a hundred indirect taxes on items such as eggs.

Despite generations of attempts to redistribute the country's wealth, in 1974 the rich owned more than ever. During the decade the increasing fraction of the pie which the wealthy held came mostly at the expense of the middle class. The poor stayed at about the same level, but the rich got richer, and those who were in the middle fell back. In 1971, for instance, 30 percent of the stock certificates were held by that 0.2 percent of the population which had incomes of more than $100,000 a year, and 50 percent of all stock certificates were held by that one percent of families with incomes of more than $50,000 a year. The other 50 percent of the stock certificates were distributed among the remaining 99 percent of the country's population. This meant that control of the corporations remained in the hands of the few in the upper-income brackets. In 1974, 80 percent of the country's families earned less than $17,500 a year—and that income bought only what $10,000 had in 1964. With prices inflated, with wages lagging behind inflation, and with the real value of property decreasing, few of the 80 percent could face the future with any feeling of economic security.

Psychologists reported that money troubles were a major contributing factor to the rising number of divorces. More men took second jobs and spent less time with their families. More women entered the work force to aid family income—and spent less time with their families. In 1960, for instance, 33 percent of the wives of blue-collar working men had jobs; by 1970 this fraction was 44 percent and rising.

Inflation sapped vitality and mobility. Union members might have risen in status to the point where they were buying houses in the suburbs, but they were more heavily in debt than their fathers ever had been, and they often found themselves no further away from being and feeling poor. Each year the officially designated poverty line crept up higher, and the middle class threatened to sink beneath it.

Inflation rubbed salt in wounds. It accelerated the middle class's disenchantment with government programs which aided the poor and the minorities. It made workers more resistant to moderating their wage demands and made the possibility that the unemployed would be hired less likely. It tore value from just those assets such as houses which had set the middle class apart from the poor.

Inflation made the generation of the parents intolerant of their children's efforts to change the work ethic. It set the blue collar against the poor, the old against the young, the middle-class managers against the working stiffs, whites against blacks, and American-born against new immigrants. Inflation was a continual shock, a permanent affliction which robbed us of our enjoyment of life and of our aspirations.

5 Don't Trust Anyone Over Thirty

As THE 1964 SCHOOL YEAR BEGAN at the largest single campus in the U.S., the University of California at Berkeley, the dean of students issued a memorandum forbidding political solicitation on a 26-foot strip of sidewalk near the main entrance to the campus. The memo was a reaction to pressure from right-wing William P. Knowland's *Oakland Tribune*, which had discovered that since the plaza was university rather than public property, under a law adopted during the McCarthy years it could not be used for political purposes.

Berkeley was what gubernatorial candidate Ronald Reagan that year called "a hot-bed of liberalism." Ten percent of the students had been involved in civil-rights protests, and the largest Peace Corps contingent came from the school. The memo provoked groups from "Friends of SNCC" to "Youth for Goldwater." Banding together to protect their First Amendment rights, they marched 500 strong to the administration building, then sat in the building all night. During the dark hours they formed the Free Speech Movement. In the morning, eight were arrested and released.

In the next few days the university refused to rescind the memo, and, in defiance of it, even more young people set up tables and solicited openly on the strip. Campus police, aided by local units, then arrested former student Jack Weinstein, who was soliciting for CORE—a group which had particularly angered the *Oakland Tribune*. Hundreds, then thousands of students surrounded the police car which held Weinstein, and prevented it from leaving the campus. Mario Savio, a friend of Weinstein's who had just returned from a summer with SNCC in Mississippi, climbed barefoot atop the police car, denounced the "machinery of the multiversity" that had precipitated such a crisis, and went off to negotiate his friend's release. Negotiations took another day, during which each side received reinforcements. By 7:30 P.M. on October 2, Clark Kerr, president of the nine-campus university, had reached an agreement with Savio that saved face, set Weinstein free, and made a plan whereby the strip would be deeded back to the city so it could be used legally for solicitation. Savio read the agreement to the crowd, asked them to accept it and to "rise quietly with dignity and go home." The students did just that.

In the weeks following, the rules were liberalized in favor of solicitation—but Savio and others were threatened with disciplinary action. Feeling betrayed, the FSM announced a mass sit-in to be held after Thanksgiving recess. The rally drew 6,000 students, Joan Baez singing "Blowin' in the Wind," and Mario Savio's famous statement:

> There's a time when the operation of the machine becomes so odious, makes you so sick at heart, that you . . . can't even tacitly take part. And you've got to put your bodies upon the gears and upon the wheels . . . you've got to make it stop. And you've got to indicate to the people who run it, to the people who own it, that unless you're free the machine will be prevented from working at all.

Eight hundred marched into the administration building, sat in, sang, played cards, attended a "freedom school," but did little to directly provoke the authorities. Kerr wanted to ignore the demonstrators, but liberal Governor Pat Brown—under pressure from a rising conservative tide—sent more than 600 police into the building at three in the morning to arrest the demonstrators. They were jailed at the Santa Rita Rehabilitation Center, known during the war as an internment camp for Japanese-Americans. Brown's action turned a local conflict into a national *cause célèbre*.

The new internees were the cream of the university—from solid backgrounds, with well-educated parents, with unusually good academic records. Most were humanities majors, white, Protestant or Jewish. (Working-class Catholic Savio was the exception.) Their jailing united the university community: within a few days, 16,000 students, faculty, and teaching assistants shut down the campus. Weinstein uttered his now-famous line, "Don't trust anyone over thirty," an unknown striker staked out future territory with a placard reading, "I Am A UC Student: Do Not Fold, Spindle, or Mutilate," and the generation gap was born.

Shortly before the Christmas recess the Board of Regents relented and agreed to most of the student demands, which were relatively harmless. The campus reopened. But things had changed: at the turn of the new year graduate students were tutoring undergrads in "socially relevant" subjects to make up for time lost in the chaos, there was a new and wilder street scene just outside the campus, and there was much more political solicitation.

On March 3, 1965, a young New Yorker arrived wearing a sign which said "fuck." He was arrested by campus police. Veterans of the Free Speech Movement demanded that charges be dropped. Students treated the matter playfully; thousands of cards with the offending word were printed and distributed; someone read aloud from *Lady Chatterley's Lover*; someone said the bad word was an acronym for Freedom Under Clark Kerr. The FSM came to stand for the Filthy Speech Movement.

These spring rites were repressed by the school administration, this time with the backing of the faculty as well as of the Board of Regents. Disgusted at the profanity and co-opting of the FSM by the joy riders, Savio dropped out. Clark Kerr, accused by some of being too liberal and soft on students, and accused by students of being an agent of conservatism, was later fired when Reagan became governor.

The Berkeley furor was the paradigm of the youth revolution—from its genesis in civil rights to its ultimate transformation into student concern with entirely personal issues. Protest, youth power, idealism, tension between right and left, confusion of issues, manipulation of symbols: all were there. To metamorphose the Berkeley incidents into a national schism the only thing lacking was the war in Vietnam.

On February 7, 1965, the USAF began to bomb North Vietnam in the campaign called "Rolling Thunder" when it became a fixed practice in March. February and March also saw the massive civil-rights confrontations at Selma, Alabama. To discuss how to protest both the government's actions in Vietnam and its nonactions in Selma, a small group of faculty met in Ann Arbor, Michigan. Sociology professor William Gamson championed a one-day strike and, in place of classes, a faculty-supervised exposition of "the concealed story of Vietnam." Along with the Bible, Gamson reasoned that the truth would make men free—or, at least, that it would stop the war.

The result of the discussions was the first teach-in, held at the University of Michigan on the evening of March 14, 1965. Observer Mark Pilsuk wrote scathingly that the faculty involved had a "dimly perceived vision of self...which permitted the concerned...to envision himself as the conqueror not of governments, but, rather, of his own sense of importance." For the students, it was not the intellectual content of the meeting that mattered but rather the experience of protest and commitment. A week later, a thousand people attended a similar teach-in at Madison, Wisconsin. The idea quickly spread to other large and "impersonal" campuses similar to Berkeley, Ann Arbor, and Madison. Later in the spring, there was a rally in Washington which 25,000 people attended. Though the ralliers had come as much to hear Joan Baez and Judy Collins as to listen to I. F. Stone and Senator Ernest Gruening, they had come, and the number of those interested in the antiwar cause grew.

At that time a poll taken on campuses reported 91 percent of the students queried supported American participation in the war, and more than half queried agreed that the U.S. would have to escalate the conflict in order to win it. Thus in 1965 the protesters were representative neither of the American people as a whole nor of American youth. They were far out in left field.

Throughout the decade the hippies, Yippies, New Leftists, communards, street people, peace marchers, and their ilk were only a small fraction of the population—but they were a vociferous and suasive minority. Especially in regard to Vietnam, they became the leading edge of dissent and ferment. Nobody liked the protesters much—but they were heard. A study by Daniel Yankelovich showed that as the late 1960s wore on, the opinions of the leading edge became those of ever-larger fractions of the campuses, then spread to the loosely knit community of intelligentsia, and finally to the population as a whole. By mid-1970, Louis Harris found 91 percent of the younger population and a majority of the population as a whole to be antiwar. In five years the students had changed the mind of the country on a fundamental issue.

Some explanation for this process can be found in the work of Robert Wuthnow. Approximately 5 percent of the Berkeley students were activists, Wuthnow found, but there were 25 percent who were in general sympathy with the protesters, and 50 percent of the campus community (including teachers and area residents) who "supported experimentation" of a fairly advanced sort both in politics and in personal life choices. This 50 percent were not themselves mounting the barricades or living in polymorphous perversity, but they tolerated such behavior without interfering with it or repressing it. Other studies in less-radical areas of the country revealed similar feelings. The majority first tolerated, then began to listen actively to the young.

In 1965 the younger segment of the population was growing by leaps and bounds. In 1964, the first year of the baby boom's majority, 1.3 million males had reached age 18; in 1965, there were 1.9 million. Increasingly more millions of 18-year-old males would be coming along in the next few years. About 50 percent of the nation's population was under age 30; soon half the population would be under age 25.

The image of Selma yielded to the image of Watts; the campaign photo of LBJ the peace candidate was superseded by the photo of the solemn president sitting with his advisors deciding to escalate the war. In part the war could be escalated because the overall draft registry was a third larger than it had been in 1963. Since the manpower pool was enormous, the hardship of military service could be spread thinly over the nation. Even so, in September young men were shocked when 27,500 were drafted— more draftees than in any month since the Korean War. Draft calls were 400 percent higher in 1965 than in 1964. Full-time undergraduates, graduate students, and fathers escaped immediate service, but the deferments were a mixed blessing; as Landon Jones suggests,

> they meant that men were vulnerable not in just one year but rather over a minefield of eight years, from their nineteenth birthday until their twenty-sixth. They had their entire student careers to worry about the draft and the injustice of the war and to build up resentments against the system that had caused it.

This meant 25 million young men at risk over the entire course of the war, rather than only a few million at risk each year.

In the fall of 1965 when the school year began, there were simultaneous rallies against the war in ninety cities. On the East Coast people burned draft cards, and two men even set themselves afire in imitation of the bonzes in Vietnam.

On the West Coast the Vietnam Day Committee in Berkeley included such veterans of the Free Speech Movement as Jerry Rubin; this year the protesters were longer-haired and of more outrageous mien. A sign of the times, they were harassed from one side by the Hell's Angels (who accused them of being Communists) and from the other by Ken Kesey's LSD–laced band of psychedelic jesters (who accused them of being too straight).

Don't Trust Anyone Over Thirty   *123*

Thanks to extensive, if still disparaging, media coverage, the protests caught the public eye and in particular the eye of the young. In the glare of what Todd Gitlin has labeled "the floodlit society," protest began to grow. Rallies were larger. SDS tripled its membership. Timothy Leary became a public guru. There was an explosion of rock music. Something was happening.

It was immediately apparent that the children of this new generation had been formed by the concatenation of three great technologies, none of which had ever been experienced in such an advanced form or by so many people in all the history of the world. The college denizens who marched in the early 1965 protests were children of the bomb, children of prosperity, and children of television. Born during the war or shortly thereafter, during their youth they had lived under the shadow of nuclear annihilation. Children of the American middle-class, they had known affluence all their days, for since the war the country had been in a prolonged boom. And they had spent more hours in front of a television set than with their schoolbooks or in the waking company of their parents. As Marshall McLuhan was pointing out just then, such a disjuncture of experience with their parents made the young different simply because they were apprehending the world in a new and different manner. They were not sober, linear readers of newspapers; rather they were ecstatic, non-rational, often passive absorbers of 40-second news "stories" and of half-hour life-and-death dramas.

For this new generation Margaret Mead had wished a moratorium period between physical maturity and the time when they began their first serious jobs. During it, they could be free "from the immediate consequences of any act," and would have "time to sleep, to grow, to experiment, to change, and to choose." Wish granted! In the United States in the late 1960s, the children of affluence (in greater numbers than anyone had imagined) were in the midst of that moratorium time. Mead had hoped for them to express "the fiercest political idealism, the hardest religious choices, the acceptance of stringent artistic discipline," and hoped they could reach "that special degree of great questioning, high dedication, uncompromising search for something greater than mankind has yet attained." Now was their time—but what would they make of it?

Some said "very little," and pointed to three obvious influences and expression of the generation: drugs, sex, and rock-and-roll.

Marijuana, common since the 1920s, was a relaxant traditionally used by jazz musicians; now it became widely used, a way to leave ordinary existence behind. The stronger drugs of LSD and peyote made greater impressions on those who ingested them. All these "psychedelics" had common effects. Drug researchers agree that under the influence of psychedelics a person's existing social and perceptual programming is altered; light, odor, and other sensations are heightened; the values and order of society appear to be arbitrary. Sociologist Hugh Gardner comments that such altered perceptions are "typically accompanied by feelings of ego-loss, godlike cosmic insight into the unity of all life, and the unmasking of society as a transparent system of games." As the drug-taker loses faith in the conventional, he changes his life plan or his career; while he constructs a new self he searches for new values and new visions of humanity.

Young people took drugs mostly in company of others, which reinforced the tendency among the young to spend more time with their peers than with older adults. Common drug experiences became the functional equivalent of religious exaltation. And since drugs were illegal, users became like outlaws—which gave to drug-taking a patina of danger and excitement.

Teenagers were maturing physically one to two years earlier than their parents had. Physical maturity and the easy availability of birth control pills allowed the young to engage in sex without fear of pregnancy and without mechanical restraints that might preclude spontaneity. To the young, marriage, children, and responsibility were far off in a perhaps-never-to-be-realized future. They saw sexual incompatibility as a cause of their parents' divorces; they believed they would have fewer hangups about sex. Virginity was a rite of passage, not a moral barrier.

Sex—like drugs—was intense, immediate, and also had the gloss of illegality. Peer pressure initiated many into sexual practice. Sexual variety became prized, the naturalness of the experience extolled. The trends were toward publicly displayed nudity, an absence of undergarments, the presence of such historically sexual symbols as long hair, baubles, bangles, and beads. Sex, too, was a ceremony, a leisure activity which helped define a life-style, an exploration of possibilities, a forbidden pleasure heretofore associated exclusively with adulthood.

Rock-and-roll, the electronically amplified *lingua franca* of the generation, was like a drug in its intensity and blurring of sensations, like sex in its heavy rhythm and passion. Its lyrics were defiantly antiestablishment, though its production reflected money, power, and corporate America. Sex, drugs, and rock-and-roll came together often, as in Jim Morrison and the Doors' rendition of "Break On Through (to the other side)." The Doors took their name from Aldous Huxley's work on mind-altering substances, *The Doors of Perception*, and the song itself was about achieving orgasm.

The music of Dylan, Joplin, Hendrix, the Beatles, the Rolling Stones, the Grateful Dead, the Jefferson Airplane, Country Joe and the Fish, and the Band explained and defined the generation. The Band sings of "The Weight," which has been dropped on the singer (a man whom Griel Marcus called "the worried man") by Miss Fanny; this weight cannot be escaped. As Marcus analyzed the song:

> We never find out who Miss Fanny is, let alone what the singer is supposed to do for her; but the music, not to mention the singing, is so full of emotion and complexity that it makes "the weight"—some combination of love, debt, fear, and guilt—a perfect image of anyone's entanglement. So the story [of the album "Music from Big Pink"] is revealed, and concealed, in flashes, dreams, pieces of unresolved incident, rumbles of doubt exiting as a joke. Yet if the music is part of the story, it is also a landscape against which the story takes place. Blurred at the edges and unsure of its center, this America is still a wilderness—the moral, social wilderness that is left even when the natural wilderness is gone. Excited and intrigued by the place for just that reason, the worried man has to get on without maps.

This exegesis, which paints a picture of a "worried man" concerned with his fellow human beings and with the paradoxes of postindustrial America, represents the best of rock and those who attempt to explain it.

More often, rock and its accouterments were simply style, a style which was anathema to older generations, in particular to that generation of middle-class parents who had spawned the new generation. The symbols and attitudes of the leading edge of youth were diametrically, and not a little perversely, opposite to those of their parents. To emphasize that the world of drugs, sex, and rock-and-roll was new, the young manipulated symbols shamelessly and brilliantly. Did the parents cultivate neatness? The kids wore long hair. Did the parents sip socially acceptable alcohol? The kids blew illegal pot. Did the parents scrimp and save for the future? The kids spent all they could beg, borrow, or steal, today. Did the parents work assiduously? The kids voluptuously embraced leisure. Did the parents revere the flag? The kids wore it on their rumps. There were deeper philosophic differences between the generations, but, in a word, the kids were anti-Establishment.

Many commentators analyzed the new world-view of youth. Charles Reich said they were the sole proprietors of Consciousness III, an advanced form of thought which floated gently above hangups and ambiguity; Theodore Roszak wrote approvingly of a whole "counterculture" that avoided the pitfalls of "technocracy." Sociologist Barbara Myerhoff suggested that in the new generation gap, the Protestant ethic clashed with the set of values derived from Locke and Rousseau:

> The themes of equality, social responsibility, democracy, liberty, and fraternity confronted the conflicting themes of the Puritan world view and resulted in a dizzying welter of confusion and paradox.... The Puritan had been taught to value above all his strength of will, his mastery and independence. Man was to obey—but he was to exert his will. He was damned, but he was responsible for his failures. He was to work, but he was not to enjoy the profits of his work. He was continually to question and evaluate himself, to scrutinize his spiritual condition which he could never know with certainty because he could never know his predestination....

The generation of the children had found a way to escape such double binds which still haunted their parents—by coming down on the side of the French Enlightenment. To Myerhoff the young were "new humanists" who espoused an "alternative interpretation of the good life." Other observers said the young were simply trying to realize those values which the parents had always held but which they had been unable to achieve in their own lives. Sociologist Lauren Langman systematized the difference between the values of "western industrial man and "counterculture child":

INDUSTRIAL MAN
1) *Rationality.* "Suppression of primary process thought, delayed gratification, avoidance of emotional (impulsive) expression."
2) *Self-reliance, independence, and individualism.* "Highly individuated ego structure. Internalized 'guilt' controls."
3) *Hard work as a moral calling.* "Material accumulation as a symbol of success."
4) *Domination over nature.*
5) *Future orientation.* "Immediate experience subjugated to long-term utility." Goal: "To enter heaven."

1) *Anti-rationality*. "Impersonal bureaucracy (rational hierarchy)" is "one of the prime evils," and "impulse expression" a prime good.
2) *Community, engagement, dependence*. "Co-operation, shared responsibility, living to help others."
3) *Hedonistic self-expression preferable to goal-oriented activity*. "Being over doing."
4) *Harmony with nature*.
5) *Present orientation*. "There may not be a tomorrow." Goal: "Immediate experience and sensation."

Engaging in the fad for apocalyptic terminology, Langman suggested that whereas industrial man was Apollonian, emergent countercultural child was Dionysian.

The explanations became quite esoteric. Y. Michael Bodeman reached into the lexicon of theology to explain the revolt of the young. They were headed for *theopoimsis*, a dissolution of the ego associated with the notions of "unlimited sphere" (of actions), of "omnilocal center" (the person as the center of the universe), and of "immediacy of salvation." While all this was undoubtedly true, it seemed wide of the mark, for sex, drugs, and rock-and-roll were earthy concerns.

For the most part the young knew where they were: in a land of temporary fantasy, and not in what they called the "real world" of jobs, marriage, children, and responsibilities. They admitted that when they came up against such realities their attitudes would be different. For the present, however, their temporary world presented them with enough problems to be dealt with and conquered.

In 1966, draft laws were changed so that class standing could be used as a basis on which to decide which students would be drafted or deferred. LSD was declared illegal. SNCC and SDS came out against the war. "Black power" scared people.

By the spring of 1967 both the youth culture and the war were firmly established. Draft calls were at 60,000 a month. In April, "peace" marches and rallies drew a half-million young people. Dr. Martin Luther King, Jr., read a "Declaration of Independence from the War in Vietnam," and heavyweight champion Muhammed Ali refused induction into the army. Tom Wicker of *The New York Times* wondered what would happen if all young men of draft age took the same position as the champ. A hundred thousand could be jailed,

But if the Johnson administration had to prosecute 100,000 Americans in order to maintain its authority, its real power to pursue the Vietnamese war or any other policy would be crippled if not destroyed. It would then be faced not with dissent but with civil disobedience on a scale amounting to revolt.

Wicker's colleague James Reston revealed that his highly placed administration sources feared just such a movement, and for that reason they were continuing student deferments: "The estimate here is that if college students were called like any other 19-year-olds, as many as 25 percent of them might refuse to serve." The administration did, however, announce that graduate deferments which directly affected 650,000 young college men would stop soon.

Pushed by the imminence of the draft, and lured by reports of new nirvanas, large numbers of young people—in the hundreds of thousands—flocked to the Haight-Ashbury section of San Francisco and to a portion of New York's Lower East Side which became known as the East Village. Much hype attended these migrations, but even when excess is discounted, these journeys remain significant cultural phenomena. The young came as pilgrims and left as apostles. They came in droves to participate in the youth scene, to experience what Jerry Rubin characterized as the "ecstasy and rainbows" of such seminal events as the January 1967 be-in at Golden Gate Park. Near the bridge the "tribes" of the Haight and of Berkeley melded under the hot sun, ingested LSD supplied by Kesey's Merry Pranksters, and played out fantasies. Rubin wrote:

> Our nakedness was our picket sign. . . . We were kids playing "grown-up games." You can be whatever you want to be when you're a kid. We were cowboys and Indians, pirates, kings, gypsies and Greeks. . . . The rock bands created a tribal, animal energy. We were a religion, a family, a culture, with our own music, our own dress, our own human relationships, our own stimulants, our own media. And we believed that our energy would *turn on the world.*

Television crews and reporter teams from national magazines ate up such events and spread the word to the young that they needed no means of entry to such fantasies other than their style and youth. Awakening—a *satori*, as those newly steeped in the short course in Eastern mysticism called it—would come to them like a thunderclap.

Ken Kesey and his California friends put LSD into everyone's punch: it was an "acid-test" of whether you were new or old, a litmus of immediate perception. On the East Coast, Rubin's compatriot (and later, with Paul Krassner, co-founder of the Yippies) Abbie Hoffman dropped something equally symbolic on equally unsuspecting squares:

> When we went in the guards immediately confronted us. "You are hippies here to have a demonstration and we cannot allow that in the Stock Exchange." "Who's a hippie? I'm Jewish and besides we don't do demonstrations, see we have no picket signs," I shot back. The guards . . . agreed we could go in. . . . When the line moved . . . we saw more newsmen than I've ever seen in such a small area. We started clowning. Eating money, kissing and hugging . . . (and) throwing money over the railing. The big tickertape stopped and the brokers let out a mighty cheer. . . . When I got out, I carried on in front of the press. . . . We danced . . . celebrating the end of money. I burned a fiver.

Hoffman did not believe that dropping dollars on "straights" would turn them into "freaks," but rather that the gesture would alert potential converts that the youth culture was both imminent and powerful. The Stock Exchange confirmed Hoffman's view that it was neanderthalic when a few weeks later it put up bulletproof glass up in the Visitors' Gallery.

For most who experienced the "summer of love" on both coasts, it was a time out of time, an idyll only slightly marred by exploitation and abuse. The young came to be seduced, to express their alienation from their parents, or simply to enjoy their moratorium time before school—or the draft—or the necessity of getting a job—took hold of their lives. Detroit was burning, but the Haight-Ashbury was alight with a glow of a different kind. The establishment was making war, but the youth were making love.

Near the end of the summer there was a brutal murder in the Haight and a march to proclaim the "Death of A. Hippie, Beloved Son of Mass Media." In the East Village there was the equally brutal double-murder of drifter Groovy and daughter-of-the-wealthy-suburbs Linda, who had run away from home in search of experience.

Vicious and sad though they were, these murders deterred few and might even have heightened the sense of danger and excitement many felt in the hippie scene. Rock groups sang of revolution and outlawry, revelation and omnipotence. With its sense of community, shared transcendence of everyday reality, and endless possibilities, the hippie experience was overwhelming. There seemed no limits to what "good heads" might do or be in life. When the summer ended, the sense of promise ran smack into the growing anxiety. A young Harvard student described how

> A peaceful campus, only marginally concerned with Vietnam suddenly became desperate. We felt boxed in. We were like the man about to go into the gas chamber, with no way out and the walls slowly but inexorably closing around him.

The war effort was nearly at flood tide, with a half-million American boys in Vietnam or on the way there. It was not the draftees themselves who were protesting—they were overwhelmingly from the lower classes, disproportionately black and brown—and so those in the leadership of the resistance felt that the most forceful and sacrificial act would be to get themselves arrested. Some 158 men and women, the men over the draft age, signed the September "Call to Resist Illegitimate Authority," which counseled young draft-eligible men to resist conscription and the war. Among those whose signatures appeared in *The New York Review of Books* and in the *New Republic*, where the ad was printed, were Dr. Benjamin Spock and Reverend William Sloane Coffin.

The October 1967 demonstrations changed the tenor of the antiwar movement from nonviolent to—at the very least—confrontational. In Oakland, California, 3,000 people surrounded an army induction center. Police charged them, and some were injured. On Friday, October 20, 10,000 demonstrators, many wearing helmets and shields, advanced on the center. Jeff Segal, later indicted for inciting a riot, wrote:

> People were mad about...the brutality they saw and were determined to make the power structure pay for what it did. They went into the streets and built barricades...would run up behind buses and rip the ignition wires out or would climb into trucks and steal the keys...start to paint things on the streets and sidewalks. The paint was really the original catalyst that loosened the people up and led to the many other great, beautiful things....They...let their imagination and newfound sense of power run wild.

Lonnie Heller, an organizer at Oakland with tear gas still smarting in his eyes, flew to Washington to exhort people to action. Spock, Coffin, and others also descended on Washington to deliver to the Department of Justice a briefcase containing 994 draft cards of men who wished to return them. Then, under the leadership of the SDS, young people came to "attack the war machine" at its seat, the Pentagon.

Fifty thousand rallied at the Lincoln Memorial; then a few thousand marched across to Virginia; then a hard core of a thousand moved onto Pentagon grounds. They planned to "levitate" the building by spiritual means. The Department of Defense had paid such scrupulous attention to the marchers that they knew better than most protesters what their tactics were, where they had come from, and how the demonstration would go. The 82nd Airborne was called in to maintain order and to guard the premises. The protesters, bedded down on Pentagon grass and tarmac, stared at fixed bayonets and watched soldiers break bottles with billy clubs. Some protesters taunted the soldiers with nudity; others offered them flowers. One Pentagon insider yelled out, "Dr. Spock, this is all your fault!" The overt anti-Americanism of the protesters, the display of Viet Cong flags, the nudity and pot, and the performing for television crews, antagonized many watchers. As at Oakland, the magnitude of the force called out to curtail the event showed that a few protesters could provoke the government into a near-absurd reaction. After these events, the tactic of confrontation was confirmed, and the battle lines were solidly drawn. It was antiwar vs. pro-war. There was no middle ground.

The antiwar forces coalesced swiftly. SDS and the Resistance (to the draft) stopped their ideological squabbling and agreed on targets. SNCC was joined by SCLC and said that halting the war was a priority for blacks. In November of 1967 the "dump Johnson" forces led by Allard Lowenstein convinced Eugene McCarthy to run for the Democratic presidential nomination. Some news media became openly critical of the war's progress.

More than 30,000 young men a month were managing to get 1-Y—medical—deferments. Applications for conscientious objector status trebled. Prosecutions for draft evasion or refusal rose to 1,500 out of the 250,000 cases a year reported to Washington by local draft boards. By the thousands, young men were fleeing to Canada and Sweden. The January 1968 indictment of Spock, Coffin, and a handful of other antidraft leaders showed to what extreme the government would go in trying to silence the antiwar sentiment.

In Vietnam, Ho Chi Minh's current tactics aimed at realizing the philosophy of the ancient Chinese warrior Sun Tzu:

The supreme excellence is not to win a hundred victories in a hundred battles. The supreme excellence is to defeat the armies of your enemies without ever having to fight them. . . . Break the will of the enemy to fight, and you accomplish the true objective of war. Cover with ridicule the enemy's tradition. Exploit and aggravate the inherent frictions within the enemy country. Agitate the young against the old. Prevail if possible without armed conflict.

Acting at least in part to exacerbate American antiwar sentiment, North Vietnam on January 31, 1968, launched the "Tet" offensive. Viet Cong and North Vietnamese forces simultaneously hit a hundred cities in the South; they gained ground initially but were repulsed afterward. The shock of the surprise attacks was manifest in the reports American television and newspaper crews sent home. In the February 7 *New York Times* James Reston asked, "What is the end that justifies this slaughter? How will we save Vietnam if we destroy it in battle?" And after a quick tour of Vietnam, Walter Cronkite of CBS summed up a February 27 documentary saying we were "mired in stalemate" and that the only rational step would be to negotiate, "not as victors, but as an honorable people who lived up to their pledge to defend democracy and did the best they could." *Time, Newsweek,* and *The Wall Street Journal* echoed these sentiments.

Now the antiwar movement stood at flood tide; it had changed the thinking of the majority. The young became emboldened. On campuses, protests escalated; many were directed against companies such as Dow Chemical, manufacturer of napalm. Phalanxes of college students stumped in the snows of New Hampshire for Eugene McCarthy, hoping to force Johnson from the race—an action they equated with ending the war.

On March 12, McCarthy came within a few hundred votes of winning the New Hampshire primary; on March 16, a potentially more formidable challenger with an antiwar platform—Senator Robert F. Kennedy—announced for the nomination. That same day European governments which disapproved of American actions in Vietnam, together with speculators who no longer believed in the dollar, caused huge drains on gold reserves and the closing of the London gold market. Westmoreland requested 206,000 more troops in addition to the current half million in Vietnam. On March 25, Johnson met with the "wise men," some of whom had advised presidents as far back as Truman. The previous fall they had counseled continuation of the war; now they told the president to send no more Americans to Vietnam. In a Gallup poll, only 36 percent of those queried supported the president's recent actions and only 23 percent approved of his handling of the war. Ever sensitive to public opinion, ill, and not willing to divide the country further, Johnson made his decision. On March 31 he announced that there would be only a token increase in U.S. forces, that South Vietnam would henceforth take over the burden of the fight, that bombing of the North would stop, that we would seek negotiations, and that he himself would not run for a second full term as president of the United States.

With Johnson's abdication, and with the "Vietnamization" of the war, it seemed that the major targets of the youth movement had been toppled. But the head of state had not been deposed, he had simply agreed to fade away; and the war had not been ended, it had been slightly de-escalated and transferred to the client state. If the youth movement sought a revolutionary change in the country, there was yet plenty to do. Still awaiting action: a more responsive political system, deep economic changes, equality among the races, heightened empathy in human relationships. But rather than storm the halls of Congress, the students stormed only the halls of the campuses.

Just a few days after Johnson's "April Fool" speech, Martin Luther King, Jr., was assassinated. There was intense reaction in black communities, a reaction suppressed by the largest aggregation of military and paramilitary forces inside the borders of the United States since the Civil War. At a Columbia University memorial service for King, Mark Rudd, leader of the campus SDS chapter, denounced the university's eulogy as hypocritical, for the officials sanctifying King were at the same time planning to exclude Harlemites from a new gymnasium under construction, and were kicking black tenants out of university-owned tenements.

A few days later, on a beautiful spring morning, there was a demonstration. The administration had told students recently that holding protest assemblies inside campus buildings was no longer allowed. A thousand people protested this ruling by trying to go inside Lowe Library. They also were protesting the university's membership in and sponsorship of the Institute for Defense Analysis, a think tank in which a dozen universities participated, and which made studies for various arms of the military. The crowd did not get into the library, which the administration had locked, and someone suggested they all go instead to the site of the proposed gym. Later, Rudd admitted that neither the gym nor the IDA was important; rather, he had needed them as targets on which to focus the students' antiestablishment anger. The gym site was a bulldozed lot at Harlem's edge. Once there, the marchers started tearing down a surrounding fence. Columbia called the New York City police to disperse the demonstrators, who, in reaction, went back to the campus and occupied some buildings. Thus began the Columbia strike.

Inside one building, a new occupant said,

> It was a community, and a very diverse one. We acted like so many "soviets"—lengthy discussions on what to do—meetings by candle-light—lots of singing—radios playing "Rolling Stones" sides. Two peo-ple got married. There was a lot of tribal stuff, and constant tension because of the fear of what would happen when the police came in. People who got involved came to an understanding of who they were; they had a feeling of *engagé*.

By the time several days later when the university invited the police to retake the campus—with nationally televised smashed heads, arrests, and high jinks—Columbia had become a model for campus revolts. "Two, Three, Many Columbias," Tom Hayden wrote. Over a hundred colleges had riots that spring, and though many of those were only tangentially concerned with Vietnam, it was clear that students were now to have a larger voice in their own destinies—at least for as long as they remained in universities. Columbia, too, was a victory for the youth movement— but, unlike the earlier victories, it was not a step on the way to further progress; rather, it was the movement's modest high point. From Columbia on, things went downhill.

Very few in the country other than high school admirers thought the students' takeovers and destruction of property were justified. Yes, the majority was now cognizant that the war had been a bad move for the United States and wanted it ended, but it found repugnant the other tenets of the hippie ethos—the anti-Establishment pose, the scruffy style, the trashing of beloved symbols, the rejection of the work ethic. Other college students, most of the young who were not then attending college, and the greater fraction of older Americans looked on the protesters with disdain and often with outrage. No substantial portion of the adult population wore its hair long or pored over Mao's aphorisms. The largest-grossing movie of the era was not *The Graduate* but John Wayne's *The Green Berets*.

At this moment, midpoint in the decade, David Mark Mantell studied two "extremes" of youth: fifty "war resisters," some of whom were under indictment for returning draft cards (not for draft evasion), and fifty "war volunteers," Green Berets, most awaiting combat duty in Vietnam, who had volunteered rather than been drafted for the war.

The families of the Green Berets were "externally intact, cohesive, and socially accepted," but were also "strongly conformistic, hard, autocratic, intolerant, and non-intellectual" as well as "emotionally isolated, rigid, tense, violent, and cold." Few of the soldiers reported having been loved at home; their fathers valued "emotional toughness" and taught the boys that "relaxation and self-indulgence were luxuries that had to be earned." Eleven of the fifty Green Berets' fathers were chronic alcoholics. By contrast the families of the war resisters exhibited "qualities of friendliness, non-violence, calmness, tolerance, and intellectuality," and the sons reported close ties to them, even though many of the families had been rent by divorce. Unlike the Green Berets, the war resisters did not fear their parents, and only a handful had ever been physically punished. Only two of the fifty war resisters' fathers drank heavily. In contrast to thirteen veteran fathers of the Green Berets, more than half the resister fathers had been on active duty in World War II, but none of the latter told adventurous war stories at home, and all agreed they had fought a necessary fight and expressed horror about the senselessness of war and of what they had seen in it.

The Green Berets had volunteered for the army and again for the Special Forces. Many of them were college dropouts, or had felt they were making no headway in careers, or had felt too pressured by girlfriends to get married; "confronted with dwindling prestige and the pressure to make something of themselves," they had "run away from their previous lives." Sexually they needed to "prove their potency over and over again with women," and used "the external paraphernalia of the Green Berets to provide them with a feeling of importance." The war resisters' reasons for their choices were highly idealistic; most were college students who had refused student deferments. To them sex was important but not of overwhelming moment; they cared little what they looked like and they abhorred uniforms.

The resisters valued autonomy while the volunteers valued deference to the leadership and judgment of others. The resisters were introspective, empathetic, and nurtured others; the volunteers were or wished to be well organized, able to endure hardships, to be lone individuals yet team players, to be aggressive and dominant.

In the study one anomaly cropped up: a behavior pattern that characterized 16 percent of the Berets and also 57 percent of the resisters and a like percentage of the (undrafted college student) control group. These men were "disoriented, perplexed, hyperactive, and idealistic." Such characteristics described an

> inner-directed person who may be seen as quite socially perceptive and sensitive to interpersonal interactions. His interest patterns are quite different from those of the average male. . . . [They] reflect such characteristics as self-awareness, concern with social issues and an ability to communicate ideas clearly and effectively. . . . The same interest pattern may reflect a rejection of masculinity accompanied by a relatively passive, effeminate, non-competitive personality.

Mantell had expected such a pattern among the educated and the cultivated, but not among the Green Berets. Looking more closely at those Berets who fit the description, he found them to be the four readers of serious literature, the one writer, the two who had almost gone into the ministry. They, along with the resisters and control group members who fitted the pattern, were the best of the lot. Mantell didn't know what to make of these young men, tormented and perceptive, idealistic yet changeable, with values so at odds with those embraced by the majority.

At this same time psychiatrist and historian Robert Jay Lifton struggled to describe a new "Protean man," who had much in common with the "disoriented, perplexed, hyperactive, and idealistic" young men of Mantell's study. Lifton wrote that breakdowns and blurring of boundaries—between life and death, man and woman, self and not-self, inner man and outer man—had been occurring at a tremendous rate since Hiroshima. More and more people were experiencing psychological processes which involved "changing self-definitions, or at least blurring of perception of where self begins and ends." There were breaks in the feeling of connectedness with symbols of family, religion, and even of the life cycle; the "flooding of imagery" produced by mass media permitted "each individual everywhere to be touched by everything." The result was Protean man, a name derived from Proteus, the mythological hero who was able to change his shape at will but who would not commit himself to a single form unless seized and chained. The Protean style, or process, was characterized by

> an interminable series of experiments and explorations, some shallow, some profound, each of which can readily be abandoned in favor of still newer psychological quests. . . . Protean style is by no means pathological

as such, and in fact may be one of the functional patterns necessary to life in our times. I would emphasize that it extends to all areas of human experience—to political as well as sexual behavior, to the holding and promulgating of ideas, and to the general organization of lives.

At the time the Protean style fitted the leading edge of youth. It would not continue to be limited to them, though it did bespeak a certain perennial youthfulness in those who embraced it.

This was perhaps because in Protean man the classic superego had disappeared, and with it the internalized criteria of right and wrong which had been transmitted to children by their parents. Protean man required a "symbolic form of fatherlessness...in order to carry out his explorations." He had a "strong ideological hunger" and was "starved for ideas and feelings that can give coherence to his world." Thus he willingly took up new political and religious convictions; such beliefs were not, however, able to "command his allegiance for more than a brief experimental interlude." Therefore he lived in a profound state of absurdity which found expression in mockery.

He mocked death, which was so omnipresent in his world. He mocked communication: the Free Speech Movement became the Filthy Speech Movement; the "Up Against the Wall Motherfucker" slogan at Columbia revivied "the flagging attention of protesters becoming gradually bored with the repetition of their 'straight' slogans and goals." He mocked affluence as "counterfeit nurturance" which was a threat to autonomy, and affluence as technology which threatened him with complete annihilation. Protean man—child of the bomb, of the boob tube, of prosperity.

The hunger made Lifton wonder. Where was Protean man to find a "meaningful inner formulation of self and life in which his actions, even his impulses, have some kind of 'fit' with the outside" world? Protean man must find such a linkage because he suffered from

> a vague but persistent kind of self-condemnation...a sense of having no outlet for his loyalties and no symbolic structure for his achievements....Rather than a clear feeling of evil or sinfulness, it takes the form of a nagging sense of unworthiness all the more troublesome for its lack of clear origin.

His pattern of seeking targets, sometimes hitting them but always moving on, was actually a psychic struggle with the idea of change itself, an innovation in the thirst for immortality, a way to die and to be born again repeatedly. Protean man might long for a mythical past of "perfect harmony and pre-scientific wholeness," but such nostalgia, Lifton warned, could be "explosive and dangerous" because it sets the time for the "restoration of politically rightist antagonists" and "energizes the transformationist totalism of the Left which courts violence."

Lifton saw a time of troubles for his new creature, just as Suzanne Langer had described an earlier period of "shifting and uncertain social circumstances" as problematical for those who lived in it. During such times, Langer wrote,

> ordinary cultural symbolism and language become incapable of adequately capturing the meaning of events and of guiding individual and collective responses. It resonates with the more familiar experiences but is not designed to help people cope with new problems and actually limits their vision of potential solutions. Therefore it is necessary to abandon the more cognitive, culturally available interpretations of events, immerse oneself personally in intense experiences, where new symbolic meanings can be developed intuitively, and then make use of fantasy, metaphor, and analogy to express the new "understandings" one has developed.

The point which Langer—and Lifton—described was reached by the leading edge of the youth movement in the spring of 1968. Fundamental, perhaps insoluble questions were coming to the fore. Should you reform the world, or reform yourself? In Prague, students were having some success in changing an ugly Communist regime. In Paris, students were assaulting the barricades of an authoritarian though democratic government. One Paris slogan of the moment was: *Une révolution que démande que l'on se sacrifice pour elle est une révolution à la papa.* "A revolution that demands you sacrifice yourself for it is one of Daddy's revolutions—" or, as Michael Ferber and Staughton Lynd interpret the statement, it is a revolution that "mirrors the society it aims to replace." In the United States, people were torn between the wish to change society and to change themselves, and the issue, wrote Ferber and Lynd (themselves veterans of protests and arrests), was this:

> Are we to forego all the playful, artistic, sexual and spiritual aspects of life—the kinds of things that will flourish in the liberated society we want—during the struggle to bring about that society? If so, then we

risk becoming unfit to bring it about or live in it if we do. Or are not the forces of creativity and festivity vital parts of the struggle itself?

In the spring of 1968 in the United States, the adversaries were melting away, the causes were being co-opted and becoming mainstream. Bobby Kennedy and Martin Luther King, Jr., who had been close to the revolutionary edge of youth, had been gunned down. With them gone, some young warriors opted out. Yet signs of struggle abounded: the Prague spring turned into a nightmare of repression; the Poor People's March ended in squabbling and mud; the U.S. Army was trying to break Cesar Chavez's grape boycott; a conservative tide was sweeping the country. None of these causes brought out in protest substantial numbers of the young. The leading edge numbered (according to SDS rolls) in the tens of thousands, as large a fraction of the population as had ever in history begun a revolution. What would they now do?

Philosopher Lionel Rubinoff suggested that to look at society and to find it inadequate and corrupt was part of the normal growing process. So was a bit of revolt. But if that revolt pinned the failure entirely on society, and did not comprehend that the society's failings had their origin in man himself, Rubinoff suggested, that was a cop-out—and one that would allow youth to dissolve its anger in "creativity and festivity." Such youth would be equating virtue with happiness—and that was not a path that led to true societal reform. Here was the point of choice, and Rubinoff left no doubt about what the hard road entailed:

> It is my view that either happiness is not the end of man, or it cannot be equated with pleasure. The salvation of man lies not in complacency or well-being but in the assumption of responsibility—no easy matter. To suffer the burden of one's responsibility is neither a matter of self-realization nor a question of forcing one's existence to coincide with one's essence. The anguish of responsibility lies in the need to wrestle with it in the face of evil. The freedom and salvation of man are accompanied not by feelings of sensuous delight but by an experience of dread which brings him to the very threshold of eternity only after having first charted a course through hell.

In the summer of 1968 the hottest show on Broadway was a "tribal love rock musical" called *Hair*, in which a group of young people, some exceedingly fuzzy around the edges, sang, danced, and appeared in one scene nude. The songs apostrophized astrological signs, be-ins, and the difficulties of being black, young, or female. *Hair* had its own company astrologer and tarot-card reader. One cast member thought her work was not just acting but "spreading the word." Another referred to the performances as therapy. Producer Michael Butler talked with the "tribe" about the necessity of going against the grain of the Establishment; it was hard, though, to maintain an anti-Establishmentarian pose when performing for the staid, mainstream audience.

Perhaps the same was true of performing for political audiences and explains why no demonstrations were planned against the Republican party convention held in early August in Miami Beach. Radical leaders wrote that demonstrations there would have made more strident and reactionary the conservative tide bearing the candidacy of Richard Nixon. Far better to try to influence one's friends.

A number of rationales were advanced as to what protesters hoped to accomplish at the Democratic party's nominating convention in Chicago during the week of August 24–29, 1968. Here are some: 1) to foster the antiwar cause, in particular the candidacy of Eugene McCarthy; 2) to "bring out a repressive response from authorities," or to stage a "spectacle of repression" which would lower "middle-class cultural fears of violence"; 3) to express the hypocrisy behind the nominating process; and 4) "to freak out the Democrats so much that they would disrupt their own convention— and meanwhile demonstrate to the world the alternative: our own revolutionary youth culture."

During that tumultuous week, when thousands of demonstrators filled the streets, threw feces at the police, and baited the police in every imaginable way, police attacked them regularly and viciously, principally at night, even when they were not threatening the peace and quiet of the city or the sanctity of the convention. "Even elderly bystanders were caught in the police onslaught," J. Anthony Lukas reported to *The New York Times*:

> For no reason that could be immediately determined, the blue-helmeted policemen charged the barriers, crushing the spectators against the windows of the Haymarket Inn, a restaurant in the [Hilton] hotel. Finally the window gave way, sending screaming middle-aged women and children backward through the broken shards of glass. The police then ran into the restaurant and beat some of the victims who had fallen through the windows and arrested them.

Jack Newfield reported to *The Village Voice*:

> At the southwest entrance to the Hilton, a skinny, long-haired kid of about seventeen skidded down on the sidewalk, and four overweight cops leaped on him, chopping strokes to his head. His hair flew from the force of the blows. A dozen small rivulets of blood began to cascade down the kid's temple and onto the sidewalk.... A doctor in a white uniform and Red Cross arm band began to run toward the kid, but two other cops caught him from behind and knocked him down. One of them jammed his knee into the doctor's throat and began clubbing his rib cage.... Demonstrators, reporters, McCarthy workers, doctors, all began to stagger into the Hilton lobby, blood streaming from face and head wounds. The lobby smelled from tear gas, and stink bombs dropped by the Yippies. A few people began to direct the wounded to a makeshift hospital on the fifteenth floor, the McCarthy staff headquarters. [Former RFK aide] Fred Dutton was screaming at the police, and at the journalists to report all the "sadism and brutality."

The "spectacle of repression" was indeed evoked from the police, but what it accomplished was not the protesters' aim. Norman Mailer expressed this in a speech he put into the mouth of an imaginary "Prince of Greed" in Chicago:

> No, do not let them march another ten blocks and there disperse on some quiet street; no, let it happen before all the land, let everybody see that their dissent will soon be equal to their own blood; let them realize that the power is implacable, and will beat and crush and imprison and yet kill before it will ever relinquish the power. To let them see before their own eyes what it will cost to continue to mock us, defy us, and resist. There are more millions behind us than behind them, more millions who wish to weed out, poison, gas, and obliterate every flower whose power they do not comprehend than heroes for their side who will view our brute determination and still be ready to resist. There are more cowards alive than the brave.

Many protesters had hoped Chicago would prove the ultimate confrontation between the "politics of ecstasy" espoused by the Yippies and the "convention of death" which they said the Democrats were holding. But even when major candidates, reporters, and bystanders were tear-gassed along with the rebels, even when Hubert Humphrey advanced the history of banality by kissing his wife's image on the television set, even when Mayor Richard Daley was caught by the camera yelling obscenities at Senator Abraham Ribicoff—even then, Chicago did not accomplish much for the youth movement. Despite the protests, the convention did nominate Humphrey and did follow the party's rules for such a nomination. The "revolutionary youth culture" made some converts, but it did not turn on the world. The freaks put their bodies on the gears and levers of the machine and slowed it, but only until their offending presence had been wiped off. Then the machine churned again.

Nixon addressed his campaign to those who hadn't ever rallied in the streets against a government policy, whose lives were uncomplicated by mind-blowing drugs, who owned property and who had jobs which they fiercely wanted to keep, whose days of youthful excess were long over. Those people did not believe the official report that called Chicago a "police riot." For them the Chicago police had been acting in the interests of preserving law and order. After Chicago the political enthusiasm of the young took a nose dive, and strength that might have been transferred from the McCarthy campaign to the Humphrey campaign dissipated—and in the end, on election day, it was Richard Nixon who reaped the ultimate benefit from Chicago's chaos.

"Bring us together," said a placard that candidate Nixon saw; he made that the theme of his campaign. For the first few months after his inauguration it seemed as if tensions between old and young were easing. The occupation of university campuses went on, but the arguments were about rules of conduct rather than rules of war. *Newsweek* conducted a poll among "middle Americans" who were the majority of the work force and found them fed up with student protests. Sociologist Michael Novak commented that the working class felt "looked down upon because their manners are untaught, and then they witness the sons and daughters of the privileged violating with impunity every inhibition they themselves had been forced to nurture," and so they condemned sex, drugs, and rock-and-roll as libidinous, and the protests (and protesters) as anti-American.

That spring, knowing his constituency unerringly, President Nixon fired salvos across the bows of campus protesters: "Force can be contained. . . . It has not been a lack of civil power, but the reluctance of a free people to employ it that so often has stayed the hand of authorities faced with confrontation." H. E. W. Secretary Robert Finch wrote to remind college and university presidents that recently passed congressional statutes forbade student loans to those convicted of crimes in campus disorders: it was an unmistakable signal to crack down. Attorney General John Mitchell's Department of Justice indicted eight well-known radicals for crossing a state line in order to incite the Chicago riots—under another statute recently passed by Congress.

The Chicago prosecution linked the Nixon administration with discredited policies of the Johnson administration. Behind the scenes another such linkage was also taking place. On his own authority President Nixon secretly ordered the Air Force to bomb enemy bases in Cambodia. This bombing both widened the war and ended the useful phase of the Paris peace negotiations. In May, when the story of the bombing leaked out, Nixon, National Security Advisor Henry Kissinger, and H. R. Haldeman wiretapped colleagues and newsmen to find the leakers. As Jonathan Schell comments:

> In the United States in which the public lived, the war was almost over, and an open, trustworthy, even "mellow" White House was turning the nation toward peaceful pursuits. In the United States in which President Nixon lived, however, the war was growing, tension was building, and the level of suspicion had become so intense that he felt driven to spy on his own subordinates.

In June the SDS met in the Chicago Coliseum for its ninth (and, as it turned out, its last) convention. Fifteen hundred delegates represented a hundred thousand members. SDS split over the future direction of the organization. The Nixon administration already had shown its commitment to continuing the war, was publicly backing away from civil rights, was working on wiretaps and was about to present to Congress a "no-knock" crime bill which would greatly infringe on the Bill of Rights. Yet the convention foundered over male chauvinism, whether or not to let in the press, and a host of lesser issues. Then it split completely apart over one fundamental issue. The Maoists wanted to continue to escalate guerrilla warfare against the state. Most of the other delegates wished to aid black liberationists in their struggle for separation from white society. The Maoists became the violence-prone Weathermen and went underground. The rest fragmented.

Meanwhile, one weekend in August, the social stream of the youth movement welled up 450,000 strong on Max Yasgur's farm in Bethel, New York, at the rock festival known thereafter as Woodstock. Food, tickets, overnight sleeping space, even sexual partners seemed to be free for the asking. The celebrants heard Jimi Hendrix, Joe Cocker, Country Joe MacDonald, Arlo Guthrie, Pete Townshend, and Jerry Garcia, all of whom agreed that the essence of the event was the enormous crowd itself. The gathering was peaceful, the supervision exemplary, and for most the experience was pleasurable. As Landon Y. Jones comments, Woodstock was not so much the obverse of the majority society as a gentle mirror of it:

> In a strange kind of reversal, the kids at Woodstock took pride in some of the very qualities they found oppressive in adult organizations.... They had created the third-biggest city in New York State, overnight. And it had fewer crimes and good medical care. Helicopters were dropping in and evacuating the wounded, oddly like Vietnam. Boasting about their free kitchens and clean-up details, the volunteers of Woodstock sounded for all the world like the Chamber of Commerce of Rochester, the real third-biggest city in New York.

Many media observers suggested in picture spreads and instant television specials that this was the birth of the children's crusade. Abbie Hoffman saw in the throng "thousands of soldiers resurrected from the Macedonian army hammering out their weapons." Rather, the crowd was full of passive consumers of packaged culture. Neither birth-yelp nor death-cry of the youth movement, Woodstock was only the symbolic midpoint of a generation's movement from energy to torpor.

In the summer of 1969 one of the pillars of modern sociology, S. N. Eisenstadt, looked at worldwide youth culture and wrote that one basic difference between old and new youth protest was that the present youth had no older models—either good or bad—from whom to take direction. As a result, they identified only with the charisma of individuals and had lost faith in traditional institutions. They loved the Kennedys, rock musicians, and gurus, but not democracy, musical harmony, or the church. Eisenstadt placed the youths' estrangement from ordinary institutions quite deep. All of us were subject to the Kafkaesque feeling of being lost in the bureaucratic mazes in anonymous organizations—but only youth felt that participation in *any* facet of modern society was meaningless. Yet they yearned for contact, to have older models, to have organizations and institutions to which they could adhere. Soon the protests themselves might become "institutionalized" in the growth of new areas of permissiveness, areas in which some people may participate fully, others in a more transitory fashion, areas which will institutionalize the possibility of extension of individuality beyond the more bureaucratized, meritocratic, occupational and administrative structures.

Hedonism itself would become a game/institution, with rules, winners and losers, and hierarchies.

As Marshall McLuhan was pointing out, people sought roles, not goals; institutions were settings, rather than paths to achievement. One became an acolyte in a new version of an ancient Eastern religion, but as one could not afford to spend twenty years in a monastery to achieve understanding, one took a magic mushroom or got a special word from a TM franchise which guaranteed that twenty minutes of meditation a day would suffice to achieve satisfaction. People dabbled in extending their sensitivity at such temples of the self as the Esalen Institute at Big Sur, where they could choose between the heady mysticism of the seer-of-the-week, or the gestalt "mind-blowing" techniques of Fritz Perls, or the physical trammeling of Ida Rolf, or the pan-sexuality of the hot-tubs, or a smorgasbord of all of the above.

Vices themselves became institutionalized and legitimatized. Sex was a quest or calisthenics. Marriage was a trial period, divorce only a rite of passage. Drugs were a ticket to join the in-group, a path not to relaxation but to awareness. Rock-and-roll was more than another style of music; it was an aesthetic before which all previous philosophies must yield.

Max Weber had shown that the great change was always from charisma to routine. Institutionalization was a way station. When free spirits gravitated to communes, when women banded together in a liberation movement, when nature lovers became ecologists—there you could see routinization in action, see "new areas of permissiveness" springing up, soon to be encrusted with tradition and rules. In the setting of a rock festival or an ecology movement, people sought not freedom (though that might have been a seeker's original goal) but order: each setting provided a way of viewing the universe that allowed both certitude and peace.

Critiques which had begun to elucidate valid points against society started to disintegrate into ideologies. SDS, which had begun out of nothing but a shared conviction that power must be given to ordinary people to more fully participate in social and economic America, split into Maoists and black-power groupies. Drug taking, which had started as a quest for expansion of the mind, had become a ritual for initiation into the youth society. The individuality of a Ken Kesey, or the spirit of the original band of Free Speech Movement people, had been transmuted into the routine of docile consumption of prepackaged freak culture.

The Vietnam War continued, despite lessened American ground-force involvement, and opposition to the war became more mainstream. In September, Nixon announced the withdrawal of 35,000 American combat troops. He did so in hopes of forestalling further antiwar protests, but on October 15, 1969, in Boston, in New York, and in Washington, D.C., tens of thousands marched to encourage a more rapid end to the war. Some 57 percent of those queried in a poll supported the marchers' aim of withdrawing all American troops from Vietnam by a specific date—an idea which Nixon opposed steadfastly.

Four days after the October moratorium, Vice-President Spiro Agnew attacked the antiwar leaders as "an effete corps of impudent snobs . . . hard-core dissidents and professional anarchists." Nixon authorized CIA group "Operation CHAOS" to infiltrate the peace movement. On October 30, Agnew suggested it was time for a "positive polarization" of the American people, the "functioning, contributing portion" against the "minority" who, the president said a few days later, were trying to impose their point of view "by mounting demonstrations in the street." In a speech, Nixon said he had a scheduled withdrawal timetable but to announce it would only aid the enemy and so it had to be kept secret, and he asked that the "silent majority" support him to end the war with a victory through withdrawal. "North Vietnam cannot defeat or humiliate the United States," Nixon said, "only Americans can do that." The implication was that the protesters were close to being guilty of treason.

When television commentators' analysis of Nixon's speech called attention to its variance from earlier promises, Agnew's attacks shifted directly to the networks. So taken aback were the networks by Agnew's assault that on November 15, when a half-million people converged on Washington to protest the war's continuation, the networks gave no live coverage to the largest demonstration in the nation's history. Nixon soon announced the withdrawal of 50,000 more troops.

Begun by the administration, the going-sour attitude on youth's protests carried over into media reaction to the rock festival held in December at the Altamont Raceway in California. There a young black man was killed by Hell's Angels, while the Rolling Stones played and sang "Sympathy for the Devil." Some characterized Altamont as a disaster and went so far as to call it the end of the youth movement, overlooking the fact that three people died at Woodstock (albeit in accidents). The misfortunes at Altamont were as much due to shoddy planning and greed on the part of the festival's planners as they were to the "bad vibes" emanating from the Stones.

Altamont, the revelation of the young American soldiers' part in the massacre at My Lai, and the discovery of Charlie Manson's psychotic mixture of murder and communal living all occurred in the winter of 1969–1970. They were enough to chill any youth movement. As 1970 began some campuses rocked with disorder, and over 500 bombs were thrown at targets ranging from banks to defense-related buildings. Ideological revolt was one thing; destruction of property and reckless endangerment of the populace was another. When a Manhattan townhouse which had served as a Weathermen bomb-factory blew up, most saw this as retributive justice for the ultraradicals, not as a tragedy in which a few bright and misguided people lost their young lives.

Public condemnation of such events fed the growing feeling at the White House that "positive polarization" was the route to political victory. At White House behest, the Federal Communications Commission and the IRS were asked to look at the networks, which consistently covered radical groups. Justice Department subpoenas were served on *Time, Life, Newsweek,* and *The New York Times,* in connection with court cases in several states, all of which involved reports about young revolutionaries.

The spring of 1970 was the time of the growing ecological consciousness, a movement swelled by the young. Some radicals charged that it was a deliberate attempt by the administration to divert attention from the Vietnam War. Few young people agreed. In the highly personal ecology movement, the young could express their commitment to ideals closer at hand than peace in Vietnam. They could use fewer machines, eat fewer processed foods, and pursue a simpler style of consumption to cleanse the world. On April 20, Nixon announced the withdrawal of 150,000 American troops from Vietnam over the course of the coming year. Perhaps this was one of the reasons that Earth Day, April 22, 1970, went so well, for it seemed as if the war was really winding down, and many thousands of young people could go with easy consciences to antipollution rallies in New York, Chicago, and Philadelphia.

However, at the same time that he announced the troop withdrawals, Nixon simultaneously (and secretly) ordered an American-led thrust into Cambodia. As he later wrote in his *Memoirs,* Nixon felt the need to clean out the Cambodian sanctuaries of the Viet Cong, to help the new right-wing Cambodian ruler Lon Nol, and at the same time "to drop a bombshell on the gathering spring storm of anti-war protest." When the incursion was in process, Nixon spoke to the nation and said he had sent American forces into Cambodia not to expand the war but rather to speed its end by making peace possible through a military victory. The incursion decision was taken without consultation with Congress, and over the objections of the most concerned cabinet secretaries and members of the National Security Council. Lon Nol, who found out about the incursion only by listening to the president's speech, declared publicly that the incursion violated the territorial integrity of Cambodia.

Viewing the sending of troops into Cambodia as a widening of the war, more than one-third of all American college and university campuses erupted in protest. Nixon and Agnew decried the protesters. Following their lead, Governor James Rhodes of Ohio said, in reaction to the burning of ROTC buildings at the Kent State campus, that he would "eradicate" demonstrators, who were "worse than the Brown Shirts and the Communist element and also the nightriders and the vigilantes. They're the worst type of people we have in America." Next day, May 4, ill-trained National Guardsmen, provoked by demonstrators throwing rocks at them, fired into a crowd. They wounded fifteen and killed four protesters, two of whom were students.

The worst had happened: American paramilitary troops, operating at government behest, had killed young and essentially unarmed civilians. In emulation, four days later on Wall Street in New York City a group of construction workers—"hard-hats"—beat up a band of young protesters. By that time shock at the Kent State deaths had inflamed campuses all over the country. The near-moribund antiwar movement mustered instanter nearly a hundred thousand people to come to Washington for a protest rally on May 9.

On the night of May 8, President Nixon, deeply moved (he wrote) by the Kent State shootings, made fifty phone calls: eight to Henry Kissinger, who would later believe that the president was then at the edge of a nervous breakdown, and others to such men as Billy Graham and Norman Vincent Peale. He sent clandestine messages of solidarity to the construction workers. He listened to Rachmaninoff's Second Piano Concerto. Finally, at 4:30 A.M. he took his valet, his personal physician, and a few other staff members and went to the Lincoln Memorial. On the steps of the memorial he spoke to clusters of young people. Later he wrote in an extensive memorandum to Ehrlichman that he did not touch directly on why the protesters had come, but steered the conversation to how he had felt as a young man at the time of Munich in 1938; then he touted the wonders of travel and how important it was for youth to see the world as he had—Mexico, Central America, Prague, Warsaw, "gray" Moscow. When a student said he was not interested in Prague but in the quality of life in America, the president shifted into talk of the environmental crisis as the challenge of the future:

> I said candidly and honestly that I didn't have the answer, but I knew that young people today were searching, as I was searching 40 years ago, for an answer to this problem [concerning the right way to act in the world]. I just wanted to be sure that all of them realized that ending the war, and cleaning up the streets and the air and the water, was not going to solve the spiritual hunger which all of us have and which, of course, has been the great mystery of life from the beginning of time. . . .

Egil "Bud" Krogh, a young aide to John Ehrlichman who accompanied the president, pronounced himself moved deeply by this dawn encounter, though Nixon told his valet, "I doubt if that got over."

In fact it had been a classic confrontation. A few months earlier, writer and disc jockey Jonathan Schwartz had envisioned a fictional dialogue between the boyish-looking actor Elliott Gould as the quintessential bright-but-failing student, and Nixon as the archetypal high-school teacher. Gould doesn't listen to the lesson and peers at a tree across the street from the classroom; teacher Nixon rebukes him, saying, "The answer isn't out the window." Yet, Schwartz wrote, Nixon was shouting clichés through "the vast Victorian chamber of his mind" at the precise moment in American history when the students were "just beginning to discover that the answer *is* out the window."

Pascal said that when men try to live without God they infallibly succumb to either megalomania or erotomania. In the opposition of Nixon and Gould, in megalomania and erotomania, we read the two extremes of the time.

It was just after Kent State that the paranoid state of mind which would eventually result in Watergate began to close down over the White House. At first it seemed reasonable for White House insiders to believe that the strident students were not in the majority: a Gallup poll showed that 65 percent of the adults queried approved of Nixon's handling of the presidency, that 50 percent approved of the decision to go into Cambodia, and that 58 percent blamed "demonstrating students" for the deaths at Kent State. The Nixon administration also took into account the stance of potential candidate Ronald Reagan, who said that a "blood-bath" might be needed to solve the student problem. To the White House, the protests over Cambodia demonstrated the need to control and coordinate intelligence about domestic dissidents. Former Army Intelligence officer Tom Charles Huston was asked to come up with a plan. He cited 40,000 bombings in the U.S. in 1970. (Senate investigators could later document 586 in the first half of 1970.) Nixon told intelligence agency chiefs that "hundreds, perhaps thousands of Americans—mostly under 30—are determined to destroy our society." The Huston plan gave these agencies the right to open mail, burglarize homes, spy on student groups, and wiretap anyone suspected of being a threat to "national security." Huston admitted that some of the suggestions were "clearly illegal," and although FBI Director J. Edgar Hoover managed to squelch the plan (because it interfered with his fiefdom), the thinking that went into the plan later became the rationale for the White House "plumbers" unit.

Among the reasons why the Huston plan was ludicrous was that the trend of youth was away from SDS radicalism and toward more personal quests. There were now three thousand rural communes in America and they encompassed a quarter-million young people.

Sociologist Hugh Gardner studied eighteen of the communes in the summer of 1970 and found that, among the communards, he "could count on one hand those who did not have a long list of experiences [with] visionary psychedelia and political defiance." Kent State and other repressive events sent the young to the wilderness to try "voluntary primitivism." When "Nixonian America openly declared war on its young," Gardner wrote, "the search for alternatives took on a desperate as well as an alienated tone." *Life* did laudatory commune articles. Communal living was celebrated in rock—"We are stardust, we are golden, and we've got to get ourselves back to the Garden" (Joni Mitchell, "Woodstock"). Sales of the *Whole Earth Catalog* jumped from a thousand in 1968 to a quarter million in 1970. The "children of prosperity" left colleges and jobs to seek a simpler life. In the best of communes what began as flight from the parental culture became introspective and revelatory journeys into the communards' selves; in the worst, the problems of the "real world" overwhelmed the experimenters. But for a time the communes were the epitome of the revolution of self that the youth movement had become in the early 1970s.

The culture of competitive individualism was dying, Christopher Lasch later wrote, and the defeat in Vietnam, the economic stagnation, the sense of impending exhaustion of natural resources produced a mood of pessimism. What was emerging was the culture of the narcissist, a person who "doubts even the reality of his own existence," and though "superficially relaxed and tolerant" is "fiercely competitive in his demand for approval and acclaim."

> He distrusts competition because he associates it unconsciously with an unbridled urge to destroy.... He extols cooperation and teamwork while harboring deeply anti-social impulses. He praises respect for rules and regulations in the secret belief that they do not apply to himself. Acquisitive in the sense that his cravings have no limits, he does not accumulate goods and provisions against the future . . . but demands immediate gratification and lives in a state of restless, perpetually unsatisfied desire.... Having no hope of improving their lives in any of the ways that matter, people have convinced themselves that what matters is psychic self-improvement: getting in touch with their feelings, eating health food, taking lessons in ballet or belly-dancing, immersing themselves in the wisdom of the East, jogging, learning how to "relate," overcoming the "fear of pleasure."

Typical of the "journeys into self" taken by the young (and not-so-young) in the early seventies was that of Jerry Rubin:

> I directly experienced est, gestalt therapy, bioenergetics, rolfing, massage, jogging, health foods, tai chi, Esalen, hypnotism, modern dance, meditation, Silva Mind Control, Arica, acupuncture, sex therapy, Reichian therapy, and More House—a smorgasbord course in New Consciousness.

For Lasch, such narcissistic adventures revealed more than self-absorption or a joyride through life; they represented a psychic formation in which "love rejected turns back to the self as hatred" and which could be considered a character disorder. Narcissists attached themselves to gurus, had value systems which were "generally corruptible," had a "fear of emotional dependence" and a "manipulative exploitative approach to personal relations" which made those relations "bland, superficial, and deeply unsatisfying." Their cult of personal relations concealed a disenchantment with personal relations; their cult of sensuality concealed a similar repudiation of sensuality in all but its primitive forms. Espousing personal growth, they were nevertheless "without faith" and radiated a "profound despair and resignation." Their adherence to the narcissist style as they got older was a refusal to mature. Such a juvenile outlook presaged a "terrible suffering" in the second half of life:

> The usual defenses against the ravages of age—identification with ethical or artistic values beyond one's immediate interests, intellectual curiosity, the consoling emotional warmth derived from happy relationships in the past—can do nothing for the narcissist.

Despite their bleak futures, Lasch suggested, narcissists rose to positions of prominence in business corporations, political organizations, and government bureaucracies, "which put a premium on the manipulation of interpersonal relations" and which "discourage the formation of deep personal attachments" while they provide the narcissist "with the approval he needs in order to validate his self-esteem."

In the more difficult economic times of the early 1970s, in the era after political activism ceased to seem efficacious, and with an evolving narcissist style, many of the young who had dropped out began to drop back in. Sociologist Lauren Langman, who had earlier written with much enthusiasm of Dionysian man, again looked at youth and saw a decline of the work ethic, but one which no longer heralded the dawn of a new society. Rather,

> the decline of the work ethic should foster the recruitment into occupational roles in which the rewards are less likely to be material and more likely to allow individual creativity, self-realization, or genuine helping of others. Such fields as education, medical services, and leisure will be able to expand because they will be consonant with countercultural values rather than with the work ethic. . . . It may therefore be that the counterculture is acting as any other youth culture in facilitating the transition to ultimate occupational roles.

Celeste MacLeod saw the return of the hippies to society in a different light: she thought they had never really been away. Having come from affluent homes and college backgrounds,

> they did not risk their futures when they deserted the Establishment because they walked away already equipped with the skills and know-how that would allow them to re-enter at a later date. . . . If they changed their minds at any time, they could return to their parents' homes, accept a job, go back to college.

Such people MacLeod called "optionaires," for they always had the option of being able to reenter society at their own level. They were not the alienated—a term better reserved for the poor and the minorities who had no options—but for a time they had been the disaffected. Their moratorium depended on society's "selective permissiveness." In the downturn of 1970–1971, when the checks from home stopped coming and the winter proved to be the worst in a quarter century, many of the communes folded. However, the countercultural values that stressed the irrelevance of money and social position, and the importance of communal brotherhood and of noncompetition, MacLeod wrote, still were

> music to the ears of young people cemented in low-paying jobs in communities where they and their families were considered nobodies. Likewise the philosophy of the hippies appealed to young people who had serious problems at home and were looking for a way to escape the family nest.

These "new migrants" wore denim and headbands, took drugs and bought rock-and-roll records, but they embraced the hedonistic part of the hippie ideology without the protection of the social and educational safety-net which in the 1970s enabled the hippies to drop in, to take up Establishment jobs, and to smoke pot only on the weekends. The new migrants were the "street people," and they numbered in the hundreds of thousands. It was they who had the highest proportion of troubles with drugs, with venereal disease, and—most of all—with employment. When times turned bad, the optionaires survived; the children of the lower classes went under and became part of that permanent core of jobless and underemployed who are still with us today.

In "Vietnamization," American troop levels dropped from a 1969 high of 544,000 to 281,000 in April of 1971. For the third spring in a row, in 1971 a new offensive took the war outside the borders of South Vietnam. Assisted by American air power, the ARVN army moved into Laos to attack enemy supply dumps and infiltration routes. American bombers also hit North Vietnam with more ferocity than they had since the bombing pause of November 1968.

The attack into Laos became the last precipitating action in a spring during which the war was brought home to the United States even as it was ending for American grunts in Vietnam. Earlier in the spring the trial of Lieutenant William Calley held the headlines. After the Laos incursion, the Vietnam Veterans Against the War made their own "limited incursion" to the halls of Congress, told of their war crimes, and threw away their bravery medals. The "Mayday tribe" disrupted Washington's routine, causing such problems that the White House directed that the protesters be taken to RFK Stadium and held there for days, unconstitutionally. Also in reaction to Laos, Daniel Ellsberg supplied to *The New York Times* and other newspapers the "Pentagon Papers," which detailed the practices and deceptions of the Truman, Eisenhower, Kennedy, and Johnson administrations in Vietnam. In response to the publication of these papers, and to the demonstrations, the White House sent burglars to break into Ellsberg's psychiatrist's office and committed other actions that later fed the Watergate scandal.

Throughout the summer of 1971 the Paris negotiations and the de-escalation of the American involvement in the war continued. By fall the American "body count" had dropped to 13 dead in two weeks, the lowest number since early 1965. The all-volunteer army was just around the corner. Draft calls were low. Nixon announced that America's offensive role in Vietnam had already ended. Coupled with administration use of some restrictive statutes, the withdrawals kept the fall demonstrations strangely mute. People were tired of hearing about the war. They spoke of the new wage and price controls. Between Christmas and New Year's, 350 bombers pounded North Vietnam daily in "protective reaction strikes" to curtail any activity that might imperil the "safety and security" of the remaining American forces.

Few objections were raised to this new bombing. Americans were no longer being killed in quantity in Vietnam, and, so long as negotiations and withdrawals continued, the public at large seemed unwilling to support more dissent on the war.

Senators George McGovern, Edmund Muskie, and Hubert Humphrey announced for the Democratic presidential nomination for 1972. McGovern's main platform issue was the war; he would end it immediately and unilaterally. His other positions—an income grant to poor families, a $30 billion cut in defense spending, support for environmental legislation—appealed to the young, who flocked to his campaign in droves and who, in the first months of 1972, helped him edge out Humphrey and Muskie. The young had hopes for a McGovern victory, since passage of the Twenty-sixth Amendment had lowered the voting age to 18 and had made a new pool of 25 million voters (including those ineligible to vote in 1968). It was clear that had such voters been available in 1968, Humphrey would have beaten Nixon. Now four million college and a million graduate student voters might give McGovern the edge.

Nixon welcomed youth's candidate McGovern, for the senator was an extremist as Goldwater had been, and youth's help in the primaries would not count for much in November. As Richard Scammon and Ben Wattenberg had pointed out,

> more than one of every three adults don't vote, and young people, poor people, and blacks are less likely to vote than the middle-aged, the wealthy, or whites.

By various "dirty tricks" the Nixonians aided McGovern's efforts to eliminate Humphrey and Muskie. During the campaign the president's stalwarts also took delight when long-haired protesters heckled the president; if there were no such protesters at a whistle stop, the stalwarts would hire some. Every obscenity hurled at Nixon (preferably televised) was worth a hundred votes for Nixon.

Hogging the center, announcing withdrawals and negotiation breakthroughs, Nixon forced McGovern further to the left and robbed him of his main issue, the war. In midcampaign a Gallup poll reported that those queried who were under 29 thought Nixon more sincere and believable than McGovern by 57 percent to 28 percent. Two weeks before the election Henry Kissinger announced that peace was at hand in Vietnam. McGovern called that a lie and said Watergate proved that the administration was corrupt on all issues—but Nixon won in a landslide. Only in the age 18–24 group did McGovern edge out Nixon; among voters 25–34 some 60 percent favored Nixon, and as the age of the voters increased, so did the percentage favoring the president. Though a high 64 percent of college students voted, those of the young who were not in school stayed away from the polls in such droves that the overall result of youth voting was to speed Nixon's reelection.

However, young voters did help Democratic and especially liberal candidates to win congressional seats, and they did help to decide many primaries. Voting scholar Louis M. Seagull counts increased participation in primaries in 1976 and 1980 as positive gain from the youth movement. Youth, Seagull wrote, also had accelerated political change in altered styles of political action (protest movements, single-issue pressure groups), and in the rise of noncentrist candidates (Wallace, RFK, McCarthy, Mc-Govern); unfortunately, youth also had contributed to the trend on the part of voters of staying away from the polls altogether, and to the erosion of the political center by both the Right and the Left.

So tied had the enthusiasm of the young been to the McGovern candidacy and the antiwar issue that when both disappeared, the youth movement seemed to fragment permanently and die. Antiwar protesters did not shout out in significant numbers when the worst carpet-bombing in history was ordered by Nixon at Christmastime of 1972—at least the youth of the United States did not shout. Shock waves of criticism did come at Washington from all over the rest of the world. They were ignored. Nixon's 1973 inaugural speech was a cruel echo of John Kennedy's: "Let each of us ask... what can I do for myself?" A counterinaugural attracted 30,000 protesters, but nobody seemed to be listening to them. And three days after inauguration, when Henry Kissinger initialed a peace treaty and Air Force bombers merely shifted their targets from North Vietnam to Cambodia, youth did not raise an effective voice in protest.

The new youth heroes of 1973—Senator Sam Ervin, Archibald Cox—were quite decidedly of the Establishment. Mao was busy shaking hands with Nixon. "Revolution for the Hell of It" appealed more now to street people and to teenagers who refused steadfastly to cut their hair and who led lunch-line protests in high schools. Sales of rolling papers for smoking marijuana were in the millions. A full 75 percent of college students reported engaging in premarital sex—in 1969 it had been only 50 percent. There were rock festivals; however, as an article about Watkins Glen (1973) asked, "Bigger Than Woodstock, But Was It Better?"

In the spring of 1974 there was Patty Hearst. Young, Berkeley-educated and enormously affluent, in her rebellion against her parents Patty had gone no further than private dinner parties and an affair with an older man. The Symbionese Liberation Army which abducted her, abused her, and involved her in a bank robbery was an ugly caricature of earlier rebel groups. The SLA was led by a drug-crazed black ex-convict with an inchoate program, and was filled out by cannon fodder of much the same ilk as had followed Charles Manson into the abyss. Dressed as "Tania," machine gun in hand, Patty was a victim in the guise of an aggressor, an appropriately inverted symbol for the end of the era in which youth had sought to change the world.

Had the youth movement done anything at all to people's attitudes about the country, about themselves, about life? Had the whole hippie trip been merely a superficial change in style which would soon be lost and was in any case irrelevant?

Professors M. Kent Jennings and Richard G. Niemi studied the political orientations of two generations of Americans in 1965 and again in 1973. In 1965 they interviewed more than a thousand 18-year-olds and a thousand of their parents; in 1973 they interviewed the same people again. Both the children and the parents, they found, had moved slightly to the political left. As only a third of the young had college degrees and 40 percent had not attended college at all, the change could not be ascribed to educational levels. Rather, the authors said, the finding showed that all had perceived national shortcomings in moral, ethical, and religious conduct, and saw the political system as failing. Both generations were growing cynical about government, the young much faster than their parents and at a rate which hinted that their faith would probably not return even when the political atmosphere became "less charged" after Watergate. The young had been brought more in line with their parents' views by marriage, families, jobs, property ownership, and belonging to organizations—and the parents' views now reflected those criticisms of society which the youth movement had so forcefully brought to bear on people's minds.

In Robert Wuthnow's study, mentioned earlier, he found that the young embodied and helped to crystallize certain long-term theological trends. These trends were away from beliefs in "theism" and nineteenth-century "individualism" to beliefs in "scientific explanations" of life and to "mysticism." Theism, a belief in God's hand in man's affairs, had been a restraint against social unrest and social experimentation. When a person began to emphasize the role of social forces rather than God's will, the blame for society's ills was imputed not to God, the individual, or fate, but to the structure; thus "justice, inequality, crime, alienation, become flaws attributable to the character of society itself." Mysticism went hand-in-glove with scientific understanding, for both stressed relaxed attitudes and tolerance to other-than-mainstream life-styles. Those who condoned social experiments were those who did not stress values of "conformity to authority and to strict moral standards."

Mike Brake, an English sociologist, studied youth rebellions the world over, and found them not much more than lavishly extended subcultures which offered their participants "a collective identity" that "magically" freed them from the "ascribed roles of home, school, and work." For years, youth might live from an "alternative script" in an "identity which separates them from the expectations and roles imposed on them," but

> Once they have made this separation, which makes a dramaturgical state-
> ment about their differences from those expectations . . . they often give
> up this identity of transformation. They reject it as "adolescent;" in a
> very real sense it is no longer them.

Was all that had happened to American youth a dramaturgical flight of fancy, followed by collapse back into the center? Brake suggests that was not all; for where a youth rebellion "has a moral edge on it, it threatens the hegemony of the state." And Wuthnow's studies show that our youth movement was the expression of deep changes in belief among many Americans—in other words, that youth were the leading edge not only of antiwar dissent, but of a deep and important moral disillusionment with the majority society.

The strength of the youth critique was in its perceptions of America's faults. The black critique had identified faults of the power structure. The youth critique identified faults of the moral underpinnings. The sons questioned the fathers' values; the questions youth asked had been asked before, but never so baldly nor by so many people at once. The questions raised the level of doubt—and in a democracy doubt is the benchmark by which the delicate balance between order and freedom is measured.

The most important question was about the Vietnam War, which youth saw as deplorable before their elders did. With a genius steeped in a television culture, the younger generation found ways to raise older folks' consciousness about the war. Testimony to youth's effectiveness was in the growth of backing for the drive to end the war, in Johnson's timing of his abdication and the change in the war's direction, in Nixon's sensitivity in scheduling troop withdrawals to defuse youth demonstrations.

The perception of the war as immoral was the youth movement's main contribution, but the war was also a moral trap for youth. The fight against the war absorbed energies and took focus disproportionate to its overall importance in the larger matter of changing America. The idealistic "unfinished business" of civil rights, saving the cities, the environmental crisis, equality for women, etc.—all of which, in the latter half of the decade, could have used a little help from their friends—remained unfinished. Opposition to the war led in a twisting path to provoking the spectacle of repression in Chicago, and to the election of conservatives. Disillusion with the political process sent many into rural communes at a time when cities were disintegrating and there was a need for urban homesteading. When the threat of youth's direct involvement in the Vietnam fighting ended, when the imminent terror of the draft receded, for many of the young the importance of the task of ending the war itself faded. And when the Watergate affair exploded and thereby—as in all crises—afforded immense opportunities for positive change, the young did not act on them.

There were other losses: student rebels obtained more relevance in their courses, more ease in their social strictures, and a say in their own governance, but these things contributed to the dilution of quality education. Similarly, they obtained hedonism but perhaps sacrificed intimacy.

Overall, there was a net gain: if the country as a whole was not greatly changed by the efforts of the young, many people had been made acutely aware of some of society's shortcomings. More people knew that if the temperature of the body politic rose high enough, the system could be made to alter course. The youth movement proved what has to be learned anew by every generation: that in a democracy all the people can be heard. More people understood that the standards of behavior which had been held for many years needed to be reevaluated, that morality must reflect the tenor of the times. More people realized that there might be a greater variety of styles in which one could spend a lifetime or a few years, and that conformity was not always precondition to happiness. The excesses of the Yippies were fine counterbalance to the narrow, fear-driven paths of the McCarthy years. After both, the pendulum could rest nearer the center. More people realized that women had been oppressed, that the earth's resources were finite. And last, more people became concerned with living in the present, rather than continuously preparing for a future that might never arrive or might not live up to their expectations.

But in this learning there was the schism: most who accepted such lessons were young; most who refused to acknowledge the legitimacy of such lessons were older. The young were committed to the "search" mode; many of the old still embraced the need to "preserve" what seemed so pervasively under attack.

On the savannah of East Africa, pain, purification, intensity, and isolation are the components of the rite of passage that transforms boy into man. Scholars guess that a purpose of the intensity and pain of the experience is to make the transformation occur quickly yet thoroughly—since to drag it out would cause untold difficulties to the tribe. In America during the decade of shocks, some privileged youth took their own sweet time for their rite of passage, and while they passed over into adulthood there was indeed trauma for everyone.

Eventually the youth in the movement passed into maturity, progressing from alienation to integration into society.

Increasingly socialized into the older population through marriage, children, vocations, responsibilities, today those of us who were young in the time of the youth movement retain many of the attitudes, life-styles, and expectations we adopted at the time. We differ far more from our parents than our parents did from our grandparents. We have different *miranda* and *credenda*—that which we admire and that in which we believe. We may not have become Dionysian or Protean, and we may be somewhat more narcissist than we would like—but having been forged in an extended time of fire, we are loath to render up our idealism. Studies of the "Woodstock Nation" and of other agglomerations of those who were young in the decade of shocks show that most of us still adhere to a left-of-center political stance and to substantial vestiges of our old life-styles. We continue to regard the "straight" world somewhat askance, and attempt to pursue lives in which we can maintain our individuality. Although quite middle class now, most of us eschew both cynicism and materialism, and still wish to pursue whatever will bring about a better world.

We soften; we age; we express our differentness in style and not so often in protest. Our megalomania and erotomania have both diminished. Recalling now the time when both the youth movement and we were young, many who participated in the marches, the demonstrations, the radical attempts to restructure society are wont to say that it was the time in our lives when we felt the most alive. We had a cause, its name was freedom, and to fight in its service with like-minded comrades was ennobling and all-consuming; we knew the passion of life. Those of us who are short on history forget that our parents said the same of their much larger fight against the Nazi menace, or do not know that philosophers since ancient Greece have been telling us that the feeling of *engagé* is the closest any of us come in our lives to defying death.

6 The Scarlet Thread

THE SCARLET THREAD of the war in Vietnam runs continuously through the Decade of Shocks, connecting the administrations of Johnson and Nixon, the youth protests, minority actions, assassinations, the growth of inflation, and nearly all the other subjects of this book. The war was the central shock of the era.

Since Hiroshima a consensus foreign policy had been in place. Its main object was the containment of Communist expansion. In search of *pax Americana* the free world had fought communism successfully in Berlin, Greece, Spain, the Philippines, Malaysia and South Korea, and unsuccessfully in China and Cuba. South Vietnam, a vulnerable Southeast Asian ally, had been considered a key country by Truman, Eisenhower, and Kennedy, all of whom had pledged themselves to maintain its integrity. Should South Vietnam fall, then, like dominoes, the other countries of the region would go rapidly Communist; such an event would threaten our allies' security and our own. We defended South Vietnam in order not to have to defend our markets and way of life in Australia, Japan, Hawaii, or in the continental U.S.

We also defended South Vietnam in order to show-case the power of the American colossus, to prove that our pledges and alliances were credible. Nuclear weapons were our ultimate threat, but they could not be used. We had to find other methods to maintain our credibility; as Henry Kissinger wrote in 1957, "all-out war has...ceased to be a meaningful instrument of policy." To demonstrate our power, we would have a limited war which we could win by means of conventional weaponry. Since communism was being imposed on South Vietnam by North Vietnam with the help of Russia and China, our war in South Vietnam would be a blow at Moscow—an indirect blow, but of the only sort possible in the nuclear era. In Vietnam, then, we would be making a demonstration of our credibility, which, as Jonathan Schell has pointed out, was

> above all, a problem of public relations, since what counted was not the substance of America's strength or the actual state of its willingness but the image of strength and willingness.... The United States, blocked by nuclear dread from using its military forces on a scale commensurate with its global size, began to use its power to strike poses and manufacture images.

As a chosen battleground, Vietnam brought out all the anomalies of our tightly reasoned posture. It led us to choose belligerent anti-communism and war over popular government and negotiation. In the six changes of Vietnam's government from 1963 to 1965 we repeatedly supported the most hard-line, pro-war of the candidates over those who campaigned for negotiation with the enemy, and once the leaders were "elected" we backed despotism. We also confused communism and anti-communism with the century-old struggle in Vietnam between Catholics and non-Catholics (primarily Confucians and Buddhists). We also neglected to assess properly the deep separations in the Communist world which affected Vietnam, such as the Sino-Soviet split of 1963 and the 1964 schism between North Vietnam and Russia. We did not take into account the extent to which most Vietnamese hated the Chinese, whom they had been fighting for a thousand years. Viewing communism as a monolithic and undifferentiated menace, we refused to acknowledge the possibility that the war being waged by Ho Chi Minh and Vo Nguyen Giap of the North might be as much a nationalist war to end foreign domination as it was a war of Communist outreach.

For thousands of years the small villages of Vietnam had been clusters of family units organized according to the tenets of Confucius. Families worshiped their ancestors whose graves were on their land; sons owed their allegiance to their fathers; in turn the fathers owed fealty to the overlords, and the overlords to the emperor. Growing pressure from French colonization, Japanese domination, Catholicism, urbanization, and West-ernization had been attacking and undermining the ancient system for most of this century. Between 1945 and 1954 there was war between various Vietnamese factions and the French; it ended after the French defeat at Dien Bien Phu. The 1954 settlement between the French and the Viet Minh (led by Ho Chi Minh) left Vietnam divided into North and South, and was fundamentally unstable. In the wake of the settlement, for ex-ample, 900,000 Catholics fled South of the DMZ, and 100,000 Viet Minh supporters went North. The North had all the industry; the South all the agriculture.

A new and larger war began, for domination of the southern region. The North's main weapon at the start was the Dang Lao Dong, a cadre of 5,000 men whom Ho Chi Minh had directed to stay in the South after the 1954 accord. They later became the National Liberation Front (NLF) and its military arm, the Viet Cong (VC). The NLF pressed a radical trans-formation of the villages. In place of the vertical hierarchy of fealty, the NLF substituted a system of lateral alliances and bonds. The restructuring was most often accomplished through selective use of terror—kidnappings, torture, assassinations—as well as through verbal persuasion. William R. Andrews studied how the NLF functioned in this "village war." Their selective assassinations of leaders and their omnipresent threats destroyed the village's social framework, and

> left the villager physically unharmed but socially isolated. His leaders had been proven incapable of surmounting the problems facing the vil-lage . . . and in order to save himself he had to find new answers that would offer stable frames of reference. Isolated and incapable of com-prehending the nature of the problems facing him, no individual or his family group could define the necessary behavior patterns required to end this disorientation. It was at this point that the Party said, in effect, "Here, do these things and act in this manner and order will be restored."

The Party organized groups of farmers, of housewives, of youth, of elders who supported the soldiers. The soldiers "protected" the village; thus the NLF built an armed force, collected taxes, established schools, regulated commerce, and dispensed justice. They also gave the peasants a coherent political philosophy, a goal, and reasons for being.

Confronted with the crumbling village structure, the Diem government of the South (and its successors) did little to combat the decay. They merely substituted government officials for the old overlords. Another fundamental difference between the government of South Vietnam (GVN) and that of the North was that the GVN did not desire unification with the North and had no coherent political philosophy or program. In the face of NLF–VC attacks and terror, the best the GVN could offer was to uproot villagers from their land, transport them to guarded "New Life" hamlets (many of which seemed little better than concentration camps) and give them what amounted to a dole.

By 1964 the NLF controlled nearly half Vietnam's land area and a quarter of its population. NLF pressure was greatest in the delta west of Saigon, in the Central Highlands, and near the confluence of the Laotian, Cambodian, and DMZ borders. Following the tenets of Mao and Ho, which subordinated military action to political goals, the VC avoided the cities, engaged the enemy only when in a superior position and with superior forces, were content to make ambushes and then to fade into the jungle, and did not mind when political cadres rather than military encounters won over villagers. By 1964 the NLF and the GVN both thought that the Communists' ultimate goal—political victory—was nearly at hand.

Believing that South Vietnam might "go under," the United States sought to prevent that from happening. First we looked for an excuse to enter the war more fully. In mid-1964, American naval forces in the Gulf of Tonkin were on a clandestine mission. They went close enough to North Vietnamese bases to evoke radar contact which allowed American technological equipment to fix on the radar and thereby locate more accurately the North Vietnamese bases and forces. One such mission resulted in "contact" between the opposing forces: the American ships were fired upon. Using the "contact" as occasion—but not disclosing that the United States had provoked the North Vietnamese—President Johnson sped through Congress the Tonkin Gulf Resolution of August 1964, which gave him authority to make reprisals against North Vietnamese "aggression."

The precipitating incident was at best a cloudy *casus belli*. A cable sent by Commander John Herrick from the destroyer *Maddox* three hours after the attack read:

> Review of action makes many recorded contacts and torpedoes fired appear doubtful. Freak weather effects and overeager sonarman may have accounted for many reports. No actual visual sightings by *Maddox*. Suggest complete evaluation before any further action.

* * *

Despite such doubts, the early "contacts" were dubbed real, and a case built up around them.

The resolution itself was also suspicious—purposely vague and shading the truth. It said that the U.S. regarded the peace and security of Southeast Asia as vital to our national interest and was prepared to assist militarily any SEATO signatory "requesting assistance in defense of its freedom." This sounded simple, but was not. In many of the countries, such a "request" would require a legislative vote. That included the United States, where the warmaking power was specifically vested in Congress. Thus the resolution was an attempt to get around the constitutional requirement that only Congress could declare war, and an attempt to fight a war without ever declaring that that was what we were doing. Convinced that the nation was in danger and that the president needed flexibility in making a response, Senator William Fulbright shepherded the resolution through the Senate 48 to 2; in the House the resolution passed unanimously. Echoing the congressional stance, a poll taken just after the resolution's passage showed that among those queried, approval of Johnson's handling of the war jumped from 42 percent to 85 percent. The president, the Congress, and the people seemed at one in favor of supporting South Vietnam by "replying" to North Vietnamese "aggression."

Immediately after the resolution was passed, Johnson, McNamara, and the Joint Chiefs of Staff drew up plans for escalating the action in Vietnam. These were secret, of course. Johnson also reaped political capital for his resolution, which showed he was capable of waging an aggressive war (should one be required) and thus took that issue away from challenger Barry Goldwater. Johnson's electoral landslide in November assured him that his designs for Vietnam reflected the majority's wishes.

At the beginning of 1965 a political settlement for Vietnam seemed possible. The Chinese let it be known that they were too busy making a cultural revolution at home to support North Vietnam in a major confrontation with the United States. Russia joined France in calling for a new Geneva sort of conference; both United Nations Secretary-General U Thant and the NLF said separately that an arrangement could be made which would obviate further bloodshed.

The signals were ignored. Both the U.S. and the government of South Vietnam now wanted war.

On February 7, 1965, Premier Kosygin of the Soviet Union was in Hanoi when the first American bombs fell on North Vietnam. This gave Russia a golden opportunity to wean the North Vietnamese from China by offering them sophisticated Russian weaponry with which to counter the American bombing.

When it "accelerated in tempo" (a typical military phrase of the period) in March, the bombing was dubbed Rolling Thunder by the USAF. When Westmoreland requested that the Marines come and defend the Da Nang air base from expected VC reprisals, General Maxwell Taylor, former head of the Joint Chiefs and at the moment ambassador to Saigon, objected. He warned that American forces were inadequately trained for guerrilla warfare, that the introduction of American ground forces would encourage ARVN forces to pass military responsibility for the war to the U.S., and that bringing in such ground forces would violate the rule we had followed in Vietnam for many years. Once a few troops were in, Taylor said, there would be no end of requests.

Despite Taylor's prescient warnings, in early March two battalions of Marines in full battle regalia made an amphibious landing on the Da Nang beaches. They were welcomed by leis and banners. But the Marines had not been officially requested by Saigon, and thus their presence technically violated even the language of the Tonkin Gulf Resolution. No matter: with the arrival of the Marines, the war changed. The faint chance that the U.S. could easily withdraw from the conflict was now gone.

"Half war," the military called it, and chafed under restrictions. The air force complained the bombing was too slow, not widely enough ranged, and so predictable that it could be countered easily by antiaircraft fire, SAM missiles, and MIG clusters. The Marines cursed that they could only fan out from bases and were not allowed to pursue the enemy into the bush. Engagements were limited, and although American forces "won" each of them (in terms of the ratio of American to VC forces killed), the victories were meaningless because territory once cleared was not continuously defended and was soon lost again.

A June, 29, 1965, State Department intelligence note concluded that the bombing was having little effect:

> Quite uniform and convincing evidence indicates that the U.S. strikes against North Vietnam have had no significantly harmful effects on popular morale. In fact, the regime has apparently been able to increase its control on the populace and perhaps even to break through the political apathy and indifference which have characterized the outlook of the average North Vietnamese in recent years.

* * *

A similar report had been made on English resistance after the Nazi blitz on London in late 1940. In 1965, CIA Director John McCone warned of another effect of the U.S. bombing of North Vietnam:

> With the passage of each day and each week, we can expect increasing pressure to stop the bombing. This will come from various elements of the American public, from the press, from the United Nations, and world opinion.

McCone counseled neither patience nor withdrawal, but harder-hitting air strikes inflicted with "minimum restraint," and more ground forces.

With a new and apparently stable government under Nguyen Cao Ky and Nguyen Van Thieu in Saigon, the time had come for an American decision on the war. Since the present level of force would not guarantee the continued independence of Vietnam, we now had to decide whether to escalate or to abandon the war.

Through the spring and summer, Johnson and his intimates wrestled with the decision. Reading the record of their deliberations amassed by Larry Berman in *Planning a Tragedy*, one is struck by how few of the advisors counseled caution or conciliation. Clark Clifford, then outside the government, wrote Johnson on May 17 that the president should keep American forces in Vietnam to a miminum and should probe "every serious avenue leading to a possible settlement." Such a settlement might not be particularly palatable, but it would undoubtedly be something we could "learn to live with." Under Secretary of State George Ball hammered repeatedly at Johnson to consider withdrawal and a negotiated settlement; once we had climbed on the dragon's back (further escalated the war), Ball said, we could not easily choose our place to dismount. Clifford and Ball were outflanked by the Bundy brothers and outranked by Dean Rusk and Robert McNamara. All six of the men looked dovish when compared to the Joint Chiefs, who wanted to end restrictions on the bombing, to call up the reserves so that large quantities of troops could be sent overseas right away, and to wipe out the VC sanctuaries in Cambodia, Laos, and the DMZ.

The course chosen by Johnson and ratified by his advisors (including George Ball) was a "slow," staged squeeze rather than a "fast/full" squeeze. The all-out war suggested by the military was rejected because it might trigger Chinese "hordes" coming to aid the North Vietnamese. Withdrawal was not seriously considered because Johnson feared that if we did withdraw the public would not stand for it, and he would become an instant lame duck, unable to push through the War on Poverty. Moderate escalation would allow both his wars to go on. He announced a commitment of 125,000 troops and secretly made plans to send up to 250,000 troops within twelve to eighteen months.

No one among the planners hazarded a guess as to what might happen if the new American effort failed to deter the Communists; even in the age of computerized military scenarios, that was not in the program. We had no fallback position.

American military strategy in Vietnam was equally fuzzy and short-sighted. In war there are three objectives: to beat the enemy's forces; to render inoperable the enemy's rear base; and to break the enemy's will to resist. The U.S. was well equipped to accomplish the first objective, but not when it was faced with a guerrilla force that wouldn't come to battle. It was not equipped to accomplish the second objective, and the third was never seriously attempted. As George C. Herring comments,

> Left on its own to frame a strategy, the military fought the conventional war for which it was prepared without reference to the peculiar conditions in Vietnam. Westmoreland and the JCS chafed under the restraints...(but) sensitive to MacArthur's fate...would not challenge the President directly or air their case in public. On the other hand, they refused to develop a strategy that accommodated itself to the restrictions imposed by the White House, but rather attempted to break them down one by one until they got what they wanted. The result was considerable ambiguity in purpose and method, growing civil-military tension, and a steady escalation that brought increasing costs and little gain.

The basic U.S. military strategy was the air war. It was massive, with 25,000 sorties against North Vietnam in 1965, 79,000 in 1966, and 108,000 in 1967—many times the number flown in World War II. And during these several years, more than twice the tonnage was dropped on South Vietnam that was dropped on the North, in attempts to kill VC and to deny them cover and sanctuary in the South.

McNamara estimated that during each week of heavy bombing, the air war was causing a thousand civilian casualties in the North. This was not good for the public image of the United States. Also, the air war was effective only sporadically in "interdicting" the ferrying of troops and supplies to southern insurgents. The U.S. bombed incessantly the Thanh Hoa bridge over the Ma River, and lost more than a hundred planes in its vicinity before the bridge was put out of action in 1972. When it was finally hit, the bridge was not repaired, and U.S. intelligence realized belatedly that for some years it had been a dummy, left standing only to draw American planes into a trap.

Other weapons in our arsenal were equally destructive but only intermittently effective. The 7,000 tons of nerve gas we dropped excited many international protests. We sprayed 83,000 tons of herbicide on vegetation. "Only You Can Prevent Forests" was the mocking motto of defoliant crews who destroyed 5½ million acres—half of all the coastal and delta mangrove forests, and a fifth of the total forested area of South Vietnam (an area the size of the state of Massachusetts). We disrupted rainfall patterns, used laser- and television-guided bombs, had helicopter machine-guns which fired 6,000 rounds per minute; we used "people sniffers" to detect the smell of human urine, heat and sound detectors to tell us when guerrillas were near.

Our major ground forces strategy was what General Westmoreland in a moment of semantic infelicity labeled "search and destroy" missions. American units were "inserted" into an area by helicopter to look for VC; often they stepped deliberately into ambushes in order to locate the enemy, engage him, and bring artillery or aircraft fire down to destroy him. A computer analysis later showed such missions to be effective less than one percent of the time.

Units were not supposed to come back empty-handed. Sometimes they killed "friendlies" by mistake: this was to be expected, Marine Brigadier-General Edwin H. Simmons wrote, for many of the local South Vietnamese hamlet-defense forces

> had the dismaying but unavoidable habit of wearing the peasant's traditional black pajamas, the uniform usually worn by the Viet Cong. Recognition of the [militia] under these conditions was sometimes fatally difficult. In desperation officers sometimes briefed patrol leaders and pilots in words to this effect: "If you can see them, they are Popular Forces [militia]; if you can't see them, they are Viet Cong."

On one sweep mission soldiers found a village deserted except for an old couple. Their pot of rice was too large for just themselves, so the soldiers concluded it had been cooked for the VC. Setting fire to the thatched roof of the couple's hut with a Zippo lighter, the soldiers were rewarded with verification. It exploded, honeycombed with bullets hidden there by the Viet Cong. There were many such "Zippo inspections," some more warranted than others. Antipersonnel bombs, napalm, and white phosphorus also were used frequently in civilian areas against Viet Cong. White phosphorus ignited buildings, stuck to human beings, and burned through flesh and bone. Such weapons were used at times in "free-fire" zones where, after all the friendlies had been evacuated, soldiers were at liberty to kill anything non-American that moved. The result in civilian deaths was appalling. According to some estimates, as many noncombatants as VC died in free-fire zones.

Some observers believed that weapons such as napalm and white phosphorus would not have been used against a Caucasian enemy, and should not have been used against an enemy so deeply infiltrated among the Vietnamese citizenry. They saw the use of such weapons as racist.

The rule of thumb in the bush, Philip Caputo reported, was "If it's dead and Vietnamese, it's VC." This assumption by working grunts may or may not have been racist—but it derived from the only acceptable criterion of success in American military operations, the number of guerrillas killed. The "body count" was a way to measure progress, a way to quantify a war which defied quantification. American brass assumed that if the number of enemy dead was high enough, the Communists would have to stop fighting. That wasn't true for the Vietnamese, but American military men didn't understand it. All too often the criterion of numbers led to padded body counts and to the labeling of friendly or civilian Vietnamese casualties as VC dead.

It was not a good war, professional military men admitted, but it was the only one they had. As in most wars, the chiefs were prepared to fight the last war. American tactics would have worked in Korea, or in slicing through Nazi Europe; they had little relevance in Vietnam's terrain or against Viet Cong tactics. As in most wars, there was scrambling to get ahead by American professionals who knew promotions came faster on the battlefield with its opportunities for demonstrating aggressiveness. What better road to success than having high body counts? Or using napalm to wipe out a village while taking minimal U.S. casualties?

The same logic was behind the command decision not to issue to the ARVN the new M-16 rifles which Americans used, but rather to give them World War II vintage M-1 rifles.

The rotation policy also made little sense. It had been designed to prevent an entire unit from being wiped out, and to let soldiers serve the minimum amount of time in an unpopular war. But the results were catastrophic. Soldiers were "rotated" home after a year in the field. In a unit, some would go home one month, others, three months later. After a year, a soldier was just becoming acclimated to fighting conditions in Vietnam. He would spend a few months as a green recruit, a few months as a hardened soldier, and his last few months lying low and less inclined to fight hard, knowing that he was "short" and could soon return home. The rotation policy added to the temptation to take fewer prisoners and to kill at a distance: prisoners could prove dangerous, and so could hand-to-hand combat.

Before such tactics had completely taken their toll, General S. L. A Marshall could report to Westmoreland in late 1965 that the morale and fighting fitness of American soldiers was as high as he had ever seen it. In nearly every engagement from 1965 to 1967, American and ARVN forces killed five to ten VC for every American or ARVN killed.

Perhaps as many as 200,000 VC died during those two years but during those same years nearly 200,000 men per year were coming of draftable age in North Vietnam, and infiltration rates to the South went from 35,000 a year in 1965 to 90,000 a year in 1967. As quickly as Americans killed off the VC, they were replaced.

General Giap wrote:

> Every minute, hundreds of thousands of people die all over the world. The life or death of a hundred, a thousand, or tens of thousands of human beings, even if they are our compatriots, represents really very little.

The statement does not bolster the American racial slur that Asians have a disregard for human life; rather, it is Giap's tenet that the deaths of individuals matter less than achieving great ideals. Before each engagement VC and NVA commanders would tell their men of its political importance and suggest that if they died in the encounter, soldiers would spring up to take their places and would not rest until they had been avenged and Vietnam was united under Communist rule. Americans never understood the persuasiveness of this logic, nor how it was used to counter the American policy of trying to wear down the enemy by attrition.

The large-scale operation called "Cedar Falls" involved many U.S. policies and everything the U.S. could throw at a concentration of enemy forces in a province not far from Saigon. In an "Iron Triangle" area there appeared, first, waves of B-52 bombers to soften up the enemy. Then, to surround the stronghold, ground forces were inserted by helicopter. Searching every hamlet, the ground forces were fired upon and managed to kill some VC, though most VC, warned of the attack, had fled into Cambodia. What indigenous villagers then remained were removed from the area and placed into a giant refugee camp. After all the friendlies were out, enormous converted bulldozers known as Rome Plows were brought in to reduce an area the size of Rhode Island to rubble: it was denuded of vegetation, then burned and bombed again to destroy any tunnels the VC might have left intact. As Vietnam veteran John Kerry later commented,

> In Vietnam, the "greatest soldiers in the world," better armed and better equipped than the opposition, unleashed the power of the greatest technology in the world against thatch huts and mud paths. In the process we created a nation of refugees, bomb craters, amputees, orphans, widows, and prostitutes, and we gave new meaning to the words of the Roman historian Tacitus, "Where they made a desert, they called it peace."

It did not go unnoticed inside the American military power structure that the war in Vietnam was at best ineffective and at worst tragic. Assistant Secretary of Defense John T. McNaughton's memo of January 19, 1966, was entirely realistic:

> The ARVN is tired, passive, and accommodation-prone. . . . The North Vietnamese/VC are matching our deployments. . . . Pacification is stalled. . . . The GVN political infrastructure is moribund and weaker than the VC infrastructure. . . . South Vietnam is near the edge of serious inflation and economic chaos. . . . *The present U.S. objective in Vietnam is to avoid humiliation.* The reasons why we *went into* Vietnam to the present depth . . . are now largely academic. Why we have *not withdrawn* from Vietnam is, by all odds, *one* reason: (1) to preserve our reputation as a guarantor, and thus to preserve our effectiveness in the rest of the world. We have not hung on (2) to save a friend, or (3) to deny the Communists the added acres and heads (because the dominoes don't fall for that reason in this case), or even (4) to prove that "wars of national liberation" won't work (except as our reputation is involved). . . . The ante (and commitment) is now very high. . . . *We are in an escalating military stalemate.*

* * *

President Johnson knew all about such a viewpoint when he met in Honolulu in January of 1966 with Thieu and Ky. The report notwithstanding, he believed that we could not get out of Vietnam and must enlarge the war. Not wanting to have the U.S. pull out, the Vietnamese leaders agreed to everything Johnson asked them for—the encouragement of democracy, better pacification programs, and the like. More American troops were committed to the war.

To Vietnamese Buddhists, Johnson's approval of Ky and Thieu condoned GVN suppression, torture, extortion, and corruption. In February the Buddhists created a massive uprising which affected the entire country. In Saigon, bonzes burned themselves to death and led mobs in the street. In Hue, they sacked a U.S. embassy and nearly took over the city. Ky sent a thousand ARVN marines to wrest Hue from the Buddhists, and the revolt was quelled, but the tenuous nature of the GVN hold was exposed for all to see. It was clear the U.S. was supporting a regime that was neither democratic nor representative nor tolerant of dissent.

The chief public relations man for the American government in Saigon, Barry Zorthian, later wrote:

> Given the situation and the nature of the war; given the way we backed into it, and the personality of LBJ... given the openness of the war; given the lack of censorship, and the letdown that the press felt... on a number of our claims... given all that, the amazing thing is not that the press was critical, but that they stuck with us so long.

After the Buddhist revolt some of the press started to question the American involvement. We were falling into ambushes in the same places the French had; pacification by evacuation was a disaster; the bombing was worthless. In turn, press reports fueled growing antiwar sentiment in the United States. Even official reports, far rosier than those of the press, made Pentagon readers question the efficacy of our actions in Vietnam. By late 1966 McNamara suggested to Johnson that the bombing was hurting us in the eyes of the audience that mattered most, the other nations of the world.

A few months later McNamara pressed Johnson to 1) halt the bombing of the North, 2) set a ceiling on troop levels, 3) shift forces from "search-and-destroy" missions to those better designed to provide security for the South Vietnamese, and 4) change our bargaining stance so we would not be obligated forever to prop up Thieu and Ky. The Joint Chiefs said McNamara's proposals would result in "an aerial Dien Bien Phu" and threatened to resign *en bloc* if Johnson acceded to the proposals.

The Joint Chiefs reminded Johnson that since the 1965 crisis South Vietnam had not collapsed, and asked for 200,000 more men and for authority to hit the Laos and Cambodia sanctuaries and to bomb Hanoi and Haiphong. Believing that McNamara's proposals were influenced by his own rival Robert Kennedy, Johnson listened to other advisors (Rusk, Rostow, Maxwell Taylor, Lodge, Clifford, the Bundys) who said a bombing halt would not stop domestic dissent, would anger hawks, and would be taken by the Communists as a sign that Hanoi would not have to bargain. Once more Johnson compromised: he approved 55,000 new troops but did not set a troop ceiling; he reviewed but did not stop the search-and-destroy strategy and began to give ARVN more responsibility for the war; he expanded the air war into more of the North but refused permission to attack the extraterritorial sanctuaries. These 1967 decisions, wrote George Herring,

> were improvisations that defied military logic and did not face, much less resolve, the contradictions in American strategy. The bombing was sustained not because anyone thought it would work but because Johnson deemed it necessary to pacify certain [hawkish] domestic factions and because stopping it might be regarded as a sign of weakness. The President refused to give his field commander the troops he considered necessary to make his strategy work, but he did not confront the inconsistencies in the strategy itself. The commitment remained open-ended. The United States continued to fight a conventional war in a limited war setting where success was unlikely if not impossible.

By mid-1967 the antiwar movement had gathered considerable force, as well as a body of doctrine based on the military infeasibility of winning the war which refuted the long-held assumptions on which the war was being fought.

Doves not only disputed the notion that the brand of communism menacing South Vietnam came from Moscow, but now also contended that communism itself might not be the terrible fate we had long insisted it was. Senator Fulbright, who had just a few years earlier shepherded the Tonkin Gulf Resolution through the Senate, wrote:

> The point I wish to make is not that communism is not a harsh and, to us, repugnant system of organizing society, but that its doctrine has

redeeming tenets of humanitarianism; that the worst thing about it is not its philosophy but its fanaticism; that history suggests the probability of an abatement of revolutionary fervor; that in practice fanaticism *has* abated in a number of countries including the Soviet Union; that some countries probably are better off under communist rule than they were under the preceding regimes; that some people may even want to live under communism.

This pulled the ground from under anti-communism. Other antiwar theoreticians argued that if South Vietnam fell, the rest of the Southeast Asian dominoes would not necessarily fall—but that even if they did, what we were doing in Vietnam reflected badly on our image and was alienating our friends and allies.

In Vietnam we had placed the evil of the world wholly outside ourselves. In fighting the war, we hoped we were doing good. Many things showed us we were not doing good but rather were using evil means toward goals which were not self-evidently good. We were being corrupted constantly by our actions: in backing a demonstrably tyrannical Saigon government, we acquiesced in its horrors; in bombing the civilian countryside, we inched up on genocide; in dehumanizing our enemy, we dehumanized ourselves. "Power," wrote Senator Fulbright,

> tends to confuse itself with virtue and a great nation is peculiarly susceptible to the idea that its power is a sign of God's favor, conferring upon it a special responsibility for other nations—to make them richer and happier and wiser, to remake them, that is, in its own shining image.

To remake countries in its own image was the wish of Hitler's Germany. Were we that bad? Fulbright could see what he labeled as the "arrogance of power" in the wish of the U.S. military to use Vietnam as a testing ground for new weaponry, and in Johnson's Honolulu Declaration, which stated that one of the reasons we were in Vietnam was to bring the American way of life to Southeast Asia.

Historian Arthur Schlesinger, Jr., wanted the United States to confront the idea of

> whether this country is a chosen people, uniquely righteous and wise, with a moral mission to all mankind, or whether it is one of many nations in a multifarious world...committed not to an American century but to

what President Kennedy used to call a world of diversity.... The ultimate choice is between messianism and maturity.

Such language gave moral fiber to dissent. If in 1967 and 1968 the government reacted strongly to the dissent, that was, Jonathan Schell suggests, because the war was being fought to uphold the nation's image:

When a government has founded the national defense on the national image, as the United States did under the doctrine of credibility, it follows that any internal dissension will be interpreted as an attack upon the safety of the nation.

As for dissent, Schell wrote,

What better way is there to oppose a public-relations war than with a public-relations insurrection? The antiwar movement was often taken to task for its "theatricality." The fact is that it was precisely in its theatricality that its special genius lay.... The demonstrations at home struck at the very foundation of the larger aims for which the war was being fought. They struck a crippling blow at the credibility upon which the whole strategy was based.

Because the public agreed with either the reasoning or the theatrics of the antiwar movement, or because it was just turned off by the television pictures of the war, by the fall of 1967 a large segment of the population was increasingly critical of the government's work in Vietnam. Nearly two-thirds of those queried in a poll thought that Johnson's conduct of the war was inadequate.

On January 20, 1968, General Westmoreland cabled the JCS that the enemy was "presently developing a threatening posture in several areas in order to seek victories essential to achieve prestige and bargaining power," and would attack around the Tet holiday. The general also told NBC that he expected the Communists might seek a "spectacular battlefield success" during Tet. Westmoreland vastly underestimated the scope of the offensive and ignored for the most part the potential date of attack, though he did persuade Thieu to limit the GVN Tet truce to 24 hours rather than six days. On January 21 the Marine base at Khe Sanh came under heavy bombardment. Westmoreland viewed this attack as a diversion. On January 30, eight towns in the Central Highlands were attacked. Westmoreland did not order countermeasures in strength. And so on the morning of January 31, 1968, the Communists' Tet offensive was a considerable surprise. That morning, a ferocious Communist assault ranged over 36 of 44 provincial capitals, five of the six largest cities, and two dozen air bases.

In a widely reported incident, a team of VC "suicide sappers" forced their way onto the grounds of the U.S. embassy in Saigon; they never got within the chancery, and in six hours all were dead, but the uproar they caused was enormous. American newsmen were astounded by the attack on the embassy. As a military historian sympathetic to the American effort concluded,

> From a strictly military standpoint, it mattered little whether or not the VC sappers had entered the chancery; from a psychological angle, it was of profound importance. To many newsmen, and thus to many people in the United States, the attack seemed to confirm that Westmoreland and President Johnson had been disseminating falsehoods. If the United States could not protect its own embassy, how could the war have reached a point (as Westmoreland had recently put it) "where the end begins to come into view"? The fact that . . . even a weakened enemy could launch small, suicidal attacks on almost any installation [was] disregarded in sensational press and television reportage.

It was not quite so straightforward. Intense fighting in Saigon lasted five full days, during which many Vietnamese believed the end of the war was nigh. Panic was the message reflected in such things as the widely reprinted picture of Saigon's Chief of Police executing with a pistol a suspected VC. JCS Chairman Wheeler was shocked by Tet, and reported to Johnson that it had been "a very near thing." Only the perspicacity of some middle-rank ARVN and U.S. commanders who had kept their forces on alert, and the power of the Air Force, stemmed the tide. The Communists held ten of the provincial capitals and Hue for some time before they were beaten back.

Forty thousand of the estimated 84,000 enemy troops who attacked one hundred cities were killed. Americans lost 2,000, ARVN forces 3,000. There were 14,000 civilian casualties and some 600,000 new refugees. In most spots the enemy was driven back after a few days. Hue proved the most difficult to recapture, taking until February 25. In Hue friendly troops were trapped in the Citadel, and since no one wanted to damage the historic city unduly, the American forces were cautious. Had they gone in more quickly, it is possible that some of the 5,000 civilians tortured, killed, and secretly buried by the Viet Cong during their hold of the city might have survived.

In World War II, American reporters had become inured to the sight of entire city blocks in rubble, but during Tet the new generation of reporters were shocked by such sights; so, too, were television audiences unable to tell whether a screen-filling image of a burning block was representative or atypical of the war as a whole. The hidden story, if there was one, was the destructive power the American forces used to drive away the enemy and recapture the cities. The firepower was immense, overwhelming, and—to many—futile. At the small town of Ben Tre, heavy American shelling leveled a quarter of the buildings, and an unnamed major told an AP reporter that "in order to save the city it became necessary to destroy it." A report later suggested that the Communists had fought deliberately near important structures—primarily religious ones—to cause American forces in the process of battle to destroy those symbols of organization among the populace.

For seventy-seven days an enormous fury beset Khe Sanh, which was near the conjunction of Laos and the DMZ: at times it was under attack by as many as 20,000 North Vietnamese regular troops. Rather than evacuate the small contingent of Marines, Westmoreland and Johnson decided to supply and reinforce them so that the U.S. would not be seen to retreat in the face of the enemy. The perimeter of Khe Sanh became the most-bombed target in military history. Some 10,000 of the enemy (and a few hundred defenders) died in the encounter, but since the remainder of the enemy simply moved into Laos, the victory was inconclusive.

Westmoreland wanted to make a major thrust immediately after Tet, arguing that the time to go after the enemy was when he was hurt and had suffered tremendous losses. Westmoreland sought many more troops and the authority to go into Cambodia, Laos, and the DMZ to finish the Communists and end the war. General Wheeler passed along the request for 206,000 more troops. It was this request which surfaced in March of 1968 and caused great controversy.

Much of the American public perceived Tet as a disaster for the United States and reasoned that even if the Communists had been defeated, the surprise and vigor of their offensive did not bode well for the American war effort. In a society grown used to the short-term presentation of the "living-room war," the impact of televised pictures of isolated violence and incursions outweighed long-term reports of immense enemy casualties and of renewed high morale among our troops and allies. If to General Westmoreland Tet was the Viet Cong's last stand, akin to the Nazi surge in the Battle of the Bulge, to the reporters and to the American public Tet was an American Dien Bien Phu.

Tet legitimatized the doves' claims, and made people believe that either the U.S. was losing the war, or that we were unable to win it, or that we were fighting a war we ought not to be fighting. After Tet, the consensus on foreign policy, which had held since the end of World War II, fell apart. As *The New York Times* later put it, the new American consensus was "that the price of rescuing Vietnam from Communism had outrun the benefit and should not be paid."

Soon after Tet, Lyndon Johnson's war came to an end.

Johnson's war had been reluctant, if ferocious; honorable, though fatally misguided. At every step up the escalator he had tried to take those actions which reflected the public consensus as he perceived it. If he continually rejected the option of pulling the U.S. out of Vietnam, he also resisted the siren call of the military for actions which would have enlarged the theater and circumstances of the war. He had used the Tonkin Gulf incidents as an excuse to pursue the war, but thereafter had committed sins of omission rather than commission—sins of the sort that, since time immemorial, governmental leaders and military chieftains have been forgiven if they win, but have never been forgiven if they lose their wars. In early 1968, when the consensus to continue the war in Vietnam evaporated, Johnson bowed to public pressure. On March 31 he authorized only a quarter of the troops Westmoreland requested, immediately began to deescalate, initiated a bombing halt—and, to add emphasis to his desire to stop the fighting, removed himself from the 1968 presidential race. With these decisions, the war changed.

General Creighton Abrams replaced Westmoreland. Some troops arrived. In place of the halted bombing of the North there was increased bombing of the South, where 50,000 civilians had already been killed by U.S. bombs. There were such spectacles as the saga of the U.S.S. *New Jersey*, a World War II ship brought out of mothballs, refurbished, and sent to Vietnam, where its 16-inch guns shelled enemy positions from the Tonkin Gulf; after a year and an expenditure of $40 million, it was declared useless and put back in mothballs.

It made little difference to American soldiers that the Viet Cong had been decimated by Tet, and that the Communists now fighting were North Vietnamese regulars. Correspondent Michael Herr overheard one American in a bar tell another his plan to end the war: "What you do is, you load all the friendlies onto ships and take them out to the South China Sea. Then you bomb the country flat. Then you sink the ships." The same disdain for all Vietnamese may help to explain the destruction of My Lai, which took place just after Tet.

Frightened in part by the Tet offensive, and by recent casualties to his unit from booby traps and snipers, Lieutenant "Rusty" Calley and his young and inexperienced squad from the American Division landed by helicopter in a free-fire zone near the hamlet of My Lai. After searching the hamlet, they executed 347 Vietnamese civilians.

Atrocities such as My Lai occur in every war—in fact, a massacre of similar though smaller proportions happened on the same day as My Lai, and in prior years in Vietnam there had been other incidents. ARVN excesses were legendary, though hushed up for the press, and the Viet Cong had just executed 5,000 civilians in Hue. Nevertheless, the murder of Vietnamese civilians at My Lai was a grisly reminder that evil belonged not only to the enemy: it was ours, as well.

After Tet, soldier-historian Douglas Welsh recalls, he and his fellow infantrymen were told that

> Tet and Khe Sanh were the enemy's last great offensives and that the United States had won the war. It was just taking time to arrange the final settlement. Believing what they were told, the soldiers' attitude changed, particularly those of the infantrymen. . . . The fear of dying in Vietnam was bad enough in itself, but that nagging fear of being the last soldier killed could not be rationalized.

This was part of what led to the "fragging" of officers (killing them with a fragmentation grenade), to the refusal of hazardous duty, to the over use of drugs—an estimated 30,000 hooked soldiers by 1971—and to the increase of antiwar activity among the troops in Vietnam.

The Thieu government was afraid the U.S. might negotiate itself out of Vietnam and leave the GVN without support. The leaders feared a bloodbath reminiscent of Hue. In the Paris negotiations the GVN dragged its feet, refused to accept the NLF as an equal participant, objected to the shape of the table, and generally obstructed progress in the belief that Richard Nixon would be more sympathetic to their cause than Hubert Humphrey.

During the campaign Nixon told Haldeman, "I'm not going to end up like LBJ, holed up inside the White House afraid to show my face in the street. I'm going to stop that war. Fast." Eisenhower, he recalled, in 1953 had forced North Korea to bargain by threatening nuclear annihilation. Nixon suggested that the North Vietnamese would

> believe any threat of force Nixon makes because it's Nixon. We'll just slip them the word that, "for God's sakes, you know Nixon's obsessed about Communism... he has his hand on the nuclear button."

He felt certain this would make the North Vietnamese negotiate in earnest. (Perhaps this was the secret plan to end the war, of which he spoke during the campaign.)

In *Foreign Affairs* for January 1969, National Security Advisor Henry Kissinger wrote that "ending the war honorably is essential for the peace of the world. Any other solution may unloose forces that would complicate the prospects for international order." America would exchange a military withdrawal for a political settlement that would leave the Thieu government in control, perhaps with the NLF as a minor party. This was the same solution Johnson had sought, but Nixon and Kissinger had two new elements to make it happen. Since their design was for a global peace, they would pressure Russia and China (in exchange for détente and trade) to make Hanoi come to terms. Also, they would now unleash the American military: maximum force would be used to bring Hanoi "to the breaking point."

Negotiations with the superpowers would take some time to mature. Military power was easier to muster. Only a few days after the inauguration, General Abrams reported that the legendary "COSVN"—headquarters for the Viet Cong effort in the South—had been definitively located in Cambodia and requested permission to bomb it. After consultation the secret, Operation "Breakfast" was launched, 48 sorties into Cambodia, an area previously off-limits to the American planes. A barrier had been broken: over the next 14 months 3,600 "Menu" bombing raids were flown against Cambodia. COSVN was not definitively found or wiped out. But the discovery of the secret bombing (in May 1969) by William Beecher of *The New York Times* caused consternation in the White House; as a result, wiretaps were placed on a dozen people's phones. In Cambodia the bombing led only to the increased presence of Communists in the country, and to the further destabilization of the Sihanouk government.

In the spring of 1969 the president withdrew 25,000 troops from Vietnam. To force further withdrawals and to heighten American casualties, Communists were doing their utmost in the field. One captured Communist document boasted that the spring 1969 offensive had killed more Americans than had the Tet offensive. By July the Cambodia bombing, the troop withdrawals, and the negotiating ploys had not moved the Paris talks an inch. Kissinger began to meet secretly with North Vietnamese negotiator Le Duc Tho. In September the National Security Council led by Kissinger drew up plans for "savage, punishing blows" against North Vietnam—the bombing of major cities, the mining of Haiphong harbor, even the potential use of tactical nuclear weapons. Kissinger privately said that before the war was settled such blows would prove necessary. Staunch opposition by Secretary of State William Rogers and Secretary of Defense Melvin Laird prevented the plans from being immediately executed.

The Nixon administration had come to power with a clear mandate to end the war and with a negotiation structure already in place. After World War I, after World War II, and after Korea far more complicated issues had been solved in months. Some said there was no progress in the Vietnam peace talks because the American withdrawal had to be carefully staged to avoid a debacle. Our government was pledged to ensure the health of the Thieu government after the U.S. left, though we knew this was an unattainable goal. The real goal of the United States, Nixon announced on November 3, 1969, was to avoid "defeat and humiliation," which might come if the antiwar faction pushed us to an overhasty retreat. Nixon called on the "silent majority" to back his program which tied American troop withdrawals to the pace of Vietnamization and to stand united so the enemy would know we were serious. By November 12, 300 representatives and 58 senators, a majority of both Houses, had expressed approval of these "new" policies for the Vietnam War.

ARVN forces were increased from 850,000 to one million, which meant that nearly every able-bodied South Vietnamese man between the ages of 16 and 40 was now under arms. The arms were new: M-16 rifles, machine guns, helicopters, ships, planes, enormous quantities of trucks. But ARVN desertion rates remained high, the officer corps' corruption notable, and the army's ability to function well without American military supervision and air support nonexistent. The "Accelerated Pacification Program" had so many militiamen guarding hamlets that it seemed as if each farmer had a personal armed chaperone to fend off the VC. Supposedly as a result of all this, progress was made in clearing roads, establishing schools, and providing a governmental infrastructure that could command loyalty as well as allegiance—but no one could be sure that the progress had not come as much from the fact that the Communists seemed to be lying low, waiting for the Americans to leave.

Today, in retrospect, many argue that at this moment the U.S. was winning the war and could have pushed on to military victory—but that the political climate was not right. At the time, General Abrams publicly voiced the view that the withdrawals were hurting the Vietnamization program. Others argued that the rapid pace of withdrawal encouraged Hanoi to stall at the Paris peace talks.

In early 1970 the president became convinced he must find a military action that would, as he put it in his memoir, "show the enemy that we were still serious about our commitment in Vietnam." Over the objections of Rogers and Laird, and with the backing of Kissinger, Nixon gave the military what it had long sought: permission to clean out the North Vietnamese sanctuaries in the Parrot's Beak and Fishhook areas of Cambodia. These sanctuaries were about fifty miles west of Saigon. We had been bombing them for a year. Why go after them now? Nixon reasoned that since the Sihanouk government had just been overthrown by the right-wing Lon Nol, a military sweep would simultaneously aid the new anti-Communist Cambodian regime and buy time for Vietnamization. On April 30 he added to these reasons his ultimate justification for the "limited incursion" of a foreign country:

> If, when the chips are down, the world's most powerful nation acts like a pitiful, helpless giant, the forces of totalitarianism and anarchy will threaten free nations and free institutions throughout the world.

Nixon's statement was straight out of the old American crusade to contain worldwide communism. But the old consensus had died, and when this old rationale was invoked to legitimatize widening the war, a firestorm of criticism broke about the Cambodian invasion even before its success or failure could be determined. There were violent campus upheavals, epitomized by Kent State. Also, and for the first time, there were congressional attempts to curb the president's power to wage the undeclared war.

Nixon pledged to remove all troops from Cambodia quickly. Despite his pledge, the Senate voted to rescind the Tonkin Gulf Resolution and nearly approved an amendment which would have cut off all funds for American military operations in Cambodia. The wish of Congress was that the war escalate no further. That Congress acted no more strongly than it did was indicative of the support which in this military crisis as in every previous one for a hundred years rallied automatically to a president who took strong military action.

The invasion was not the greatest military exploit since MacArthur's landing at Inchon, as Nixon suggested to a group of businessmen, but it did locate and destroy 8,000 bunkers and much matériel. However, there were many civilian casualties, and Vietnamese long resident in Cambodia fled to avoid having their homesites become a battleground, thus creating 100,000 new refugees for the tent cities. William Shawcross noted another result:

> The invasion pushed the battlefields [for the two sides currently contesting Cambodia] farther westward into the heavily populated villages and rice fields around and beyond the Mekong river. The Lon Nol government proved itself unable to defend the country, and it entered into a dependence upon foreign aid that would eventually choke it. In Peking, Sihanouk was now encouraged by his new sponsors to form a government in exile containing a preponderance of his recent enemies from the Khmer Rouge.

In seeking to shorten the war, Nixon had widened it; in seeking to circumvent dissent by a military victory, he had broadened its base. Four out of the five NSC members who had discussed the invasion with Kissinger resigned. Secretary of the Interior Walter Hickel wrote the well-known letter which led to his being fired. About this period following Cambodia and Kent State, Chuck Colson later recalled:

> Within the iron gates of the White House, quite unknowingly, a siege mentality was setting in. It was now "us" against "them." Gradually, as we drew the circle closer around us, the ranks of "them" began to swell.

It was at this time that new alliances formed in the ranks of dissent. For the first time, unions entered the lists; whole church congregations marched with groups as diverse as businessmen, Chicanos, blacks, women, etc. The antiwar movement took on the breadth, depth, and high-minded moral stance that reminded observers of the early days of the civil-rights movement. Here was moral leadership, but it did not appeal to everyone. As Senator George McGovern noted, while the demonstrations undoubtedly focussed national attention on the Vietnam tragedy... in the present context [1970] they probably do not bring the war's end closer; on the contrary, they may make it more elusive by identifying peace efforts with activities the majority finds repugnant.

In response to dissidence Nixon stepped up surveillance of antiwar groups, became midwife to the Huston Plan, and acquiesced in the cover-up of the secret bombing in Cambodia. Half the people Louis Harris polled now questioned Nixon's credibility on the war, and more than half disagreed with his handling of the war. The better-informed National Security Council seemed to feel the same way. Even with four of its doves gone, the NSC late in 1970 concluded that the U.S. was neither able to coerce nor able to persuade the North Vietnamese from South Vietnam's soil—in other words, that both military punishment and the peace talks were failing. By the time of the 1970 election the number of U.S. forces in Vietnam had shrunk to half what they had been when Nixon took office. However, on the battlefield the outcome had not changed; all that had altered was the proportion of blood spilled: it was more than ever Asian. And as that became the case, Americans forgot about the war more and more. Dissent peaked with Kent State, then declined.

After the 1970 elections, acerbic observers suggested that Nixon would have no incentive to end the war before his own reelection bid in 1972— a canard which drew from the administration retorts about lack of patri- otism. The problem, the White House said, was that the North Vietnamese had no incentive to end the war so long as the U.S. pulled out its troops unilaterally.

In order to break the battlefield and peace table stalemates, the president and his advisors suggested a new offensive for spring 1971. To counter a possible NVA invasion, to cut the Ho Chi Minh Trail, and to provide a test of Vietnamization, the ARVN would go into Laos, backed by U.S. air and logistics support. "Lam Son 719/Dewey Canyon II" took off on January 30, 1971. Ten thousand American support and air troops ferried 20,000 ARVN ground-fighting troops into Laos. The target area was di- rectly west of Khe Sanh, and no heavy resistance was expected.

The ARVN went into a trap set by 36,000 NVA regulars with new Russian-made tanks and fortified antiaircraft positions. In the most intense fighting of the war, nearly every American helicopter was used. Alexander Haig from the NSC office, Ky, Thieu, and Abrams kept in close touch with the fighting. After six weeks the ARVN withdrew. Though NVA casualties were listed at 13,000, of whom 5,000 were killed by American air strikes, the ARVN lost nearly *half* of its own men and many of its seasoned commanders. Ky blamed the Americans for inadequate support; Haig and Abrams blamed the ineptness of the Vietnamese. The Ho Chi Minh Trail was scarred but not cut, and the whole affair was judged a signal disaster for Vietnamization.

American domestic reaction to the jaunt into yet another country, Laos, was full of anger: Harris polls showed that 71 percent of those queried now thought we had made a mistake in sending troops to Vietnam in the first place, 58 percent regarded the war as "immoral," only 31 percent approved of Nixon's handling of the conflict, and a majority favored pulling all our troops out of Vietnam by the end of 1971 even if that meant a Communist takeover of the country.

Incensed by the invasion, defense analyst Daniel Ellsberg gave the "Pentagon Papers" to reporters. The Vietnam Veterans Against the War (VVAW) staged "Dewey Canyon III," a "limited incursion into the country of Congress" during which they testified to their own war crimes, some of which echoed those of recently convicted Lieutenant Calley. Continuous television coverage of the many April 24 demonstrations gave to the protests the air of a countrywide town meeting on the war. The "Mayday Tribe" caused disruptions that were among the worst in Washington history.

In counterreaction the Nixon White House rounded up the Mayday protesters with actions later judged illegal, ordered Calley released from prison with the suggestion that the president would favorably review his conviction, tried to evict the VVAW from sleeping on the Mall, and secured an injunction to prevent the dissemination of the "Pentagon Papers" on the ground that their publication would hamper the president's ability to wage war. The pace of troop withdrawals also was stepped up.

In Paris, Henry Kissinger made a concession to the North Vietnamese: the U.S. would agree to withdraw its own troops without requiring a mutual withdrawal of northern troops from South Vietnam. In return Le Duc Tho suggested that the North would release American POWs as the last U.S. forces left the South, provided the U.S. would drop its insistence that the Thieu government lead the postwar political settlement of Vietnam. The talks broke down over the issue of support for the Thieu government. When Thieu removed Ky and General Duong Van Minh from the ballot of an interim election, it was clear the U.S. would not be able to budge

Thieu from the leadership prior to a total settlement. Thus stymied, Nixon and Kissinger turned for a solution in Vietnam to China and Russia.

In late 1968, Mao had beaten back the challenges to his own regime and had announced that China could learn to live peacefully with the United States. In early 1969, China initiated a series of border clashes with the U.S.S.R. These escalated so much that Soviet Marshal Grechko soon ranked China with Germany and the U.S. as major enemies of the Soviet Union. As more countries of the world normalized relations with China, the Sino-Soviet rift continued to widen. While pursuing China, the United States started up the SALT negotiations and moved toward long-term trade agreements with Russia. On March 15, 1971, the same day a crucial phase of SALT was resumed, Washington also lifted travel restrictions on American nationals who wanted to go to China. A Ping-Pong team made the journey. In September the SALT negotiations were concluded. By October of 1971, China had been admitted to the United Nations and Nixon had announced visits to both Moscow and Peking for 1972. As a consequence of all these moves, Moscow and Peking were asked to pressure Hanoi to end the war.

Even as the superpowers began negotiations, the war quietly widened. For some time the U.S. had been supporting anti-Communist forces in Laos. After the spring 1971 ARVN incursion into Laos, General Abrams cut down on his bombing support for the Laotian anti-Communist forces. Without air support, these government forces lost ground, and by late 1971 the Communists had extended their control from the Plain of Jars to many other portions of the country, leaving the government to hold only the western lowlands. The balance that had been maintained for years was tipped toward a Communist victory.

Less than 175,000 Americans remained in Vietnam, and most were support and logistics, not front-line grunts. Yet the Vietnam War had metastasized into an Indochina war. The various governments and rebels in the area—Vietnamese, Laotian, Cambodian—had more than two million men in their armies. In South Vietnam half the population sat in virtual military occupation over the other half; with a military economy, the country became wholly dependent on the American taxpayer. More than a half-million South Vietnamese had been killed since 1964; tens of thousands were dying in refugee camps and in cities where cholera, typhus, and other diseases stalked the choked streets.

As the agony went on, the Paris negotiations continued. In them, according to John Ehrlichman, Kissinger and Nixon would play "good guy, bad guy." Kissinger would say the North Vietnamese must deal with him, the reasonable man, or "this crazy fellow" Nixon would do something rash, such as unleash more bombs. In the winter of 1971, when the negotiations faltered, the "bad guy" ordered a carpet-bombing of the North, then revealed to the public that secret talks had been going on for two years but had proved fruitless. Certain that the president's scheduled visits to Moscow and Peking at midyear would force Hanoi to compromise, the administration sat back and waited for the North to respond.

The response was an invasion: on March 30, 1972, some 120,000 NVA regulars with tanks and rocket launchers swept down out of the DMZ and from Cambodia toward Saigon in an offensive that again caught American and ARVN forces by surprise. The invaders threatened Quang Tri in the north, Kontum in the Highlands, and An Loc in the south. When ARVN forces went to rescue those cities, VC regiments assaulted the Mekong Delta.

Reviving the "savage, punishing blows" scenario, Nixon sent waves of B-52s at the DMZ and at Hanoi, and had Kissinger warn Brezhnev personally that the U.S. would hold the Soviets responsible for the invasion. Nixon told aides in his newly bugged Oval Office, "The bastards have never been bombed like they're going to be bombed this time." In addition to the bombing, the president ordered the mining of Haiphong harbor, where Soviet supply ships were at anchor, and the bombing of rail lines that led from China into North Vietnam. In doing so he risked escalation of the conflict into a true global confrontation. For some days the threat of war between the superpowers hung over the world. Nixon's gamble was that Peking and Moscow would understand that détente could mean more to them than the continuation of aid to North Vietnam. The gamble worked. Soon Nixon was sipping vodka in Moscow and making plans to eat duck in Peking—while the blockade and the bombing continued.

Nixon had also gambled that Americans would flinch less when our bombs hit an enemy than they did when American soldiers were being killed—and he won that gamble, too. The American response to the bombing and blockade was muted and ineffective.

During the course of the summer of 1972 an ARVN counteroffensive and the intense and accurate American bombing, which included new "smart" bombs guided by television, turned the tide of the invasion. An estimated 100,000 Communist casualties were recorded along with 25,000

ARVN dead. By summer's end there was a virtual military stalemate. Experts such as British guerrilla-fighter Sir Robert Thompson now argued that the U.S. and South Vietnam could press their advantage and quickly win the war. Reports from the field showed that since all their seasoned troops had been killed, wounded, or captured, the NVA was fighting with teenagers.

Hurt by the failure of the offensive, and pressured by Moscow and Peking, North Vietnam began to negotiate in earnest. In three weeks the essential agreements were hammered out: within 60 days of a ceasefire all U.S. troops would be withdrawn and all POWs returned; a tripartite council of GVN, VC, and neutralists would then hold an election; should Thieu wish to be a candidate in it, he would first have to step down; several foreign powers would oversee the election and the maintenance of the agreement. No mention was made of withdrawal of any Communist troops from South Vietnam's soil. These were terms to which the United States could have agreed at any moment during the previous four years; Hanoi had given barely an inch.

Kissinger made ready to initial the agreement in Hanoi on October 22. But Thieu strenuously objected to the settlement, and Nixon decided to put off further action until he had a new elective mandate. In early November, after the landslide, Kissinger told Le Duc Tho to settle now, or all hell would break loose, and he told Thieu that the U.S. would if necessary settle without him. More negotiations followed, but by December, Kissinger had tired of their pace and he and Nixon decided on one last paroxysm of force. (Kissinger later wrote that he had not agreed to the Christmas bombing; Ehrlichman wrote that Kissinger had emphatically agreed to it.) Nixon told the new JCS Chairman, "I don't want any crap about the fact that we couldn't hit this target or that one. This is your chance to use military power to end this war." For twelve days near Christmas 1972, the U.S. dropped 36,000 tons of bombs—a destructive force well in excess of the power unleashed at Hiroshima—on Hanoi and Haiphong. It devastated factories, power plants, transport terminals, residential districts, and a hospital. There was an outcry the world over that the U.S. had become bloodthirsty and that the bombing was insensate; in fact, it was extremely accurate and not particularly bloody, for between one and two thousand people died in it—as many people had been killed in a single night during the 1940 German blitz of England. The bombing of Hanoi and Haiphong might have gone on longer than twelve days, except that the JCS, alarmed that we had lost so many B-52s in the raids, warned that the raids must stop or America's capacity to fight in the air elsewhere might soon be entirely crippled.

Though youth seemed to have given up their anger, congressmen were so incensed over the bombing that they indicated that when they reconvened they might well cut off military funds for the war. When on January 2, 1973, North Vietnam called for renewed talks, Washington immediately returned to the bargaining table, and after twelve days an agreement was reached. On January 14, 1973, the undeclared war between the United States and North Vietnam was over.

Some said the terms were fair, others said they bore no relation to the realities of the situation. A third group, primarily of the American military, pointed out that as the U.S. and the GVN now had the enemy on the run, the peace treaty managed to snatch political defeat from the jaws of military victory. Old China hand O. Edmund Clubb wrote in *The Nation* that the ceasefire terms reflected no new understanding of what had gone on during the years of war:

> The policymakers in Washington never really understood, from beginning to end, what the Indochinese revolution was all about—that it was inherently a *political*, not a military struggle. Blinded by this error, the United States tried to dominate and suppress the Indochinese revolutionaries—and failed ingloriously.

The agreement was formally signed January 27. Thieu never assented to it. Nonetheless, American forces were soon pulled out, and within a month there were ceasefires (of varying kinds) in Laos and in Cambodia, and the POWs returned home. Large U.S. forces remained on carriers and at nearby bases, and air strikes against Laos and Cambodia continued, as did military aid to anti-Communist forces throughout the region. Nixon wrote secretly to Thieu that he would respond with air power should the Communists move on Saigon, but in the summer of 1973, with Watergate scandal headlines all about, Congress curbed Nixon's ability to live up to his promise. The Case-Church amendment prohibited

> any funds whatsoever to finance directly or indirectly combat activities by the United States military forces in, over, or from off the shore of North Vietnam, South Vietnam, or Cambodia.

* * *

Also, over Nixon's veto, Congress passed the War Powers Act, which required a president to inform Congress within 48 hours of any deployment of U.S. forces and to withdraw such forces if in 60 days Congress had not endorsed their use.

Even if there would be little further U.S. help for South Vietnam, the GVN air force was the fifth largest in the world, and the ARVN had immense quantities of superior arms and a huge number of men. Battles continued at a pace similar to that which prevailed before U.S. involvement. During 1973 the Communists rearmed, began construction of a 25-foot-wide highway from the DMZ to within a few miles of Saigon, and turned Khe Sanh into a SAM (surface-to-air missile) base. Saigon's inflation rate reached 90 percent a year. The country's economy was in chaos, food supplies were inadequate, people left the country in droves, and desertion from the ARVN ranks reached 250,000 men a year. In August of 1974, just at the time Nixon was resigning, Congress cut back military aid to Vietnam to $700 million for fiscal 1975. This forced the dismantling of 11 of the GVN's 15 air squadrons, and mandated other equally debilitating cuts.

The final Communist onslaught began in early 1975. ARVN soldiers and air power managed to contain it for some time. But then the GVN made military blunders: it abandoned Hue and the Central Highlands. In the opinion of some military historians, had the government contested those areas, Saigon would not have fallen, and in light of the relative weakness of the NVA forces the GVN might even have won the war in 1975. Others feel that the GVN mistakes were inevitable, that a rout had been in the cards from the moment the United States pulled out, and that nothing could have prevented it.

By the end of 1975, South Vietnam, Laos, and Cambodia had all fallen to Communist forces. They toppled as if they were the dominoes the policy makers had imagined them to be in the years after World War II—but they fell as much from United States intervention as they did from outside Communist agitation.

In the late 1970s an entire symposium on the "lessons of Vietnam" focused on the need to redefine military policies and strategies. It charged that "inflexible" bureaucracies were responsible for "ineffective" work in Vietnam, and suggested the United States had to come up with new ways of dealing with Communist insurgencies around the world.

Ithiel de Sola Pool of MIT argued at the conference that "we were more culpable for our errors because we had greater freedom to act better," and implied that a totalitarian regime would have ignored the (democratic) restraints that stood in the way of military victory. The generals, foreign service officers, and military tacticians drew from the symposium one clear lesson: in the future, the U.S. must limit the use of American military power to situations in which it could be effective. Professor Earl Ravenal was in the minority when he observed:

> There is an implicit presumption here...that, had we learned those lessons, the campaign might have been more successful; and were we to learn those lessons we would avoid certain kinds of mistakes in the future....Whether we win or lose a war has a good deal to do not so much with the objectives that we hold for the war, as with something that goes beyond objectives. That is, not *what* we are trying to accomplish, but in a larger sense, *why* we are trying to accomplish it. When we begin to ask the question in that form, it seems that we are not yet clear about Vietnam.

What we tried to accomplish in Vietnam was the winning of a moral crusade to contain the spread of communism. Why we went into Vietnam was, primarily, to demonstrate our power. It was in Vietnam that the "what" and the "why" became confused, that the relationship between our morality and our power turned sour.

In 1927, Julien Benda wrote that Establishment intellectuals of his time had become moralists of realism. For them, acts which served the goals of power were invested with moral righteousness simply because they were associated with power. Much as Socrates had, Benda deplored this, for it meant that intellectuals were no longer upholding the autonomy of morality. Socrates had insisted that truth was absolute, that it could be defined, known, and agreed to by men. In his time the Sophists had argued that truth was relative, that it depended on a man's opinion. It is a short jump from "truth is relative" to the pragmatism of "might is right." Benda reasoned that when intellectuals became pimps for power, they replaced the autonomy of morality by the morality of power; then the exercise of power became its own justification and reward. In Vietnam the autonomy of our morality yielded to the morality of our power.

The antiwar consensus demonstrated that morality could be autonomous and need not inevitably yield to power. For instance, Henry Steele Commager pointed out to us that in other eras we had known some absolutes, some fixed concepts of the "good." Traditionally, he wrote, we had been committed to negotiating rather than resorting to force; in the nineteenth century we had been committed to supporting rather than to stifling revolutions; at Nuremberg we had established humane standards for the conduct of war and had prosecuted those who had not acted in accordance with our standards. In Vietnam we used force, stifled a revolution, and committed acts on the battlefield that we would have been punished for by hanging at the end of World War II. As a nation, Commager observed, we had been long committed to the supremacy of civil authority over the military, to an open government which accomplished its aims with a minimum of deceit and secrecy—yet during the Vietnam era "evasion, distortion, and duplicity" had become the "almost official policy of the government from the White House down through the whole executive department and military establishment." As a result, we paid a heavy price at home:

> Loss of faith in the integrity of our government; loss of confidence in the ability of the press and television to retain their independence; erosion of the guarantees of the Bill of Rights and of the habit of taking those rights for granted; and worst of all, perhaps, denial of that access to information which the Founding Fathers rightly deemed essential to the operations of a democratic society.

During the Vietnam War we claimed to love peace but caused great destruction; we claimed to champion democracy but backed corrupt and despotic governments; we claimed to value free speech but suppressed dissent. We championed morality and embraced a sordid reality—and when the war revealed that double standard, our claims to innocence, destiny, and moral superiority were shattered.

Philosopher Lionel Rubinoff suggests this happened because we tried to rationalize the irrational. When power erupts in massive bombings, napalm, and free-fire zones, it becomes an irrational destructive force that is characterized by the random way it spews death. In Vietnam we used not the rationalized retributive power of the state that we direct to execute a murderer, but the naked power which leveled a village without consideration of the villagers' individuality. Rubinoff calls such power not only irrational but pornographic, defining pornography as a perversion of a true act, a substitute form of gratification in which one "represents one's action as other than it is." During the war we consistently represented our actions as other than they were; when we wished to loose bombs to destroy the enemy before he could possibly destroy us, we called it a "protective reaction strike." Unable to use our great power because it was tied to the nuclear threat, we perverted it into a limited, ultraviolent war that in the end could be completed only by the defeat which our president called "peace with honor."

Some say we did not lose in Vietnam. They contend that we withdrew when in a position of strength, and thus we were never beaten on the battlefield. But we did lose in Vietnam. We were defeated on the battlefield because while we remained numerically superior, we did not win—and when we withdrew we did not achieve our objective, and in war that is tantamount to losing. We were defeated because our vaunted soldiers were stymied by enemy soldiers who were "inferior" to our own in every category except the will to prevail.

Evidence of our defeat showed in the shabby manner in which we greeted our returning Vietnam veterans. Never before in history had we turned our collective back so solidly on our soldiers, as if blaming them for the loss of Vietnam. We made them, if not scapegoats, then at least sacrificial ghosts; we did not wish to see them because they reminded us so forcefully of our failure.

Why have some people fought against admitting our defeat in Vietnam? Perhaps because we are a nation used to winning, and we do not like to admit a loss. Football coach George Allen's dictum that "Every time you lose, you die a little" expresses one of the truisms by which America lives. Certainly if we admit that we lost in Vietnam, we must admit that we died a little.

But death is a part of life, and if through being defeated in Vietnam we come now to accept this, it is only high time. To continue the football metaphor, it is usually those teams tempered in defeat who are fully mature. Perhaps in that sense the United States required a twentieth-century battlefield defeat. As a nation we had not been seriously hurt since the Civil War. In World War I, we missed most of the fighting. In World War II, Europe and Japan were destroyed, but our continental soil was not touched; in that war Russia lost 20 million people, and we lost half a million. Thus we had "won" many conflicts at the cost of only a small fraction of our resources. In Vietnam we were bloodied. Our allies learned to hate us, our people were confused and split, our economy was wrenched into a phase of ruinous and long-lasting inflation. The number of our soldiers killed was in a sense the least of our losses: more young American men were killed each year of the war on our highways than in combat in Vietnam. In Vietnam our national psyche was tainted, and our arrogance was humbled.

The Vietnam War showed us that we were not, *ipso facto*, morally superior to the rest of mankind. We could rationalize aggression with as much aplomb as had dictators and colonial powers of the past. We could be racist, we could blow away the gooks, slopes, and yellow-bellies with little regard for their humanity. We could terror-bomb. We could corrupt. We could call oligarchy democracy. We could do evil. Vietnam was an important—one hesitates to say "good"—defeat, for it exposed these rationalizations which in the heat of victory might have been reforged into certitudes.

The defeat in Vietnam made apparent to us that we could so bend the processes of our own governmental system as to come near being ruled by a home-grown oligarchy. All too often, during the Vietnam era, our military and political leaders acted without consultation of our representatives or of the citizenry. We had leaders who lied to us, who manipulated us, who stifled criticism in the name of patriotism. It was not precisely that we had been near a military *coup d'état*, but rather that an all-important power had been ceded into the hands of those who were in thrall to the military. As De Tocqueville had pointed out long ago, the military does not have to stage a coup in order to hold sway:

> War does not always give democratic societies over to military government, but it must invariably and immeasurably increase the powers of civil governments; it must automatically concentrate the direction of all men and control of all things in the hands of the government. If that does not lead men to despotism by sudden violence, it leads men gently in that direction by their habits.

In 1968 the United States had decided that it wanted out of the Vietnam quagmire, even at the cost of defeat. Such, surely, was the lesson of the year, and of Nixon's election. Yet the Nixon administration carried on the war four more years, at the cost of hundreds of thousands of lives and billions of dollars, in what must surely go down in history as the most avoidable destruction of the century.

The Nixon administration's actions were part of a pattern of abuse of power which had been growing since the start of the Second World War, so Johnson, Nixon, and their inner circles cannot shoulder all the blame for Vietnam. Throughout the long war the Congress (as a whole) did very little to curb presidential excesses or to protest the progress of the fighting, except to question its small details. Certainly during the Nixon years, there was no extensive agitation in Congress to speed the settlement process.

For quite some time after the war began the American populace remained complacent about it. Not many people were really aroused until late 1967 or 1968, and even when aroused, the citizenry did not make its wishes known in such a way as to halt the abuses of power or to curb the prolongation of the war. Docile, trusting, and basically of the same anti-Communist and military-solution beliefs as the policy makers, we as a people did little to stop the pornographic uses of our power in Vietnam, and so we must be judged as having collectively shared in the excesses of that power. We were caught in a paradox described succinctly by Emil Fackheim in 1948, after the fight against nazism:

> In the twentieth century, men—all of us—find themselves compelled to commit or condone evil, for the sake of preventing an evil believed to be greater. And the tragedy is that we do not know whether the evil we condone will not in the end be greater than the evil we seek to avert— or be identical with it.

This is one guess as to why the real debate over our Vietnam policy came very late in the conflict, and after a great deal of damage had already been done.

Late though it was, when it came that debate served purposes beyond the raising of important questions about the war. "The art of government is not to let men go stale," Napoleon wrote to Carnot, and the dissent on the war served just that purpose, to end the complacency with which we assented to the consensus foreign policy of the postwar years. Dissent helped us see that we had compromised the aura of invincibility, that we had made a mistake, that we had alienated our friends and made people hate us, that the war was having intolerable repercussions at home, that we needed to question seriously what our government was doing, that we could not realize our goals through military might. Dissent showed that the war was being lost, and that perhaps it ought to be lost because it was being waged for the wrong reasons against the wrong adversary at the wrong time.

Blaise Pascal wrote that we are made virtuous not by our love of virtue but "by the counterpoise of two opposite vices." The antiwar movement only revealed much truth to America when it went beyond conventional and polite dissent to become obnoxious and outspoken. Many times, in polls, Americans said they agreed with the dissenters' goals but found it hard to sympathize with the dissenters' methods. When the antiwar movement contended that the United States was rotten to the core and that the degradation of Vietnam was the only thing we could accomplish in the world, that was outrageous exaggeration. But perhaps we needed such demagogic exaggeration, for without shocking dissent the war would undoubtedly have gone on and on and on. By its stinging and often vitriolic dissent the antiwar movement gave to the country that "counterpoise of two opposite vices" which allowed us to come to our senses and to abandon the war—in fact, to lose the war—and thereby to achieve that return to stability and to a deeper virtue that was victory enough.

7 The Magnificent Bribe

In 1957, Dr. Harrison Brown of Cal Tech reported the conclusions of many scientists and engineers in a book entitled *The Next Hundred Years*:

> If we are able in the decades ahead to avoid thermonuclear war, and if the present underdeveloped areas of the world are able to carry out successful industrialization programs, we shall approach the time when the world will be completely industrialized. And as we continue along the path we shall process ores of continually lower grade, until we finally sustain ourselves with materials obtained from the rocks of the earth's crust, the gases of the air, and the waters of the sea.

Predictions of technological utopia were common in the postwar years. The forecast for tomorrow—other than the possibility of a mushroom cloud looming up unexpectedly—seemed rosy. If there was something we couldn't accomplish now, we could certainly do it within ten or twenty years, or at the latest by the turn into the twenty-first century. We were using the chemical insecticide DDT to eradicate malaria, transforming many previously uninhabitable places around the globe into safe and productive areas. We were working to eliminate smallpox. We were about to discover not one, but two "vaccines" for polio. We were augmenting the world's food supply. The Pill was under development. Computers were just coming into their own. The new "science" of systems management was revolutionizing business. Leisure time was being filled with television, instant photography, swift airplanes, and the like. In terms of our consumption of electricity, natural resources, and calories, and in terms of how little manual labor we performed, and in terms of our increased good health and life-spans—as well as our mobility, communications, and possessions—we enjoyed a standard of living previously known only by pharaohs and other godlike rulers.

Former Interior Secretary Stewart Udall also recalled this period:

> Whatever was technically feasible would (we believed) ultimately be economically affordable; because of cheap energy, unlimited economic expansion and global industrialization seemed to be rational goals.

The only thing holding us from instantly achieving technological nirvana was the shortage of trained scientists and engineers. The 1960 Rockefeller Panel on National Goals endorsed the idea of a "supertechnology" world in which the United States would continue to play the leading role. A 1962 National Academy of Sciences panel recommended to President Kennedy that the country shift away from a philosophy of conserving scarce resources (which policy had been recommended to Truman by a commission ten years earlier) and pursue the "wise management of plenty." New breakthroughs had already allowed mankind to provide "dramatic increases" in food and energy for the world; and in the future, should we run out of a basic resource, the NAS panel thought that technology would come forth with a better and probably cheaper substitute. Such a "belief in omnipotent science," Udall later wrote, "shaped efforts and expectations, both in Washington and in the country as a whole."

Udall might as well have written that it shaped all of Western society. Historian Lynn White, Jr., later traced our attitude directly to the Judaeo-Christian "traditional" attitude toward the earth and its creatures. As expostulated in Genesis 1: 28, man is commanded to

> be fruitful and multiply, and fill the earth and subdue it, and have dominion over the fish of the sea and over the birds of the air and over every living thing that moves upon the earth.

White wrote that in the Christian tradition man was at the center of the universe, and as a consequence felt he could "exploit nature in a mood of indifference to the feelings of natural objects." This expression of superiority and indifference typified the worst excesses of the Protestant ethic as each man felt able to war against others and against his environment to achieve and consume more worldly goods than his neighbor. For the Puritan, the physical surround was to be disregarded; life was a matter between a man and his God—and so a man's body, his fellow creatures, even the temporal world about him were secondary to goals of the spirit. All that mattered was progress toward an ultimate heaven.

Progress was an idea central to the American identity. For three hundred years, America had been the place on earth where the frontier was continually conquered. The direct descendant of the lone pioneer who went into the primeval forest to hew a home for himself was the rugged individualist. American men had confronted the wilderness and had made it "work." We hacked down trees, dug coal, conquered distance with railways and telephones, used every machine we could invent or find. The notion of interchangeable parts was conceived in Europe but was first put into practice by Americans in the nineteenth century. We were the first people to take to the assembly line—to produce automobiles that transformed our society. We were the first to use electricity extensively to raise the level of comfort of both urban and rural populations. We were the first to use our scientists to tame and direct the force of the atom. A relatively new country (by world standards), and one not encumbered by tradition, we developed a love of innovation and an admiration for all things new. We were the masters of know-how; give us a problem, we would say "can do" and invent a device to "fix" it. We put much energy into developing technology to produce more goods for less money with less physical labor. It was only fitting that the country that in the 1950s many people were already describing as entering the postindustrial society, should believe deeply in progress—and in progress as measured through material goods.

"Progress is our most important product." That was how actor Ronald Reagan summed up our aims in the 1950s, when he was the television spokesman for General Electric. We came to understand the slogan in its larger context to mean that the production of newer, more efficient, more ingenious household gadgetry—or faster cars—or better medicines—was leading toward the ultimate perfection of mankind.

French philosopher Jacques Ellul was appalled that technology seemed likely to define man's future. The villain, he thought, was *la technique*, which he defined as "the totality of methods rationally arrived at and having absolute efficiency...in every field of human activity." Efficiency was the key: it was more efficient to know how to make fire than to carry it, more efficient to use an automobile than to use a horse, more efficient to use an atomic bomb than to use a howitzer. *La technique* was leading to man's subjugation of self to the larger community, to behavior modification, to systems management—as well as to the more obvious "machine transformations" of natural resources such as the undue reliance on electric power with all its comforts. *Technique* was the source of alienation, the source of the increasing dichotomy between the haves and the have-nots of the world.

Ellul worried that technique was self-aggrandizing and drew everything into its orbit. People wanted ever-more-sophisticated refrigerators—and so, as time went on, refrigerators began to include water faucets and other kitchen gadgets. People who had no refrigerators envied those who had simple ones, and those who had simple ones envied those with fancier ones—and deprivation came to be measured on a scale of the possession of technology. Our civilization seemed committed to the continual enhancement of the means without taking into account the aims. *Technique* was the ultimate means: in fact, *technique* transformed means into ends. "Know-how" became prized for itself, not for what it could accomplish. Rationality disappeared. We made faster racing cars and 100-story buildings because we could; we built atomic bombs because we feared others might do so first; and we spent $25 billion on a project to send a man to the moon—because we wanted to attempt the impossible. *Technique*, wrote Ellul, "transforms everything it touches into a machine," and then "integrates the machine into society."

City planner and historian of science Lewis Mumford didn't term all technology bad—just that part of technology which was not life-enhancing. He divided "technics" into two categories: those that were "democratic," by which he meant humanitarian, small-scale, craft-oriented, and good for people; and those that were "authoritarian" and led inevitably to the control of man. He believed we had a predominance of authoritarian technics in our lives—not just atomic bombs but also such economic entities as factories, which were as coercive as armies. Mumford wrote that mechanization, automation, and cybernetic direction were "marvelously dynamic and productive," able to greatly conserve manual labor and ease life for millions. But the bargain they offered to the community was "a magnificent bribe." By accepting the bribe, every member of the community might claim every material advantage, every intellectual and emotional stimulus he may desire, in quantities hardly available hitherto even for a restricted minority: food, housing, swift transportation, instantaneous communication, medical care, entertainment, education. But on one condition: that one must not merely ask for nothing that the system does not provide, but likewise agree to take everything offered, duly processed and fabricated, homogenized and equalized, in the precise quantities that the system, rather than the person, requires.

As we entered the Decade of Shocks, most people realized that we had already accepted the magnificent bribe—but we did not fully understand the price we might soon have to pay. Our standard of living, five times higher than the world's average, was predicated on a per capita consumption of energy six times higher than the world's average. We saw nothing wrong in that. Since Edison had perfected the lightbulb in 1879, our demand for electric power had doubled every ten years. Our society was besotted with electrically run devices, and we had made many accommodations to them. For instance, as engineer Roy V. Hudson reflected,

> The air conditioner was a boon to the worker who had to spend hot summers in a city office building. Since open windows lead to inefficiencies in the use of air conditioners, architects built structures with windows that didn't open. Such buildings were also cheaper and stayed cleaner. But without air conditioning, these offices are unbearable in summer. So the electric utilities are forced to increase generating capacity to meet the air conditioning demand. This inevitably results in more thermal pollution and probably in greater air pollution. All because we tried to better the worker's standard of living.

Raising the standard of living could lead to more than pollution. At 5:11 o'clock, during the evening of November 9, 1965, there was an unexpected power surge through one of the small relays of the Sir Adam Beck hydroelectric station just west of Niagara Falls in Canada. The device had been set for 1963 load demands, and had not been reset in two years. When the surge came, a circuit breaker was tripped and cut out the line, which overloaded other lines at the station; this, in turn, overloaded lines throughout Ontario and sent the power southward; a cascading overload effect knocked out the generating stations, the lights, and everything else dependent upon electric power in an 80,000-square-mile area of the north-eastern United States and two Canadian provinces. Overall, thirty million people were affected by the Great Northeast Blackout of 1965.

Some 800,000 commuters were trapped in subways, in trains, and on elevators. Office equipment froze. Factories stopped. The contents of freezers thawed. Airplanes landed by the grace of a full moon. Stores shut down and some were looted. Prisoners rioted. Panic-stricken people jammed the still-working telephone lines, looking for information and for reassurance. Television sets went blank; traffic lights went black. There were massive traffic jams in cities, and these and other blackout-related problems were eventually solved by ordinary people with flashlights and candles. Within the area of the blackout, and until power was restored the following day, modern civilization came grinding to a halt.

It was as if the alarm clock had rung on the American dream, but most people simply pushed the "snooze" button and settled back into comfortable sleep. Americans railed against our mechanized and electrified civilization, but when power had been restored for a few weeks they put the candles away in drawers and forgot where they had put them. As *The New York Times* put it, we were all "recaptured and brought back submissively to the prison farm of modern technology."

At that moment in 1965, all future housing projects in New York were scheduled to be heated and cooled by electricity. Many people were already living in all-electric houses. The trend was toward continued increase in the use of electric power. That year, the Federal Power Commission reported that utility regions of the country had an average 23 percent reserve margin of power. When the reserve dropped below the 20 percent mark, the FPC warned, shortages might occur. In the ensuing years, 8 percent and 10 percent drops in power generation occurred quite regularly; during these "brownouts," power flowed at a reduced rate, causing machines to stutter and lights to dim. Each brownout was a new warning signal but was treated rather as an inconvenience. For a time the regions borrowed power from one another. During one summer crisis New York's salvation came from the Tennessee Valley Authority. Soon, however, all the regions' demands were so high that the borrowing had to stop.

The federal government and private utilities had seen the soaring demand curve and had extrapolated from it the potential need for electric power. They tried to prepare for increased demand. The problem was that they had pinned their hopes for the future on the generation of electricity by the use of atomic power.

In the early 1960s the Atomic Energy Commission projected that by the year 2000 half of all the electric power in the country would be generated from nuclear fuel. This use of the "peaceful atom" would help to conserve fossil-fuel resources. At that time 43 percent of the country's electric power was obtained from oil-powered generators, 33 percent from gas, 19 percent from coal, and 4–5 percent from hydroelectric dams; in other words, 95 percent of the power was being generated by nonrenewable fossil-fuel resources.

The start-up costs to generate electricity by use of nuclear fuel were inordinately high; nevertheless, the need for power was so great that by 1966 half of the new generators being built or in the planning stages in the United States were nuclear. Most of these were "light water" reactors which used uranium fuel much in the way conventional plants used fossil fuels. Since it took relatively little uranium to operate these plants, it was hoped they would soon be cost-effective, even with their large start-up charges. There were even greater hopes for the "breeder" reactor; this device would generate electricity, but at the same time, through a complicated series of chemical and radiation reactions, it would generate more fuel than it used up. The breeder was potentially the most economical way of obtaining electric power. The first such breeder was the Enrico Fermi plant, on Lake Erie between Detroit and Toledo, and it began operation at low power levels in January of 1966.

But in the years between 1949 and 1966, during which nuclear electric power generators had been tested, there had been nine serious reactivity accidents. Fuel cores had been destroyed or seriously damaged; three of the reactors had been permanently shut down. However, because of the positive publicity efforts of the nuclear industry, the Atomic Energy Commission, and all others concerned with nuclear electric power, the public knew little of these accidents.

The fuel core at the Enrico Fermi breeder plant contained about a half-ton of U-235, or enough fissonable material to make forty Hiroshima-sized atomic bombs. Near three in the afternoon of October 5, 1966, the power coming out of the Enrico Fermi reactor suddenly doubled. Radiation alarms went off in the plant and in sheriffs' offices around the area. Something was wrong with the reactor, and the temperature kept rising. Automatic devices sealed off the buildings. Six safety rods were with difficulty inserted into the core, and the chain reaction was halted, rendering the plant inoperable. Police officers who had been on the verge of trying to evacuate the entire city of Detroit were told that the emergency was over and that the danger was past.

In fact, an enormous disaster had been narrowly averted. A portion of the core had melted down. Had more of it melted, the containment vessel might not have held; in that case there might have been a "China syndrome" (in which the core could melt deep into the earth), and great quantities of radiation would have been released to the atmosphere. These were not incredibly remote possibilities, but near ones. As one chastened observer concluded, "We almost lost Detroit."

It took investigators a year to figure out that a small piece of internal coating had come loose in the reactor and had blocked the action of a coolant. That had allowed the temperature to rise so quickly. For several years the reactor was out of commission, and eventually it was dismantled. The AEC did not commission any other breeders for some time—but the AEC also publicly dismissed the Fermi accident as minor.

According to a secret AEC report which summed up experience with working reactors to 1972, among 30 reactors there had been 850 "abnormal occurrences," 40 percent of them due to design and manufacturing errors, 60 percent attributable to operator error and faulty maintenance. Five of the 30 reactors were experimental prototypes that failed and were shut down; another two were experimental models never designed to produce power; one, Elk River, was shut down in 1969 after a series of quality-control problems. In addition to the "abnormal," there were such "normal" occurrences as the loss to the air, by a California nuclear plant in 1967 and 1968, of 900,000 curies of radioactive gases; these releases were within the AEC's permissible limits but were considered by many scientists to be vastly excessive and dangerous.

Nuclear electric power was the ultimate technological fix—the way to have enough generating capacity to fill the needs of the ever-more-modern world. But the Fermi accident, and the other accidents, emissions, and problems with storing wastes that would remain radioactive for thousands of years, etc., confirmed the fears that nuclear electric power was neither so simple nor so safe as scientists, utility people, and government bureaucrats had told us to believe. If we were to have nuclear electric power, it was now clear, we would have to live with certain risks: that was our Faustian bargain.

We had made lesser bargains in the past—some, we had hardly been aware of making. We had, for example, welcomed the automobile with undisguised pleasure, as in this rosy forecast in a 1899 issue of the *Scientific American*:

The improvements in city conditions by the general adoption of the motor car can hardly be overestimated. Streets clean, dustless and odorless, with light rubber-tired vehicles moving swiftly and noiselessly over the smooth expanse, would eliminate a greater part of the nervousness, distraction and strain of modern metropolitan life.

Cars had brought many unanticipated problems and precious little relief. They had also caused some irrevocable damage, a fact just coming to light in the 1960s. Examples of other fallout from civilization's progress also were coming to public attention with great frequency at that time, perhaps because the damage had become so great in certain instances that it could no longer be ignored.

Case in point, Lake Erie, the huge inland sea around which 13 million people lived. Millions of cars were forged in the lake's border cities of Detroit and Toledo. Much of the auto industry's garbage found its way into the lake; so did agricultural fertilizers and chemicals; so did uncounted tons of raw sewage; so did the detritus of many generations of gas- and oil-fired boats. By the mid-1960s Lake Erie's swimming beaches were closed; sewage floated in plain sight of them; mounds of algae and decaying fish piled up on its shores. Oil discharged into its tributary river, the Rouge, periodically burst into flames. The fish catch dropped to nil. The lake could no longer be used for fresh water. Scientists called Lake Erie's disease eutrophication: overfertilization had caused tremendous algae growth, and a lack of oxygen at the bottom killed small insects and animals, which, in turn, caused the starvation and destruction of the fish population. The lake had "aged" far beyond the capabilities of science to reverse the process. It could still be used as a dumping ground, but for little else. Many said the death of Lake Erie had been inevitable, part of the price we paid for progress.

The price of other aspects of our progress was still being determined. For instance, chemical fertilizers. Since 1940, by making possible a higher yield per acre, chemical fertilizers had allowed the United States to take out of cultivation some 50 million acres of farmland. Through the use of chemicals, we could feed our expanding population and still export food to the rest of the world. Chemical fertilizers came under attack as prime villains in eutrophication and were also implicated in the poisoning of some water supplies.

The partner of the chemical fertilizers was the insecticide DDT, which protected crops by killing pests. In 104 countries and tropical territories around the world DDT also was used to kill anopheles mosquitoes in order to stamp out malaria. As a prophylaxsis against the swamp disease, DDT had been phenomenally effective. In Ceylon, for instance, there had been two million cases of malaria annually; in 1963, after a few years of DDT spraying, there were only 17 cases. By the mid-1960s, malaria had been all but wiped out in several dozen countries.

But around the same time, scientists began to find disturbing evidence that those very properties of DDT which made it an effective insecticide— its stability, mobility, and insolubility in water—also made it dangerous to other forms of life. DDT in agricultural runoff was affecting reptiles, birds, and small animals. Since DDT concentrated as it went up the food chain, from insect to fish to fish hawk, the successively higher concentrations were killing some larger animals and were affecting the ability of others to reproduce.

Birds that had ingested DDT in quantity were laying eggs with thinner shells. These eggs could not withstand the process of incubation as well as thicker-shelled eggs could, and as a consquence populations of peregrine falcons, hawks, eagles, and other birds of prey were rapidly diminishing. A number of species were declared "endangered," or facing the possibility of extinction. DDT was discovered in the fat of Antarctic penguins, and in the fat of Arctic Eskimos. DDT was tested and found carcinogenic when ingested in high concentrations. It also was suspected of having deleterious genetic effects in animals and possibly in man.

Looking at the evidence, many scientists agreed with the position of Dr. Charles F. Wurster, who wrote:

> I have been studying the effects of DDT on birds and other organisms for some time and I have long been convinced that we must stop its use completely in the United States because it is harmful to birds, fish, and other wildlife, because it is a hazard to human health, and because adequate or superior alternatives are available.

These alternatives were the use of less hazardous compounds, and the substitution of "natural" predators for the chemical insecticide.

Not everyone agreed with Wurster's position—not even all scientists. For instance, Dr. Norman E. Borlaug, Nobel laureate for developing the strains of cereals that fostered the "Green Revolution," wrote that he had seen people try to use natural predators in place of DDT and fail miserably.

When the World Health Organization tested 1,400 chemical compounds to find those safer and more efficient than DDT in combating malaria, they could find none. When DDT use was stopped in Ceylon in 1966, malaria sprang back to epidemic proportions by 1969—two million cases a year.

Dr. Borlaug wrote that there was no conclusive proof that DDT was genetically harmful to humans. Furthermore, if it had thinned bird egg-shells, well, bird populations had also dropped precipitously in the 1880s and 1890s because of "human encroachment," and 99 percent of all the species that had ever lived on the earth had sooner or later become extinct. Weighed against DDT's contribution to the world, the loss of several bird species had to be seen as of small consequence. One-half the earth's population was starving, Borlaug wrote, and a large portion of the other half was malnourished. The Green Revolution would help feed people, but its continued success hinged upon

> whether agriculture will be permitted to use the inputs—agricultural chemicals—including chemical fertilizers and pesticides, both absolutely necessary to cope with hunger. If agriculture is denied their use...then the world will be doomed but not by chemical poisoning, but from starvation.

Because of DDT's great value to the world in terms of lives saved, its environmental consequences could perhaps be borne—but what of other products of the technological era? Our economic growth following World War II was heavily tied to the use of technologically intensive products such as nonreturnable soda bottles, synthetic fibers, air-conditioner units, household gadgets, and consumer electronics. Food and clothing production had risen at the same rate as the population, but the production of technologically intensive products was sky high. Biologist Barry Commoner pointed out that these new products were not only technologically intensive but also pollution-intensive—that is, they produced more waste and potentially harmful byproducts than previous products. Commoner showed that the new technologies had replaced natural products with synthetic ones:

> Soap powder has been displaced by synthetic detergents; natural fibers (cotton and wool) have been displaced by synthetic ones; steel and lumber have been displaced by aluminum, plastics, and concrete; railroad freight

has been displaced by truck freight....On the farm...fertilizer has replaced land. Older methods of insect control have been displaced by synthetic insecticides such as DDT, and for controlling weeds the cultivator has been displaced by the herbicide spray. Range-feeding of livestock has been displaced by feedlots.

All this "progress" had greatly increased the impact of man on his environment. Just how large the impact really was had not yet become known: understanding would come after a series of shocking accidents and incidents.

In March of 1967 the 974-foot "jumboized" oil tanker *Torrey Canyon* struck a reef 16 miles off the southwest corner of England and spilled 118,000 tons of oil into the sea. The ship had been sailing from southern Africa toward England, under a Liberian flag, though it was owned by a cardboard Bermuda company and an American oil giant. It was the largest tanker ever to be wrecked, and the great volume of oil it carried created a large-scale disaster. Beaches of Cornwall in England, Brittany in France, and—three weeks later—Cape Cod and New Jersey in the United States were all heavily polluted. The Royal Air Force had to bomb the wreck to finish it off and to burn up some of the 30 million gallons of spilled oil. Beach clean-up efforts involved thousands of people and hundreds of thousands of gallons of detergents. Scientists began to speak of the destruction of the infinitesimally small phytoplankton, organisms which are the food for much larger life in the sea.

In the three previous years 91 tankers had been stranded and 238 involved in collisions; a potentially serious accident to a tanker occurred once every two weeks. The next year, 1968, the Liberian-flag tanker *Ocean Eagle* broke in two off San Juan, and the Greek tanker *General Coloctronis* foundered off the Bahamas; both caused large oil spills. Crossing the Atlantic in a small craft a while later, Thor Heyerdahl observed:

> Clots of oil are polluting the midstream current of the Atlantic Ocean from horizon to horizon....During 27 days of sailing so far, oil lumps in varying quantities have been observed every day....It is entirely possible that the pollution area spans the entire ocean, from the coast of Africa to the coast of tropical America.

Scientists had long warned that the routine pumping of oil and gas from offshore wells presented far more possibilities of spills and accidents than did the oil tankers. Despite such warnings, and ignoring pleas for the creation of a series of marine sanctuaries in the Santa Barbara channel area, the Department of the Interior leased much of the oil-rich continental shelf there to a consortium of American oil companies. The reason was money. Leases there brought the U.S. Treasury $61 million, and revenues to the government for 1968 from the shelf brought in another $600 million, plus a one-sixth royalty on the market price of each barrel of oil sold. California officials who had at first objected to the drilling were assured by the federal government and the private companies that the technological devices for preventing accidents at the wells were foolproof.

On January 28, 1969, six miles offshore in the Santa Barbara channel, a rig erupted. When operators withdrew a dulled drill bit to replace it with a sharp one, high pressure from the undersurface deposit forced oil and gas sideways through fissures and out through cracks in the ocean floor. Hot crude oil bubbled to the surface and made an 800-mile-long slick on the water. Altogether, 235,000 gallons of oil escaped—far less than the 30 million gallons released by the *Torrey Canyon*—but the tides concentrated the oil along a heavily populated 80-mile-wide stretch of shoreline, where it produced considerable damage and consternation. Beaches, marine life, and a luxurious style of living were affected. For months, oil companies daily sent their employees to clean up the residue on the beaches. Pleasure boats were befouled. Animals ranging from barnacles to sea lions died in great numbers. However, because of the narrow area of the spill, the overall population of the animals was soon able to recover.

Again, scientists advanced explanations about the fragility of the balance of nature, the interconnectedness of the various plants and animals, the food chain: all were affected by the oil spill.

Public outcry over the spill was large and sustained; there was major coverage by television news units, newspapers, magazines. The notion of "ecology" began to filter out from the realm of science and take up residence in the mind of the lay person. In the Santa Barbara incident, Americans could see how their environment could be affected by what was, after all, a relatively small technological mishap.

It took twelve days and 900 sacks of cement to cap the well. After that was done, the danger continued, for 68 small earthquakes had been recorded in the area in the preceding year, and a new one might dislodge the cement cap or force the oil and gas out from another exit on the sea floor.

When the spill occurred, newly appointed Secretary of the Interior

Walter Hickel flew over the site and announced that drilling here and on 70 adjacent sites would be suspended. A few days later he was astounded to find that bureaucrats in his own department had allowed the oil companies to quietly resume pumping in all but one damaged site. In California the consortium led by Union Oil, which owned the well, paid property owners $4.5 million in damages and various city and county entities another $9 million. However, the Santa Barbara municipal court dismissed 342 counts against the companies and allowed them to plead guilty to one: each company was fined $500 for "criminal pollution." President Nixon appointed a panel to look into the spill, but it consisted only of Interior men and oil industry officials. They blamed the spill not on technological malfeasance but on unanticipated quirks of Mother Nature, and said the best way to prevent future spills was to deplete the reservoirs of subsurface oil—in other words, to pump out the oil, a process which would take ten years and in the interim would not appreciably lessen the possibility of new spills. Hickel later concluded that there was "some truth" in the allegations that the Department of the Interior was "in the pocket of big business."

The ultimate lesson of Santa Barbara was not about technology but about oil. At great expense and with the newest techniques, oil had been sought and pumped in the Santa Barbara channel because other, more easily accessible sites and supplies were rapidly diminishing. In the postwar years the United States had a surplus of oil. In 1957, when the Suez Canal had been seized, the U.S. had so much reserve oil that we not only weathered the shortage but also managed to export enough oil to cover the needs of our European allies. In the intervening years we had given oil producers generous depletion allowances and had given domestic producers incentives to get rid of their oil. We became seduced by the low price of imported oil, and increasingly dependent upon supplies from the Middle East. The Arab-Israeli war of 1967 put a crimp in our supplies, and the requirements of the Vietnam War dented them severely. We no longer had a surplus of oil. A few warnings were raised, to the effect that we were becoming vulnerable to oil, and that we must realize that worldwide deposits of oil were finite.

The finite nature of all our resources was emphasized in one of the era's most striking images, the photograph taken by an early Apollo mission which showed the "whole earth." Vibrant with color, dominated by the blue oceans, the planet floats in a dark void, beautiful, breathtaking and yet a bit frightening to behold, for the huge expanse of the oceans emphasizes the tininess of the continents. Nothing of man's civilization can be seen. From a hundred thousand miles up, even the atmosphere is invisible.

In 1969 the American space program was about to put a man on the moon, to fulfill the age-old dream of breaking the physical bonds which tied man to the earth. To make the voyage possible it had taken $25 billion, the efforts of 20,000 companies and 300,000 workers, the will of 200 million people. It also took, rocket designer Werner von Braun suggested, the contemporaneous maturation of the technologies of computers, microelectronics, rocket propulsion, and advanced communications. Apollo 11's task was not only to bring back a few rocks and soil samples, Von Braun said on the eve of the launch; rather, the whole expedition was the ultimate expression of the human urge to transcend our own limits.

The space program had had its share of accidents. During the decade problems plagued nearly every space shot. Some 20,000 malfunctions were recorded; the most tragic was the 1967 fire on the launching pad which killed astronauts Virgil Grissom, Ed White, and Roger Chaffee. That accident shut down manned space flights for 21 months. After it, some in the community of engineers and technicians who made up the space program heaved an anguished sigh of relief: they knew the program had been pushed too far too fast, and believed the accident had been almost statistically inevitable. After it, there could be, and were, thorough reevaluations of every minute part of the machines and systems designed to take men to the moon.

The space program helped compress technological developments and innovations; what might otherwise have taken a quarter-century was accomplished in about ten years. The culmination of all the effort came in July of 1969. In a feat which held the rapt attention of more than 500 million people around the globe, the United States landed the Apollo 11 *Eagle* and two astronauts on the surface of the moon, and shortly thereafter brought them back to safe landing on earth. Man set foot on another planetary body: this was eloquent testimony to the greatness of the powers which man had manufactured for himself. Through technology, man had extended himself to the heavens.

"We came in peace for all mankind," read the plaque which the astronauts left on the moon's surface. But the triumph was a purely American exploit, as much a consequence of our frontier-conquering, nature-dominating mythology as it was an outgrowth of the politico-military race to beat the Russians in the Cold War. Though by winning the race we merely did what we had been expected to do by the rest of the world, most Americans agreed that the race had been worth running and that we could not have afforded to lose.

Widening the triumph to include all mankind was never truly considered. We rejected possible cooperation with the Russians; Congress, in fact, specifically forbade it. We also rejected the idea that the flight be placed under the aegis of the United Nations, or even that a UN flag be placed on the moon—Congress also expressly forbade that. Going to the moon was a secular and provincial triumph.

After we landed on the moon, there seemed nowhere else to go. We had wanted to see if the feat could be accomplished. Once over, the great adventure did not spur us on to further journeys or to much greater utilization of space. We could send a man to Mars and back—it was technologically feasible, but it would take a generation. We could build a permanent station in space, but what for? After the landing, interest in the space program declined precipitously; NASA's budget had already been cut before the landing. It was an acknowledgment that more acute problems still remained on earth.

In the heyday of the space program the question was often asked: If we could put a man on the moon, why couldn't we solve the problems of our decaying cities? Going to the moon was a task capable of definition and accomplishment by technological means alone. To do the job we already possessed a backlog of know-how, decades of education in science and technology, a governmental bureaucracy that could control the process, and large companies that were oriented toward accomplishing technological feats. To resuscitate a city was a more complex task, and one less susceptible to solution through technological fixes. Efficiency, the watchword of *la technique*, would not suffice to rejuvenate a city.

And so going to the moon was a turning point for the United States. Perhaps only by actually going there, by spending all that money and by making that tremendous effort, could it become possible for us to wonder whether technology had taken us as far as it could, to question whether technology could ever do more for humanity than it already had. So what if a few men had kissed the sky and set foot on the moon? The vast majority of people felt themselves more than ever tied to the earth, to their homes, their societies, their bodies.

Charles Lindbergh, himself a pioneer some fifty years before the Apollo 11 astronauts, reflected on the new voyage. It was, he wrote, a part of man's history of extending his awareness outward through the universe by the use of technological devices. But Lindbergh felt that the "assistance" received from such technological devices was countered

> by restrictions they place upon us, and the same scientific knowledge that constructs our spacecraft informs us of apparently insurmountable physical limits. We find the speed of light and the vastness of space to be incompatible with biological time. We begin to realize that a point arrives after which the distraction and destruction caused by technological enterprise reduce man's awareness. We become apprehensive of the direction in which our twentieth-century heading leads. Is it toward an affluent and spiritual utopia or a bleak dead end?

The gathering realization of the limits of technology came at the same time as, and was a part of, the explosion of concern about the environment which erupted as the 1960s ended and the 1970s began. "Ecology"— roughly, the study of the links among all forms of life on earth—covered many emerging worries about pollution, about the exploitation and rapid depletion of natural resources, the degradation of many facets of the environment, the endangerment of various animal species.

Television cameras went to garbage dumps and examined the heaps as if they were new phenomena. Our eyes were opened to all sorts of possibilities—mostly dark—which we had never before considered. An electric toothbrush could be seen as utilitarian, but also as a waster of precious energy. Smoke billowing from factory stacks had been a symbol of economic health; now we saw smoke as a pollutant which endangered the community's physical health and the beauty of the countryside. Many values were shifting. Lead had been what made engines run smoothly; now we began to realize it was a lethal element which when emitted from cars could poison a child's lungs. Seat belts became articles of faith. Cars were, as Ralph Nader wrote, "unsafe at any speed." Even the most seemingly innocuous articles were found to be potentially dangerous: who could have imagined, when pressing the button on a deodorant can, that he or she was releasing aerosol propellant which when it reached the upper atmosphere was compromising our envelope of air?

It was a deep shock for us to discover that the world was polluted and that our resources were dwindling fast, a shock akin to that experienced when a person finds out his body no longer moves with the fluidity he had in his youth. We were aghast to learn at what high cost nature had been dominated and frontiers conquered.

For years, doom-sayers had been prophesying a time when the earth would smother in its own rubbish, or overpopulate to the point of starvation, or burn up its resources so that machine-age civilization would end abruptly. Most Americans had always believed these possibilities to be remote. But as more and more examples of pollution, exploitation, and degradation came to light, we could no longer ignore the evidence nor the possibilities of destruction they suggested.

To sum up the danger dramatically, people cited a French riddle for children. It was an explanation for exponential growth, and the suddenness with which such growth approached a fixed limit:

> Suppose you own a pond on which a water lily is growing. The lily plant doubles its size each day. If the lily were allowed to grow unchecked, it would completely cover the pond in 30 days, choking off other forms of life in the water. For a long time the lily plant seems small, and so you decide not to worry about cutting it back until it covers half the pond. On what day will that be? On the twenty-ninth day, of course. You have one day to save your pond.

It seemed to be dawning on more and more people—most of them young—that the twenty-ninth day was fast approaching.

Such an awareness underlay the celebration of the first "Earth Day" on April 22, 1970. In the United States, demonstrations and rallies were held in many cities, and projects as diverse as the generation of solar power, the closing of urban streets to automobiles, and the instigation of recycling efforts for paper products were celebrated. Diverse speakers blamed the present sad condition of the environment on politicians, technology, overpopulation, businessmen's greed, man's innate aggressiveness, and excessive American affluence.

These villains seemed most villainous to the young, who were already quite dissatisfied with the society they saw around them, but there was enough villainy to go around. Everyone was able to point the finger at everyone else and to say, only quietly, *mea culpa*.

In succeeding months and years there was a frenzy of standard setting, regulation, damage assessment, legislation, and lawsuits. Each member of Congress had a pollutant axe to grind. The orgy of regulation-making produced a hopeless jumble for businessmen, government bureaucrats, and consumers alike—but there were some successes. The air, the water, and even some of the land became cleaner. A technique was evolved that would allow coal to be strip-mined and then the "overburden" of topsoil replaced so no unsightly scars were left on the landscape. There was research into recycling. Demonstration projects used garbage for fuel.

The principal pollution targets were the most visible: the local belching smokestack, or the local discharge of untreated sewage. But such problems, argued Denis Hayes of the Worldwatch Institute, were simply "those that appeared most solvable," and whose solutions were technical:

> Devices have been attached to automobile exhaust pipes, to industrial chimneys, to sewage pipes—all in an effort to remove certain pollutants from the effluent. The pollutants thus removed have not always been the most dangerous, but they have been the most "removable." For example, the large particles in industrial smoke are now routinely removed, but small particulates—which are more hazardous but more difficult to control—are still emitted in large quantities. The tonnage of pollution has thus decreased dramatically, as has its visibility. But much of the danger remains.

It was a fundamental rule of physics, Hayes pointed out, that nothing was ever consumed, it was merely transformed. Air pollutants removed from smokestacks became solid wastes. Pollution had to be seen as "resources out of place."

The real problem was how much pollution we were willing to accept relative to the value society received from using up or transforming the resources. Take fossil fuels: as a society we needed fossil fuels so much that we seemed willing to deplete our reserves rapidly and to sustain whatever environmental damage was caused by using them up. In consideration for the pollution they produced, we curbed our appetite for them only slightly.

Some concerns defied equations. For instance, paving over a hectare of California farmland with a freeway reduced the carbon-monoxide removal capacity of the hectare by 440 kilograms a day, and also reduced the hectare's oxygen output. How much farmland could we afford to turn into freeways before the overload of poisonous carbon monoxide in the area would render the site uninhabitable? The answer was only partially obtainable through calculation. The remedy would not be in the form of a technological fix. The trade-offs had to be considered in a more than scientific context. Thus environmental problems leapt out of the bailiwick of the scientist and landed in the realm of policy and priorities.

A single human being might not be able to affect whether or not a freeway was built, but he or she could control certain environmental concerns on a personal level. Younger people, and highly educated families, began to buy and use "natural" foods and to reject where possible packaged and processed food products. (This was exceedingly difficult to do, since most people lived away from areas of pure food production; also, as large companies saw the market potential in "natural" foods, they labeled their products "natural.") Some city dwellers changed their buying habits, especially where such changes brought them into cooperative contact with others. Many people participated in recycling programs, though the one which had the greatest success was the recycling of aluminum, which was sponsored (and paid for) by industry.

Despite its co-optation by American business, the "ecology" movement served many individuals well, providing a tangible (if muddy) philosophy on which to base their lives. Interestingly, the ecology constituency cut across traditional political lines. Many conservatives became champions of the untrammeled wilderness; many liberals found it important to forsake the usual liberal emphasis on progress (which in the past had been accomplished with the help of machines) and fought against further mechanization. Environmental protection made for strange bedfellows.

This was evident in the local politics of many areas. Pressure from the public forced the cancellation of a jetport close to the Florida Everglades, and the slowdown of development of the New Jersey wetlands. Around Lake Erie, the consensus helped to form multigovernmental agencies which tried to reverse the eutrophication process.

On a national level, the ecology consensus was reflected in three Senate actions in the spring of 1971. A majority of senators voted against further governmental support for the as-yet-unproven American supersonic transport; this vote effectively killed the SST. More than a defeat for a particular enterprise, the vote was an American retreat from sheer infatuation with machinery, and a signal that in the future the environmental impact of any new technology would be assessed before such projects could go very far.

In a second action, Senator Sam Ervin's subcommittee held hearings on what might happen if the government went ahead with a planned computer data bank. The new bank was supposed to fight crime; through computers linked to various points around the country, tabs would be kept on many millions of Americans who were potential or actual lawbreakers. Testimony showed that such a data bank would invade the privacy of millions of innocents, and also would restrict dissenters' civil liberties and work to suppress the legitimate claims of the poor.

A third Senate committee considered whether to ban completely the use and sale of American-made DDT. This exercise assumed that the growing ecological consciousness in the U.S. was repeated in the rest of the world. In the developing countries, it definitely was not. Developing countries had to ignore such thorny issues as the effect of DDT on the environment, or the disturbance of natural flood patterns caused by a hydroelectric dam; if they did not ignore them, there would be no progress. Only a nation as industrially advanced as the United States could afford to pose such questions and to answer them on the environmentally conscious side. Only in a postindustrial service economy could a people afford to pick their luxuries and to worry about the distant future.

Here was one more piece of evidence that the world's power alignment was no longer simple and bipolar. In the postwar years the world had seemed divided into camps led by Russia and the United States (the Warsaw Pact versus NATO countries), plus a large in-between clutch of "Third World" nations. Through the 1950s and 1960s seventy former colonial areas in Asia, Africa, and the Caribbean became sovereign states; during much of that time it was assumed that the U.S. and the U.S.S.R. were battling for the economic souls of those poor, illiterate, and nonaligned states. Thus it was a defeat for the U.S. when Russia built the Aswan dam for Egypt. We and our western European allies gave the "developing" nations aid, Alistair Buchan writes, partly from a sense of conscience, partly from fear of the influence the Communists would gain were the aid not given, and partly in an attempt to safeguard sources of raw materials. Later, Buchan points out, things changed:

> One salient characteristic of the late 1960s was the relative decline in the flow of American and other Western resources to the developing world, compounded partly by the disenchantment of both political and expert opinion with the social achievements of fifteen years of development aid, partly of diminished fear of Soviet or Chinese encroachment in the developing countries, partly of the re-direction of private investment towards Europe. The level both in 1970 and 1971 of American official aid amounted to only just over .3% of the GNP . . . and the total flow of resources to the developing world (public and private) to .65% of the GNP of the United States.

The Magnificent Bribe 221

By this time, also, the nonaligned countries had themselves altered considerably. In 1971 two leaders of the formerly nonaligned, India and Egypt, signed pacts with Russia, but the U.S. did not initially overreact* as if these nations had fallen forever to the Red menace—for, indeed, they had not. India and Egypt felt capable of taking aid from Russia without completely compromising their political position vis-à-vis the U.S. in part because the world's axis was no longer East-West, but North-South. There were more differences between India and Russia than there were between Russia and the United States.

In the Northern Hemisphere most countries were industrialized, technology-rich, and wealthy in material goods. In the Southern Hemisphere countries were for the most part unindustrialized, technology-poor, and lacking in material goods. This gulf between haves and have-nots had been apparent for some time, but during the 1960s the industrial states added $700 billion to their annual real incomes, a sum far greater than the total combined incomes of all the countries in Asia, Africa, and Latin America. Per capita income in the northern latitudes rose by $300 per person per year; in the southern latitudes it rose by $10 a year. Such a disparity was accentuated by the problems which beset the Southern Hemisphere: overpopulation, scarcity of food, lack of capital for development, lack of a skilled work force. For instance, India had been growing at a rate greater than the industrialized countries—but its industrial gains were negated by its rapid increase in population, which created new mouths to feed faster than food could be processed to satisfy them.

Seeing what the wealthy countries had in terms of technology, the have-nots wished to share in the wealth. To slake such wants, and to expand their own markets, American and other multinational companies urged technological products on the poor nations. In many cases the technology could not simply be transferred, for it was inappropriate. In a country of many small subsistence farms, huge harvesting combines built for use on vast unbroken acreages were useless; in a state with few paved roads, trucks and automobiles were confined to rapidly choking cities; in an urban district where there was no electricity, remote-controlled color television sets were superfluous.

Until the overwhelming problems of food, shelter, and income had first been solved—until an industrial civilization had been created—technology could not be used to good effect. But during the early 1970s the

---

*A U.S. overreaction came later, as the Nixon administration made a "tilt" toward Pakistan in the conflict between India and Pakistan.

basic problems of the Southern Hemisphere worsened. Populations continued to increase. The growth spurt in cereal food production began to level off as the first fruits of the Green Revolution were absorbed by growing populations. South American countries which had been food exporters became food importers. Drought in the Sahel region of Africa spread across the broadest part of the continent from the Atlantic to the Indian Ocean; hundreds of thousands of people died. A more lasting result was the death of millions of cattle and the subsequent condemnation to permanent starvation of whole tribes and populations. The world over, forests began to disappear as people used firewood to keep warm. When a desperate rural family substituted animal dung for fire fodder, they used up their supply of available fertilizer and diminished the yield of the following year's crops.

One of the great tragedies of our age was that this process of continual degradation was actively encouraged by the developed countries. Many southern nations were pushed from broad-based, varied economies which had a chance of self-sufficiency toward economies dependent upon outside sources. Thus a food exporter in South America became a food importer. Thus a former colony in Africa full of nomadic tribes came to base its national economy on tourism.

In 1972, crops failed all over the world except in the North American breadbasket. Despite increases in population, the world food reserves had for some years hovered around the 70-day mark. They now fell precipitously. The sub-Saharan drought worsened, producing famine in Mauritania, Senegal, Mali, Upper Volta, Chad, Niger, Sudan, Somalia, Ethiopia, Kenya, and Tanzania—all of them poor nations. At this very moment, however, the United States was building a policy of détente; taking the Soviet Union's disastrous harvest as an opportunity, the U.S. sold enormous quantities of wheat to the Communists. The message to the southern countries was clear: although the U.S. helped to provide some food for the drought- and famine-stricken countries of Africa (mainly through international agencies and private relief organizations), it was obvious that the U.S. considered a deal with Russia more important than providing food to prevent the starvation of millions in the Southern Hemisphere.

The wheat deal had another important consequence: within months it caused the world price of wheat to double, making the precious cereal too expensive for some southern nations to buy or even to have bought for them. The wheat sale also contributed to the surging of worldwide inflation, and the countries most deleteriously affected by inflation were the have-nots. Inflation placed the price of high-technology products even further beyond the reach of the poor.

To survive, to prosper, to industrialize and achieve their political goals, the southern nations had come to realize that they must force the industrialized nations of the North to share the world's wealth. To push the North the have-not nations possessed only two weapons—weapons which, in the past, they had been reluctant to use. However, in the early 1970s they began to use these weapons more frequently, and their use delivered shocks to the world.

The model for the southern nations in the Decade of Shocks was North Vietnam. Ho Chi Minh's nation began small and poor; it had only recently thrown off colonial rule. Through the decade, in the war for the hearts and minds of the Vietnamese people, in the struggle for self-sufficiency as a nation, in the fight for approbation of worldwide public opinion, North Vietnam did very well. With more zeal than technological wherewithal, North Vietnam was keeping the United States at bay, and was steadily working toward achieving its long-term political goal of unification of the country and people, free from all foreign domination. True, North Vietnam accepted help from Russia and China, but it remained quite independent in its outlook. The main bulwark of North Vietnam was not the antiaircraft weapons from Moscow but the determination of native foot soldiers. North Vietnam's triumph was a victory of the have-nots over the haves.

The two North Vietnamese weapons of interest to southern nations were 1) mobilization of resources in place, and 2) use of terrorism. Both were antitechnology tactics. Hanoi did not need technology to withstand U.S. bombing attacks—the people were organized to dig tunnels, and that helped them survive. When food and fuel supplies were cut off, they somehow managed to continue. Hanoi did not have an atomic bomb, nor did it need one to win the war. Through individual terrorism the NLF and VC showed villagers that the technological superiority of the Americans could not protect them.

The Arab countries were one particularly cohesive bloc of have-not nations. They had thrown off colonial rule; they had some important political goals, among them the establishment of a homeland for the tens of thousands of Palestinian refugees displaced by the establishment of the state of Israel; and they had an important resource in place, oil.

Highly industrialized nations had become more and more dependent upon assured supplies of oil, copper, tin, manganese, uranium, and other ores and abstracts. This fact was understood by Marxists and by leftist nationalists. In 1970 Chilean President Dr. Salvador Allende nationalized Chile's copper mines. As an isolated action this did not mean much, since at the time copper was in copious supply throughout the world. But Allende's next move had larger implications: he revitalized the moribund Andean Pact. This treaty bound Peru, Chile, Bolivia, Ecuador, and Colombia together and drew up for them a common charter on foreign investment. Steel, banks, and other major industries would henceforth be allowed no foreign investors, and many important commodities would be mined and sold only by the governments. As Louis Turner suggests, the impact of such nationalization was "traumatic."

> Other countries followed suit, like Bolivia, which nationalized Gulf Oil's assets. But the [multinational] companies were possibly most disturbed by the realization that a country like Chile could democratically elect a Marxist president, who would then work with other countries to formulate terms seriously affecting private investment—by imposing limits on equity participation and repatriation—and get away with it.

The Andean Pact and Allende's moves served to set the stage for an even more important cartel, based on oil. Modern industrial civilizations ran on oil; it fueled the production and transport of machines, the use of telecommunications equipment and of electrical technology. The scale of energy consumption—actually, the use of oil—was central to the "standard of living" index.

In 1970 the demand for oil in the United States was nearly insatiable. As a consequence of new environmental protection legislation which set pollution-control standards, giant utilities such as New York's Con Edison were gobbling up low-sulfur oil. In September of 1970 Colonel Muammar el-Qaddafi, in power just a year, forced up the price Libya received for its low-sulfur oil. This stimulated other member states of the Organization of Petroleum Exporting Countries (OPEC) to ask for higher prices for their own crude oil. OPEC had been founded in 1960 by an ecology-minded Venezuelan who preferred bicycles to automobiles. For ten years the thirteen-member meetings seemed to be mostly Arab-dominated social gatherings. After the 1967 Arab-Israeli war, the Arab countries had attempted to shut off the flow of oil to Western supporters of Israel, but their action had had little effect. As late as January of 1971, the price of OPEC's Arab Light oil was $1.80 per barrel. The Teheran Agreement of February 1971 sent it to $2.18 a barrel, and later in the year the tab went higher when

Nixon devalued the dollar. Faced with a broken pipeline and a blocked Suez Canal, American companies and consumers had little choice but to pay the higher prices. The rise in price of oil, the consequence of an OPEC action taken after decades of docile acceptance of domination by technology-rich nations, was a signal that the have-nots had understood just how much power their resources could command in the modern world.

On October 6, 1973—Yom Kippur, the holiest day of the Jewish year— Israeli territory was attacked from the south by Egypt and from the north and west by Syria. After four days of the war, and of large Israeli losses, President Nixon ordered American resupply of the Israelis. The Soviets were already supplying the Arab countries. America poured into Israel a thousand tons of weapons, spare parts, and other munitions a day; these helped the Israelis turn the initial tide of battle. On October 17, Nixon requested Congress pass a $2.2 billion emergency aid bill for Israel. In response the OPEC ministers voted to reduce crude oil production, and a few days later Abu Dhabi, Libya, Saudi Arabia, Algeria, and Kuwait imposed total oil embargoes on the United States. By early November 1973, the war was at a stalemate, and through combined U.S. and U.S.S.R. pressure, the fighting phase ended. As the shooting stopped, however, the embargo continued, and was soon followed by a series of stiff oil price rises. During the war the posted price of Arab Light went to $5.12 a barrel. On January 1, 1974, OPEC raised that price again, to $11.65 a barrel.

Although only 7 percent of the oil needs of the United States was supplied by the Middle Eastern countries, enormous difficulties arose. As Robert Engler discovered, the large oil companies and some large consumers of oil such as the airlines exacerbated the shortages; as a result, Americans had a hard time:

> Sweating out heating fuel deliveries (which, like voltage reductions and brownouts, had begun for some in previous years) and lines at the service stations were jolting if fleeting experiences for a people heretofore assured that the consumption of more and more was their birthright.

There were layoffs in oil-related industries such as automobiles and petrochemicals, airline price hikes, and increases in the prices of food. The GNP for the first quarter of 1974 showed a 7 percent decline. Furthermore:

> Highway blockades by truckers and walkoffs by coal miners resenting soaring fuel costs and allocations emphasized the dependence upon pe-

troleum and showed how a disturbance in its flow could bring people to the edge of violence and martial law. There were even suggestions of a new war between the states. The governors of Louisiana, Oklahoma, and Texas hinted they might cut off shipments of oil and gas to the big consuming regions if the latter continued to resist exploration and refinery construction in their own backyards in order to preserve their beaches and air. The Department of Defense, which early in 1973 had difficulty in buying the 50% of its petroleum requirements usually obtained from domestic refineries, now reported that the Arab embargo had cut its foreign supplies drastically and that its stocks were at a dangerous low.

It was later found that oil industry profits went up 70 percent in 1974. The embargo also became the excuse for the trucking industry to call for the use of larger trucks, and for the auto industry to advocate the rollback of environmental legislation and emission standards; it even gave politicians an excuse to call for not using school buses to achieve racial integration on the grounds that the vehicles used up too much precious fuel.

After the immediate crisis eased, supplies returned to "normal," but the consequences of the oil shock remained. The era of cheap energy was over. This meant higher bills for generating and using electricity, for transport, for making fertilizers, and for creating the "energy-intensive" myriad manufactured products of advanced civilizations. The bank balances of the world's countries shifted. Saudi Arabia had earned about $1.8 billion for its oil in 1971; it earned $22.5 billion for its oil in 1974; and overall in 1974 the OPEC nations took in about $100 billion. As the technology-rich, machine-endowed nations of Western Europe, Japan, and the United States paid dearly for the oil without which they could no longer operate, the OPEC nations became fabulously wealthy and one of the great centers of world economic power.

Along with the growth of the OPEC cartel as an economic power, there was also the growth of the Palestine Liberation Organization (PLO) as the foremost purveyor of acts of terrorism. The PLO was not an arm of the Arab oil countries, yet the political objective which the PLO sought was also openly advocated by the Arab countries. For several years following the 1967 war, the PLO conducted isolated acts of terrorism, mostly against Israeli targets. These attracted attention; indeed, attracting attention seemed to be their main function. As the Vietnamese NLF had habitually made opportunities for their cause to be known to "audiences" other than those countries directly involved in their struggle, so the PLO constantly performed terrorist acts for the benefit of countries outside the Middle East.

The era's quintessential act of terrorism involved all these elements.

On September 5, 1972, in the early morning hours, eight PLO guerrillas dressed as athletes entered a dorm for Israeli competitors at the Olympic Village in Munich. They killed a few men on the way in, then holed up with eleven of the athletes as hostages. The guerrillas called themselves the "Black September" group, and were outfitted with hoods, grenades, and machine guns. They demanded the release of 236 "political prisoners" then held in Israeli jails, and said they were prepared to kill their hostages and to die themselves if the demand was not met.

It was later discovered that the Black September group had lived in the Gangsgatan district of Stockholm, had been financed partly with money from an Italian leftist, had ties to terrorists as far away as Japan and South America. All during 1972 there had been terrorist attacks throughout the world. The Tupámaros had provoked civil war in Uruguay. Japanese terrorists had killed pilgrims at Israel's Lod airport, and there had been a particularly bloody attack in Japan itself. The existance of terrorists inside Germany was well known; some had been operating in the open since 1968.

At Munich in 1972, the television audience was worldwide. The seizure of eleven Israelis by an Arab terrorist group astounded people, and the world watched while, for 22 hours, negotiations went on. Tunisia, Egypt, and the Arab League tried to mediate. Israel would not give up the jailed men, and Germany could not force Israel to do so. There were strange echoes of Dachau, the Nazi concentration camp only nine miles from Munich. That Jews could be killed again on German soil worried all, but Germany was determined not to simply export the problem by allowing the terrorists and their hostages to leave the country. The television spotlights added to the sense of paralysis. At last the German authorities, in cooperation with the Israeli secret service, attempted to ambush the terrorists at the airport to which they had brought the hostages. The ambush was a disaster. All eleven of the hostages were killed by the terrorists, and five of the eight terrorists also died. Two months later, other Black September stalwarts hijacked a Lufthansa plane from Damascus, Syria, and forced Germany (this time acting without Israel) to release the three terrorist survivors of the attack. Since Munich, such terrorist attacks have been frequent, if not as spectacular.

Munich showed how vulnerable a complex, technologically oriented society had become to attack by a handful of fanatics. They paralyzed whole nations—that was the whole point. George Habbash, the Palestinian physician who helped to create the Black September group, had often said that the enemy was not just Israel but also worldwide "imperialism" of the sort that had spawned Israel and continued to back the Jewish state. "To be honest," Habbash said, "what we want is a war like Vietnam's."

In the wake of Munich it became clearer than ever that governments were limited in their ability to protect the lives of citizens from seemingly random violence—whether at an airport or in a private home. Those who valued something more than they did their own lives could easily disrupt the technological society.

After Munich, after oil prices had quintupled, after technology had been shown wanting, after people had switched to wheat germ from white bread—then what? Had there been only a cosmetic change, or had people really come to question progress-through-technology? Was the change in thought processes deep? Could it last?

There were signs of a lasting impact. Glenn T. Seaborg, apostle of nuclear electric power and former chairman of the Atomic Energy Commission, spoke out in 1974, when he was president of the American Association for the Advancement of Science. He counseled the public to think seriously about converting America to a "re-cycle society" which would emphasize conservation, re-use, and the manufacture of higher-quality and more durable products. Also in 1974, orders for new nuclear plants virtually stopped. In the wake of the oil shock, nuclear plant orders might have been expected to jump, but they disappeared. The Faustian bargain was called into question. New regulations, rampant inflation, and fears of apocalypse all combined to make nuclear electric power appear less feasible and less attractive.

Seaborg's call, the stoppage of nuclear plant construction, the re-arrangement of the world's economic polarities subsequent to the oil price hikes, the general retreat from technology—all reflected profound changes close to the heart of modern civilization. These were realizations about the limits of machinery, the limits of economic growth, and the limits of man imposed by the environment.

These limits were interrelated. We have encountered them several times before in different places, earlier in this book. But it is in the nexus of technology, ecology and the shift from the East-West to the North-South axis that they stand out most starkly.

The scientists and extrapolators of trends in postwar America had predicted utopia. They drew their graphs and charts and saw a work-free, ecstasy-filled, painless environment for the long-lived, healthy, wealthy American. There were hosts of future-gazers—what was an American, if not someone constantly looking toward the future?—and the majority of them believed in the triumph of technology and all that such a triumph entailed. Slowly, over the course of the Decade of Shocks, the gleaming picture of the future lost its gloss and was shown to be merely one science fiction scenario among many. In place of the chrome-and-glass dream, we came to imagine with just as much ease the specter of decay—of limits, entropy, routine, failure, even of death. We had always known the limits were there, had known full well that machines could not perfect the society of man, but for a time we had suspended our disbelief and expected too much.

For a time the technological harvest was indeed bountiful: automation, computerization, biomedicine, and communications technologies altered our lives in numerous ways. A few people would admit, here and there, that some technology or other was unnecessary or harmful—but no sane person would want to live without electricity, or to have polio stalking the young again, or to be unable to own a high-powered car or to shop without credit cards.

We had reached a new level of comfort. If, however, our struggles were no longer for food, shelter, and work, they had entered a different realm. Now we had to battle for meaning and worth. Having taken the magnificent bribe and satisfied our basic comforts and then some, we could now ask questions which had never before been posed by so large a percentage of humanity at once, questions of values, policies, the breadth and depth of institutional change. Emmanuel Mesthene, director of Harvard's Program on Technology and Society, pointed out that the problems which technology raises for advanced societies are not the ones solvable by newer or improved machines or techniques:

> If we are to rationalize our institutions and make them more adequate to technological pressures while at the same time preserving our values, then we must be clear about our values.... [Technological change's] main direct effect is to stimulate changes in the hierarchy of a society's commitment to different values by making some values easier or less costly to achieve than others. Thus, labor-saving technology can lead to a shift in which leisure comes to be valued above hard work, and new medical technologies can reinforce a commitment to material comfort at the expense of the value of courage in the face of adversity.... Any

effort to rationalize society's institutions and processes tends to bring out value conflicts among different groups in society and increases the pressure to resolve them.... Another effect of a high-technology, densely-populated society is that values once held in high esteem become no longer appropriate and may actually become harmful if commitment to them remains strong. The value of individualism inherited from the America frontier... especially in its extreme form once called "rugged individualism"... clearly cannot be allowed free rein in a society in which every act increasingly has unintended or unforeseen consequences on third parties and where actions taken for individual benefit may carry social costs that will impoverish everyone in the end.

Many of the tensions of the society, Mesthene believed, existed because people held on to values long after they had been superseded by events.

Throughout the decade, these tensions were evident; but also, some attitudes were altered.

First, we now questioned whether or not we should accomplish all that was technologically feasible. For instance, there were techniques available to desalinate part of the Pacific Ocean to obtain fresh water, power, and minerals—but a scientific council advised Nixon to abandon a pilot desalination project because the money could be better used elsewhere. Similarly, we agreed that some things which were biomedically feasible—the artificial extension of life after brain death, or the gross modification of people's behavior—were best left undone. We could send men to Mars, but we didn't do it. A new hesitancy, a prudence and caution, became the order of the day.

With that hesitancy also came the necessity for taking into account, by testing and extrapolating the results, the future consequences of our actions and new technologies. Trial and error in these matters had produced: the Navaho missile ($750 million spent, obsolete before use); the nuclear-powered aircraft ($1 billion spent, proved not practical); and the nuclear-powered space booster ($2 billion spent, proved not practical). As a select panel in 1969 told the House of Representatives committee considering the "Assessment and Choice" of technology, in the past we had not made such studies:

The panel believes that in some cases the injection of the broadened criteria urged here might have led... to the selection or encouragement of different technologies, or at least modified ones—functional alternatives with lower social costs (though not necessarily lower total costs). For example, bioenvironmental rather than primarily chemical devices might have been used to control agricultural pests or there might have been design alternatives to the purely chemical means of enhancing engine efficiency, or mass transit alternatives to further reliance upon the private automobile.

At the level of national debate, no one had ever seriously questioned the impact of the automobile on the environment. To now regulate exhausts was helpful, but it was a bit like closing the barn door after the horse had fled. We needed to evaluate technologies before the harm was done, before society could be irrevocably changed. A first tentative step in this direction was taken by the scientific community and the government-regulated laboratories that were genetically altering the *E. coli* bacteria: a misapplication of this research could lead to bacterial poisoning of whole populations—and therefore it was strictly controlled.

This sort of planning for the future would at least encompass some of the tenets of ecology, whose principles were most simply stated by Barry Commoner:

> 1) Everything is connected to everything else; 2) everything must go somewhere; 3) nature knows best, and 4) there is no such thing as a free lunch—every gain is won at some cost.

The greatest shock that came from the realization of technology's limits was the discovery that the most dangerous threat to our future came not from natural disasters like typhoons or earthquakes but from the fragility of the web of life. All life in the biosphere was intensely vulnerable. Our new technologies had greatly increased each person's power, but they had also increased society's vulnerability because that heightened power was the ability of each person to affect everyone and everything else—for good or ill. One man could invent a vaccine and save many. One man could blow up an airliner and kill many. To become acutely aware of our interactions, and of the potential consequences of our power, meant we had to change what it was we valued in the world.

It was at the very peak of our economic prowess that the ecology movement surfaced. Perhaps only when the economic goals of a majority of Americans had been met could it become possible to postulate goals on a different plane. Ecology was something championed by youth, who were not firm or old-style believers in the ethic of consumption which dominated the United States in the early postwar era. Young people believed one need not be concerned only with winning bread but must also treat with meaning and purpose and pay attention to the nuances of becoming a well-rounded human being. Subtly, this line of thought began to influence the wider public. We began to state official goals which had more to do with the conservation of resources than with the growth of the economy.

For us, this meant the death of the progress ideology. But in giving up the precept that "progress is our most important product," we would be dangerously close to subverting the basic tenet of American capitalism— that growth was equivalent to economic health. Rufus E. Miles, Jr., suggested that all growth economies, whether those of *laissez-faire*, Keynes, or Marx, would soon have to stop growing:

> Further economic growth of the overdeveloped world, insofar as it depends on further increases in the consumption of energy, will be dysfunctional both from the most crucial standpoint of the preservation of the biosphere and from the secondary standpoint of achieving a reasonably stable society, yielding the benefits that societies are supposed to produce. The Marxists with their panacea of abolishing private property and production for profit, and substituting government ownership of the means of production, continue to be wedded to the obsolescent fallacy that the world's growth potential is virtually unlimited.

In fact, Miles wrote, no economic theory could provide adequate future guidelines for societies that prized freedom and representative government. In a world of limited resources and rising demands, economic policies could not continue to be the means of achieving the personal and political goals of freedom and democracy. Therefore, the value systems of Americans "must either undergo a major change in the direction of living more rewarding lives with fewer material demands, or the nation is headed toward endless and escalating crises."

It was a matter, the Rockefeller Commission on the Quality of Life suggested, of altering our orientation from emphasis on "standard of living" to emphasis on "quality of life." The former could use calorie consumption as a measure, but how could you measure a person's degree of happiness? Sociologist Peter L. Berger suggested that it might not be possible to measure degrees of happiness, but it was possible to know the components of the good life. The Founding Fathers had held certain "truths" to be "self-evident," and had provided us with a set of values to which we could still adhere. Berger wrote that it hardly mattered what set of values we used as long as we used some set, for "the inevitable consequence of our inability to objectively say what constitutes the good life" would be nihilism:

> If we are unable to distinguish between good and bad, then it would seem not to matter what kind of life we choose. That is precisely what nihilism asserts. . . . If nothing is true, everything is permitted. In other words, nothing matters and everything goes. A life devoted to lechery, a life devoted to the murder of the Jews, a life devoted to the relief of man's estate—there is no self-evident hierarchy among these because it makes no difference what we do, and only some obscure drives or hesitations would lead us to prefer decency to indecency, assuming such terms retain any meaning.

After a century in which destruction was rampant and after a startling decade of environmental shocks, technological degradations and rude awakenings—we had nihilism in our bones. Whatever innocence and naiveté the progress ideology had given us, we had lost. Harvey Cox pointed out that the technological triumphs had occurred at the same time as society-wide breakdowns in the cultural and psychological grounds of meaning. As we went to the moon, for example, there was a collapse of "transcendence," and a loss of "any culturally or psychologically operative sense of an objective realm of reality toward which one is governed, punished, or saved." This did not mean that we had collectively lost faith in God, but it did mean that in the light of new technological breakthroughs and a relatively new set of circumstances for the world, we could not leave uninterpreted the value-guiding canons of older religions. It was right and proper that our values change. Emmanuel Mesthene agreed:

> It is not existing values that are valuable but the continuing human ability to extract values from a changing experience and to use and cherish them.

Since we had come to accept that we were the proximate, if not the ultimate, makers of our own destiny, we would have to choose our future in line with our changing values. Thus it became necessary for us to define— once again—what we considered to be the good life.

Having overrun our frontiers; having overcome the simple necessity to make a living; having pushed resources to the point where we saw them begin to dwindle; having reached the realization that all human society was intertwined—we reached the point where we could not escape the ethical questions. The ways in which we could consider and provide answers for those questions reflected our interpretations of the events and lessons of the decade. We had interpreted many shocks in the past; now our explanations would shape our future.

Many people believed that our way of life was a good way, perhaps the best way ever known to mankind, and they wished to "preserve" what we had. They wanted to pass that way of life on to their children.

To preserve our current way of life, however, meant (with perhaps a few modest restraints) continuing to use the world as our ashtray. It meant that the resources of the world would be fed to us at the present rate, and that we would consume them approximately in the quantities and at the rate that we were currently consuming them. If, because of the finite limits of those resources, this meant some people would have more and others would have to settle for less—sobeit. In accepting the preserve modality its champions were tacitly supporting the idea that some people, namely Americans, were better or more deserving than others. Pursuant to this logic, they believed that sooner or later everyone would have to recognize that in a world of diminishing resources in which Americans planned to give up nothing, there would be widening gaps between rich and poor.

To continue our wealth at present levels, however, would mean that 1) we would need increasing monetary wealth, for in the future the have-nots would charge us ever more dearly for the resources they held; 2) if we did not wish to pay hyperinflated prices for such resources, we might have to go to war to obtain them; 3) within our own culture we would similarly and increasingly be divided into rich and poor, for to keep one group wealthy would mean denying existing wealth to the other group or even the opportunity to create much new wealth.

As resources diminished and needs expanded, maintaining wealth might require greater social control within the country. The poor could not be expected to remain docile about their inability to share in the wealth. In our cities there would be enclaves of the very rich and ghettos of the very poor; the enclaves for the wealthy might become armed camps; the tactics of the poor might turn more often to taking wealth from the "haves" with little compunction about legality. In such a system, unable to encompass differing rules for the rich and the poor, democracy would become meaningless. It would be a relic to be discarded as inadequate to the central tasks of government—the preservation of in-place concentrations of wealth. Wealth might be preserved, but democracy would go. We would become a neo-Fascist society with a government devoted to the maintenance of the *status quo* and to the unbroachable division between the rich and the poor.

The "search" modality of thought took as a basic premise that in regard to man's environment we needed new solutions to the problems of pollution, allocation of resources, and the utilization of technology. The most accessible solution was the humanistic "one world" concept. Some would allow that world zero growth, some would allow limited growth, some would allow growth in underdeveloped countries but not so much in the developed. Whichever permutation of the solution was embraced, all involved a serious diminution of our current way of life.

The converging crises of energy, pollution, overpopulation, lack of food, and disparities in productive capacities and incomes the world over, emphasized that we now had to deal with one interconnected and complex crisis of world development. In a world so interconnected, what was good for one individual or one country was often not good for all. New strategies for production and consumption seemed necessary, and the fact that they had not yet been found did not deny the need for them. In the future, there would have to be limits to uncontrolled growth—limits to population, to consumption, to whole economies. Such limits would have to be imposed by man before they were forced upon us by nature. In turn, this would mean a redefinition of the levels of need and luxury for individuals, for nations, and for our global human civilization. As the wealthiest nation in the world, we would have to be intimately involved in those new definitions.

If growth were curtailed or sharply limited, the current American economic system would change radically. For example, the stock market—a place for trading futures—would disappear, for the future would be planned and not hoped-for. Other consequences might be more dire. Limiting growth might condemn our own have-nots to the status of suppliants who must rely only on some central authority for advancement. Initiative would no longer make a man wealthy. We would have to accept that our children's lives would be less comfortable than our own. It would be not only a matter of condemning people to gas lines; they might have to accept state control of whether or not they could own a car. The limiting of growth would indubitably mean some serious limitations on personal freedom. To control pollution, consumption, and the like, there would have to be powerful restraints on the capacity of individuals, corporations, and even nations to pollute, consume, or even to propagate and make new consumers. In order to make such laws, and then to enforce them, there would have to be institutions that could make such social control workable. Almost certainly such institutions would have to be large, central, and authoritarian. Out of the "search" modality of thought, then, would come an engorged state. It might be Socialist or Communist or some new form of social compulsion mixed with egalitarianism—but it would not be democratically based. The wishes of the majority are most often for their own aggrandizement; in the new future society those individual wishes could not be allowed to interfere with what the designated central authority would construe as the greatest good for the greatest number of people worldwide.

8 The Quiet Revolution

In 1872, women's movement leader Susan B. Anthony wrote:

> I do pray, and that most earnestly and constantly, for some terrific shock to startle the women of the nation into a self-respect which will compel them to break their yoke of bondage and give them faith in themselves; which will make them proclaim their allegiance to women first.... The fact is, women are in chains and their servitude is all the more debasing because they do not realize it. Oh, to compel them to see and feel and to give them the courage and the conscience to speak and act for their own freedom, though they face the scorn and contempt of all the world for doing it!

The shock Susan Anthony sought never arrived during her lifetime. After a period of intense activity during the "progressive" years around the turn of the century, the women's movement lacked for victories, and went into a kind of hibernation. In American society, women were the shock absorbers, not the shock generators. During the difficult years of the Depression and World War II, women kept households together, took jobs when men could fine none, or were at war. Yet, for all their work, women received little approbation and seemed unable to alter their status within society. After the war Rosie the Riveter simply moved aside to let a returning serviceman take over her factory job, and retired to the baby farm.

In the postwar era, one of the most significant trends was the rate at which the country became suburbanized. In the era, the suburbs absorbed an additional 10–15 percent of America's families. By the 1950s more than a third of the population lived in "bedroom communities." The families who moved to the suburbs were by and large those with young children. The parents were the progenitors of the "baby boom." Women were marrying younger; they were having more children (the average number of children per household in 1957 was nearly four); and they were staying home more than any women had since the turn of the century. In 1955, Adlai Stevenson told "you girls" of the graduating class at Smith College for Women, that it was their task to "restore valid, meaningful purpose to life in your homes," and "to influence us, man and boy," in order to keep the husbands of America "truly purposeful."

Only a minority of women would have disagreed with Stevenson's prescription for their lives, for Stevenson was simply restating the prevailing mythology of the day. Those who were unhappy being the perfect helpmeet, many psychologists were suggesting, were more than a bit sick. In the 1947 best-seller *Modern Woman: The Lost Sex*, Ferdinand Lundberg and Marynia Farnham contended that since men worked away from the home, and since children left the home at an early age to attend school, women who remained at home had "no certainty of status...no security...as a woman, a female being." Rather than rail against their fate and wish they were men or could do as men did, the authors suggested, women should acknowledge the dominance of the male, embrace passivity and dependence, and celebrate the roles of wife and mother. Created biologically and physiologically submissive, the women should accept their fate. To restore the prestige of sexually ordained roles for women, Lundberg and Farnham urged a government-sponsored propaganda campaign that would bolster the image of the family, give cash subsidies to women who bore more children, and award annual certificates to women who were excellent "moms."

All three campaigns had been firmly in place in Hitler's Germany, where they were aimed at producing more soldiers for war. In the United States in the postwar era the campaigns were again being pushed but not by government edict. We did not require more soldiers. We kept women at home because we needed them as directors of consumption for the American home: that was the message in the pages of such magazines as *Good Housekeeping*, *Redbook*, and *McCall's*. Paeans to motherhood and wifedom began to appear with regularity in such magazines in the 1940s and 1950s, sandwiched in between interminable articles on how to cook, how to sew, and how to keep a man when your looks were fading—and bordered by hundreds of advertisements for products which could be consumed in the home. The drive for better and more costly refrigerators, and for larger homes with "family rooms," relied on continual blandishments to women to buy themselves comfort, security, and status. A woman's field of action might be limited to the home, but within its confines she could sharply affect the directions of family life and family spending.

Just as the suburban home was extolled as the best the country had to offer, the nuclear family which inhabited such homes in the 1950s was celebrated as the best possible family. In the nuclear family, the husband worked so the couple could live, while the wife kept the house and raised the (two or more) children. The children were the future; adults lived for them and through them, expecting their children's lives to be better than their own. The nuclear family was divided into clear and separate masculine and feminine spheres. He ruled the head, she, the heart; he was a man of the world, she was unsullied by the world's dirt and therefore pure and noble; he took part in business, she was the embodiment of culture; he was the breadwinner, she was the emblem of his achievement.

The realm of the personal was thus as polarized as the realm of global relations. With such clear role distinctions between the sexes, for a woman every choice became a matter of choosing "femininity" or rejecting it. If a woman was conflicted about a job and marriage and a family, the stereotype of the "truly feminine" would push to make the choice on the side of capturing a man, raising children. Women who were graduating from college unhesitatingly chose to get married rather than to enter the job market. As late as 1962, Claire Cox could report that mating rituals at colleges had reached disturbing extremes. When senior sorority members sat down for their last breakfast on the University of Missouri campus, any young lady who was neither engaged nor pinned was required to eat a lemon. One graduate told Cox it was shocking to "see how many girls got pinned or engaged just to avoid the lemon torture." At Chicago's Northwestern University, when a girl received a fraternity pin,

> the recipient's sorority goes into a kind of seance at which the members stand in the dark in a circle while the housemother passes a lighted candle from girl to girl. When the candle reaches the girl who has been pinned, she blows out the flame, thus announcing that she is the lucky one. After the cries and squeals of delight have died away, the girl's sorority sisters

seize upon her and drag her fully-clad to the nearest shower and thrust her under a stream of cold water.

Anthropologist Ashley Montagu took a harsh view of such activities; they were "an absurd tribalism...part of conformity, a wrong sense of values....Going steady in my view is an evidence of insecurity and also what goes with immaturity." Montagu suggested that the brightest and best-rounded students sloughed off the social scene and concentrated on their studies. Not so: polls taken of college graduates from academically oriented campuses in the late 1950s and early 1960s showed that a great many women graduates married and had children soon after graduation. As one Barnard graduate wrote to a Columbia researcher, Mirra Komarovsky,

> The plunge from the strictly intellectual college life to the 24-hour-a-day domestic one is a terrible shock. We stagger through our first years of child-rearing wondering what our values are and struggling to find some compromise between our intellectual ambition and the reality of everyday living.

While most young mothers resolved their conflict in favor of becoming good homemakers, those who did go to work felt universally guilty about working, and worried that while they did their jobs their homes suffered and that they were bad or inadequate wives and mothers.

If a woman really wanted what a man had—a job, achievement, the satisfaction of supporting herself—she ran the large risk of cultural disapproval. Those who could not settle comfortably into being good little homemakers nearly always felt out of step with their world. The irony was that the nonworking suburban woman, and the nuclear family of the 1950s and early 1960s had not always been the norm for all of American society. Earlier generations had not married so young, or differentiated roles quite so completely, or had families with so many living children that the mothers were forced to be perpetual baby-sitters. It wasn't an absolute necessity for women to marry young, have several children, and be unable to enter the work force—rather, it was a cultural bias.

Suburban homemaking was well publicized. The fact that women were entering the postwar work-force in unprecedented numbers was not publicized nearly so well. New, paperwork-intensive industries needed office workers; new fast-food chains and shopping malls needed part-time sales help. By 1960 twice as many women were at work as in 1940; female employment was increasing four times faster than male employment. Of all women over the age of sixteen, 40 percent held a job. This included 30 percent of the wives in the country, and nearly 40 percent of all mothers with children aged six to seventeen.

The catch was that the magazines and television shows and politicians sang no paeans to women workers, and the American marketing community ignored working women and still considered the stay-at-home housewives the prime consumers of the country.

In 1960, in more than ten million homes, both the husband and the wife worked; that figure had increased 333 percent in twenty years. Most of the women who stayed at home and did not work were either late middle-aged, or mothers with very young children. The median age of women workers had risen to 41. Women were increasingly returning to the labor force after their last child left home. Those women who were childless and who did not work were a shrinking fraction. By the beginning of the 1960s the postwar baby boom was about over; each year more and more women sent their last child off to school and began to look for work.

In the world of work there were vast gender-based inequalities. For comparable jobs women were paid about 50 percent as much as men. And most jobs were not comparable. Women were secretaries, assistants, sales clerks, grade-school teachers. (This, too, was a change from the past: in the 1930s, for example, there had been a greater percentage of women teachers in colleges than there were in the 1950s and 1960s.) Women were almost totally excluded from occupations such as truck driving, from high executive positions, from skilled crafts such as directing films or plays. A male college graduate might be a junior management executive in a large company; with similar credentials his wife might be a secretary or an underpaid social worker. In the workplace as well as in the home, there remained a sharp distinction between male and female domains.

Betty Friedan was a suburban housewife and a writer of articles, primarily for the women's magazines. In the early 1960s she looked around her—both in the world of the women's magazines and in suburbia—and identified

a strange stirring, a sense of dissatisfaction, a yearning that women suffered in the middle of the twentieth century in the United States. Each suburban housewife struggled with it alone. As she made the beds, shopped for groceries, matched slipcover material, ate peanut butter sandwiches with her children, chauffeured Cub Scouts and Brownies, lay beside her husband at night—she was afraid to ask even of herself the silent question—"Is this all?"

Looking through several years of recent women's magazines, Friedan saw that women had been taught to conform to an image of docile femininity, and to "pity the neurotic, unfeminine, unhappy women who wanted to be poets or physicists or presidents." As a consequence of having to give up their dreams, women were suffering; suburbia was a trap, Friedan wrote in *The Feminine Mystique*, a luxurious trap, but a real one. The chains that bound the suburban woman were "chains in her own mind and spirit...chains made up of mistaken ideas and misinterpreted facts, of incomplete truths and unreal choices." The "feminine mystique" which required women to be passive and accepting of their subservient status had resulted in a "stunting or evasion of growth," for "our culture does not permit women to accept or gratify their basic need to grow and fulfill their potentialities as human beings." Women had directed their considerable energy to their husbands and families, in the process often suffocating or distorting themselves and the families. Friedan dismissed out of hand the Freudian idea that anatomy was destiny, that a woman's identity could be solely determined by her biology, and wrote that more and more women were becoming aware of an "identity crisis" in their own lives,

> a crisis which began many generations ago, and will not end until they, or their daughters, turn an unknown corner and make of themselves and their lives the new image that so many women now so desperately need.
>
> In a sense that goes beyond any one woman's life, I think this is the crisis of women growing up—a turning point from an immaturity that has been called femininity to full human identity. I think women had to suffer this crisis of identity, which began a hundred years ago, and have to suffer it still today, simply to become fully human.

In her book Friedan primarily addressed women of her own socioeconomic group—middle-class, suburban, educated housewives. But the book appealed to more women than that group. *The Feminine Mystique* was an incantatory tract which opened people's eyes to the burdens under which women labored both at home and in the marketplace.

If women responded to it with fervor, however, they did so because the ground was well prepared. The time of the sole ascendancy of the suburban housewife and family was about over, as evidenced by the rising number of women already at work outside the home. Under the stimulus of the Kennedy tax cut, the economy was soon booming. There were new jobs available for women. Technology had eased some workplace requirements for brute strength which had heretofore kept many tasks outside the capabilities of women. Technology also eased the burdens of housework, and made more time available for women to do other tasks.

The technological revolution also produced the Pill. This contraceptive allowed women to control whether or not they became pregnant, a matter which had consequences far beyond the ability to control childbearing and thus whether or not women could work. A woman without such control was subservient to a man; with such control, she could realize many new possibilities. For one, women could make sexual demands upon men in the way men had always made such demands on women, but now without having to court pregnancy as a consequence of spontaneity. The Pill fostered a new emphasis on sexuality, on premarital and extramarital sex. In turn these affected the number of divorces and nonmarriage living arrangements.

Helping to push the nuclear family from the pedestal it had occupied in the 1950s and 1960s were the number of working women, the new moral climate that placed less disapprobation on divorce, and the fact that fewer families seemed to have young children who needed constant mothering.

Though no new model of rectitude arose to take the place of the nuclear family, the old model was less in style.

With its emphasis on the difference between the young generation and their parents, the youth movement encouraged young women to perceive the possibilities of having lives that were radically different from those of their mothers. And the civil-rights movement helped many women see that they, like blacks and all other "minority" groups, were oppressed and discriminated against, exploited by men, treated as second-class citizens, and patronized as childlike.

The drive toward women's liberation, then, was only the most visible symbol of a quiet revolution that changed many aspects of Americans' personal lives. This was a revolution without cataclysmic public shocks. However, the private shocks were incremental and accumulated over a period of time. They came at work, in the home, in the bed, in the discourse among friends, in the relations with children and with parents. The quiet revolution encompassed new definitions of sexuality, new ways of child-rearing, new familial alignments, new living arrangements, and new career strategy. All of work, leisure, and individuality were affected.

Although these changes had begun in the early 1960s, the pace began to accelerte in 1964. A provision forbidding discrimination on the basis of sex was inserted into the Civil Rights Act at the last minute, in the hope that it would result in the act's defeat. When the act was passed, it forbade discrimination on the bases of race, creed, country of national origin, and sex. Through the Civil Rights Act, the Equal Employment Opportunities Commission (EEOC) was set up; this evolved into the major forum in which sex discrimination cases could be aired, and through which redress could be granted.

In June of 1966 a Washington conference of state commissioners was held on the status of women. Many of the conferees were unhappy with the inattention given to the provisions of Title VII of the 1964 Civil Rights Act, which guaranteed nondiscrimination rights to women. When the conferees were told by Johnson administration officials that the commissioners had no power to take action on women's behalf, and no power even to offer a resolution on the subject of Title VII, Betty Friedan, Aileen Hernandez (of the EEOC), and other leading women in and around the conference formed the National Organization for Women (NOW). Their purpose was to "take action to bring women into full participation in the mainstream of American society now, exercising all the privileges and responsibilities thereof, in truly equal partnership with men."

During the remainder of the 1960s the women's movement, as represented by NOW and by other, less organized groups, grew slowly. People were concerned more with the Vietnam War, civil rights, and new boundaries for youth, so that during the years of ferment and hope women's issues appeared to be of secondary importance. Day care was seen as primarily an issue for the poor and the black, rather than for all women. Women spoke out on the war, but the war was an issue that affected all of the young.

In the various movements that characterized the late 1960s, women were not well treated. When asked what was the proper position for women in the black movement, Stokely Carmichael answered "prone." In antiwar groups women were most often relegated to providing moral and sexual support—or to menial jobs such as running the mimeograph machines. Even so, many younger women were radicalized by first becoming sensitized to oppression in such movements.

Ellen Willis's was a typical yet sensational journey. She graduated from Barnard in 1962 and married shortly thereafter. She and her husband moved to Berkeley and went to graduate school, with her husband aiming toward a government job overseas. Willis was a writer, but she was also a housewife, and for the first years of her marriage she felt that her future was tied to her husband's. In California she could find only a low-paid job writing promotional copy for textbooks. She went to CORE meetings and did not feel welcome. She was an enthusiastic partisan of the Free Speech Movement, but didn't join the sit-ins because she felt too old (and too married) to be a hanger-on. When the couple moved to Washington, D.C., so her husband could train to go to Africa, the only work she could find was typing, and she took it rather than sit at home. She wrote in a diary that she and her husband had begun to have fights about the housework:

> I want to eat in restaurants all the time. My husband thinks it's a disgusting extravagance. I insist that we have more than enough money, what are we saving it for? Which doesn't stop me from feeling guilty. (It's his money.) (Good wives cook.) (It isn't as if he never helps me.) (Why am I being nasty and causing trouble over something so trivial?)

> I think I'm looking forward to going overseas and that I've accepted my marriage because...life is like that, they say.... But on some level I feel a confrontation is approaching. If I go to Africa it's a commitment, I can't pick up and go home. I get very moody. Write poems about suicide, murder, and mental breakdowns. Fantasize.

Willis had an "infatuation" with another man, and when her husband went to Africa, she "made the break" and moved to New York. (Between 1960 and 1970 the divorce rate doubled, and was especially high among young childless couples; also, sexual activity outside of marriage increased dramatically.) In 1966 Willis got an assistant's job at a small magazine, and once again had "tentative skirmishes" with men:

> I realize I'm suspicious of men. Something else to feel guilty about. It's so unliberated, the old double-standard hangup, fear of being used, fear of being a conquest.... What I don't want is for this or that promising guy to think I'm cold, naive, straight, not turned on by him, or conversely desperate, undiscriminating, over-involved, etc.

At the magazine she did her boss's work for him (a common complaint among professional women), but when she tried to turn her writing and editing talent to job advantage, she was blocked and lost her position. She turned down a job as associate editor at another magazine because the supervisor told her she also would be required to answer the telephone.

Trying to focus her growing anger at the system, Willis joined radical groups, but "telling Puerto Ricans in the Avenue D housing project how the corporations are oppressing them" struck her as foolish and patronizing. In 1967, Vietnam was the overwhelming issue for her, pushing other concerns into the background; she looked to Marxist theory as a way to understand the world, but something essential, she felt, was missing from the Marxist dialectic:

> When they consider sexual problems at all it's only to dismiss them as the affliction of a decadent bourgeoisie, to be swept away by the emerging proletariat. But no proletarian revolution has yet been able to sweep them away. What we need is an analysis that can connect the politics of nations with the politics of our own bodies.

Young women like Willis looked around them and saw that they were competent, well trained, and energetic, and pressed for better and better jobs. (Kindergarten enrollment doubled from 1965 to 1970, as women sent their children to school earlier so they could go out and get jobs.) By 1968, Willis was reviewing rock music for a major publication, working on a book, and living with a sympathetic male writer. She wondered why she usually took rejection calmly but had a hard time accepting praise for her work. (Fear of success haunted many women.)

A young woman whom she knew only through friends came to stay with Willis while she got an abortion, then an illegal operation. The woman was bullied by the illegal abortionist, then by Bellevue doctors who had to repair the damage done by the abortionist, and then by clinic pharmacists who would dispense the woman only a single month's supply of birth control pills at a time.

Going west in 1968, Willis stopped in Chicago and took part in the demonstrations, but found them full of "machismo" and unsatisfying. She read about a feminist protest at the Miss America pageant. (There, "feminists" picketed the proceedings and sang a song:

> *Ain't she sweet,*
> *Makin' profit off her meat;*

She's just America's prime commodity,
Ain't she sweet.)

The protesters had burned no bras (the image of militant feminists was anathema to most women) and when compared to demonstrators for other causes, they were remarkably polite. Still, Willis wrote,

> I'm dubious—won't people think they're just ugly, jealous women? But I remember what it's like to be examined and compared at a party, and I'm proud that women are in the papers for fighting.

She considered living alone. (Increasing numbers of women were living alone; one-person households were up sharply from 1960 to 1970.) She rejected loneliness and she knew she was definitely heterosexual. In San Francisco she read a New York radical women's journal; the tone struck her as "frighteningly bitter," but after attending a women's group meeting in San Francisco, she resolved to join the authors of the radical tract on her return to New York. When she met them, she found them "nothing like my fantasies of anti-sex fanatics . . . no different from other women, except friendlier." As with many women, Willis had never talked openly with other women about her problems. (Women were expected to be competitive with other women for men, and thus not to share difficulties, for to do so was thought to lessen their competitive advantage.) After a few consciousness-raising sessions, Willis felt like a veteran:

> New women keep coming in, women who are just discovering their oppression, asserting for the first time their independence from husbands and lovers, overwhelmed that here they are listened to, *respected*. They want to talk about everything, their jobs, their husbands, their childhoods, their abortions, their attitudes toward other women. So we talk. Sometimes it's great, sometimes it's bullshit, but I learn something at every meeting.

In January of 1969 Willis was in the vanguard women's liberation contingent at the Nixon counter-inaugural, but felt used and betrayed when the radical groups at the event would not pursue women's rights along with black issues and the need to end the Vietnam War.

The Quiet Revolution   249

Until now I've . . . assumed that women's liberation was part of the radical movement, that one of our essential functions, in fact, was to bring masses of women into the left. Washington destroyed that illusion. How can it be good for women to join a movement whose ideology, history, and practice have been created by their oppressors? We need not only separate groups but a separate movement, free of preconceptions, which will build an analysis of women's oppression that is rooted in our day-to-day experience and base on that analysis our own revolutionary programs.

It was clear to her that alliance with men would come only when "sexism sickens them as much as racism." In February she and her group disrupted a New York State hearing on abortion when it refused to hear the "real experts" on the subject, the women themselves. In March she became a charter member of the Redstockings, an even more radical group. Her private life was disrupted by her beliefs; she found herself becoming humorless, then enraged by slights and evidence of sexism, then nearly ready to commit bloody acts for what she believed.

Friedan spoke to suburban housewives; Willis represented the group of fairly radical young women; the studies of Robert Blood and associates speak about the third major component of the emerging women's movement—working wives and mothers. In 1970, nearly half of all women in the country were working, and the majority of these women were wives and mothers. Blood studied the power structure of the home. He found that a woman's contribution to the decision-making process of her household correlated directly with how she was valued by the outside world. If she worked, she was valued; if she had a well-paying position, she was more highly valued; however, if she stayed at home, she was less valued. Through working she gained authority over how the family spent money, even if she lost some control over household concerns. Rather than being confined to the arena of supermarkets, bridge games, and Girl Scout troops, women who worked were in the "real" world, and in it they gained confidence and experience. They could hold arguments with their husbands on more nearly equal bases; they could insist that husbands do a share of the housework. "A working wife's husband listens to her more," Blood wrote. "She expresses herself and has more opinions. Instead of looking up into her husband's eyes and worshiping him, she levels with him. Thus her power increases, and, relatively speaking, her husband's falls."

In the consciousness-raising sessions that involved all three subgroups of women, and in the literature that was addressed to them, throughout the late 1960s and early 1970s there was forged a women's critique of American society. The critique was as fundamental and as deep as those posited by blacks, youth, the antiwar movement, and by ecologists. Its prime tenet was that all women in our society suffered from economic and sexual exploitation. As Marlene Dixon wrote in 1969,

> Clearly, for the liberation of women to become a reality it is necessary to destroy the ideology of male supremacy which asserts the biological and social inferiority of women in order to justify massive institutionalized oppression.... The phenomenon of male chauvinism can only be understood when it is perceived as a form of racism (in which) the nature of women, like that of slaves, is depicted as dependent, incapable of reasoned thought, childlike in its simplicity and warmth, martyred in the role of the mother, and mystical in the role of sexual partner. In its benevolent form, the inferior position of women results in paternalism; in its malevolent form, a domestic tyranny which can be unbelievably brutal.

The central tenet of the women's critique was that women were perceived as inferior. All else followed from that perception.

Economic exploitation began in the home, to which women had been restricted because of the nature of childbearing, and, later, because of the need to maintain a home, and, still later, because of the kinds of jobs available to women outside the home. A 1969 study showed that the work which a mother of two children performed for her husband, children, and home encompassed more than a dozen job categories (chef, chauffeur, seamstress) and was worth (figured at the minimum wage per hour) about $8,000 per year. Margaret Benston suggested that the real productivity of the homemaker was denied by the commonly held assumption that the wife-and-mother was dependent upon her husband for her sustenance:

> In sheer quantity, household labor, including child care, constitutes a huge amount of socially necessary production. Nevertheless, in a society based on commodity production, it is not usually considered even as "real work," since it is outside of trade and the marketplace. This assignment of household work as the function of a special category "women" means that this group *does* stand in a different relationship to production.... In a society in which money determines value, women are a group who work outside the money economy. Their work is not worth

money, is therefore valueless, is therefore not even real work. And women themselves, who do this valueless work, can hardly be expected to be worth as much as men, who work for money.

The valuation of a woman in the home—as a consumer—was perverse. It tied a woman's success to her ability to goad her husband into the purchase of vast amounts of socially questionable goods.

The housewife-mother who worked was doubly exploited, expected to work for low wages in the marketplace, and to continue her endless multifarious homemaking tasks without substantial assistance from husband or children. In the marketplace she was stigmatized and passed over for promotion because the power structure felt she had first allegiance to husband and children; at home she was stigmatized because she wasn't always there.

Eschewing Marx, who saw the basic problem of Western society as the inequity devolving from the concept of private property, the women's critique saw the basis for women's economic inferiority in the fundamental unfairness of the patriarchal society. The quintessential "rugged individualist" conquered nature, practiced a capitalism which exploited all minorities, and passed on his property to his son. In patrilineal descent women were excluded—as they had been excluded in America for generations. Women were excluded from equity in property ownership, equivalency in work and pay, excluded from obtaining credit, etc. American mythology cherished men who were independent and aggressive (qualities necessary in the workplace) and women who were gentle and passive (qualities useful in the home). But the women's critique pointed out that this was not the only possible sexual division of traits. It was not an incontrovertible fact of life that women were better at child rearing or that men were more naturally suited to the work world; such traits were societally conditioned— and so the possibility existed that roles assigned to sexes could change. Women could become aggressive and independent; men could be taught to be gentle and nurturing.

Women could legitimately aspire to being brain surgeons rather than nurses; men could receive as much approbation from teaching kindergarten as they did from being auto mechanics. Moreover, child rearing could be performed by institutions and would not have to take up quite so much of either parent's time. Housework tasks could be divided among those available to do them. The implications went even further. Families themselves could consist of people other than husband-wife-and-two-kids: people could live alone, families could share child care or household help, communities could take on tasks that were formerly the sole province of families.

In the personal realm, relationships between men and women had to diverge from the patriarchal model. It was strict adherence to roles that had encouraged the archaic chivalry and debasement that passed for the exaltation of women, and which also had served as incubator for the double standard in sexual relations.

A woman who was promiscuous was considered a tramp, while a man who was promiscuous was given tacit societal approbation. Sexual "liberation" as such had not done much for women; it simply made them more available to men. What was needed for true sexual liberation was freedom from all stereotyping and from the application of different standards to men and women who engaged in similar behavior. As Kate Millet wrote in *Sexual Politics*, the whole subject of sex was so covered with shame, ridicule, and silence, that

> any failure to conform to stereotype reduces the individual . . . to an abysmal feeling of guilt, unworthiness and confusion. Unalterably born into one group or another, every subject is forced, moment to moment, to *prove* he or she is, in fact, male or female by deference to the ascribed characteristics of masculine and feminine. There is no way out of such a dilemma but to rebel and be broken, stigmatized and cured. Until the radical spirit revives to free us, we remain imprisoned in the vast gray stockades of the sexual reaction.

Sociologist Alice Rossi wrote that women who were homebound focused too much of their energy on their children, who could use a dose of "healthy inattention." Sex stereotyping institutionalized the tyranny of the bedroom and made for unhappiness and for faulty rationalizations; it encouraged dependence and dominance, rather than cooperation. Studying 400 marriages over twenty years, teams of sociologists found that sex stereotyping and enforced specialization of roles fostered divorce and family dissolution. Liberating women did not produce divorces, but preventing them from being liberated did.

Indeed, there were more divorces, and many of them could be attributed to failed expectations. For years women had been traumatized into being happy with their lot, no matter how miserable it actually was. The new revolution had its own rising expectations, its own anger, its own thrust toward breaking the bonds of traditional relationships. Incompatibility in sexual matters became a permissible factor in divorces. Then, too, as experience with sexuality increased, more and more people, especially among the young, experimented with homosexual liaisons. The stigma attached to being "gay" (or even bisexual) began to fade slightly. Stereotyping became the last refuge for both extremes of the moral spectrum: the "total woman" was one who devoted herself entirely to the welfare of her husband and who used the new sexuality to bait her trap; there also were some radical feminists who were pushed into lesbianism is order to prove their commitment to the total liberation of women.

As roles and stereotypes became understood, it was possible to see that on a society-wide level, adherence to the patriarchal myth had deprived the United States of such (stereotypically female) qualities as compassion, intuition, nurturance, emotionality, artistry, and nonrational thinking. Our aggressiveness and unrelenting drive to dominate the world in the postwar years, our insistence upon rational and strict economic hierarchies, had led the nation into a thicket of continual difficulties. How could we soften and deepen our outlook? The women's critique suggested that if male-identified characteristics had gotten us into trouble, then female-identified qualities might help us achieve a more balanced view of the world.

By 1970, women's issues had reached a level of public consciousness which they had not enjoyed in a half-century. America already had been hurt and was feeling vulnerable, less "male" and less dominant. It was ready to hear the women's critique, and major newsmagazines and television networks gave extended coverage to the emerging movement. The new generation of women, looking homeward, saw the inability of their mothers to free themselves from sexual stereotyping, and vowed it wouldn't happen to them. With the new economic downturn, it became imperative for more and more women to work, and this also pushed the consciousness of women's issues to the fore.

After having languished for several decades on congressional back burners, the Equal Rights Amendment (ERA) finally passed in the House of Representatives. On the other hand, President Nixon vetoed measures for child care and for abortion reform, vetoes which were sustained in Congress. And a women's march in honor of the fiftieth anniversary of the 1920 amendment which had obtained the vote for women received as many jeers as it did cheers.

It was evidence that only some women agreed with the women's critique. There were still many who associated women's liberation with lesbian bra-burners, who felt their homes and marriages threatened by what the "libbers" were saying and doing. In various polls taken in 1970 and 1971, about 60 percent of those queried said they were satisfied with their lives as homemakers. While more women agreed than disagreed with the goals of the women's movement ("equality" and "recognition"), most of the women polled disagreed with the methods and angry stances of those leading the movement. Most believed that women were biologically different from men, and that such goals as equal pay for equal work would never be fully realized. At this time far less than a majority of the country's women were self-supporting; only about a third held full-time jobs. In general it was the nonworking women who resented the implication that their lives had less meaning or completeness than did the lives of those who were "free" or who were wholly absorbed in their paid work. Such women—and they were the large majority of women—felt their basic needs for love, for a man's companionship, children, and a home, were under attack, and they resisted that attack even though in resisting it they seemed to support and accept obviously odious and inequitable divisions between the sexes.

The women's movement appealed more to the young than to the old, more to the better-educated than to the working class. It has been called a middle-class revolution, but the base was larger than that. Even among the 600,000 teenaged Future Homemakers of America, the tenets of women's liberation exerted a "definite influence," an FHA spokesperson said in 1971, for teenaged girls now believed that fulfillment of women depended as much on holding a meaningful job as it did on having a home, a husband, and children.

Women's issues were emotional, involving sacred institutions such as marriage and the family, and control over the body. One of the most important issues was abortion. Between 1968 and 1970, seventeen states passed reform statutes on abortion, and by 1970 more than 200,000 women were receiving legal abortions each year, a 1000 percent increase over the 1968 figure. Some people thought this was a positive step, while others considered it anathema. Pro-abortion groups said it was a matter of women's rights, of women's control over their own bodies, a matter of choice. Anti-abortion groups said it was a matter of the right of the as-yet-unborn child, and a matter of society's concern for the children which was of greater importance than any individual's concern for her own body. In the early 1970s as many groups were at work to overturn the recently liberalized abortion statutes as were at work to extend such statutes to states which did not have them.

On January 23, 1973, the Supreme Court under Chief Justice Warren Burger ruled, in *Roe vs. Wade*, that a state could not prevent a woman from having an abortion during the first six months of a pregnancy. The 7–2 ruling overturned laws to the contrary in forty-six states, and for all practical purposes legalized abortion nationwide. Given the generally conservative bent of the Court and the age of the justices—and their sex—women's liberation groups concluded that the ruling was a victory, that the Court had had its consciousness raised. Actually, *Roe vs. Wade* came at a time when the reverberations from thalidomide and the German measles epidemic of the middle 1960s were still being felt, and when many doctors had called for a statute which would allow them to intervene to save a woman's life or to remove an obviously damaged fetus prior to natural birth. The new technology, then, influenced the judges as much as the movement tenet that women should have the right of control over their own bodies. This Supreme Court decision came as something of a shock to most Americans, the most visible sign of the influence of the women's movement during the decade, a major advance in the status of women, and one which safeguarded a woman's right to privacy and self-determination.

Roe vs. Wade spurred development of more abortion clinics but also galvanized anti-abortion groups, which began working through state legislatures to get around the ruling in various ways. Strong opposition to abortion was evidence that just as women's liberation was hitting its stride, a backlash had developed that mitigated against further change in the relationships between men and women. Another sign came from the visible slowing of the pace toward adoption of the ERA. After Senate passage, the amendment had been quickly adopted by a majority of the states; just a few more were needed for a two-thirds majority. By 1974 some states which had previously passed the ERA had rescinded their positive votes and others were considering doing so—and time began to run out on the first version of the amendment.

There were many explanations: bad times; too-pushy women; a conservative tide; the feeling that the family was being fatally weakened. Common to all of these was the idea that in the realm of the truly personal, more so than in other spheres, change and complexity were difficult to accept. Loss of economic hegemony, loss of authority as a nation, loss of leadership—none of these was palatable, but each could be understood and endured as long as the rock of home and marriage still stood. Loss of authority for men, and all that followed from the questioning of patriarchal dominance, was more difficult to bear.

Those who wished to "preserve" the home, the family, and marriage crouched down and resisted the various tenets of the women's critique. They characterized liberationists as people who aimed to break down the sanctity of home, marriage, and children. The defenders cited moral and Biblical justifications for their positions on abortion, child care, the primacy of man, and women's appointed place in God's plan for life.

Those who embraced the women's critique were, in general, those who wished to "search" for different and more equitable ways of life. They tended to be younger women, the women who had been forced into the job marketplace and who were not being treated with concomitant respect at home. Sometimes gently, sometimes stridently, those who agreed with the women's critique would point out to those who rejected it that the defenders were protecting a surrogate institution—the suburban version of the nuclear family—that was not gospel-based but simply a variation of reality that was untenable in the modern age.

The facts of the decade bore out the searchers' insistence that many aspects of male-female relationships were changing. More women than ever before were working in 1975; family size had diminished from nearly four children per family to 2.6; childbearing was being routinely postponed by women until their careers were under way; and more and more women were returning to work soon after their children were born. These women were holding jobs as doctors, were filling many places in law schools, were returning to assembly lines and blue-collar occupations. In the home, and in the structure of families, the changes were no less stark. In contrast to the 1950s, only a bare majority of the country's children now lived in homes in which both of the natural parents were present together. Some 20 percent of children lived with a single parent. Far fewer two-person households were made up of young marrieds or childless couples: there were more couples living together without benefit of marriage. There were more acknowledged variants of sexual couplings. There were a great many individuals living alone. More marriages were taking place when the participants were older.

In families where the mothers worked, daughters were scoring lower on tests of "traditional" femininity. These same daughters had higher expectations of themselves and of the men with whom they associated. They routinely expected those men to take part in housework, to participate in childbirth and child rearing, to accept that at times the tasks of the marketplace would be more important to the young women than the tasks of the hearth.

As for themselves, the young women now increasingly believed they could accomplish anything a man could—that they could be architects or jockeys or skid row bums—because their lives would not be circumscribed by outmoded degrees of expectation. They inhabited a world in which much of male authority was being questioned, and in which the authority of schools, religions, and other traditionally socializing influences was waning. If women still garnered only two-thirds of the salaries that men earned, there was no indication that the new generation of women would long be satisfied with wage, power, freedom or any other inequity.

9 The Double Standard

AMONG THE ASSUMPTIONS we shared at the start of the era were a belief in America's position as the main world bulwark against communism, a belief that we were and should at any cost continue to be Number One in world affairs, and a belief which equated growth with success in business. Common to the three assumptions was the notion of power.

Americans respected power. Money, sexual attractiveness, political clout, the ability to harm someone and escape punishment for the action—these were some of its forms. Power had to answer to no one; the only requirement for using power was to hold it. Power stratified the country. We recognized that a double standard existed in regard to power, that there was a set of rules for those who had power, and a different, far more restraining set for those who did not. Those who held or who were in close touch with power could accomplish anything; those without access to power were unable to change their lot, "powerless."

One of the more apparent macro-trends of the postwar world was the centralization of power. The federal government continued the expansion that had begun under President Franklin Roosevelt; for example, as the years went by, the federal budget became an ever larger fraction of the gross national product, with the inevitable result that decisions made in Washington took on increasing weight and importance. There was a similar trend toward consolidation and size in business. Since the turn of the century, when U.S. Steel and AT&T were created, companies had been growing in size. During World War II there had been centralized production in the hands of relatively few firms. After wartime restrictions were lifted, those firms made considerable profits, and were in position to fulfill the orders of the Cold War. It was at this time that many multinational companies began to come to the fore. Only giant companies with the proper kind of facilities could supply products in great quantities to the government's largest purchasing division, the military, and only giant firms could produce the bulk of the products consumed by American and overseas customers.

A third centrifugal force was the intensifying competitiveness of the American system. With the need to sell ever more products and to maintain "growth," capitalism seemed to be, as Marx said, the war of all against all. Supermarket shelves could hold only so many brands of laundry detergent; ICBMs could be made by only a few companies; Congress could have only a handful of representatives. In such a competitive atmosphere it seemed reasonable for competitors to try anything to get the "edge" that would put one ahead of another. When the stakes were high and the competition was fierce, what might enable one competitor to win out over another was not necessarily ability, innovation, or preparation for the job— but could rather be a matter of power, influence, political clout. It might not always be the best man or the best country that conquered the second-best; more often than not it was the man or the country that had somehow found the "edge."

During the Cold War era that "edge" grew to include tactics originally appropriate only in the arena of military combat. At that time, both liberals and conservatives believed that the Communists were trying to take over the world, and that they must be fought to a standstill in foreign countries and at home by every available means. Abroad, we encouraged many nefarious tactics on the part of the newly formed Central Intelligence Agency, and at home we allowed the Federal Bureau of Investigation to circumvent certain provisions of the Bill of Rights in order to keep ourselves safe from insidious foreign influences. Some of these tactics for gaining the edge were secrecy, deceit, and viciousness. All had to do with power.

Secrecy was often necessary to military victory. Possession of secrets was a perquisite of power; only those who had power, for instance, had access to Top-Secret documents. During the Cold War it seemed appropriate to conceal much from public scrutiny. One of the prime objectives of the CIA was to find out the enemy's secrets.

To maintain secrecy the agency used deceit, misdirection, concealment.

A distinction between public face and private action went hand-in-glove with CIA work. Certainly a spy could not register as such at a Moscow hotel; certainly a saboteur had a need for a weapon disguised as a cigarette lighter.

Viciousness, too, went with the Cold War operations. To disrupt an enemy's position, maximum force might have to be used. It might not be enough to simply overthrow a government by political means; it might be necessary to assassinate the government's leader so his party could not later regroup and return to power.

To keep one secret meant to make many more; to deceive successfully mandated ever-more ingenious methods of concealment and ever-larger doses of force. Tactics appropriate to dealing with Moscow also were used to deal with satellite countries, then to deal with countries in which communism was a threat but had not taken full control. As such tactics spread, so did the CIA's sphere of operations; the agency continually pushed into areas where zeal had a high probability of exceeding the requirement for action. Then the CIA style and world view came to be adopted by the FBI. Frank J. Donner suggests that in this era FBI agents acted as "full-fledged ideological zealots" and that an agent habitually saw himself as

a nation-savior, a front-line defender of the patriotic faith. Inevitably countersubversive investigation becomes a highly personalized function, unfettered by professionalism or, for that matter, the norms of legality and accountability. This dualism is distilled in the term "responsibility," which regularly emerges as an "anything goes" justification for counter-subversive abuses.... Denver agent Theodore Rosack in 1976 told a federal grand jury investigating the Bureau's acquisition of documents stolen from the Socialist Workers' Party by one of its informers [under a program that operated from 1956 to 1971], that "it is our responsibility ...to investigate... [an] organization which does not have the best interest of this country at heart"—as though this somehow was a defense of the agency's complicity in the burglary.

Eventually the tactics appropriate in the arena of global combat proved so seductive (and powerful) that they came to be used not only by the CIA and FBI, but also by various other arms of the government including other bureaus of the Department of Justice, the Internal Revenue Service, and by the White House.

When dealing with these later abuses it is important to remember that

The Double Standard   *261*

many of them were present in muted form at the outset of the era. In 1963, for instance, the CIA was already deeply involved in Indochina and helped along the coup which overthrew and executed Ngo Dinh Diem. With President Kennedy's assent, the CIA had attempted to assassinate Fidel Castro and other leaders of left-leaning countries. Under the leadership of Attorney General Robert F. Kennedy, the Department of Justice was busy tracking the machinations of Teamster Union president Jimmy Hoffa and was prosecuting some companies for antitrust violations, but was ignoring other unions' racketeering practices and other giant companies' restraint-of-trade actions. The Attorney General had approved FBI Director J. Edgar Hoover's plan to wiretap various hotel bedrooms occupied by Martin Luther King, Jr. Vice-President Lyndon Johnson, while he was rising through the congressional hierarchy, had used his political muscle to create a personal fortune in communciations; former Vice-President Richard M. Nixon was currently using his political connections to make his own fortune representing the interest of corporate clients such as Coca-Cola—on whose behalf Nixon was in Dallas on November 22, 1963.

Abuses of power grew swiftly. Although the CIA's charter specifically forbade it from operations inside the United States, when it was thought that foreign Communists were subverting U.S. organizations, the prohibition was not enforced. During a twenty-year period which encompassed much of the Decade of Shocks, the CIA looked at 28 million pieces of mail in New York City alone; of these it photocopied the exterior of 2.1 million, and actually steamed open more than 200,000 before sending the mail on its way overseas. No foreign influences were documented.

In 1967, President Johnson asked the CIA to find out whether American youth groups at the forefront of antiwar activity were backed by or infiltrated by foreign Communist agents. In response the agency formed Operation CHAOS. The acronym was a joke, and stood for nothing, but during the following seven years, until March 1974, CHAOS collected files on more than 300,000 Americans, paid undercover spies and *agents provocateurs*, etc. Associated divisions of the CIA went into the pornographic movie business, fed LSD to unsuspecting citizens, and concealed its stocks of exotic poisons even after directly ordered by President Nixon to destroy them. (Later the Rockefeller Commission, reporting to President Ford, would label all these actions as "plainly unlawful . . . [infringing on] the rights of Americans.")

The CIA produced several reports on the antiwar groups, all of which were rejected by Presidents Johnson and Nixon because they didn't say the right things. For instance, when Director Richard Helms wrote Henry Kissinger in 1969, enclosing a copy of an agency report which concluded that student protest had come from the students' social and political alienation, and was not sponsored by foreign governments, Helms said that spying on students and on New Leftists was

> not within the charter of this Agency, so I need not emphasize how extremely sensitive this makes the paper. Should anyone learn of its existence it would prove most embarrassing for all concerned.

Helms's note might have been designed to get the CIA out of the domestic spying business, but the Nixon administration's reaction to the report itself was to order Operation CHAOS to continue to look for Communists in the woodwork. Obedient, the CIA penetrated a thousand different organizations, some as wide of the subversive mark as the Women's Strike for Peace, the Southern Christian Leadership Conference, and Grove Press. It was not until 1974, when new director William Colby was worried about the CIA's links to Watergate, that CHAOS was canceled.

FBI excesses followed the same pattern. At the behest of various presidents, the FBI had been at the business of wiretapping and eavesdropping on Americans since 1939. The United States had no national police force, so most people—and presidents—had been content to have the FBI investigate possible domestic subversion. More wiretaps were installed under President Eisenhower than under Presidents Johnson and Nixon combined—but in the later years reasons for suspicion were more flimsy, and the excesses committed against those tapped and watched seemed less forgivable.

As an example of the transformation of the FBI from information gathering to "operational" missions, there was COINTELPRO. During World War II, the FBI had managed to prove that the Socialist Workers party was subversive, as the term was then defined by the Smith Act. When that act was later declared unconstitutional and the SWP was exonerated, the FBI's enmity to the organization continued. The FBI's Counter-Intelligence Program (COINTELPRO) began in 1956 as a new attempt to compromise the Socialist Workers. From 1960 to 1966, about once every three weeks Bureau agents burglarized SWP offices; Bureau agents also infiltrated the party and one even ran for national office on its platform.

Stolen SWP documents were fed to other government agencies such as the Civil Service Commission in order to disbar SWP members and contributors from government jobs.

From the SWP the Bureau moved on to the civil-rights movement. In the 1950s, FBI agents helped local southern police harass freedom riders while simultaneously refusing to adequately investigate abuse of civil-rights workers. The 1963 wiretap on Martin Luther King, Jr. was initially justified on FBI Director J. Edgar Hoover's repeated contention to Robert Kennedy that one of King's top men was a Communist. Communism, however, was merely an excuse, and the surveillance quickly extended into more personal areas. Logs of tapes were offered to newsmen and an actual tape of King's alleged sexual misconduct was sent to Mrs. Coretta King. King himself was sent an anonymous letter which tried to push him to commit suicide before he could accept the Nobel Peace Prize.

COINTELPRO also worked to disrupt the black organizations at the forefront of change, such as SCLC, SNCC, the Nation of Islam, the Black Panthers. Agents tried to set the Chicago Blackstone Rangers against the Black Panthers, and were deeply implicated in the murders of Fred Hampton and Mark Clark in the Panthers' Chicago headquarters. A Bureau agent/informant was head of the Chicago Panthers' security and provided police with a floor plan of the apartment. Another informant was head of security for the American Indian Movement (AIM) and helped lead an armed takeover of a state office building in Iowa; still other informants tried to subvert the Puerto Rican independence movement. In Seattle, invoking the name of a black nationalist organization, FBI infiltrators firebombed civic and university buildings; they also paid $75 to a young man to pull off a robbery which ended in the young man's death in a police ambush. In New York, FBI–trained police provided a black group with the explosives they planned to use to bomb the Statue of Liberty. In San Diego agents set two rival black groups against one another and provoked a war which ended in a half-dozen deaths. Also in San Diego the FBI converted a nearly disbanded right-wing paramilitary group, the Minutemen, into the Secret Army Organization (SAO) and furnished the group with a leader, firearms, explosives, and funds. The SAO committed repeated acts of violence and terrorism against leftist groups and antiwar activists; once an FBI informant and SAO colleague wounded a young woman in an antiwar professor's house; next day the informant gave the gun and some clothing to his FBI supervisor, who concealed them until after the San Diego police had, on their own, broken up the SAO.

Testimony before congressional oversight committees in the late 1970s makes clear that the FBI instigated a portion of the violent acts originally attributed to the antiwar movement. The movement groups were a particular target of FBI infiltration. In 1970, a Bureau memo recommended that the age for COINTELPRO informants be lowered from 21 to 18, because

> Never in our history have we been confronted with as critical a need for informant coverage. Terrorist violence is all around us and more has been threatened. Even our own doors are being threatened by Weathermen fanatics. Bombings, assassination of police officers, kidnapping and torture murder are all part of the picture. These violence-oriented black and white savages are at war with the Government and the American people.

Such Bureau paranoia fed into the paranoia which permeated the highest levels of government. President Johnson was a man long used to secrecy, deceit, and viciousness. In his congressional career, he had often called on the resources of the FBI, and was a neighbor of Director Hoover. In 1964 he asked the Bureau to infiltrate and bug the Democratic convention. He was interested in forestalling the efforts of Martin Luther King, Jr., and others to seat the dissident Mississippi Freedom Democratic party, which he thought had an outside chance of leading the convention to reject him, the incumbent president, and to nominate his rival, Robert F. Kennedy. Johnson was a shoo-in, but he used the FBI to get an even greater edge on his competition. In succeeding years he had the FBI and CIA work into groups which opposed his policies, and in 1968 asked that the FBI once again infiltrate the Democratic convention to help maintain his iron control of the nominating process. At his behest, the FBI also wiretapped a few phone calls made by Agnew's people in Denver.

Richard Nixon had been a crony of Director Hoover's since the 1940s, when the Bureau had 1,500 informants within the American Communist party. As committed an anti-Communist as Hoover, and a man who habitually found conspiracies around him, Nixon encouraged the Bureau's various crusades. Johnson's men—Nicholas Katzenbach and Ramsey Clark—had stymied Hoover somewhat, but Nixon's Attorney General, John Mitchell, was more attuned to the director's style. Beginning in 1969 the FBI accelerated its efforts to disrupt the peace and civil-rights movements. Even after FBI files were stolen from the Media, Pennsylvania, field office and many FBI projects were made public, the attempts at disruption did not halt. In 1971 the Media files revealed that 40 percent of FBI time was spent on investigating dissident groups, and another 14 percent on looking into military desertion and draft resistance. Only one percent was devoted to combating organized crime. Even after Director Hoover died in 1972, such practices continued; for example, FBI informants egged on black demonstrators to violent protests against Nixon's renomination at the Republican convention in Miami.

The continual encroachment by the CIA and FBI into forbidden territory was mirrored by the steady aggrandizement of presidential power during the decade. In situations such as the Cuban missile crisis it seemed impossible to follow constitutional requirements to obtain a congressional declaration of war before committing U.S. forces. In the brush-fire wars, the constitutional limits to presidential power were also blurred. It was the national goal in this era to make "credible" the power of the United States, and Vietnam provided the setting for this; it was at once the quintessential brush-fire war, an arena for secrecy, deceit and viciousness and a continually expanding theater of operations for presidential power.

Johnson's credibility gap was a result of what he perceived to be the military necessity of saying one thing and doing another in regard to Vietnam. Because he had to have the wherewithal to back up U.S. interests in Vietnam, LBJ believed he must mislead Congress while seeming to seek its approval in the Tonkin Gulf Resolution. Similarly, LBJ's attempts to ignore and then to suppress dissent came out of his belief that the dissenters did not understand the desperate nature of the battle being fought, and thus were not acting in the best interests of the country. It was easy for Johnson's men to conclude that only they who knew the situation clearly could be trusted to make the proper decisions on the country's behalf.

On taking office, Nixon had an opportunity to end the secrecy, deceit, and viciousness which had characterized the later Johnson years. He did not seize it. Rather, a few days after taking office, Nixon approved the secret Menu bombing of Cambodia. Not only did this bombing have deleterious effects on the Paris peace talks, but it also helped to create within the Air Force a hierarchy devoted to keeping the bombing orders and reports out of the usual files. An entire furnace was used each day to burn the bombing records. William Beecher's report on Menu in *The New York Times* in May 1969 precipitated the first series of wiretaps on newsmen, National Security Council members, and sub-Cabinet officers. All but one of the taps were placed by the FBI, on orders from John Ehrlichman and with names supplied by Henry Kissinger. Many of the men tapped could not have been the source of the leak, but by tapping them Kissinger and the White House upper-echelon staff were able to obtain information which enabled them to keep Cabinet officers in line. The last tap, on news analyst Joseph Kraft, was placed by White House "special investigators" John J. Caulfield and John Ragan, and were paid for with money left over from the 1968 Nixon campaign chest.

In 1968, when the country had been besieged by protesters, Congress passed a law which gave the Justice Department the power to wiretap, provided a court warrant was obtained for each individual case. Deeming the law unconstitutional, Johnson's last Attorney General, Ramsey Clark, declined to use the wiretap power. In 1969 a Supreme Court ruling suggested that defendants in trials had the right to know whether any of the evidence against them had been obtained by wiretapping. The Justice Department, under new Attorney General John Mitchell, objected vociferously to this ruling, and in June filed a brief in connection with the Chicago conspiracy trial that explained its objections. The brief admitted that the government had wiretapped some of the men indicted for conspiracy in connection with the demonstrations at the 1968 Democratic convention, and asserted the government's right to wiretap anyone who was out to "attack and subvert the government by unlawful means"—even without a warrant. The outraged defendants' attorneys replied to the brief, writing:

> For the first time in American history, a member of the President's Cabinet has publicly—and proudly—stated that he has, in open violation of his own oath of office, taken the law into his own hands.

Many times in many ways, during its first year in power, the administration took the law into its own hands. The Justice Department testified for the adoption of the D.C. Crime Bill, with its "no-knock" and preventative detention provisions. Senator Sam Ervin, Jr., called the bill "repressive," and said it should be entitled "A Bill to Repeal the Fourth, Fifth, Sixth, and Eighth Amendments to the Constitution." During the summer of 1969 the Justice Department refused to enforce civil-rights laws, shelved court-mandated busing programs, and tried to halt the extension of the 1965 Voting Rights Act. In the fall, the president declined to comply with a Supreme Court decision on desegregation because, he said, he disagreed with it.

Johnson's ire at antiwar demonstrations had led to information gathering by the CIA and FBI; Nixon's anger at the renewed dissent of 1969 led to permission for Operation CHAOS to go operational—to plant agents in the antiwar movement to stir things up, rather than only to report on what was being planned. To combat the potential impact of new demonstrations, H. R. Haldeman orchestrated a drive on newspapers, magazines, and television networks. The aim was to prevent the media from sympathetic reporting of the antiwar cause. The Federal Communications Commission was asked to monitor the networks' fairness; the Justice Department was asked to start antitrust suits against them; and the IRS was asked to investigate their tax returns.

In response to Nixon's speech about the war in November of 1969, and Agnew's attacks on the "effete corps of impudent snobs" who dared to make commentary on television and in the press about the speech, White House aides rigged a massive campaign of letters, telegrams, and telephone calls which poured into press and network offices, and seemed to reflect spontaneous and enthusiastic support for the government's policies. Soon the letter-writing program became known inside the White House as the "silent majority" program, which was cranked up for the many different occasions on which the administration needed support. Public opinion was not to be trusted, especially when it could be manufactured.

On April 30, 1970, President Nixon, in the boldest move of his administration thus far, announced on national television that American forces were going into Cambodia to wipe out North Vietnamese and Viet Cong sanctuaries. In his speech Nixon carefully linked the actions abroad with dissent at home. "Anarchy abroad and at home" threatened both American universities and the small nations in the path of totalitarianism; therefore, "It is not our power but our will and character that is being tested." Should we fail to meet the challenge, "all other nations will be on notice that despite its overwhelming power, the United States, when a real crisis comes, will be found wanting." That real crisis, to which Nixon referred but did not name, was the possibility of nuclear war—which he sought to forestall by waging a limited war. Jonathan Schell wrote that the speech revealed Nixon's convoluted aims:

In his thinking, a momentous struggle was under way, and it was not only between the United States and Communism, but between the President and those at home who would wrest from his hands the nation's chosen weapons for its defense in the nuclear age, and would thereby "defeat or humiliate" the United States even before the "real" struggle overseas had begun in earnest. And so it had become necessary, according to his way of thinking, to do what he had in fact been doing almost from the moment he arrived in office: to make war against Americans.

There soon began a thorough reorganization of the executive branch of the government which aimed at consolidating power in the White House. The reorganization was carried out amid great secrecy. Each night, left-over trash was put in "burn bags," and the Roy Ash committee members were forbidden to take their work home. The results were a domestic affairs council which began to supersede the work of some Cabinet departments, the enlargement of the spheres of presidential assistants Haldeman and Ehrlichman, and the aggrandizement of the role of National Security Advisor Henry Kissinger with the consequent diminution of the roles of Secretary of State William Rogers and Secretary of Defense Melvin Laird. The Supreme Court was flooded with inferior candidates such as Harold Carswell and Clement Haynsworth, and Congress was consistently outflanked and bypassed.

The most direct attack on the people was contemplated in the "Huston Plan" for an interagency spy group. White House aide Tom Charles Huston had previously pushed the IRS to question the tax-exempt status of left-leaning organizations; at his request the IRS reviewed such organizations' backgrounds and audited their contributors ten times more often than they did other Americans in the same tax brackets. In the Huston surveillance plan—initiated and approved by President Nixon in June of 1970—the CIA, FBI, NSA, and Defense Intelligence Agency, abetted by personnel from the State, Justice, and Treasury departments, were to form a secret corps to commit illegal acts (warrantless wiretaps, surreptitious entry, black-bag jobs) at the behest of the White House. When asked in 1977 whether he had given his approval to this plan which contemplated doing illegal acts, Nixon replied, "Well, when the President does it, that means that it is not illegal...if the President...approves an action because of a national security, or...because of a threat to internal peace and order of significant magnitude, then the President's decision in that instance is one that enables those who carry it out to carry it out without violating a law." The plan did not go directly into operation, however; it was sidetracked on technicalities by J. Edgar Hoover. But the techniques suggested in it were already being used by the agencies involved, and were later used by the White House.

In 1970, in efforts to stop the reelections of Ted Kennedy and George Wallace, Nixon's personal attorney Herbert Kalmbach disbursed hundreds of thousands of dollars in leftover 1968 campaign funds. Though not strictly illegal, these contributions were used for a purpose that the original donors had never intended. Soon after the 1970 elections, the president's men began reaching out to the dairy industry, to ITT, and to other corporate giants for 1972 campaign contributions. A deal was arranged whereby the dairy industry would contribute a quarter-million dollars to Nixon's re-election campaign in exchange for a Nixon reversal of a decision of the Department of Agriculture; as a result milk price supports were raised. When Nixon, Haldeman, and Mitchell arranged favorable settlement of an antitrust suit then pending against ITT, that company agreed to put up $400,000 toward the president's reelection.

All these things were done in secret, and in order to consolidate power. Such misuses of power came to characterize high-echelon business dealings as well as the machinations of individuals in the political process: they skirted the morality expected of the masses, in pursuit of goals of which the masses might not approve.

When in 1971 some of the men who had been earlier wiretapped by the White House went to work for Democratic frontrunner Senator Edmund Muskie, a new opportunity arose. By continuing the taps long after they had failed to reveal any national security violations, the administration hoped to obtain politically sensitive information to help the president's reelection. At about the same time the president had secret taping systems installed in his offices in the White House, the Executive Office Building, and at Camp David. Now he was taping his friends as well as his enemies.

On June 13, 1971, *The New York Times* began to print excerpts from the "Pentagon Papers" supplied to them by Daniel Ellsberg. The Justice Department, claiming that national security considerations ranked above the rights of the press derived from the First Amendment, obtained a restraining order on publication of further excerpts. When the Supreme Court ruled against this prior restraint, the Justice Department indicted Ellsberg for violation of the Espionage Act and for theft of government property. Unwilling to let the Justice Department alone handle Ellsberg, the White House hired E. Howard Hunt and G. Gordon Liddy to work with Ehrlichman deputy Egil Krogh and Kissinger deputy David Young, as well as with high-level representatives of various government depart-ments, to use various illegal means to "get" Ellsberg. These means included burglaries of the offices of Ellsberg's psychiatrist on one coast and of Mrs.

Ellsberg's psychiatrist on the other coast. The CIA contributed a "psychological profile" of Ellsberg and provided disguises and spy devices to the White House burglars. In other escapades, Hunt and Chuck Colson doctored old cables (of the type reprinted in the "Pentagon Papers") and made them read as if President Kennedy had personally ordered Diem's execution. Colson also asked John Caulfield to firebomb the left-wing Brookings Institution; this project was headed off by White House Counsel John Dean and John Ehrlichman. Hunt also visited ITT lobbyist Dita Beard and attempted to get rid of Beard's incriminating memos which detailed the ITT–Justice Department deal.

The pace of the attacks was stepped up. In the White House a comprehensive "enemies list" was compiled; John Dean wrote that its purpose was to explore ways to "use the available federal machinery to screw our political enemies . . . e.g., grant availability, federal contracts, litigation, prosecution, etc." Career civil servants in the federal bureaucracy were replaced by Nixon loyalists convinced of the necessity for cooperation with the White House. President Nixon had vast improvements made at public expense to his Key Biscayne and San Clemente homes. He made a donation of his vice-presidential papers to a library and had the deed illegally backdated. By the bequest his tax burdens for several previous years were brought down to under $1,000. Herbert Kalmbach, Nixon's personal attorney, grew wealthy as airlines, conglomerates, and firms with business before government agencies put his law firm on retainer. Vice-President Agnew continued to receive kickbacks and gratuities (which included a weekly delivery of free groceries) in payment for services he had rendered friends during his days as Maryland's governor.

In the early months of 1972 the quasilegal and extralegal activities of Nixon's inner circle multiplied. The finance arm of the Committee to Re-Elect the President (CREEP) levied a tithe of one percent of corporate profits on each of several hundred companies. In exchange for these contributions, some companies received specific deals which involved actions by government regulatory agencies; most corporations, however, paid up mainly to avoid future unnamed difficulties with the administration. Many of the contributions came illegally from corporate coffers and had to be hidden.

By April 7, after which date contributions and disbursements had to be listed with the Federal Elections Commission, some $20 million had been accumulated by CREEP, much of it in untraceable cash, some of the rest already "laundered" in Mexico.

Meanwhile the political arm of the committee undertook sabotage, burglary, forgery and wiretapping campaigns to sow dissension in the Democratic ranks. John Mitchell, along with top White House officials, planned these illegal activities and pored over their results. On a night in early June when the president was making a triumphant speech in Moscow, men hired by CREEP broke into the Watergate headquarters of the Democratic National Committee, photographed documents, and installed two wiretaps. They made several more trips to collect information and to tinker with the taps before the night of June 16–17, when they were finally caught. The burglars were soon identified as former CIA agents, and their paymaster was quickly linked to CREEP and to the White House. An immediate cover-up was planned and meticulously executed by Nixon associates. John Mitchell resigned from the reelection committee to devote more time to the cover-up efforts, and the president directed the White House's efforts, though day-to-day supervision of the cover-up mainly involved his two chief aides, Haldeman and Ehrlichman, together with John Dean. These men managed to compromise the integrity of the FBI's investigation, to involve the CIA in the burglars' defense and to otherwise compromise the agency, to get lower-rank CREEP and White House officials to burn evidence, to pay hush money to some of the burglary defendants, to suborn perjured testimony at grand jury hearings, and to limit the Justice Department's investigation to the prosecution of the original defendants. It was imperative for the Nixon men to contain the matter, because they knew if it were not contained, what John Mitchell referred to as the "White House horrors"—the illegal acts which since mid-1969 had been going on at the president's behest—would be revealed.

Because of the lassitude of the Justice Department, the Congress, and the press, and because of the immense amount of time and effort put into the cover-up by the White House, the concealment worked spectacularly well. Even after October 10, 1972, when *The Washington Post* printed damaging allegations about a cover-up and illegal acts, there was no sustained public outcry against the administration. On the day that Hunt, Liddy, and the burglars were indicted, John Dean was able to report to the president that nothing would come "crashing down" about Watergate until after the elections. Nixon congratulated Dean. At the same time, on the president's suggestion, an investigation by Wright Patman's House Banking Committee was derailed, partly by Minority Leader Gerald Ford. In November, Nixon was overwhelmingly reelected.

Immediately afterward, the president obtained blank resignations from

2,000 members of his administration and accepted those of the more liberal of his remaining appointees so he could send many strict Nixon loyalists to various Cabinet departments where they could spy on their bosses. He planned some repressive legislation, such as a bill that would prevent the release of any classified information at any time, cut "Great Society" programs to the bone, vetoed a string of appropriation bills as "budget busters," and impounded some monies already approved by Congress because he disagreed with their prospective disbursement. "Congress' separate power is an obstacle to modern policymaking," wrote a former Nixon Justice Department employee. "Today, the whole Constitution is up for grabs," said a current one. Many people were beginning to agree with Senators McGovern and Muskie, who said that the U.S. was closer to one-man rule than ever before in its history.

In the early months of 1973, weekly and sometimes daily, Watergate revelations surfaced. *The Washington Post* and other papers uncovered many facets of the crimes; there were grand jury leaks; tidbits emerged at the confirmation hearings of Acting FBI Director L. Patrick Gray III. In February the Senate formed the Ervin Committee and scheduled its hearings for May. Judge John J. Sirica pressured the original Watergate defendants until James McCord admitted the higher-ups' collusion in the burglary. When congressional pressure mounted for Nixon aides to testify before Senate committees, Attorney General Richard Kleindienst maintained that the principle of separation of powers would permit Nixon to prevent all 2.5 million executive branch employees from testifying. Kleindienst said Congress had only one way to move against the president: impeachment.

Nixon soon announced the resignations of Ehrlichman, Haldeman, Dean, and Kleindienst. He said there was nothing wrong with what they had done but said he would appoint a Special Prosecutor to look into Watergate. His new Attorney General, Elliot Richardson, pledged at his own confirmation hearings that if that Special Prosecutor were not allowed to investigate freely, he, Richardson, would resign.

Hunt, McCord, Jeb Magruder, and John Dean were talking to the prosecutors. On the West Coast the trial of Ellsberg was rocked by revelations of attempts to burglarize his psychiatrist's office. Citing this and a White House effort to influence his decision with an offer of the directorship of the FBI, Judge Matt Byrne declared a mistrial.

The Ervin hearings began. For thirty-five days beginning on May 17, 1973, in front of a television audience numbered in the tens of millions, thirty seven witnesses, from minor functionaries to major Nixon administration personalities, laid out the dimensions and minutiae of the Watergate affair. These included subversion of the Constitution, wiretapping, espionage, sabotage, extortion, blackmail, forgery, burglary, perjury, bribery, obstruction of justice, illegal offers of executive clemency, and other crimes. As painted in the Ervin hearings, the scandal was of a scale and scope never previously encountered in American history.

The arrogance and contempt of witnesses Mitchell, Haldeman, and Ehrlichman evoked public outrage that went beyond anger at specific illegal acts. It was clear that the president's men had continually placed above the law, the political survival of Nixon and that the vast majority of Americans whose lives were ruled by law were appalled. When the revelations had begun, public opinion had been sympathetic to the president; now it turned sharply against him. If Nixon's own guilt had not yet been proved beyond doubt, the obvious guilt of his closest associates had tainted him.

When the existence of the White House taping system became known, Special Prosecutor Archibald Cox and the Ervin Committee both demanded access to tapes which would reveal either the guilt or innocence of many of the witnesses and participants. The president refused to give up the tapes, and the Special Prosecutor and the Ervin Committee started to press for them, the Committee by legislative means and the Special Prosecutor through the courts. Trying to walk a middle ground, Judge Sirica ruled that the president should give the tapes to him, and that he would decide which to forward to Cox and which should be kept confidential and not released. Nixon refused to comply with Sirica's order, and the case went to the Court of Appeals.

On October 10, Vice-President Agnew resigned after pleading *nolo contendere* to charges stemming from his years of kickbacks and income tax evasion. On October 12 the court ruled that Nixon must turn over the tapes to Sirica. During the next week all parties tried to head off a confrontation between the White House and the Special Prosecutor's office, but could not. Deceiving the Ervin Committee and Richardson as to his intent, Nixon tried to force a compromise in which Senator John Stennis, but not Sirica or Cox, would listen to the tapes. When Cox refused to go along, Nixon ordered him fired. A new war in the Middle East had begun, and a world alert of U.S. forces was ordered. In the midst of both the domestic and the international crises, on Saturday evening, October 20, Richardson and his deputy William Ruckelshaus both refused to fire Cox and resigned; then Solicitor General Robert Bork fired Cox and followed the president's orders to abolish, lock, and guard the office of the Special Prosecutor. Nixon believed this action would silence Cox's request for the tapes and solve his court problem.

The Saturday Night Massacre released an avalanche of letters, telegrams, and phone calls—real, this time, and not rigged—in which the public called for Nixon's impeachment. On October 25, Kissinger revealed the previous U.S. forces alert; the accusation was made that Nixon had put the forces on alert to help him with his domestic crisis; the accusation was vigorously denied. Soon after, the president's attorneys said he would now deliver the tapes to Sirica.

Nixon had installed the taping system to control the future writing of history, through records of what transpired in the Oval Office which only he would know of and hear. In the fall of 1973, the tapes were rapidly becoming the instrument of his political suicide. In this last spasm of the Decade of Shocks, a technological toy was enabling a president to assassinate his own character.

In defending his right not to release the tapes, the president provoked a constitutional crisis which threatened to pit the executive branch against both Congress and the courts. In early November, the president's attorney told Sirica that there was a "gap" of 18½ minutes in a crucial tape which contained an extended Nixon-Haldeman conversation three days after the break-in. Later a group of experts testified that the missing portion had been manually erased between five and nine times. John Dean speculated that Nixon, a particularly clumsy man, had himself made the erasures.

Several impeachment resolutions were introduced in the House of Representatives. Many people called for the president to resign, but Republican Senator George Aiken said, "To ask the President now to resign and thus relieve the Congress of its clear congressional duty amounts to a declaration of incompetence on the part of Congress."

Nixon hardened his stance and refused to furnish those who stalked him with the evidence that would convict him. The Judiciary Committee's impeachment inquiries went forward simultaneously with those of new Special Prosecutor Leon Jaworski, who threatened to take his request for the tapes to the Supreme Court. On March 1, 1974, the grand jury indicted Haldeman, Ehrlichman, Colson, Mitchell, and others for the cover-up and named Nixon as an unindicted co-conspirator; the grand jury also requested that its information (and tapes) be submitted to the Judiciary Committee.

The committee subpoenaed additional tapes and threatened to hold Nixon in contempt of Congress if he did not supply them. Contempt of Congress would be an impeachable offense. On April 29 the president announced on television that he was releasing, not the tapes, but 1,200 pages of "transcripts" of the tapes. Appalled, Judiciary Committee Chairman Peter Rodino wrote the White House that the president had not complied with the subpoena.

The transcripts were startling. In copious detail they limned the depths of desperation to which the president and his men had sunk to cover up and put the best face on their misdeeds. In the many pages there was a void where morals might have been. Comparing the transcripts with some of the tapes turned over by the grand jury, the Rodino Committee found that in nearly every spot where potentially damaging material was located, the transcripts had been fudged. The president's version of the March 21, 1973, tape had Nixon tell Dean that, in respect to Hunt's demands for hush money, "His price is pretty high, but at least we can buy time on that." The Judiciary Committee's version had Nixon say that "his price is pretty high, but at least, uh, we should, we should buy time on that, uh, as I pointed out to John." And the president's version of March 22 excluded any mention of his telling Haldeman, Ehrlichman, Dean, and Mitchell, "I want you all to stonewall it, let them plead the Fifth Amendment, coverup, or anything else, if it'll save—save the whole plan. That's the whole point."

"I am not a crook," Nixon told an audience in a speech. Many no longer believed him. The drive for impeachment gathered force. Charges were brought before the House that Nixon had obstructed justice, compromised the FBI and CIA, spied on private citizens without warrants, approved the subornation of perjury and the payment of bribes, shown repeated contempt of Congress and the courts, refused to honor subpoenas, and had in many and various ways failed to observe his duty "to see that the laws be faithfully executed." Nixon maintained that these crimes could be attributed only to excess zeal on the part of subordinates, but the as-yet-unreleased tapes implicated him too deeply in the planning to allow him to realistically deny responsibility for the actions.

As the Rodino Committee started to marshal its evidence to present to Congress, Jaworski asked the Supreme Court to rule on whether the president could keep 64 additional tapes from him. While the Court deliberated, Nixon toured the Middle East and Russia, as if to demonstrate his importance to the country and to act as if his crimes were peccadillos when measured against his international achievements. Little was accomplished on these trips. Public business came to a virtual halt as the constitutional crisis continued without resolution.

Ramifications of Watergate were everywhere. Scandals came to light about nursing homes, industrial work conditions, academic finances, fraud and mismanagement in the stock market, incompetence in the judiciary. Information surfaced abroad about activities of U.S. companies which were implicated in Watergate. This would eventually lead to the downfall of the Tanaka government in Japan and to the disgrace of Prince Bernhard in the Netherlands.

On July 24, 1974, the Supreme Court ruled 8–0 that Nixon must yield the tapes to Jaworski. That same day the Judiciary Committee began its televised presentations. The reasoning of Barbara Jordan and Elizabeth Holtzman, and the anguished appraisals by Republicans such as William Cohen and William Railsback, convinced many remaining skeptics of the necessity of impeachment. Nixon had few defenders left. He released the tapes. When the newly released tapes showed a clear illegality—that a few days after the break-in Nixon had personally ordered that the CIA obstruct the FBI's investigation—all remaining congressional support disappeared. On August 8, 1974, Nixon announced his resignation, which took effect next day at noon as he flew toward San Clemente and as Vice-President Gerald Ford was being sworn in as the next president.

The Watergate affair left many unanswered questions. Before the Ervin hearings, why did the public fail to react strongly to the misdeeds? After those hearings why did it take Congress so long to act? What was it about the men around Nixon that made them so willing to involve themselves in sordid deeds? And what was it in Nixon that made him order illegal activity, then amass the evidence that could convict him, then refuse ever to admit his guilt?

Many people saw the mind of Nixon as the sole villain of the piece, forgetting that the public was a partner in Nixon's actions. Despite their misgivings about Nixon's character, time and again people had elected him to successively higher offices, and so had to bear a share of the blame for the whole affair. Sociologist Richard Sennett, comparing our times to earlier ones, in the wake of Watergate concluded that the most striking characteristic of the modern era was its concentration upon the personal.

What seemed to happen to us, Sennett wrote, was that we converted all social and political matters into matters of personality; this gave them meaning for us. In ancient Greece, in medieval times, in Revolutionary

America, there had been a deep belief in "public culture"; there, issues could be discussed—democracy, capitalism, social conditions—without reference to the personality of those discussing them. Gradually, as personality became more important in public affairs, the "audience" lost faith in its own ability to judge politicians by their stands on the issues, and became, instead of participants in the political process, merely a crowd of spectators approving or disapproving various politicians' behavior. The media, especially television, exacerbated this trend toward audience passivity and dependence upon personality. The result of exalting personality in politics was to suppress the need for each member of the public to actively express and consider issues. Now, wrote Sennett, "Political conflicts are interpreted in terms of the play of political personalities; leadership is interpreted in terms of 'credibility' rather than accomplishment."

In a sense Nixon continually brought out the "personal" in order to avoid the public issues. In the Checkers speech of 1952 he asked Americans to overlook his slush fund because his wife didn't own a mink coat and because he liked dogs. In the Watergate affair Nixon asked people to overlook his crimes because they were no worse than anyone else's.

The tie between Nixon and the public was a deep one, psychiatrist Leo Rangell has concluded. Nixon, he writes, was elected because of his contradictions and duplicitous character; his half-truths and appeals to fear proved to be better vote-getters than the solid platform planks of his opponents. In Nixon's speeches, Rangell writes, the president appealed to emotions, not to logic, and to gut reactions, not to fine distinctions. Nixon lied repeatedly about Watergate, then had a spokesman say the lies were "inoperative." He threw sand in our eyes by saying the presidency had to be protected when what he meant was that he, personally, had to be protected. When he said executive privilege must be sacrosanct, or that national security was involved, Nixon was merely using such concepts to safeguard the secret conversations of the co-conspirators. With such appeals to emotion, Rangell writes,

> Nixon invites regression. . . . His communications, his affect, the content of what he conveys and the manner in which he delivers it, encourage in the listener what psychoanalysts call "primary process thinking." This is a type of cognitive and intellectual activity which is irrational rather than rational, and . . . in normal life this type of thinking takes place in sleep and in dreaming, in daydreaming, in reverie states, and in fantasy life . . . without being checked by reality. . . . "Primary process thinking"

characterizes the normal irrationality of the unconscious, where contradictions and inconsistencies exist side by side...[and] result on the outside in fuzziness, lack of clarity, ambiguity, or confusion. Suggestibility is increased. In the sum total of these messages...and warnings Nixon delivers to the people, he invites them to think and respond at these levels of psychic functioning.

Rangell contends that the roots of Nixon's condition, that condition which he invited the public to share, lay in a split between Nixon's ego and superego. The rejection of the superego by the ego (the individual's rejection of society's restraints) characterized Nixon's behavior. It also characterizes narcissism. Our supreme presidential narcissist combined grandiosity, a feeling of omnipotence, exhibitionism, and a craving for power with a need for approval that could never be satisfied. Without a strong superego, Rangell writes, Nixon had no firm sense of right or wrong, and only the wish to satisfy his cravings. "Narcissism unbridled is the enemy of integrity," Rangell writes, and Nixon's integrity was so fundamentally compromised that he could never even admit guilt or personal responsibility for illegal actions.

A second level in the compromise of integrity involved the forty or so men under Nixon who went to jail for Watergate. These ex-advertising men, for-sale lawyers, and clever-bright young assistants were far from the best men of their day. They derived their power and sense of worth from being in Nixon's shadow, and steadily compromised their integrity in the service of his reelection and, later, in order for him to survive in office. Rangell suggests these men had often wished to do "bad things," and that the president's power, proclivities, and sanctions gave them opportunities to do bad things and feel good about them. Barbara Tuchman suggests that these aides and accomplices left a stunning impression of

something missing—some ordinary, familiar component of the human make-up, taken for granted when present but sinister by its absence....[But] these men are not peculiar to the Nixon White House (although it evidently attracted a high concentration of the raw arrogance of the parvenu). They are what happened to America and to our time. The same contempt for the rules is visible in street people who relieve themselves on doorsteps, and muggers who murder without a blush, and Mets fans who treat a visiting team throughout with howling hostility and swarm like a lynch mob over the field, trampling on people in their

The Double Standard   *279*

eagerness to wreck and vandalize. Conventions such as fair play and courtesy have evolved in the long civilizing process up from savagery in order to make human society bearable, just as political rules and the laws of life and property have evolved in order to make it safe. Without conventional restraints man becomes dangerous or unpleasant whether in the White House or in Shea Stadium.

Dr. Karl Menninger wrote that being without a sense of sin was pervasive in the modern era. Being without shame, people were willing to long overlook others' absence of shame—and by continually looking the other way the public shared in the compromise of integrity that was Watergate.

The majority did not cry out, and continually avoided remarking on the obvious. Both the majority and its representatives in Congress were passive. By their inaction they condoned much of what was done by the Nixon defenders in the White House. Lulled by appeals to the emotions, and knowing their own lapses of integrity—income tax violations, "cheating" on spouses, small lies, a will to look the other way—the American public let the sins of the White House grow until they were so glaring and noxious that they could no longer be ignored. Rangell writes:

> I feel that the distortions which took place on such a global scale, the denial of perceptions, the suspension of critical faculties, the repression of anxiety, and the exaggerated position of innocent receptivity, were part of an unconscious process, born out of wish and fear and hope, a wide-spread regression which spread by contagion and shared need.

That shared need was each person's hunger to feel more privileged than the next, often characterized as *ressentiment*. Edgar Z. Friedenberg, following Nietzsche, conceives of *ressentiment* as

> a free-floating disposition to visit upon others the bitterness that accumulates from one's own subordination and existential guilt at allowing oneself to be used by other people for their own purposes, while one's own life rusts away unnoticed.

We all have a need for power. By playing on *ressentiment*, Nixon transposed that need into political capital. He divided people into supporters and detractors—and thus conquered them. Nixon administered a system which punished enemies and rewarded friends; he proselytized an American way whose promise became no more than the use of naked force. The public shared in Nixon's power by acquiescing in his actions; by sharing that power, Nixon supporters felt superior to those who might be the subjects of Nixon's wrath. Over the years that wrath was directed against Vietnamese citizens, campus protesters, ghetto inhabitants, Democrats, and, later, against any who disagreed with administration policies. All the while, Nixon cloaked his actions in protestations of his own humanity and in declarations of moral worth. The end result was a public seduced into tacit approval of abuses of power virtually without precedent in a democratic state in times of peace. As De Tocqueville wrote, "To commit violent and unjust acts, it is not enough for a government to have the will or even the power; the habits, ideas, and passions of the times must lend themselves to their committal."

Henry Steele Commager wrote that as Jefferson represented the era of American Enlightenment, so Nixon represented contemporary America, "reflecting its arrogance, its violence, its passion for manipulation, its commercialism, but not reflecting its generosity or idealism or intellectual ferment." Jefferson believed the United States had a mission, to set the world a moral example. Nixon, Commager wrote, believed America's mission would be achieved not through reason or moral purity but through power:

> force at home to whip the recalcitrants into line, force abroad to whip lesser breeds into line—force in such little things as breaking into safes, force in such big things as building the greatest arsenal in the history of the world.

The force that mired us in the quicksand of Vietnam was the force that catapulted us into the pit of Watergate. We had believed we were the saviors of the world; it turned out that we had become a nation as capable of begetting tyrants as any other. "The one pervading evil of democracy," Lord Acton wrote in 1907, "is the tyranny of the majority, or rather of that party, not always the majority, that succeeds, by force or fraud, in carrying elections." The Nixon men were carried to their worst excesses by the wish to prevail in the 1972 election; Watergate was an attempt to prevent the American people from making a free and informed choice as to who would lead them.

Such corruption of power, the decade showed, could be found in the jungles of Vietnam, in business clashes, in the dealings of Congress, and in the actions of the FBI, CIA, and the Plumbers' Unit and its masters. We had wanted to believe that our best men could not be corrupted by power. Watergate showed that the legitimatizing sanction of power could still corrupt absolutely. "When watching men of power in action," Eric Hoffer had written some years before the era,

> it must be always kept in mind that, whether they know it or not, their main purpose is the elimination or neutralization of the independent individual—the independent voter, consumer, worker, owner, thinker— and that every device they employ aims at turning man into a manipulatable "animated instrument" which is Aristotle's definition of a slave.

Power, therefore, was always the enemy of liberty.

"The system works," many people crowed when Watergate was straining toward a conclusion. They lauded the checks and balances which ended the crisis. But did the system work? The reassertion of the primacy of the government of laws over that of the government by a particular band of men took quite some time, and was not particularly well done. Only a tiny fraction of the press was involved in stumbling over what later proved to be a veritable mountain of illegal acts and data. Congress was incredibly slow to act. Infested with a penchant for collective blindness and a desire to accommodate the president which bordered on the conspiratorial, the legislators deserved as much censure for inaction as applause for their final moves. As with Nixon himself, the Congress seldom did anything unless forced to do it. A relative handful of men, such as Sirica, Ervin, and Cox, pushed things ahead despite congressional and executive branch indolence. And the public was more than gullible. We seemed all too willing to completely institutionalize a two-tier system of governance in which there would be laws for those who held power and different laws for those who had none. For example, polls taken near the end of the Watergate affair showed a seemingly irreducible minimum of 25 percent of the people queried who believed that the president ought not to be impeached and that his already-convicted associates ought not to be punished by imprisonment.

Those who took the stance of "my president, right or wrong," and who believed that Nixon should stay in power and be forgiven his excesses, were far out on the limb of the "preserve" modality. In the 1950s and into the late 1960s they might have believed they were protecting the system in allowing the FBI and CIA to take extraordinary measures in pursuit of

Communists, but the latterly goals of the Nixon administration—suppression of dissent, the reelection of the president at any cost—were tantamount to tyranny and not so easily defended. To preserve the in-group's power, hegemony, and continuity meant to champion different rules for those in power and for those out of power. After knowledge of Nixon's methods and goals had come to light, to support him meant embracing secrecy, deceit, and viciousness; it meant believing that might makes right, and that there were no objective standards by which the conduct of those in power might be judged. This truly put die-hard Nixon defenders out on a limb, for if they championed Nixon's actions and methods, what was to ensure them that they would long remain on the side of the winners, and not tomorrow be on the side of the losers?

A large segment of the population wished to see Nixon jailed for his crimes; an even larger segment of the country—the clear majority, according to polls—agreed with President Ford that Nixon should be pardoned and that the country should return to normal.

But it was not easy to come back to normal governance, because Ford was in many ways an illegitimate executive, a man chosen by the disgraced former president and by a body of his congressional cronies—not by the American public. Also, we had ceased to believe that our leaders were good men, or even that we as a people were quite so good as we once had thought. We had lost our claim to moral superiority.

When Ford pardoned Nixon, he announced the act as a deed of compassion, but it smacked of a deal. In pardoning Nixon the new president short-circuited any true inquiry into the roots of the problems which had flowered into Watergate. Moreover, by pardoning Nixon, Ford accentuated his own illegitimacy. Because Ford would not allow discovery and purging—a true catharsis—the Watergate affair was not in the Greek sense of the idea a tragedy. When as a country we were let off the hook by the pardon, we were excused from the difficult work of self-inquiry and from the possibility of learning more about ourselves than we wanted to know.

Only a tiny fraction of people in the country wanted to go that deep, to learn, through Watergate, what was at bottom of America's problems. Most people thought Watergate revealed nothing new about the system except the extent of its rot. But there was evidence of a large network of difficulties connected with Watergate: there was, for instance, the collusion and co-option of business, of the military, of the press, even of Congress by the White House hierarchy. Had it merely been Nixon and his handful of cohorts who were guilty of subverting the nation's institutions, or were the institutions themselves outmoded and inadequate? Compromises of institutional integrity buttressed the arguments of those who embraced the "search" modality, and who maintained that the double standard had not come to the United States only with Watergate but rather was tied in to the fundamental ways in which modern American society went about some of its most important business.

For the searchers, Watergate validated the radical nature of the decade's great critiques—those voiced by the blacks, the youth, the ecologists, the women—and the decade's great losses—assassinations, inflation, the loss of authority, the debacle of Vietnam—and tied them all together. Watergate was the final, melodramatic debacle which showed up the outmoded and even dangerous nature of the fundamental assumptions of the postwar era.

In the aftermath of Watergate it was finally possible to see that the expression of those assumptions had led to many of our crises and problems. In exercising power as he had, Nixon acted as a man who was completely rooted in the American assumptions current at the decade's outset. He never changed his rootedness in those assumptions. In the service of an outmoded objective he extended a lost war beyond endurance; he showed to what lengths a man could go to remain "Number One"; he said America would be helpless if we could not invade a small foreign country when we felt like it; he fueled inflation to serve his own needs; he hid a shoddy pattern of behavior behind the facade of an outwardly correct nuclear family life; he laced his intimate conversations with racial and ethnic epithets. By taking power to its constitutional and ethical limits and beyond, Nixon, his henchmen, and all who sailed with them, made obvious by their activities the moral bankruptcy of the era's underlying assumptions.

10 Legacies

THE SHOCK OF PRESIDENT KENNEDY'S ASSASSINATION provoked two reactions from Americans: the first, a need to preserve what was left of a crumbling world-structure, the second, an equal need to search for the root causes of the disaster. Both reactions were in the service of preventing like disasters from happening in the future. Often a single individual would cherish both modes of thought, even though they were seemingly antithetical. As the later waves of shocks beset Americans, people sought to understand what was happening to them, and tended to perceive these later shocks according to the explanation they had initially embraced, either the "preserve" or the "search" formulation. Along with each new shock, then, came reinforcement for the individual's predilection for seeing the shock in the context of the mode of thought already established. What was at first advanced as an explanation for an inexplicable event was transformed into a pattern that encompassed all subsequent events.

Each shock, each hammer blow on the American psyche, drove a wedge of explanation deeper between Americans, accentuating the separation of groups on matters political, social, and personal. At the beginning of the decade there had been a set of beliefs on which most Americans could agree and from which they derived rules for the conduct of their lives and their government's policies. At the decade's end that common ground had all but disappeared. Though many longed for the common ground, they found themselves forced to take sides with extreme positions, or not to have opinions or explanations at all.

The homogeneous, harmonious, unified country which had stood as triumphant colossus at the end of World War II was now fragmented and argumentative. There were no longer many ideas on which Americans of varying stripes could agree.

In the political arena this was reflected in general voter apathy, and in decreased support for traditional political parties, and in the support for "splinter" candidates. There was a general trend toward liberalism among many people, but it did not translate into support for any particular political party. Rather, each faction seemed to have grown radical edges: the ultra-radical Left moved so far as to espouse solutions which were anathema to most, and the ultra-radical Right seemed to do the same.

All demarcations were sharpened. The separation between inner cities and suburbs was more clearly delineated; so was the distance between the old industrial North and the new "sunbelt" South; between feminists and "traditional" women; between rich and poor. The hardening of stances could easily be seen in the personal arena: on one side there was a strident reassertion of Biblical morality, while on the other there was what seemed to be moral laxity or a belief in the irrelevance of moral codes.

Sharply delimiting stances seemed required on every issue, but a legislator (or an individual arguing with another individual) had to take such hard positions that there was no room left to join his ideas with anyone whose position was at variance with his own. Those who thought the police were handcuffed by the courts in dealing with criminals had difficulty making law or common cause together with those who thought restraints on police powers were imperative for a free society. When issues became too much for us to decide, we pushed them into the courts, where, in adversarial proceedings, one side was bound to win and the other to lose. No middle ground was elucidated; few compromises were made.

All issues became politicized. During the decade women, blacks, and other "minority" groups brought into the political arena issues of employment and educational practices previously the province of private enterprise, and issues of medical treatment previously matters between patients and doctors. Abortion, gun control, educational quotas: all were political footballs.

Today, as more of politics includes private and highly emotional matters, we no longer debate on the high plane of the Federalist Papers. We do not expect rational argument; politic is no longer the civilized proceedings in which a man initially persuaded by the logic of Alexander Hamilton could change his allegiance on a public issue because of the equally persuasive logic of Thomas Jefferson.

In the wake of shocks, the public arena has become buffeted by winds of rabid partisanship, extreme emotion, charged personalities. Reason and logic suffer. We try to decide on the thorny question of what sort of nuclear defense system to have for the United States, but public debate is shifted to the issue of whether a particular configuration of missiles is to be considered a victory or a defeat for President Reagan. While the majority of the public yearns for a middle ground on such issues, the choices forced upon us are increasingly of the "either/or" variety in which each alternative is fraught with unacceptable drawbacks.

We have become inured to shocks. We expect them. We have to have ever-higher levels of shock in order to respond. Many people did not find Watergate shocking until the scandal had been directly and irrevocably tied to upper-echelon White House officials. Many others did not find the attempted assassination of President Reagan shocking because it did not succeed, and because we had witnessed the spectacle so many times before.

After a Decade of Shocks, ordinary problems no longer give us a rise; only "real" shocks can do that. Our attention span, so often abused, has shortened. We were aghast at the oil crisis when there were lines at gas stations, but when the immediacy of that shortage passed—or when controls on the economy were lifted—or when the Vietnam War was declared over—or when Nixon left office—or when the U.S. hostages came home from Teheran—people went back to their old ways of behavior. Whatever had roiled the surface had been quieted, and, since the crisis was past, we didn't want to know about the crisis any longer; we didn't want to be roused from our lethargy. During the initial gasoline crisis we eagerly embraced the idea of "energy independence," but when the crisis eased, we were no longer willing to suffer the hardship that would be involved in becoming independent of imported fossil fuels, and the new energy policy never materialized. Today the long-term problems illustrated by the energy crisis, inflation, and the Vietnam War are still unresolved. "Shock is a ritualized substitute for change," wrote the authors of a study of assassination. As we recoiled from a great many shocks, we resisted change. Now, as we react to nothing unless it is of the magnitude of an assassination, a war, or a riot, we suffer from our "crisis mentality." Our minds are cemented to the present. We rely on simplistic explanations and on short-term fixes—and, in an era of complex problems with complex solutions, such a crisis mentality does not help us. It forces our reactions into instant and nonreflective modes of thought. We react viscerally, not intellectually; we become prey to demagogues.

We understand that in the midst of a shock or crisis there is usually no time to consider fully the ramifications of options open to us, but our leaders use this understanding for their own purposes. When President Jimmy Carter sought to arouse the American public to the dangers of dependence on foreign oil, he deliberately shocked us by using the phrase "the moral equivalent of war" to describe the battle we had to fight for energy self-sufficiency. We were ready to react, but the shock did not continue. The country seemed at that moment to have adequate oil supplies, and since what Carter was proposing would involve sacrifice, the war fizzled out. Similarly in 1981 when inflation was at a rate so high as to be a continual shock, President Reagan went on television to declare that a crisis was at hand. He asked the public to choose between his economic program and what he described as disaster. Our reaction to his either/or proposal had less to do with long-term solutions and rational consideration than it did with our perception of the crisis of the moment, with the emotional overtones in which the issue was presented to us, and with the medium through which the presentation of the choice was made.

The shocks of the decade served to accelerate various social trends. During the times of crisis, there were giant increases in government and in bureaucracy at all levels. It was a time when idealism was everywhere eroded by cynicism, when adversarial models replaced conciliatory ones, when the rugged individualist yielded at last to the corporate gamesman. It was a time when independence was seen to be less valuable than inter-dependence. All these movements are in a single direction: along the arc from charisma to routine.

Weber's arc moves from the belief in the unlimited possibilities of the future, to the acceptance of death and the continuation of the system. We no longer believe that our children will be better off than we are; the vision of the future as a wonderland is fading. But is this bad?

"Americans frequently voice the fear that their world is falling apart," James Oliver Robertson wrote in his 1980 study of American myths:

> The specter of war threatens either imminent atomic holocaust or con-
> tinuing Vietnams. There is fear that the wealth and productivity of Amer-
> ica may decline or cease to exist. There is great ambivalence among
> Americans, increasingly conscious and obvious, concerning government

of all kinds, the Presidency, the military and defense, and the availability and consumption of American resources. There are conscious, public discussions of and ambivalence about the fundamental distinctions between life and death, and human and animal life. . . . The sense that the present world is in increasing crisis, that the wars and weapons, the waste and pollution, the reforms and revolutions, the exhaustion of resources and the economic crises of contemporary life are signs that today's world is very different from the past, has led to a sense that the ideals and perceptions, the interpretations and explanations of reality, upon which Americans seem always to have depended, no longer apply.

That is to say, the assumptions which characterized the postwar era and which underlay our attitudes at the outset of the Decade of Shocks are no longer articles of faith.

Let me briefly restate those assumptions, as set forth in greater detail in chapter 1. They are:

1. A belief in the safety, sanctity, and legitimacy of our leaders.
2. A belief, grounded in the idea of the gradual nature of change, that minorities would stay in their "place."
3. A belief in the basic health and superiority of the American economy.
4. A belief that we were, and would continue to be, militarily superior to the rest of the world.
5. A belief that small nations could not by themselves affect their own future nor alter the world's strategic balance.
6. A belief that our environment and natural resources were virtually limitless.
7. A belief that the problems of the day would be solved through the application of technology.
8. A belief that youth would take its place, as previous generations had, and without undue upset, on the accepted ladders to success.
9. A belief that the supremacy of the nuclear family in our society would not appreciably alter.
10. A belief that our society was the best possible configuration we could have to realize our potential, and that ours was a model for the rest of the world.

The Decade of Shocks showed that these assumptions were not inflexible laws. Under pressure of events, the assumptions crumbled. They were shown to be inadequate to the task of explaining or ordering a more modern world.

Take, for example, our loss of charismatic leadership. With the assassination of President Kennedy, I have argued, we began to factor death into our understanding of the political system, an understanding that was reinforced by other assassinations. For a while there were no positive, charismatic leaders rising up to take the places of those who had been murdered. Nixon was charismatic only in his ability to evoke and direct *ressentiment*, a negative factor. With the fall of Nixon, with the absence of charismatic leaders, the system became more prominent than the man. The system was revivified, and now we understand its capacity to survive both the depredations and the achievements of individuals.

Despite what happened during the Decade of Shocks, many people in the United States still hold to the old assumptions. They contend that what was challenged and found wanting during the era was not our beliefs but rather our will and nerve, and that if we reassert our will and nerve we can once again attain military, economic, and moral superiority.

Thus the Reagan administration pursues a military buildup of great magnitude, measured in the hundreds of billions of dollars and designed to provide the United States with superiority to the Russians in missiles, to give us a navy capable of dominating several oceans at once, etc. In the international economic sphere we begin to enact tariff barriers and to bring sanctions against our foreign competitors in order to bolster our flagging economy. Taxes are cut with an eye to encouraging people to spend money. This is done despite already-enormous and burgeoning federal budget deficits which help keep interest rates so high that business investment is discouraged and plant capacity remains idle. The personal tax cuts are skewed toward the wealthy in the hope that their money will "trickle down" to the other strata of society. To replace social programs that aid the needy, Reagan asks for private sector assistance—charity—which nowhere matches previous governmental support. In Congress, a majority of votes is swung behind cutbacks in the funding of social programs at the same time that a level of poverty is reached—one out of seven Americans—which has not been seen since the early 1960s. Welfare benefits for the working poor are rescinded or cut back; Medicaid is eliminated for people who are slightly above the poverty line. School lunches are taken away from 2.6 million children. Prior commitments to build low-income housing units are canceled. Black leaders said such cuts hurt blacks more than whites, because the black poverty rate was 32.4 percent. President Reagan encourages those who are challenging federal court decisions in the area of civil rights, and in other socially explosive areas. According to *The New York Times*:

> The President supports a constitutional amendment to permit officially sanctioned prayer in public schools. The Supreme Court forbade such prayer 20 years ago, saying it violated First Amendment guarantees of freedom of religion. Mr. Reagan has also urged Congress to approve antiabortion legislation, which would permit states to reimpose restrictions removed by a 1973 decision of the Supreme Court.
>
> In addition, Mr. Reagan has fought against school busing and the use of numerical hiring goals even though the Court has approved such remedies for school segregation and employment discrimination.

In January 1983, the Justice Department asked a federal court to overturn a decision involving the hiring of minority firefighters in Boston, and is pursuing other reversals of previous "affirmative action" policies.

The administration proposes deep cuts in public health services, education supports, and in funding of basic scientific research. Programs for developing alternative energy sources and achieving energy independence are shelved, while development of nuclear-fuel reactors is encouraged even in the face of new and disastrous accidents such as Three Mile Island. Secretary of the Interior James Watt extends offshore oil leasing and contemplates opening up public lands for further mineral exploration and exploitation. Watt's positions on this and other issues are at such an extreme from those of environmental groups that they circulate petitions for his removal from office. Safety and health regulations are relaxed in fields ranging from sewage treatment to auto emission standards, in order to "free" businesses to operate and to heat up the economy. There is a full-scale retreat from the consumer-oriented practices written into law in the late 1960s and early 1970s, and the Environmental Protection Agency is under legal fire from Congress for laxity in enforcing existing laws. Government classification of information is intensified, not lessened as mandated by Freedom of Information statutes, and within government agencies there is more secrecy than existed a few years ago.

The Equal Rights Amendment has failed on its first attempt at passage, and women's salaries are once again declining when compared to men's.

Women's progress to the higher echelons of American business is stalled, and President Reagan has suggested that if more women were to stay at home, there would be more jobs for men and less unemployment. Many people comment that President Reagan and his supporters wish to return the country in spirit and in substance to the time of Eisenhower, before all the shocks began, when the world seemed a simpler and more understandable place.

But the shocks of the decade 1963–1974 were of the sort described by the phrase "the genie is out of the bottle." The expression was first used in speaking of the effect on the world of the existence of atomic weapons. Once the genie has escaped, he can never be put back into the bottle again. Once a shock has occurred, its ramifications are not easily undone. Perhaps another fable will put it into perspective: in "The Emperor's New Clothes" the monarch parades through the streets in the belief that he is wearing beautiful new clothes. A shock wave goes through the crowd as a child points out that the emperor wears no clothes—that is to say, that the emperor's assumption or belief is invalid. We need to perceive with equal force that the assumptions of the postwar period have been rendered inoperative by the events of the Decade of Shocks. They are dead, and it is time we buried them.

As Richard J. Barnet suggests in his 1981 study *Real Security*, the immense power of the American colossus of the postwar era was a "wasting asset." Because we did not use it well to achieve permanent world stability but rather directed it into an unwinnable crusade against communism, the decline of our power was inevitable. The emerging nations' drive for survival, the Soviet Union's thrust for military parity, and the inherent limitations of nuclear weaponry all saw to that decline. Real security, Barnet suggests, will be achieved only when all nations feel secure enough not to threaten one another—that is, in a multipolar world.

That multipolar, multifaceted world can come about only when we have recognized our own limitations, seen that we are no longer invincible but vulnerable. We are vulnerable militarily, we are vulnerable economically, and we can choose to be vulnerable socially to the legitimate demands of the less-favored sectors of our population. To be vulnerable now is proper, because we were never truly invincible—we just saw ourselves that way.

To have seen ourselves as the morally superior and omnipotent power around which everything and everyone revolved was juvenile. In the postwar era our posture resembled that of the powerful adolescent who feels his strength and looks for ways to demonstrate it; our assumptions about the world reflected our egocentricity. By shocking us out of these assumptions, the events of the decade served to make us grow up. As a country, as a people, we matured. Such was the forcing-house nature of the decade that we matured in a remarkably short period of time. During a few short years we learned what it took England a hundred and more years to discover while the British Empire crumbled. We learned the hard way our limits, our vulnerability, the requirements of many competing factors for our attention, the necessity of a society based on equal provision for those who had less than the majority.

At the time, if we had looked carefully, we might have seen that our assumptions were at variance with the declared values of the United States' form of government and shape of society. We might have seen that the assumptions were pushing us to courses of action which were directly contrary to our values. Near the end of the decade, in 1973, Henry Steele Commager wrote:

> What we sometimes overlook is that it is not only the material heritage we lay waste with our exploitations, our strip-mining and pollution, it is the political and moral heritage as well. How little thought our government, our Corps of Engineers, our great corporations, our roadbuilders and "developers" give to posterity; but how little thought, too, those who are prepared to sacrifice the Constitution, the Bill of Rights, the principle of due process of law, the idea of even justice, the integrity of the ballot box, the dignity and privacy of the individual human being, give for posterity.

Commager pointed out that in our history the people most concerned for posterity were the Founding Fathers.

The animating principle of a true republic, Montesquieu had written, was virtue. It was to virtue that such men as Jefferson adhered, and in their works they provided for the future by constructing a system that would nurture many generations of liberty-loving people. In his 1801 inaugural, Jefferson told his audience that a "wise and frugal government" would work to guarantee "equal and exact justice to all men," would guarantee the various freedoms assured under the Bill of Rights, as well as "peace, commerce, and honest friendship with all nations," and would not "take from the mouth of labor the bread it has earned." To effect such guarantees "should be the creed of our political faith, the text of civil instruction, the touchstone by which we try the services of those we trust." For Jefferson, the Constitution was not only a political document but also was a personal code of ethics. A country's morality could be no better than that of its people.

But the Constitution is an amalgam of two different pools of thought— values from the French Enlightenment that primarily deal with equality among men, and values from English mercantilism that primarily deal with property. Historically, when these two value constellations interact, the intersection has been uneasy. In the postwar era the entrepreneurial spirit seemed to be stronger than the humanist spirit. In the 1940s, 1950s, and early 1960s the "achievement ethic" came to dominate the United States. We pursued success with such vigor that sociologists such as Robin Williams, Jr., could view the achievement ethic as the most important element in the modern American character. But, as Lionel Rubinoff suggests, the achievement ethic is

> governed by a set of values which will appeal only to those whose interests are best served by holding onto these values, namely those who are members of the entrepreneurial or middle class.... The achievement ethic... is therefore an ethic of technology and progress rather than an ethic of humanization.

Attempts to order our lives by following the tenets of the achievement ethic (as detailed in the list of assumptions) led us astray. We moved inexorably into the steady subversion of constitutional guarantees, of traditions such as firm civilian control of the military and of a government which pursues peace rather than domination. Not planning for future generations, we despoiled our resources, overly stratified our society, and tried to keep various sections of the population in economic and social bondage.

In this light, the decade's violent upheavals appear not as attempts to overthrow our institutions, but rather as illustrations of the need to reassert in our system the values derived from the French Enlightenment. "The system works," people said when Lyndon Johnson smoothly assumed the presidency after Kennedy's assassination. "The system works," people said proudly when blacks' grievances were partly redressed. "The system works," people said in astonishment when antiwar sentiment forced us out of Vietnam. "The system works," people said with relief when Congress and the Supreme Court put an end to the usurpation of power by the Nixon White

House. In fact what people saw working were those guarantees of liberty, equality, democracy, and fairness which the framers of the Constitution had deliberately incorporated into the system.

What had not worked was the achievement ethic. Rather than solving the world's problems, it had exacerbated them. Domination over nature, the premium placed on technological progress and on unlimited economic growth, the flaunting of the United States' military might and moral superiority—all these reflected a claim of privilege, and the great critiques of the Decade of Shocks rejected those claims of privilege and proclaimed humanism's primacy in our way of life. They insisted on the necessity of the idea of the brotherhood of man considering before any assertion that the United States is constituted mainly to preserve and protect those entrepreneurial rights which devolve from ownership of property.

The questions raised by the great critiques have not been fully answered, and the goals of the blacks, the youth, the women, the ecologists have not been met. They may never be satisfied, but that does not negate the power of the questions. The sentiments of these groups may not be the sentiment of the majority of the American people, but, as Ibsen has Dr. Stockmann say in *An Enemy of the People*,

> The majority *never* has right on its side. Never, I say! That is one of those social lies against which an independent, intelligent man must wage war. Who is it that constitutes the majority of the population in a country? Is it the clever folk or the stupid? I don't imagine that you will dispute the fact that at present the stupid people are in an absolutely overwhelming majority all the world over.... (*Uproar and cries.*) Oh, yes—you can shout me down, I know! But you cannot answer me. The majority has *might* on its side—unfortunately; but *right* it has not.... The minority is always in the right. (*Renewed uproar.*)

If today we are in the midst of renewed uproar over questions of privilege, fairness, and future planning—an uproar in which emotions run high, in which the center is not holding—it is because we have not yet assimilated the lessons of the Decade of Shocks. The time speaks to us about our priorities, about the ways in which we interact with one another, and the ways in which our nation should interact with the other nations of the world.

For the past ten years we seem to have been sleepwalking, adrift without a clear, positive philosophy to direct us. Today we try in various ways to recover the past, and to act as if the assumptions of the postwar years have not been proven specious. The realities of the 1980s are far more complex, multifaceted, and interdependent than those of even a few years ago. Fashioning a policy toward the Middle East is far more complicated than was getting out of Vietnam. Deciding how to apply triage to the requirements of the entitlement society is more difficult than was deciding to encourage black voter registration and lowering the voting age.

Yet certain principles have come out of the Decade of Shocks with renewed vigor, and we need to pay attention to them as a guide in choosing our courses of action. If the exact approach to contemporary problems is not always obvious, what is certain is that we cannot solve those problems by recourse to the discredited assumptions of privilege. We cannot act as if the shocks had not occurred. The genies are out of the bottles, and no appeals to patriotism, militancy, or attempts at simplistic solutions will be able to wave them away and allow us a return to past patterns. It will not be possible—nor is it desirable—for the United States to return to the position of arrogant world supremacy and flawed moral superiority which was once the basis for our actions. Having outgrown our youth, we must now act out of our maturity.

ACKNOWLEDGMENTS

Many people have given generously of their time, skills, and memories to aid me in this book. I am particularly indebted to my wife, Harriet Shelare, for her help in clarifying much of my thought, and for her continual encouragement. In the late 1960s I worked on the CBS documentary series "The 21st Century," and I would like to belatedly thank my colleagues there for the opportunities they provided to observe the country's scientific and cultural phenomena, and for our continual discussions of what it all meant. Agent Mel Berger and editor Ann Patty have been constant sources of help. I would also like to thank Roger Ailes, Mark Bloom, Ann Jackowitz, Peter Leeds, John Lord, Gail Pellett, Gus Reichbach, Betty Shabazz, my father Leon Shachtman, and David Stiffler. Many others whom I hereby thank have asked to remain anonymous. My work on this book was aided by the resources of the Wertheim Room of the New York Public Library, the Bobst Library at New York University, and the library of the Museum of Broadcasting in New York City. These efforts notwithstanding, the errors in this book are mine.

Notes

These notes refer to books and periodicals listed in the bibliography, by author. The numbers refer to the text page on which the cited material appears. Where there is more than a single entry under a name in the bibliography, I have also included in the notes the name of the book or article cited. References for the speeches of Presidents Kennedy, Johnson, and Nixon can be found in the various volumes of their published speeches, and I have not cited them in the notes. I have cited daily newspapers only where direct quotations of some length have been used.

Foreword

13 Commager.
13 Sissman.
14 Lambert.
15 Sennett.
15 Graubard.

Chapter One

17 Williams.
19 Hsu.
19 Niebuhr, in Smith, ed.
27 Mead, in Ginzburg, ed.
28 Pope, in Ginzburg, ed.
34 ADA quote, in Wittner.
36 Hayden, in Cohen and Hale.

39 Stone, in Middleton, ed.

40 Rubinoff.

41 Truman.

41 Mead, *op. cit.*

42 Janeway, in Ginzburg, ed.

42 Pope, *op. cit.*

Chapter Two

45 Housewife, quoted in Greenberg, ed.

46 Wolfenstein, ed.

47 Television critic Jack Gould, *New York Times*, Nov. 27, 1963.

48 Coleman and Hollander, in Greenberg, ed.

48 Durkheim, quoted in Thompson.

50 Wolfenstein. *loc. cit.*

51 Malcolm X.

53 King, quoted in Wofford.

53 Kennedy, quoted in Schlesinger, *Robert Kennedy and His Times*.

56 Havens, *et al.*

Chapter Three

66 Baldwin.

67 Simmons, in Smith, ed.

70 Hoffer.

70 De Tocqueville, quoted in Hoffer.

72 Conot.

72 King-Rustin dialogue, in Rustin.

72 Rustin, reported in Newfield.

74 Wagstaff.

75 Button.

78 Kerner.

79 Nixon, quoted in Wittner.

85 Button.

86 Gwaltney.

87 Sartre, *Anti-Semite and Jew*, Schocken Books, 1948.

88 Rubinoff.

88 William Ryan.

Chapter Four

95 Hendrickson.

97 Johnson to Ackley, quoted in Manchester.

100 Maynard and van Ryckeghen.

102 Heilbroner and Thurow.

102 Keynes, quoted in Krefetz.

107 McCracken to Congress, quoted in Miller and Williams.

109 Blinder.

112 Lewis.

113 Nieburg.

113 Heilbroner.

114 Charge Account Bankers, cited by Krefetz.

Chapter Five

120 Savio, quoted in Heinrich.

123 Jones.

124 Mead, in Ginzburg, ed.

125 Gardner.

126 Marcus.

127 Myerhoff.

127 Langman.

128 Bodeman.

128 Wicker and Reston articles quoted in Ferber and Lynd.

129 Rubin.

130 Hoffman, quoted in Brooks.

131 Harvard student quoted in Mehnert.

131 Segal, quoted in Ferber and Lynd.

132 Sun Tzu, quoted by William C. Westmoreland, introduction to Bonds, ed.

135 Interview, Gus Reichbach.

135 Mantell.

137 Lifton, *Boundaries*.

139 Langer.

139 Ferber and Lynd.

140 Rubinoff.

140 Davis.

141 Rubin.

141 Lukas and Newfield articles quoted in Mailer, *Miami and the Siege of Chicago*.

142 Mailer, *Miami*.

143 Novak, quoted in Lemon.

144 Schell.

145 Jones.

145 Eisenstadt.

149 Rhodes, quoted in Michener.

150 Nixon.

150 Schwartz, *New York Times,* 12, 9, 70.

151 Gardner.

152 Lasch.

154 MacLeod.

156 Scammon and Wattenberg.

158 Wuthnow.

159 Brake.

Chapter Six

163 Kissinger, quoted in Schell.

164 Schell.

165 Andrews.

166 cable quoted in Pusey.

168 Taylor statement in *Pentagon Papers*.

169 State Department, McCone, Clifford, and Ball, all quoted by Herman.

170 Herring.

171 Simmons.

172 Caputo.

173 Marshall, in Thompson and Frizzell, eds.

173 Giap, quoted in Pike.

174 Kerry.

174 McNaughton memo, *Pentagon Papers*.

175 Zorthian in Thompson and Frizzell.

176 Herring.

176 Fulbright, quoted in Petit.

178 Schell.

178 Westmoreland, *loc. cit.*

179 Military historian Charles B. MacDonald, in Bonds, ed.

180 AP report, *idem.*

182 Welsh.

182 Haldeman.

183 Kissinger, quoted in Shawcross.

186 George McGovern, introduction to Rosenberg, *et al.*, *Vietnam and the Silent Majority*.

190 Ehrlichman.

190 Nixon, quoted in Shawcross.

192 Clubb.

194 De Sola Pool, in Thompson and Frizzell, eds.

194 Ravenal, in Thompson and Frizzell, eds.

194 Commager.

195 Rubinoff.

197 De Tocqueville.

198 Fackheim, quoted in Rubinoff.

Chapter Seven

201 Harrison Brown, quoted in Catton.

202 Udall, introduction to Catton.

202 Lynn White.

203 Ellul.

204 Mumford, in Kranzberg and Davenport, eds.

205 Hudson, in Olsen, ed.

208 AEC report cited in Fuller.

208 *Scientific American* article cited by Dubos.

210 Wurster and Borlaug articles, in Olsen, ed.

211 Commoner.

212 Heyerdahl, quoted in Cowan.

216 Lindbergh, introduction to Collins, *Carrying the Fire*.

218 riddle in Meadows, *et al.*

219 Hayes, *Worldwatch* #27, "Pollution."

221 Buchan.

225 Turner.

226 Engler.

230 Mesthene.

232 Commoner.

233 Miles.

233 Berger, in Rockefeller Commission report.

234 Mesthene.

Chapter Eight

239 Anthony, quoted in Elizabeth Lady Stanton, Susan B. Anthony, correspondence, writings, speeches, New York 1981.

240 Stevenson, quoted in *New York Times*, 6, 18, 55.

240 Lundberg and Farnham.

241 Northwestern coed and Montagu, quoted in Cox.

242 Komarovsky, quoted in Chafe.

242 statistics in Taeuber, ed.

243 Friedan.

247 Willis.

250 Blood, cited in Chafe.

251 Dixon.

251 Benston, quoted in Dixon.

Bibliography

A true bibliography of the "Decade of Shocks" would run into the thousands of items—perhaps the tens of thousands. The books and articles listed below I found particularly accurate or insightful. In addition to these, I also consulted many issues of newspapers from the years 1963 to 1974, among them *The New York Times*, *The Washington Post*, and the *Christian Science Monitor*. I also used what records remain in public hands of television news broadcasts of the era, principally at the Museum of Broadcasting in New York City.

Andrews, William R. *The Village War*. University of Missouri Press, 1973.
Arendt, Hannah. *Crises of the Republic*. Harcourt Brace Jovanovich, 1972.
Armstrong, Neil, Michael Collins, Edwin E. Aldrin, Jr., Gene Farmer, and Dora Jane Hamblin. *First on the Moon*. Little, Brown, 1970.
Baldwin, James. *The Fire Next Time*. Dial Press, 1963.
Barnet, Richard J. *The Economy of Death*. Atheneum, 1969.
———. *Real Security*. Simon & Schuster, 1981.
Barret, Marvin, ed. *Surveys of Broadcast Journalism*, vols. 1–7, 1968–1974. Grosset & Dunlap.
Belfrage, Sally. *Freedom Summer*. Viking, 1965.
Bell, Daniel. *The Coming of Post-Industrial Society*. Basic Books, 1973.
Berman, Larry. *Planning a Tragedy*. W.W. Norton, 1982.
Blackstock, Nelson. *COINTELPRO*. Random House, 1975.
Blair, John M. *The Control of Oil*. Random House, 1977.
Blinder, Allan S. *Economic Policy and the Great Stagflation*. Academic Press, 1979.

Block, Richard, and Lauren Langman. "Youth and Work: The Diffusion of 'Countercultural' Values," *Youth and Society*, vol. 5 #4, June 1974.

Bodeman, Y. Michael. "Mystical, Satanic and Chiliastic Forces in Countercultural Movements," *Youth and Society*, vol. 5 # 4, June 1974.

Bonds, Ray, ed. *The Vietnam War*. Crown, 1979.

Brake, Mike. *The Sociology of Youth Culture*. Routledge & Kegan Paul, 1980.

Braungart, Richard G. "Status Politics and Student Politics," *Youth and Society*, vol. 3 #2, Dec. 1971.

Brooks, John. *The Go-Go Years*. Gill & Macmillan, 1972.

Brooks, Thomas R. *Walls Come Tumbling Down*. Prentice-Hall, 1974.

Brown, Lester R. *The Twenty-Ninth Day*. W.W. Norton, 1978.

———. *Building a Sustainable Society*. W.W. Norton, 1981.

Brown, Michael E. "The Condemnation and Persecution of Hippies," *Trans-Action*, Vol. 6 #10, Sept. 1969.

Buchan, Alistair. *The End of the Post-War Era*. E.P. Dutton, 1974.

Bullock, Paul, ed. *Watts: The Aftermath*. Grove Press, 1970.

Burke, John G., ed. *The New Technology and Human Values*. Wadsworth Publishing, 1972.

Button, James W. *Black Violence*. Princeton University Press, 1978.

Campbell, Angus, Philip E. Converse, and Willard L. Rogers. *The Quality of American Life*. Russell Sage Foundation, 1976.

Caputo, Philip. *A Rumor of War*. Holt, Rinehart & Winston, 1978.

Catton, William Robert. *Overshoot*. University of Illinois Press, 1980.

Chafe, William H. *The American Woman*. Oxford University Press, 1972.

Clubb, O. Edmund. "The Cease-Fire," *Nation*, vol. 216 #7, Feb. 12, 1973.

Cohen, Mitchell, and Dennis Hale, eds. *The New Student Left*. Beacon Press, 1967.

Collins, Michael. *Carrying the Fire*. Farrar, Straus & Giroux, 1974.

Commager, Henry Steele. *The Defeat of America*. Simon & Schuster, 1974.

Commoner, Barry. *The Closing Circle*. Knopf, 1971.

Congressional Quarterly. *The U.S. Economy: Challenges in the Seventies*. CQ, 1972.

Conlin, Joseph. *The Troubles*. Franklin Watts, 1982.

Conot, Robert. *Rivers of Blood, Years of Darkness*. Bantam, 1967.

Constantin, Edmond, and Kenneth Hanf. "Environmental Concerns and Lake Tahoe," *Environment and Behavior*, vol. 4 #2, June 1972.

Cowan, Edward. *Oil and Water*. J.B. Lippincott, 1968.

Cox, Claire. *The Upbeat Generation*. Prentice-Hall, 1962.

Crowe, Kenneth C. *America for Sale*. Doubleday, 1978.

Dasmann, Raymond F. *Planet in Peril*. World, 1972.

Davis, Fred. "Why All of Us May Be Hippies Someday," *Trans-Action*, vol. 5 #2, 1967.

Davis, Lorrie, with Rachel Gallagher. *Letting Down My Hair*. Arthur Fields Books, 1973.

Denisoff, R. Serge, and M.D. Pugh. "Consciousness III or Counterculture: A Preliminary Study," *Youth and Society*, vol. 5 #4, June 1974.

Denison, Edward F. *Accounting for U.S. Economic Growth, 1929–1969*. Brookings Institution, 1974.

Dickstein, Morris. *Gates of Eden*. Basic Books, 1977.

Dixon, Marlene. "Why Women's Liberation?," *Ramparts*, Dec. 1969.

Donner, Frank J. *The Age of Surveillance*. Random House, 1981.

Donovan, John C. *The Politics of Poverty*. Western Publishing, 1967.

Dubos, René. *Reason Awake*. Columbia University Press, 1970.

Ehrlichman, John. *Witness to Power*. Simon & Schuster, 1982.

Eisenstadt, S.N. "Changing Patterns of Youth Protest," *Youth and Society*, vol. 1 #2, Dec. 1969.

Ellul, Jacques. *The Technological Society*. Knopf, 1964.

Emerson, Gloria. *Winners and Losers*. Random House, 1976.

Engler, Robert. *The Brotherhood of Oil*. University of Chicago Press, 1977.

Erikson, Eric. *Identity: Youth and Crisis*. W.W. Norton, 1968.

Fellner, William, ed. *Economic Policy and Inflation in the Sixties*. American Enterprise Institute for Public Policy Research, 1972.

Ferber, Michael, and Staughton Lynd. *The Resistance*. Beacon Press, 1971.

Ferkiss, Victor. *Technological Man*. Braziller, 1969.

FitzGerald, Frances. *Fire in the Lake*. Atlantic–Little, Brown, 1972.

Foss, Daniel. *Freak Culture*. E.P. Dutton, 1972.

Friedan, Betty. *The Feminine Mystique*. W.W. Norton, 1963.

Friedenberg, Edgar Z. *The Disposal of Liberty and Other Industrial Wastes*. Doubleday, 1975.

Frost, David. *I Gave Them a Sword*. Morrow, 1978.

Fulbright, J.W. *The Pentagon Propaganda Machine*. Liveright, 1970.

Fuller, John G. *We Almost Lost Detroit*. Reader's Digest Press, 1975.

Gans, Herbert J. "Why Did Kennedy Die?," *Trans-Action*, vol. 5 #10, 1968.

Gardner, Hugh. *The Children of Prosperity*. St. Martin's Press, 1978.

Gastil, Raymond D. "Homicide and a Regional Culture of Violence," *American Sociological Review*, vol. 36 (3), 1971.

Gay, Anne, and George Gay, "Haight-Ashbury: Evolution of a Drug Culture," *Journal of Psychedelic Drugs*, vol. 4 #1, fall 1971.

Ginzberg, Eli, ed. *Values and Ideals of American Youth*. Columbia University Press, 1961.

Gitlin, Todd. *The Whole World Is Watching*. University of California Press, 1980.

Glasser, William. *The Identity Society*. Harper & Row, 1975.

Gofman, John W., and Arthur R. Tamplin. *Poisoned Power*. Rodale Press, 1971.

Goldman, Eric. *The Tragedy of Lyndon Johnson*. Knopf, 1968.

Graubard, Stephen R., ed. *A New America?* W.W. Norton, 1978.

Greenberg, Bradley, and Edwin S. Parker, eds. *The Kennedy Assassination and the American Public*. Stanford University Press, 1965.

Greer, Germaine. *The Female Eunuch*. McGraw-Hill, 1970.

Gregor, A. James. *The Fascist Persuasion in Radical Politics*. Princeton University Press, 1974.

Gwaltney, John Langston. *Drylongso*. Random House, 1980.

Halberstam, David. *The Best and the Brightest*. Random House, 1972.

Haldeman, H.R., with Joseph DiMona. *The Ends of Power*. Times Books, 1978.

Halstead, Fred. *Out Now!* Monad Press, 1978.

Hamilton, David. *Technology, Man, and the Environment*. Scribner's, 1973.

Hapgood, David. *The Screwing of the Average Man*. Doubleday, 1974.

Harmon, James E. "The New Music and Countercultural Values," *Youth and Society*, vol. 4 #1, Sept. 1972.

Harris, Louis, *The Anguish of Change*. W.W. Norton, 1973.

Havens, Murray Clark, Carl Leiden, and Karl M. Schmitt. *The Politics of Assassination*. Prentice-Hall, 1970.

Hayes, Harold, ed. *Smiling Through the Apocalypse*. McCall Publishing, 1969.

Heilbroner, Robert. "Second Thoughts on the Human Prospect," *Challenge* vol. 18 #2, May–June, 1975.

———, and Lester Thurow. *Economics Explained*. Prentice-Hall, 1982.

Heinrich, Max. *The Beginning: Berkeley, 1964*. Columbia University Press, 1968.

Hendrickson, Robert A. *The Cashless Society*. Dodd, Mead, 1972.

Herring, George C. *America's Longest War*. John Wiley & Sons, 1979.

Hersey, John. *The Algiers Motel Incident*. Knopf, 1968.

Hodgson, Godfrey. *America in Our Time*. Random House, 1976.

Hoffer, Eric. *The Ordeal of Change*. Harper & Row, 1963.

Hofstadter, Richard, and Michael Wallace, eds. *American Violence: A Documentary History*. Knopf, 1970.

Hole, Judith, and Ellen Levine. *Rebirth of Feminism*. Quadrangle, 1971.

Hope, Karol, and Nancy Young. *Out of the Frying Pan . . .* Doubleday, 1979.

Horowitz, Irving Louis. "Kennedy's Death—Myths and Realities," *Trans-Action*, vol. 5 #10, 1968.

Howard, Gerald, ed. *The Sixties*. Washington Square Press, 1982.

Hsu, Francis L.K. "American Core Values and National Character," in *Psychological Anthropology*. Homewood Dorsey, 1961.

James, Bernard. *The Death of Progress*. Knopf, 1973.

Janeway, Elizabeth. *Between Myth and Morning*. Morrow, 1974.

Jaros, Dean. "Children's Orientation Toward the President," *The Journal of Politics*, vol. 29 #2, May 1967.

Jeffries, Vincent, Ralph H. Turner, and Richard T. Morris. "The Public Perception of the Watts Riot as Social Protest," *American Sociological Review*, vol. 36 (3), 1971.

Jennings, M. Kent, and Richard G. Niemi. "Continuity and Change in Political Orientations: A Longitudinal Study of Two Generations," *American Political Science Review*, vol. 69, Dec. 1975.

Johnson, Lyndon Baines. *The Vantage Point*. Holt, Rinehart & Winston, 1971.

Jones, Landon Y. *Great Expectations*. Coward, McCann & Geogehan, 1980.

Joseph, Peter. *Good Times*. Charterhouse, 1973.

Kahn, Roger. *The Battle for Morningside Heights*. Morrow, 1970.

Kail, F.M. *What Washington Said*. Harper & Row, 1973.

Keniston, Kenneth. *The Uncommitted*. Harcourt, Brace & World, 1965.

———. *Youth and Dissent*. Harcourt Brace Jovanovich, 1972.

Kerber, Linda, and Jane De Hart Mathews. *Women's America*. Oxford University Press, 1982.

Kerner, Otto (Chairman). *Report of the National Advisory Commission on Civil Disorders*. Bantam, 1968.

Kerry, John, and The Vietnam Veterans Against the War. *The New Soldier*. Macmillan, 1971.

Kopkind, Andrew, and James Ridgeway, eds. *Decade of Crisis*. World Publishing, 1972.

Kranzberg, Melvin, and William H. Davenport, eds. *Technology and Culture*. NAL, 1972.

Kraus, Sidney, ed. *The Great Debates*. Indiana University Press, 1962.

Krause, Patricia A., ed. *Anatomy of an Undeclared War*. International Universities Press, 1972.

Krefetz, Gerald. *The Dying Dollar*. Playboy Press, 1972.

Kunen, James Simon. *The Strawberry Statement*. Random House, 1969.

Lambert, T. Allen. "Generations and Change," *Youth and Society*, vol. 4 #1, Sept. 1972.

Langer, Suzanne K. *Philosophy in a New Key*. Harvard University Press, 1957.

Langman, Lauren. "Dionysius—Child of Tomorrow," *Youth and Society*, vol. 3 #1, Sept. 1971.

Lasch, Christopher. *The Culture of Narcissism*. W.W. Norton, 1979.

Lemon, Richard. *The Troubled American*. Simon & Schuster, 1970.

Levitan, Sar A., William B. Johnston, and Robert Taggart. *Still a Dream: The Changing Status of Blacks Since 1960*. Harvard University Press, 1975.

Lewin, Leonard. *Report from Iron Mountain*. Dial Press, 1967.

Lewis, Jordan D. "Technology, Enterprise, and American Economic Growth," *Science*, vol. 215 (5), Mar. 1982.

Lifton, Robert Jay. *Boundaries*. Random House, 1969.

———. *Home from the War*. Simon & Schuster, 1973.

Loory, Stuart H. *Defeated: Inside America's Military Machine*. Random House, 1973.

Lorenz, Konrad. *Civilized Man's Eight Deadly Sins*. Harcourt Brace Jovanovich, 1973.

Lowenthal, Richard. "Unreason and Revolution," *Encounter*, 23, Nov. 1969.

Lundberg, Ferdinand, and Marynia Farnham. *Modern Woman: The Lost Sex*. Harper, 1947.

Mack, Raymond W. *Transforming America*. Random House, 1967.

Maclear, Michael. *The Ten Thousand Day War*. St. Martin's Press, 1981.

MacLeod, Celeste. *Horatio Alger, Farewell*. Seaview Books, 1980.

Magruder, Jeb Stuart. *An American Life*. Atheneum, 1974.

Mailer, Norman. *The Armies of the Night*. NAL, 1968.

——. *Miami and the Siege of Chicago*. NAL, 1968.

——. *Of a Fire on the Moon*. Little, Brown, 1970.

Malcolm X, and Alex Haley. *The Autobiography of Malcolm X*. Grove Press, 1965.

Manchester, William. *The Glory and the Dream*. Little, Brown, 1973.

Mantell, David Mark. *True Americanism: Green Berets and War Resisters*. Teachers College Press, 1974.

Matza, David. "Rebellious Youth," *Youth and Society*, vol. 1 #4, June 1970.

Maynard, Geoffrey, and W. van Ryckeghen. *A World of Inflation*. Barnes & Noble Books, 1975.

McGinniss, Joe. *The Selling of the President, 1968*. Trident Press, 1969.

McKay, David (Chairman). *Attica: The Official Report of the New York State Special Commission on Attica*. Bantam, 1972.

McLuhan, Marshall. *Understanding Media: The Extensions of Man*. McGraw-Hill, 1964.

Meadows, Donella H., Dennis L. Meadows, Jorgen Randers, and William L. Behrens III. *The Limits to Growth*. (Club of Rome study.) Universe Books, 1972.

Mehnert, Klaus. *Twilight of the Young*. Holt, Rinehart & Winston, 1976.

Mesarovic, Milhajlo, and Eduard Pestel. *Mankind at the Turning Point*. (Club of Rome II.) Dutton, 1974.

Mesthene, Emmanuel G. *Harvard Program on Technology and Society, 1964–1972, A Final Review*. Harvard University Press, 1972.

Michener, James A. *Kent State: What Happened and Why*. Random House, 1971.

Middleton, Neil, ed. *I.F. Stone's Weekly Reader*. Random House, 1974.

Miles, Rufus E., Jr. *Awakening from the American Dream*. Universe Books, 1976.

Miller, Roger Leroy, and Raburn M. Williams. *The New Economics of Richard M. Nixon*. Harper & Row, 1972.

Mines, Samuel. *The Last Days of Mankind*. Simon & Schuster, 1971.

Moore, Barrington, Jr. "Thoughts on Violence and Democracy," *Proceedings of the Academy of Political Science*, 29 (1968).

Morison, Elting E. *From Know-How to Nowhere*. Basic Books, 1974.

Myerhoff, Barbara G. "New Styles of Humanism," *Youth and Society*, vol 1 #2, Dec. 1969.

Nathan, Richard P. *The Plot That Failed*. John Wiley, 1975.

National Commission on the Observance of International Women's Year. *American Women Today and Tomorrow*. 1975.

Newfield, Jack. *Bread and Roses Too*. E.P. Dutton, 1971.

Newman, Dorothy K., Nancy J. Amidei, Barbara L. Carter, Dawn Day, William

J. Kruvant, and Jack S. Russell. *Protest, Politics, and Prosperity*. Pantheon Books, 1978.

Nieburg, H.L. *In the Name of Science*. Quadrangle, 1966.

Nixon, Richard M. *The Memoirs of Richard Nixon*. Grosset & Dunlap, 1978.

Novick, Sheldon. *The Careless Atom*. Houghton Mifflin, 1969.

Oberdorfer, Don. *Tet!* Doubleday, 1971.

Olsen, Fred A., ed. *Technology: A Reign of Benevolence and Destruction*. Mss Information Corporation, 1973.

O'Neill, William L. *Coming Apart*. Quadrangle, 1971.

Pascarella, Perry. *Technology: Fire in a Dark World*. Van Nostrand Reinhold, 1979.

The Pentagon Papers as Published by The New York Times. Bantam, 1971.

Perelman, Louis. *The Global Mind*. Mason-Charter, 1976.

Petit, Clyde Edwin. *The Experts*. Lyle Stuart, 1975.

Pike, Douglas. *The Vietcong Strategy of Terror*. U.S. Mission to Vietnam, 1970.

Pinkney, Alphonso. *The Etiology of Violence*. Random House, 1972.

Polner, Murray. *No Victory Parades*. Holt, Rinehart & Winston, 1971.

Pomper, Gerald M. *Voters' Choice*. Dodd, Mead, 1975.

Pusey, Merlo. *The Way We Go to War*. Houghton Mifflin, 1969.

"Rabbit, Peter" (pseud.). *Drop City*. Olympia Press, 1971.

Rangell, Leo. *The Wind of Watergate*. W.W. Norton, 1980.

Reich, Charles A. *The Greening of America*. Random House, 1970.

Reichley, A. James. *Conservatives in an Age of Change*. Brookings Institution, 1982.

Revelle, Roger, and Hans H. Landsberg, eds. *America's Changing Environment*. Beacon Press, 1970.

Richmond-Abbott, Marie. *The American Woman*. Holt, Rinehart & Winston, 1979.

Robertson, James Oliver. *American Myth, American Reality*. Hill & Wang, 1980.

Rockefeller, Nelson A. (Chairman). *Critical Choices for Americans*, vol. 7, *Qualities of Life*. Lexington Books, 1975.

Rosen, Sumner, ed. *Economic Power Failure: The Current American Crisis*. McGraw-Hill, 1975.

Rosenberg, Milton J., Sidney Verba, and Phillip E. Converse. *Vietnam and the Silent Majority*. Harper & Row, 1970.

Roszak, Theodore. *The Making of a Counter Culture*. Doubleday, 1969.

Rothman, Sheila M. *Women's Proper Place*. Basic Books, 1978.

Rubin, Jerry. *Do It!* Simon & Schuster, 1970.

Rubinoff, Lionel. *The Pornography of Power*. Quadrangle, 1968.

Rustin, Bayard. *Down the Line*. Quadrangle, 1971.

Ryan, Mary P. *Womanhood in America*. Franklin Watts, 1979.

Ryan, William. *Blaming the Victim*, rev. ed. Random House, 1976.

Sack, John. *M*. NAL, 1967.

Sale, Kirkpatrick. *SDS*. Random House, 1973.

Sales, Stephen M. "Authoritarianism," *Psychology Today*, vol. 6 #6, Nov. 1971.

Santoli, Al. *Everything W'e Had*. Random House, 1981.

Scammon, Richard, and Ben Wattenberg. *The Real Majority*. Coward-McCann, 1970.

Schell, Jonathan. *The Time of Illusion*. Knopf, 1976.

Schlesinger, Arthur M., Jr. *A Thousand Days*. Houghton Mifflin, 1965.

———. *Robert Kennedy and His Times*. Houghton Mifflin, 1978.

Schrag, Peter. *The End of the American Future*. Simon & Schuster, 1973.

———. *Test of Loyalty*. Simon & Schuster, 1974.

Schurmann, Franz, Peter Dale Scott, and Reginald Zelnick. *The Politics of Escalation in Vietnam*. Beacon Press, 1966.

Scott, Donald M., and Bernard Wishy, eds. *America's Families: A Documentary History*. Harper & Row, 1982.

Seagull, Louis M. *Youth and Change in American Politics*. Franklin Watts, 1977.

Seeman, Melvin. "On the Meaning of Alienation," *American Sociological Review*, vol. 24, Dec. 1959.

Sennett, Richard. *The Fall of Public Man*. Knopf, 1977.

Servan-Schreiber, Jean-Jacques. *The World Challenge*. Simon & Schuster, 1980.

Shachtman, Tom. "Technology: Challenge and Promise," *Electronic Age*, vol. 29 #3, 1970.

———. "The Power Crisis," *Electronic Age*, vol. 30 #3, 1971.

———. "A Summer of Brownouts," *Ecology Today*, vol. 1 #4, July 1971.

———. "Getting More Power to the People," *Ecology Today*, vol. 1 #5, Sept. 1971.

———. "Nuclear Energy and Electric Power," *Ecology Today*, vol. 2 #2, Mar. 1972.

Shannon, William V. *They Could Not Trust the King*. Collier-Macmillan, 1974.

Shawcross, William. *Sideshow: Nixon, Kissinger and the Destruction of Cambodia*. Simon & Schuster, 1979.

Silberman, Charles E. *Crisis in Black and White*. Random House, 1964.

Silk, Leonard. *Nixonomics*. Praeger, 1972.

Simmons, Brig. Gen. Edwin H. "Marine Operations in 1965–1966," *Naval Review*, 1968.

Sissman, L.E. *Innocent Bystander*. Vanguard Press, 1975.

Sitkoff, Harvard. *The Struggle for Black Equality, 1954–1980*. McGraw-Hill, 1981.

Skinner, B.F. *Beyond Freedom and Dignity*. Knopf, 1971.

Skolnick, Jerome. *Trans-Action*, vol. 5 #10. 1968.

———, and Arlene Skolnick. *Family in Transition*. Little, Brown, 1971.

Slater, Philip. *The Pursuit of Loneliness*. Beacon Press, 1976.

Smith, Huston, ed. *The Search for America*. Prentice-Hall, 1959.

Sobel, Lester, ed. *Inflation and the Nixon Administration*. Vol. 2, 1972–1974. Facts on File, 1975.

Sochen, June. *Movers and Shakers: American Women Thinkers and Activists, 1900–1970*. Quadrangle, 1970.

Stebbins, Richard P. *The United States in World Affairs, 1967*. Council on Foreign Relations/Simon & Schuster, 1968.

Sterling, Claire. *The Terror Network*. Holt/Reader's Digest, 1981.

Sundquist, James L. *Politics and Policy: The Eisenhower, Kennedy, and Johnson Years*. Brookings Institution, 1968.

Sussman, Barry. *784 Days That Changed America*. NAL, 1982.

Taeuber, Conrad, ed. *America in the Seventies: Some Social Indicators*. Annuals of the American Academy of Political and Social Science, vol. 435, Jan. 1978.

Thompson, W.I. *At the Edge of History*. Harper & Row, 1971.

Thompson. W.S., and D.D. Frizzell, eds. *The Lessons of Vietnam*. Crane, Russak, 1977.

Thurber, James A., and Evan D. Rogers. "Some Causes and Consequences of Student Political Participation," *Youth and Society*, vol. 5 #2, Dec. 1973.

Truman, David B. "The Politics of a New Collectivism," *Trends in Modern American Society*, Clarence Morris, ed. University of Pennsylvania Press, 1962.

Toqueville, Alexis Charles Henri Maurice Clérel de. *Democracy in America*. Oxford University Press, 1947.

Toffler, Alvin. *Future Shock*. Random House, 1970.

Tse-tung, Mao. *Primer on Guerilla Warfare*, trans. Col. Samuel B. Griffith. *Marine Corps Gazette*, n.d.

Tufte, Edward R. *Political Control of the Economy*. Princeton University Press, 1978.

Turner, Louis. *Multinational Companies and the Third World*. Hill & Wang, 1973.

Urban America, Inc., and The Urban Coalition. *One Year Later*. Praeger, 1969.

Wagner, Stanley P. *The End of Revolution*. Barnes, 1970.

Wagstaff, Thomas. *Black Power: The Radical Response to White America*. Glencoe Press, 1968.

Walker, Daniel (Chairman). *Rights in Conflict*. The Official Report to the National Commission on the Causes and Prevention of Violence. NAL, 1968.

Warren, Bill, ed. *The Middle of the Country*. Avon, 1970.

Wattenberg, Ben. *In Search of the Real America*. Doubleday. 1976.

Weber, Max. *The Protestant Ethic and the Spirit of Capitalism*. Scribner's, 1977.

Weiner, Rex, and Deanne Stillman. *Woodstock Census*. Viking, 1979.

Welsh, Douglas. *The History of the Vietnam War*. A&W Publishers, 1981.

Wheeler, Michael. *Lies, Damn Lies and Statistics*. W.W Norton, 1976.

White, Lynn. "The Historical Roots of Our Ecological Crisis," *Science*, vol. 155, Mar. 1957.

White, Theodore H. *Breach of Faith*. Atheneum, 1975.

Whyte, William H. *The Organization Man*. Simon & Schuster, 1956.

Wicker, Tom. *A Time to Die*. Quadrangle, 1975.

Williams, Robin M., Jr. *American Society: A Sociological Interpretation*. 2nd ed., rev. Knopf, 1960.

Willis, Ellen. *Up from Radicalism: A Feminist Journal*. Bantam, 1969.

Wise, David. *The American Police State*. Random House, 1976.

Wittner, Lawrence S. *Cold War America*. Praeger, 1974.

Wofford, Harris. *Of Kennedys and Kings*. Farrar, Straus & Giroux, 1980.

Wolfe, Tom. *The Electric Kool-Aid Acid Test*. Farrar, Straus, 1968.

Wolfenstein, Martha. *Disaster: A Psychological Essay*. Free Press, 1957.

————, and Gilbert Kelman, eds. *Children and the Death of a President*. Doubleday, 1965.

Woodward, Bob, and Carl Bernstein. *All the President's Men*. Simon & Schuster, 1974.

Worldwatch Institute Papers.

    #2. "The Politics and Responsibility of the North American Breadbasket." Lester R. Brown. Oct. 1975.

    #5. "Twenty-Two Dimensions of the Population Problem." Lester R. Brown, Patricia L. McGrath, Bruce Stokes. Mar. 1976.

    #13. "Spreading Deserts—The Hand of Man." Erik Eckholm, Lester R. Brown. Aug. 1977.

    #27. "Pollution: The Neglected Dimensions." Denis Hayes. Mar. 1979.

    #34. "Inflation: The Rising Cost of Living on a Small Planet." Robert Fuller. June. 1980

Wuthnow, Robert. *The Consciousness Reformation*. University of California Press, 1976.

Yankelovich, Daniel. *The New Morality*. McGraw-Hill, 1974.

Index

Abernathy, Ralph, 53
abortion, 248, 250, 254
  legalization of, 255–56, 290
Abrams, Creighton, 181, 183, 185, 187–188, 189
Accelerated Pacification Program, 184–85
achievement ethic, 17, 294–95
Ackley, Gardner, 97
Acton, Lord, 281
Aeschylus, 54
Agnew, Spiro T., 55, 265
  antiwar movement and, 147, 149, 268
  kickbacks received by, 271, 274
Ali, Muhammad, 128
Allen, George, 196
Allende, Salvador, 225
Altamont Raceway, rock concert at (1969), 147–48
"American Core Values and National Character" (Hsu), 19
American Indian Movement (AIM), 264
Americans for Democratic Action (ADA), 34
American Society (Williams), 17–19
Andean Pact, 225
Andrews, William R., 165
Anthony, Susan B., 239
anti-communism, 30–31
  nefarious tactics in, 260–62, 264
  War on Poverty and, 68
  see also Cold War
antiwar movement, 121–24, 128, 131–37,

141, 148–51, 175, 264, 294
  assessment of, 159–60, 198–99
  Cambodian incursion and, 149, 185–87
  confrontational stance adopted by, 131–132
  demise of, 148, 155, 157
  draft and, 123, 128–29, 131, 132
  majority views and, 122, 147, 155, 178, 186–87
  media coverage of, 124, 147, 268
  moral arguments of, 176–78, 181, 194–195
  North Vietnamese tactics and, 132–33
  surveillance and infiltration of, 147, 151, 187, 262–63, 265–66, 268
  teach-ins in, 121–22
  unity of, 132
  U.S. servicemen in, 155, 182, 188
  women's role in, 246, 249
Apollo mission, 214–16
Arab-Israeli War (1967), 214, 225
Arab nations, political goals and weapons of, 224, 225–29
Aristotle, 282
Army, U.S., in riot control, 78, 79
Army of the Republic of Vietnam (ARVN), 168, 172, 174, 175, 176, 179, 182, 184, 190–91, 193
  Laotian offensive of, 187–88
Ash, Roy, 269
assassinations, 45–64
  authority questioned after, 62

Committee to Re-Elect the President (CREEP), 271–72
Commoner, Barry, 211–12, 232
Common Market, 112
communes, 151–52, 154
communism:
  antiwar movement views on, 176–77
  monolithic view of, 164
  see also anti-communism; Cold War; Vietnam War
Community Action, 82
competition, 260
conformity, 18, 31–33
Congress, U.S., 80, 97, 109, 280, 282, 290, 291
  aggrandizement of presidential power and, 266, 267, 269, 272, 273
  black poverty and, 68–69, 74–75, 76, 81
  civil-rights bills in, 38, 66, 68, 69
  ecological concerns in, 218, 220–21
  elections of 1960 and, 33
  elections of 1962 and, 36, 37
  impeachment hearings in, 275–76, 277
  Kennedy's initiatives and, 34, 38, 39, 66
  space program and, 216
  tax issues in, 98–99
  technological issues in, 231
  Vietnam War and, 149, 167, 185–86, 188, 192–93, 198, 266
  Watergate hearings in, 110, 273–74, 277
  women's movement and, 254, 256
Congress of Racial Equality (CORE), 67–68, 119, 247
Connally, John, 108
Connor, "Bull," 67
consciousness-raising sessions, 249
Constitution, U.S., 21, 274, 294, 295
  Bill of Rights to, 21, 144, 260
  ERA and, 254, 256, 291
consumption, homemakers as directors of, 240–41, 243
containment policy, 163
Coolidge, Calvin, 32
Cost of Living Council (COLC), 108, 109, 110
Council of Economic Advisors, 96–97
counterculture, *see* youth movement
Counter-Intelligence Program (COINTEL-PRO), 263–65
Cox, Archibald, 157, 274–75, 282
Cox, Claire, 241–42
Cox, Harvey, 234
credibility doctrine, 163–64, 178
credit cards, 95–96, 114–15

"credit crunch" (1966), 97, 98
crime:
  in black communities, 79, 86
  Nixon's policies on, 80, 267
  rate of, 52, 61–62
crisis mentality, 287–89
Cronkite, Walter, 133
Cuba, Bay of Pigs invasion in, 35
Cuban missile crisis, 24, 36–37, 266

Daedalus, 16
dairy industry, milk price supports for, 270
Daley, Richard, 143
data banks, 220-21
DDT, 209–11
  ban on, 221
  beneficial effects of, 201, 210, 211
  dangers of, 210–11
Dean, John, 271, 272, 273, 275, 276
death, inevitability of, 58–59
Debs, Eugene, 18
Declaration of Independence, 21
Defense Department, U.S., 132, 227
defense spending, 96, 98, 100, 105, 115–116, 290
deficit-spending policy, 104–5, 109
democracy, 17, 233
  preservation of wealth and, 235–36
Democratic Convention (1964), 265
Democratic Convention (1968), 265
  demonstrations at, 141–43, 144, 267
demonstrations and protests:
  antiwar, 122, 128, 131–32, 133, 147, 149–50, 155, 188
  on college campuses, 119–21, 134-35, 143–44
  at Democratic Convention (1968), 141–143, 144
  Earth Day (1970), 148, 218
  feminist, 248–49
  see also riots
Depression, Great, 23, 24, 41, 94, 104, 239
détente, 183, 190, 223
Detroit riot (1967), 76–78
Dewey Canyon III, 188
Diem, Ngo Dinh, 38–39, 165–66, 262, 271
Dillon, Douglas, 34
disasters, large-scale, impact of, 46–47
divorce, 146, 245, 247
  money troubles and, 117
  women's movement and, 253–54
Dixon, Marlene, 251

eutrophication, 209, 220
Evers, Medger, 82

Fackheim, Emil, 198
family:
  assumptions about, 28–29
  black, crumbling structure of, 73
  nuclear, 28–29, 241, 242, 245
  structural changes in, 252–53, 257
Family Assistance Plan (FAP), 80–81
Farnham, Marynia, 240
Federal Bureau of Investigation (FBI), 272, 277
  nefarious tactics of, 81, 260, 261, 263–266, 268, 269, 282–83
Federal Communications Commission, 148, 268
Federal Power Commission (FPC), 206
Federal Reserve Board, 97, 98, 100, 102–104, 105, 108, 109
Feminine Mystique, The (Friedan), 244
femininity, 241, 257
feminism, *see* women's movement
Ferber, Michael, 139–40
Fermi, Encrico, breeder reactor, 207–8
fertilizers, chemical, 209
Finch, Robert, 143–44
food, "natural" vs. processed, 220
food prices, rise in (1972), 110
food production, 211, 223
food shortages, 223–24
Ford, Gerald R., 62, 262, 272, 277, 283
Ford, Henry, 18
Foreign Affairs, 183
fossil fuels, 219
France:
  dollar holdings sold by, 99, 106
  Enlightenment in, 21, 127, 294
  in Vietnamese conflict, 165
freedom, 17, 233
  limiting of growth and, 236–37
  misapprehensions of, 21
free-fire zones, 172
Free Speech Movement (FSM), 119, 120, 121, 123, 138, 147, 247
Freeze II, 110
French Revolution, 70
Friedan, Betty, 243–44, 246, 250
Friedenberg, Edgar Z., 280
Frost, Robert, 39
Frye, Marquette, 71
Fulbright, J. William, 167, 176–77
Future Homemakers of America (FHA), 255

Galbraith, John Kenneth, 34
Gamson, William, 121
Gardner, Hugh, 125, 151
generation gap:
  birth of, 120–21
  see also youth movement
George III, king of England, 21
Germany, Nazi, 240
Germany, West:
  currency of, 105–6, 108, 110
  technological breakthroughs in, 112
ghettos:
  educational expectations in, 89
  function of, 87
  police power in, 85–86
  see also riots
Giap, Vo Nguyen, 164, 173
Gitlin, Todd, 124
Golden Gate Park, San Francisco, be-in at (1967), 129–30
gold prices, 108, 110
gold reserves, 133
  dollar stability and, 99, 106
  paper value of, 108
Goldwater, Barry, 156, 167
gold window, closing of, 106, 107, 108
good life, defining of, 233–34
Gould, Elliott, 150
government, growth of, 115, 259
gradualism, 100
  belief in, 22–23
Graham, Billy, 149
grain sales, to Soviet Union, 110, 223–24
Graubard, Stephen R., 15–16
Gray, L. Patrick, III, 273
Great Britain, government workers in, 115
Great Society, 68, 73, 74, 76, 84, 90, 97, 273
Greek Way, The (Hamilton), 53
Green Berets, study of war resisters vs., 135–37
Green Berets, The, 135
Green Revolution, 210, 211, 223
grief, stages of, 60
Grissom, Virgil, 215
gross national product (GNP):
  declines in, 102, 104, 111, 226
  potential vs. actual, gap between, 93, 94
  spending as percentage of, 96, 109, 115, 116, 221, 259
growth, economic, 26
  limiting, 232–33, 236–37
Gruening, Ernest, 122
gunshots, responses to, 63
Gwaltney, John Langston, 86–87

Habbash, George, 229
Haig, Alexander, 187–88
Haight-Ashbury, San Francisco, 129, 130
Haiphong harbor:
    bombing of, 176, 191–92
    mining of, 184, 190
Hair, 140–41
Haldeman, H. R., 144, 268, 269
    in Watergate, 272, 273, 274, 275, 276
Hamilton, Alexander, 287
Hamilton, Edith, 53
Hampton, Fred, 264
Hanoi, bombing of, 176, 190, 191–92
Harburg, Ernest, 77
Harlem, education experiment in, 89
Harris, Louis, 122, 187
Havens, Murray Clark, 56
Hayden, Tom, 36, 135
Hayes, Denis, 219
Haynsworth, Clement, 269
Head Start, 74
Hearst, Patty, 157–58
Heilbroner, Robert L., 102, 113–14
Heller, Lonnie, 131
Hell's Angels, 123, 147
Helms, Richard, 263
Hendrickson, Robert A., 95–96
herbicides, 171
Hernandez, Aileen, 246
Herr, Michael, 181–82
Herrick, John, 166
Herring, George C., 170, 176
Heyerdahl, Thor, 212
Hickel, Walter, 186, 214
Hiss, Alger, 30
history, great men vs. great moments in,
    56–57
Ho Chi Minh, 132–33, 164, 165, 166, 224
Ho Chi Minh Trail, 187–88
Hoffa, Jimmy, 262
Hoffer, Eric, 70
Hoffman, Abbie, 130, 145
Hollander, Sidney, 48
Holmes, Oliver Wendell, 43
Holtzman, Elizabeth, 277
homemakers, 240–41
    career ambitions of, 242
    as directors of household consumption,
        240–41, 243
    dissatisfaction of, 243–44
    valuating work of, 251–52
homosexuality, 254
Honolulu conference (1966), 175, 177
Hoover, J. Edgar, 53, 103, 151, 262, 264,
    265, 266, 269

Hopkins, Harry, 104–5
households, power structure of, 250
housework, 252, 258
housing projects, 89
Hsu, Francis L. K., 19, 21
Hudson, Roy V., 205
Hue, 193
    VC attack on (1968), 179–80, 182
Humphrey, Hubert, 62, 182
    as presidential candidate, 54, 55, 58,
        142–43, 155–56
Hunt, E. Howard, 270, 271, 272, 273, 276
Huston, Tom Charles, 151, 269
Huston Plan, 151, 187, 269
Huxley, Aldous, 126

Ibsen, Henrik, 295
"identity crisis," 15, 244
imports:
    surcharge on, 106, 107
    tariff barriers and, 290
income:
    median, of blacks vs. whites, 83
    real, inflation and, 101–2, 109–10
    redistribution of, 84–85
income-tax surcharges, 98–99, 100
India, alignment of, 222
individualism, 18, 231
inflation, 23, 76, 93–117, 288
    assumptions challenged by, 111–17
    budget cuts and, 99–100, 109, 110
    consumer credit and, 95–96, 114–15
    consumer demand and, 95
    deficit-spending policy and, 104–5, 109
    distorted perception of, 101–2
    double-digit, 110
    as global phenomenon, 110
    money supply and, 97, 98, 99–100,
        102–4, 105, 109, 110
    new phase of, 100
    1964 tax cut and, 93–94
    Nixon's reelection bid and, 108–9
    pressure on dollar and, 99, 105–7
    productivity and, 101
    real incomes and, 101–2, 109–10
    short- vs. long-term industrial planning
        and, 112
    tax measures against, 96–99
    unemployment and, 100–101, 104
    U.S.-Soviet grain sale and, 223–24
    Vietnam War and, 96–98, 196
    wage and price controls and, 104, 106–
        111
insecticides, *see* DDT
Institute for Defense Analysis (IDA), 134

Index   *321*

integration:
  black views on, 74
  popular opposition to, 67
  as unworkable goal, 84
  Wallace's opposition to, 54–55
integrity, compromised in modern era, 279–280
Interior Department, U.S., 213–14
Internal Revenue Service (IRS), 148, 261, 268, 269
investment tax credits, suspension of (1966), 98
Iron Triangle, 173–74
Israel:
  Arab wars with, 110, 214, 225, 226
  terrorism against, 227–29
ITT, antitrust suit against, 270, 271

Jackson, Jesse, 53
Janeway, Charles, 42
Japan:
  currency of, 105–6, 107, 108, 110
  technological breakthroughs in, 112
  U.S. import surcharge and, 107
Jaworski, Leon, 275, 276, 277
Jefferson, Thomas, 281, 287, 293–94
Jennings, M. Kent, 158
Johnson, Lyndon B., 58, 83, 166–81, 193, 198, 246
  antiwar movement and, 133, 263, 268
  contradictory Vietnam strategies under, 169–70, 175–76
  credibility gap of, 266
  domestic initiatives of, 68–70, 74, 97
  "dump Johnson" forces and, 132, 133
  economic policies of, 93, 97–99, 105, 109, 167
  election of, 69, 109
  in escalation of Vietnam War, 123, 166–167, 169–70
  Kennedy assassination and, 46, 47, 49, 51, 62, 294
  opinion polls on, 133–34, 167, 178
  power abused by, 81, 262, 265, 266, 268
  reelection not sought by, 54, 79, 99, 134, 159, 181
  riots and, 78
Joint Chiefs of Staff (JCS), 167, 169, 170, 175–76, 178, 192
Jones, Landon Y., 123, 145
Jordan, Barbara, 277
Judaism, 202
Justice Department, U.S., 83, 131–32, 144, 148, 272

civil-rights movement and, 38, 55, 291
nefarious tactics of, 261, 262, 267, 268, 269, 270–71

Kalmbach, Herbert, 270, 271
Katzenbach, Nicholas, 265
Kennedy, Edward, 58, 270
Kennedy, Jacqueline, 29, 46
Kennedy, John F., 22, 33–40, 157, 178, 202
  admiration for, 29–30
  advisors to, 34
  business community and, 35, 36
  domestic initiatives of, 34, 37–38, 49, 65–66, 68
  economic policy of, 93–94, 245
  election of, 33, 34, 39
  emerging nations as viewed by, 24–25
  evangelical rhetoric of, 39–40
  foreign policy of, 35, 36–37, 38–39, 155, 163, 262, 271
  inauguration of, as start of new era, 33–34
  lionization of, 61
  military buildup under, 34–35
  young people galvanized by, 35–36, 37
Kennedy, John F., assassination of, 45–51, 62, 290, 294
  analyses of, 50–51
  energy dissipated after, 48, 56, 61
  groups most affected by, 49–50
  nature of loss in, 48–49
  reactions to learning of, 45–46
  "search" vs. "preserve" modality and, 63–64, 285
  as shocking event, 45, 46–47
  as start of Decade of Shocks, 13–15
  television coverage of, 46, 47–48
  transference ritual after, 60
  see also assassinations
Kennedy, John F., Jr., 46
Kennedy, Robert, 37, 62, 176
  assassination of, 50, 54, 56, 58, 60, 62, 63, 80, 140
  as attorney general, 38, 55, 262, 264
  King's assassination and, 53–54
  as presidential candidate, 54, 80, 133, 157, 265
  social issues and, 38, 54, 55
Kent State University:
  demonstration at (1970), 185, 186, 187
  shootings at, 149, 151
Kerner, Otto, 78
Kerner Commission, 78–79, 90
Kerr, Clark, 120, 121

Nhu, Ngo Dinh, 39
Niebuhr, Reinhold, 19–21, 59
Nieburg, H. L., 113
Niemi, Richard G., 158
nihilism, 234
Nixon, Richard M., 62, 182–93, 214, 226, 231, 249, 290
  aides of, integrity compromised by, 279–280
  anti-black stance of, 79–81, 82
  antiwar movement and, 147, 149–51, 157, 159, 186–87, 188, 263
  bombing of North Vietnam and, 157, 191
  Cambodian operations and, 144, 148–49, 185–86
  campus protests and, 143–44
  economic policies of, 99–100, 102–11, 114
  in election of 1960, 33, 39
  in election of 1968, 55, 79–80, 101, 107–8, 156
  in election of 1972, 108, 109, 141, 143, 156–57, 187, 271–72
  impeachment hearings on, 275–76, 277, 282
  McCarthyism and, 30
  opinion polls on, 150–51, 188
  paranoia of, 149–51, 186–87
  pardon of, 283
  peace negotiations and, 183–84, 189–90, 191, 192–93
  personality of, 278–79
  power abused by, 197–98, 262, 265, 266–84, 294–95
  resignation of, 13, 277
  social policies of, 57–58, 254, 273
Nobel Peace Prize, 52, 69, 264
"no-knock" provisions, 80, 144, 267
nonviolence, 52, 66–67
North Atlantic Treaty Organization (NATO), 24, 221
North Vietnamese Army (NVA), 173, 181, 187–88, 190, 191, 193
Novak, Michael, 143
nuclear reactors, 25, 206–8, 229
  accidents at, 207–8
nuclear test ban treaty (1963), 37
nuclear weapons, 163–64, 204, 268–69
  "baby boom" generation and, 124
  considered in Vietnam War, 183, 184
  developed by Soviet Union, 35, 37

Oakland, Calif., antiwar demonstration in (1967), 131, 132

Oakland Tribune, 119
Office of Economic Opportunity (OEO), 80, 82, 84, 90, 99
offshore oil wells, 212–14
oil, 25
  energy crisis and, 287
  as political weapon, 224, 225–27
  U.S. vulnerability and, 214, 288
oil embargoes, 226–27
oil prices, 110
  raised by OPEC, 225–26
oil spills, 212–14
  from offshore wells, 212–14
  from tankers, 212
"optionaires," 154
order, see "law and order"
Organization for Afro-American Unity, 51, 57
Organization of Petroleum Exporting Countries (OPEC), 110, 111, 112, 225–27
Oswald, Lee Harvey, 46, 48, 54, 61, 63

Palestinian Liberation Organization (PLO), 227–29
Palestinian refugees, 224
Palmer, A. Mitchell, 30–31
Paris, student protests in (1968), 139
Paris peace talks, 144, 155, 156, 182–83, 187–92, 266
  agreement reached in, 157, 191, 192
  Chinese and Soviet pressure in, 183, 189, 190
  secret negotiations in, 184, 188, 190
  U.S. offensives as incentives in, 183, 187–88, 190–92
Parker, William H., 71
Pascal, Blaise, 150, 198–99
patriarchal dominance, 252, 254, 257
Pay Board, 108, 109, 110
Peace Corps, 34, 35, 119
peace movement, see antiwar movement
Peale, Norman Vincent, 149
Pearl Harbor, 48
Penn Central, bankruptcy of, 103–4
Pentagon, antiwar demonstration at (1967), 132
"Pentagon Papers," 155, 188, 270
Perls, Fritz, 146
personality, public culture replaced by, 277–78
peyote, 125
"Phillips Curve," 100
Pilsuk, Mark, 122

Planning a Tragedy (Berman), 169
"plumbers," 151
police:
   at Chicago demonstrations (1968), 141–142, 143
   in ghettos, order as function of, 85–86
   in riot control, 71–72, 77–78, 85–86
   southern, segregationist ethic of, 67
"politico-cultural consciousness," formation of, 14–15
politics:
   demise of rational argument in, 286–87
   new issues in, 286
   personality stressed in, 277–78
   sharply delimiting stances in, 286
Politics of Assassination, The (Havens, Leiden, and Schmitt), 56
pollution, 25, 205, 211, 217
   acceptable levels of, 219
   controlling, 101, 218–19, 225
   of Lake Erie, 209, 220
   oil spills and, 212–14
   see also ecological concerns
Pool, Ithiel de Sola, 194
Poor People's March (1968), 52–53, 60, 140
Pope, Liston, 28, 42
population growth, 222, 223
Port Huron statement, 36
"positive polarization," 147–48
posterity, lack of concern for, 293
poverty programs, 68–70, 73–75, 97, 117, 170, 290
   appropriations for, 68, 74, 99
   backlash against riots and, 76, 85
   black family life and, 73
   conservatives' critique of, 85
   goals of, 68
   liberals' critique of, 84–85
   "maximum feasible participation" in, 74
   victim blaming in, 88–89
Powell, Adam Clayton, 82
power, 20, 259–84
   centralization of, 259–60
   corruption as outcome of, 281–82
   countersubversive abuses of, 81, 260–66
   double standard for, 259
   liberty endangered by, 282
   morality and, 194–95
   presidential abuses of, 197–98, 261, 262, 266–84
   prevailing world-view and, 24–25
   public's need for, 280–81

reorganization of executive branch and, 269
respect for, 259
world, East-West vs. North-South axis of, 221–24
Prague, student protests in (1968), 139, 140
prayer in public schools, 291
"preserve" modality, 81, 161, 285
   black critique and, 91
   ecological concerns and, 235–36
   Kennedy assassination and, 63, 285
   riots and, 75
   as symbol, 48–49
   Watergate and, 282–83
   women's movement and, 257
Price Commission, 108, 109, 110
price controls, see wage and price controls
"primary process thinking," 278–79
prison, rehabilitation programs in, 89
productivity rate, 101
progress:
   as central American ideal, 18, 19, 26, 203
   price paid for, 205–14
   refuted by ecology movement, 233
   see also technology
Protean man, 137–39
Protestant ethic, 203
protests, see demonstrations and protests
psychedelics, 125
Puerto Rican independence movement, 264
Puritanism, 203

Qaddafi, Muammar el-, 225
quality of life, 233

racism, 78, 86–90
   egalitarian ideal subverted by, 86, 87
   ghettos and, 87
   male chauvinism as, 251
   "naive dualism" and, 87–88
   victim blaming and, 88–90
   in Vietnam War, 172, 173
Ragan, John, 267
Railsback, William, 277
Rangell, Leo, 278–79, 280
Ravenal, Earl, 194
Ray, James Earl, 61
Reagan, Ronald, 119, 121, 151, 203, 288, 290–91, 292
   attempted assassination of, 287
Real Security (Barnet), 292
recessions, 100, 104, 108
recycling, 220

rediscount rate, 97
Redstockings, 250
Reich, Charles, 127
Reisman, David, 32–33
Republican Convention (1968), 141
research and development (R&D), 112
Resistance, 132
resources, 217
    allocation of, 235–36
    finite nature of, 214–15
    Judaeo-Christian tradition and, 202–3
    scarcity of, 202
    viewed as limitless, 25
    as weapons of Third World nations, 224–227
    see also ecological concerns; oil
ressentiment, 280, 290
Reston, James, 129, 133
Revenue Expenditure and Control Act (1968), 99
Revolutionary War:
    "Continentals" printed in, 96
    witch-hunts after, 30–31
Rhodes, James, 149
Ribicoff, Abraham, 143
Richardson, Elliot, 273, 274–75
riots, 70–79, 80, 84
    at Attica (1971), 82
    backlash against, 76, 79–80, 85
    beneficial outcomes of, 85–86
    businesses as targets of, 71, 77
    in Detroit (1967), 76–78
    Kerner Commission report on, 78–79
    after King's assassination, 54, 56, 57, 79
    liberal vs. conservative explanations for, 75
    of 1966, 75–76
    television coverage of, 71, 75–76
    see also demonstrations and protests; Watts riot
Robertson, James Oliver, 288–89
Robeson, Paul, 31
Rockefeller, Nelson, 82
Rockefeller Commission on the Quality of Life, 233
Rockefeller Panel on National Goals, 202
rock music, 124, 125–26, 146, 157
Rodino, Peter, 276
Roe vs. Wade, 256
Rogers, William, 184, 185, 269
Rolf, Ida, 146
Rolling Stones, the 147–48
Rolling Thunder, 121, 168
Rome Plows, 174

Roosevelt, Franklin D., 21, 30, 47, 104, 259
Roosevelt, Theodore, 55
Rosie the Riveter, 239
Rossi, Alice, 253
Rostow, Walt, 34
Roszak, Theodore, 127, 261
rotation policy, 172–73
Rousseau, Jean Jacques, 127
routine, Weber's concept of, 57, 59, 146, 288
Rubin, Jerry, 123, 129, 152
Rubinoff, Lionel, 40, 88, 140, 195–96, 294
Ruby, Jack, 46
Ruckelshaus, William, 275
Rudd, Mark, 134
Rusk, Dean, 34, 169
Rustin, Bayard, 72, 73
Ryan, William, 88–90

Saigon, U.S. embassy in, VC attack on (1968), 179
Sartre, Jean-Paul, 88
Saturday Night Massacre, 274–75
Savio, Mario, 120, 121
Scammon, Richard, 156
Schell, Jonathan, 144, 164, 178, 268
Schlesinger, Arthur, Jr., 34, 177–78
Schmitt, Karl M., 56
Schwartz, Jonathan, 150
Scientific American, 208–9
Seaborg, Glenn T., 229
Seagull, Louis M., 157
"search and destroy" missions, 171–72, 175, 176
"Search for America, The" (television series), 19
"search" modality, 81, 161, 285
    black critique and, 90
    ecological concerns and, 236–37
    Kennedy assassination and, 63–64, 285
    riots and, 75, 78
    Watergate and, 283–84
    women's movement and, 257
Seattle, Wash., unemployment in (1970), 104
secrecy, in CIA work, 260–61
Secret Army Organization (SAO), 264
Segal, Jeff, 131
self-definition, Protean process and, 137–39
Selma, Ala., voter registration drive in (1965), 69, 121
Sennett, Richard, 15, 277–78

service industries, rise of, 101
sex discrimination, 246
sexual mores, 29, 245, 247
    divorce rate and, 253–54
    double standard in, 253
    of youth culture, 124, 125, 146, 157
Sexual Politics (Millet), 253
Shawcross, William, 186
shock:
    inurement to, 287
    as ritualized substitute for change, 56,
        287
    stages of, 47
Sihanouk, Norodom, prince of Cambodia,
    183, 185, 186
"silent majority" program, 268
Simmons, Edwin H., 171
Simmons, William, 67
Sirhan, Sirhan, 54, 61
Sirica, John J., 273, 274, 275, 282
Sissman, L. E., 13–14
Smith Act (1940), 263
Socialist Workers' Party (SWP), 261, 263–
    264
Social Security, 109, 110, 116
Societal assumptions:
    disagreements over, 286–86
    disrupted by Decade of Shocks, 15, 22–
        30, 285, 289
    moral bankruptcy of, 284
    need for rethinking of, 292–96
Socrates, 194
Sophists, 194
sororities, mating rituals at, 241–42
Southeast Asia Treaty Organization
    (SEATO), 24, 167
Southern Christian Leadership Conference
    (SCLC), 57, 132, 264
Soviet Union, 21, 112, 226
    Chinese split with, 164, 189
    grain sold to, 110, 223–24
    nonaligned countries and, 221, 222
    nuclear arsenal of, 35, 37
    Vietnam War and, 164, 167–68, 183,
        189, 190, 224
space program, 214–17, 234
    accidents in, 215
    political aspect of, 215–16
    technological advances in, 215, 216–17
Spock, Benjamin, 131–32
Sputnik, 22, 32
stagflation, 111
standard of living, 93, 202, 205, 225
    quality of life vs., 233
State Department, U.S., 24, 269

Statue of Liberty, 264
Stennis, John, 274
Stevenson, Adlai, 240
stock certificates, ownership of, 116
Stock Exchange:
    demonstration at (1967), 130
    Penn Central crash and, 103–4
    price decline on (1970), 103
Stone, I. F., 14, 39, 122
Strategic Arms Limitation Talks (SALT),
    189
Student Nonviolent Coordinating Committee
    (SNCC), 67–68, 128, 132, 264
Students for a Democratic Society (SDS),
    36, 124, 128, 132, 151
    split in, 144, 146
suburbanization, 240
success:
    fear of, 248
    value placed on, 17
Suez Canal, seizure of (1957), 214
Sun Tzu, 132–33
supersonic transports (SSTs), 220
Supreme Court, U.S., 66, 256, 267, 269,
    270
    Watergate tapes and, 275, 276, 277
Sutherland, Elizabeth, 73
Symbionese Liberation Army (SLA), 157–
    158
synthetic materials, 211–12

Tacitus, 174
Tanaka, Kabuei, 277
tax cuts, 290
    of 1964, 93–94, 245
    of 1971, 106, 107
taxes:
    bracket creep and, 109
    business vs. personal, 116
    in control of inflation, 96–99
Taylor, Maxwell, 168
teach-ins, 121–22
technologically intensive products, 211–12
technology, 26, 201–37
    anti-, weapons, 224–29
    cautionary views of, 203–5, 217
    consequences considered in, 231–32
    loss of U.S. superiority in, 112
    "magnificent bribe" of, 204–5
    North-South world power alignment and,
        221–24
    realizing limits of, 229–30, 232
    traditional American values and, 202–3
    utopian predictions for, 201–2, 229–30

value system and, 230–37
women's role and, 245
see also ecological concerns; progress;
    space program
Teheran Agreement (1971), 225–26
television, 15–16, 49, 228, 278
"baby boom" generation and, 124
ecological concerns and, 216
field of information narrowed by, 59–60
inflation distorted on, 102
Kennedy assassination and, 46, 47–48
riots reported on, 71, 75–76
Vietnam War and, 132, 147, 180–81,
    188
White House pressure on, 147, 148, 268
youth revolution and, 129
terrorism, 224, 227–29
Tet offensive (1968), 133, 178–81, 182
public perception of, 99, 179, 180–81
Thant, U, 167
theism, 158
theopoimsis, 128
Thieu, Nguyen Van, 169, 175, 178, 187–
    188
postwar political role sought by, 182,
    183, 184, 188–89, 191, 192
Third World nations, 221–29
alignment of, 221–22
deteriorating conditions in, 222–24
resources in place as weapons of, 224–27
in simplistic world-view, 24–25
technology transferred to, 222
terrorism as weapon of, 224, 227–29
U.S. aid to, 221
Tho, Le Duc, 184, 188, 191
Thompson, Sir Robert, 191
Thurmond, Strom, 55
Thurow, Lester, 102
Time, 133, 148
Tocqueville, Alexis de, 21, 58–59, 70,
    197, 281
Tolstoy, Leo, 56–57
Tonkin Gulf Resolution, 166–67, 168, 176,
    184, 266
Torrey Canyon, oil spilled from, 212, 213
transference rituals, 60
Truman, David B., 40
Truman, Harry S, 22, 30, 155, 163, 202
Tuchman, Barbara, 279–80
Tufte, Edward, 108
Turner, Louis, 225

Udall, Stewart, 202
unemployment, 105, 108, 111, 117

anti-inflationary measures and, 100–101,
    104
of blacks vs. whites, 83, 104
1964 tax cut and, 93–94
Union Oil, 214
United Nations, 216
upward mobility, 27
U.S. Steel, 35, 259–60

values:
as battleground of 1960s, 42
dormant contradictions in (early 1960s),
    17–22, 293
extracted from changing experience, 230–
    231, 234
questioned by young people, 159, 160
technology and, 202–3, 230–37
of western industrial man vs.
    counterculture child, 127–28
van Ryckeghen, W., 100
victim blaming:
examples of, 88–89
motivation for, 89–90
Viet Cong (VC), 169, 191
headquarters for (COSVN), 183
tactics of, 165, 166, 173, 224
Tet offensive of, 133, 178–81, 182
U.S. tactics against, 170, 171–72, 174,
    184
Vietnamese civilians and, 171–72
Viet Minh, 165
Vietnam:
division of, 165
social structure of, 164–65
Vietnam, North:
bombing of, 121, 155, 157, 167–69,
    170–71, 175, 176, 181, 190, 191–92
military strategy of, 132–33, 165
as model for southern nations, 224
Soviet Union and, 164, 167–68, 183,
    189, 190, 224
see also National Liberation Front; North
    Vietnamese Army; Viet Cong
Vietnam, South, Government of (GVN),
    166, 174, 175, 182, 191, 192, 193
see also Army of the Republic of
    Vietnam
Vietnam Day Committee, 123
Vietnamization program, 134, 154–55,
    184, 185, 187–88
Vietnam Veterans Against the War
    (VVAW), 155, 188
Vietnam War, 52, 55, 73, 135, 163–99,
    214, 281

ABOUT THE AUTHOR

Tom Shachtman's previous books have concentrated on points of drastic change in American twentieth-century history. These include *The Day America Crashed* (1979), *Edith and Woodrow* (1981), and *The Phony War, 1939–1940* (1982). He has written documentaries for ABC, CBS, NBC, PBS, and for local stations and syndication. A number of his films, including the *Children of Poverty* trilogy, have won major awards. He also has written books for children and has had plays produced Off-Off-Broadway.